Foreign Bodies

Oceania and the Science
of Race 1750-1940

Foreign Bodies

Oceania and the Science of Race 1750-1940

Edited by
Bronwen Douglas
and Chris Ballard

ANU
THE AUSTRALIAN NATIONAL UNIVERSITY

E PRESS

ANU
E PRESS

Published by ANU E Press
The Australian National University
Canberra ACT 0200, Australia
Email: anuepress@anu.edu.au
This title is also available online at:
        http://epress.anu.edu.au/foreign_bodies_citation.html

National Library of Australia
Cataloguing-in-Publication entry

Title: Foreign bodies : Oceania and the science of race 1750-1940 / editors:
                Bronwen Douglas, Chris Ballard.

ISBN: 9781921313998 (pbk.)
                9781921536007 (online)

Notes: Bibliography.

Subjects: Ethnic relations.
                Race--Social aspects.
                Oceania--Race relations.

Other Authors/Contributors:
                Douglas, Bronwen.
                Ballard, Chris, 1963-

Dewey Number: 305.800995

Cover design by Noel Wendtman.

For Charles, Kirsty, Allie, and Andrew

and

For Mem, Tessa, and Sebastian

Table of Contents

Figures

Front cover

Adrien-Hubert Brué, 'Océanie ou cinquième partie du monde comprenant l'Archipel d'Asie, l'Australasie, la Polynésie, &.ª ... 1814'. In *Grand atlas universal* ..., carte 36 (2nd edition, Paris: Desray 1816). Engraving.

Antoine Maurin after Louis-Auguste de Sainson, 'Nlle. Irlande: 1. Habitant de Tonga;... 4. Habitant du Havre Carteret'; 'Moluques. 1. César, jeune papou de Gilolo'. In Jules-Sébastien-César Dumont d'Urville, *Voyage de la corvette l'Astrolabe exécuté pendant les années 1826-1827-1828-1829 ... Atlas historique*, pls 114, 129 (Paris: J. Tastu, 1833). Lithographs.

Introduction

1. Adrien-Hubert Brué, 'Océanie ou cinquième partie du monde comprenant l'Archipel d'Asie, l'Australasie, la Polynésie, &.ª ... 1814'. Engraving.
2. Ambroise Tardieu, 'Carte pour l'intelligence du mémoire de M. le capitaine d'Urville sur les îles du grand océan (Océanie)' (1832). Engraving.
3. Charles V. Monin, *Océanie: divisions de l'Océanie* (1834). Engraving.

Part 1 Emergence: thinking the science of race, 1750-1880

4. Anon., 'Crania collectionis meae quina selectissima adumbrat, ad totidem generis humani varietatum principalium diversitatem demonstrandam: 1. *Tungusae*; 2. *Caribaei*; 3. Feminae juvenis *Georgianae*; 4. *O-taheitae*; 5. *Aethiopissae Guineensis*' (1795). Engraving.
5. [Alphonse] Vien, 'Le craniographe de M. Broca' (1860-3). Engraving.

Part 2 Experience: the science of race and Oceania, 1750-1869

6. Anon., 'Développement du dynamomètre de Cit^{en}. Regnier' (1798). Engraving.
7. Jean Louis Denis Coutant after Antoine Chazal, 'Crânes de Papous' (1824). Engraving.
8. Jules-Louis Le Jeune, 'Papou de L'Ile ~~Bougainville~~ Bouca' [1823]. Pen and wash drawing.
9. Jules-Louis Le Jeune, 'Nlle Irlande' [1823]. Pen and wash drawing.
10. [J.-B.?] Léveillé after photograph by [Louis-Auguste?] Bisson of Pierre-Marie Alexandre Dumoutier, 'Ma-Pou-Ma-Hanga. Native de l'Ile de Manga-Réva, Archipel Gambier (Polynésie)' (1846). Lithographed photograph of plaster bust..
11. [J.-B.?] Léveillé after photograph by [Louis-Auguste?] Bisson of Pierre-Marie Alexandre Dumoutier, 'Guenney. Natif de Port-Sorelle, (Comté de Dévon),

Côte-Nord de la terre de Van Diemen (Mélanésie)' (1846). Lithographed photograph of plaster bust.

12. Jules-Louis Le Jeune, 'Habitants du Port Dori. Nouvelle Guinée' [1823]. Pen and wash drawing.
13. George Windsor Earl, 'Seats of the Papuan Race in the Indian Archipelago' (1853). Engraving.
14. W.H. Lizars, 'A Papua or Negro of the Indian Islands; Kătut a Native of Bali one of the Brown complexioned Race' (1820). Engraving.
15. William Daniell, 'A Papuan or Native of New Guinea 10 years old' (1817). Aquatint.
16. Alfred Russel Wallace, 'Physical Map of the Malay Archipelago ... 1868'. Engraving.

Part 3 Consolidation: the science of race and Aboriginal Australians, 1860-1885

17. Anon. after Prince Roland Bonaparte, 'Jenny' (1885). Engraved photographs.

Part 4 Complicity and Challenge: the science of race and Evangelical humanism, 1800-1930

18. Anon., 'Our Two Mandates' (1921). Poster.

Part 5 Zenith: colonial contradictions and the chimera of racial purity, 1920-1940

19. Anon., 'Michael Leahy in the Wahgi Valley, 1934'. Photograph.
20. Robin Anderson, 'Clem Leahy and his Mother, Yamka Amp Wenta, 1983'. Photograph.
21. Anon., 'Samoan Patriots' (1929). Photograph.

Back cover

'Céphalomètre du Dr. Dumoutier, construit par Mr. Gravet, ingénieur mécanicien du Dépôt des Cartes et Plans de la Marine Nationale d'après les indications de l'auteur'. In [Pierre-Marie Alexandre Dumoutier], *Voyage au pôle sud et dans l'Océanie ... pendant les années 1837-1838-1839-1840 ... Atlas anthropologique*, pl. 48 (Paris: Gide, 1846). Engraving.

Preface

This book had its distant genesis in the editors' discovery nearly a decade ago that we shared intellectual interests in early European encounters with indigenous people in the Pacific Islands (Douglas) and in Papua New Guinea and the Indonesian provinces of Papua and West Papua, then Irian Jaya (Ballard). Significantly, we found that we also shared a then somewhat inchoate sense of the need to go beyond empirical, utilitarian readings of representations of such encounters to take serious account of the ideas and discourses which informed them. The idea of race inevitably loomed large in any such investigation but our approach to its history was deeply inflected by our own experience and present orientations. One of us, an enthusiastic demonstrator for antiracist and anticolonial causes in the 1960s and 70s, could hardly utter the word except in verbalized quotation marks. The other, an experienced fieldworker, was disturbed by the hydra-headed tenacity of the euphemized racial attitudes he consistently encountered: amongst Australian ex-colonizers and postcolonial Indonesian neo-colonizers and in indigenous strategies of identity and resistance. Gripped by the triple imperative to throw past light on ambiguous present usages, to dereify the concept of race, and to keep encounters and local agency at the forefront of analysis, we organized a pair of exploratory workshops on racial science in Oceania. They were held in 2000 and 2001 at The Australian National University with generous funding from the Humanities Research Centre and the Division of Pacific and Asian History, Research School of Pacific and Asian Studies. Most of the contributors to this collection gave work-in-progress papers at one or both workshops.

At that time, however, the editors' primary research commitments were to other projects. Then illness (in Douglas's case) and children (in Ballard's case) supervened to keep our work on race on the back burner until 2006 when the award of an Australian Research Council Discovery grant enabled us to launch a team project on 'European Naturalists and the Constitution of Human Difference in Oceania: Crosscultural Encounters and the Science of Race, 1768-1888'. This book is the first major outcome of that project. The hiatus between its conception and completion was primarily a result of the editors' realization that a thorough historical understanding of the complex intersections of racial ideas and regional praxis requires more than a general grasp of imperial and colonial discourses on 'the savage'; that we needed to immerse ourselves in contemporary theoretical writings as well as in the accounts of European voyagers and fieldworkers. The ultimate shape of the volume, then, testifies to the lengthy, detailed programs of research we have undertaken on the natural history of man, the history of anthropology and ethnology, and the science of race, in addition to our ongoing work on specifically Oceanic materials.

The collection investigates the reciprocal significance of Oceania for the science of race, and of racial thinking for Oceania, during the two centuries after 1750, giving 'Oceania' a broad definition that encompasses the Pacific Islands, Australia, New Guinea, New Zealand, and the Malay Archipelago. We aim to denaturalize the modernist scientific concept of race by means of a dual historical strategy: tracking the emergence of the concept in western Europe at the end of the eighteenth century, its subsequent normalization, and its practical deployment in Oceanic contexts; and exposing the tensions, inconsistencies, and instability of rival discourses. Under the broad rubrics of dereifying race and decentring Europe, these essays make several distinctive and innovative contributions. First, they locate the formulation of particular racial theories and the science of race generally at the intersections of metropolitan biology or anthropology and encounters in the field — a relatively recent strategy in the history of science. We neither dematerialize ideas as purely abstract and discursive nor reduce them to social relations and politics, but ground them personally and circumstantially in embodied human interactions.

Second, the essays demonstrate the heuristic significance of Oceanian people in providing examples, proofs, and disproofs for varied strands of the eighteenth-century science of man and for the subsequent science of race and its opponents. Great diversity in human appearance and manners was reported by Portuguese, Spanish, Dutch, British, and French travellers in Oceania from the early sixteenth century. With the inception of scientific voyaging by France and Britain in the 1760s, the region's inhabitants offered Enlightenment philosophers and natural historians a kaleidoscope of 'nations', 'races', or 'tribes' to think on, debate about, and contrast themselves with. Ethnocentric Europeans positioned indigenous Oceanian groups differentially along a presumed universal human developmental trajectory from primitive to civilized; and they compared or identified the people described in voyage texts with other non-Christians or non-whites, including the enslaved and increasingly despised 'Negro' or the patronized but sometimes idealized 'Indian'. Yet, most such thinkers took original human unity for granted, attributed current physical diversity to the direct but reversible impact of climate and milieu on a single migrating species, and assumed a common human potential to progress towards the civilized state or for salvation.

From the end of the eighteenth century, however, almost all naturalists and anthropologists challenged purely instrumental environmentalist explanations for diversity on physiological or anatomical grounds while an increasing number used the refutation to deny the venerable monogenist premises of common human origin or present specific unity. As the concept of a race acquired its modernist scientific meaning of a discrete, biologically determined major grouping with innate physical and mental characters, polygenists reconfigured human races as distinct species. Oceanic materials influenced and were invoked by both sides of debates for and against human unity as Enlightenment holism gave way to taxonomy and 'primitive savages' were globally redefined as 'inferior races'. In the process, the polemic against climatic determination of human variation drew particular sustenance from a signature feature of the settlement of Oceania: the occurrence of great physical diversity, often contiguously, within common climatic zones. From about 1800, certain Oceanian people, notably Aboriginal Tasmanians and Australians, were consistently positioned closest to 'the brutes' as allegedly the most inferior of all human races or species, uncivilizable, and doomed to imminent extinction.

After 1860, the hoary conflict between monogenists and polygenists was partially resolved or superseded with the application of evolutionist theory to man. Evolutionism yoked very long-run adaptation to milieus with heredity to explain human speciation and seemed to confirm the thesis of inevitable disappearance of Darwin's less 'favoured races in the struggle for life'. Darwinism's empirical debt to Oceania is patent in the biographies of Darwin himself and of Wallace and Huxley, each of whom undertook formative fieldwork in the region and later pronounced authoritatively on the certainty of racial extinctions. With respect to extinctions, as with the related, equally emotive theme of interracial coitus, the science of race anticipated, imbibed, informed, and at times violated popular, especially colonial attitudes which resonated with longstanding scientific disputes about hybrids as the key signifiers of specific boundaries and as racially regenerative or transgressive. Such intersections of science and public opinion were invincibly racialized: even celebrations of 'hybrid vigour' usually took for granted the attenuation or disappearance of the 'lower' indigenous element; while in Australia in the 1930s, hybridity was arguably promoted as a eugenicist vehicle for racial extinction of Aborigines, since the official policy of assimilation envisaged 'breeding out the colour' of the expanding half-caste population — ironically, in the teeth of much popular disapproval of miscegenation on racist grounds.

The third important innovation in this collection is to bring British humanitarian perspectives squarely into the frame of a history of race and raciology. In the late eighteenth century, copious reports from the Pacific Islands of the moral 'degradation' of fellow human beings far removed from 'true' religion profoundly shocked Evangelicals and served as a major impulse for the great Protestant overseas missionary enterprise of the next century. Two chapters in the volume specifically address humanitarian opposition to scientific arguments in favour of unbridgeable racial difference, polygeny, or the incapacity of certain races for salvation, especially with respect to familiar Oceanian people with whom missionaries lived and worked. Yet these chapters and the collection generally also chart humanitarian complicity in the naturalization of the idea of race, the congealing of racial discriminations, and the legitimation of social evolutionism during the nineteenth and early twentieth centuries. The question of the perfectibility or aptness for civilization of different races in Oceania was a key point of cleavage between Enlightenment and nineteenth-century positions and between humanitarians and racial scientists. But widespread hardening of racial attitudes in Europe and its colonies, increasing pessimism about the civilizability of certain races, and the generalization of particular instances of demographic decline into a universal scientific law eventually led many humanitarians to concur regretfully in the prospect of racial extinction, especially in Australia and some Pacific Islands. Debilitating repercussions of the discourse of extinction still impinge on many indigenous communities across a region where, in a particularly bitter irony, the threat of overpopulation has now widely supplanted that of depopulation.

Editors and contributors all acknowledge the moral perils of writing on an issue as fraught as race and the necessity to navigate scrupulously between the opposed temptations of excessive outrage or of desensitization to the revolting language of much raciological discourse. One possible strategy is to ignore or bury racially obnoxious representations. However, to do so empowers racist ideas and reasoning by leaving them unchallenged. An alternative strategy — evidently the one we have chosen — is to locate such language historically and epistemologically and subject it to rigorous critique. This approach denaturalizes racialism by revealing the historical contingency of its concepts, semantics, and discourses while it also discredits such discourses by exposing their absurdity and illogicality. Our approach has several pragmatic corollaries. We use 'racial' as a relatively neutral term connoting 'race' in its modernist biological sense. 'Racialist' is our preferred term to label derogatory attitudes expressed towards persons or groups on the basis of supposedly collective physical characters. The grossly overdetermined term 'racist' is generally avoided except with reference to certain modern contexts. Related to these choices and also for aesthetic reasons, we use inverted commas minimally: they are included on first mention of a specialized English term in its contemporary sense and are then omitted, except for direct quotations; but they are consistently implied in the case of now problematic terms — notably 'race' but also (racial) 'type', 'half-caste', 'hybrid', 'nature', 'civilization', 'savage', 'primitive', 'Negro', 'Lapp', 'Hottentot', 'Papuan', 'Pygmy', 'native', 'pagan', 'heathen', 'black', 'white', 'man' (in the inclusive sense of humanity), 'the West', etc.

Unless otherwise indicated, all translations are our own. The personal names of French authors follow the international standard recommended by the Bibliothèque nationale de France.

Editors' Biographies

Bronwen Douglas is a Senior Fellow in Pacific and Asian History at The Australian National University. Her major research interest is the history of race since the late Enlightenment, focusing on the interface of metropolitan discourses, field encounters, and local agency in the representation and classification of indigenous Oceanian people. She also has longstanding interests in the intersections of Christianity and gender in Melanesia and the colonial history of New Caledonia and Vanuatu. She is the author of *Across the Great Divide: Journeys in History and Anthropology* (1998); editor of *Women's Groups and Everyday Modernity in Melanesia* (2003); and co-editor with Nicholas Thomas and Anna Cole of *Tattoo: Bodies, Art and Exchange in the Pacific and the West* (2005).

Chris Ballard is a Fellow in Pacific and Asian History at The Australian National University. His research focuses on concepts of race in colonial encounters and on indigenous Melanesian historicities – their transformation through cross-cultural encounters; representation through various media, including film and fiction; and articulation with contemporary challenges such as land reform, large natural resource projects, and cultural heritage management planning. His regional interests are in eastern Indonesia, Papua New Guinea, and Vanuatu. He is co-author of *Race to the Snow: Photography and the Exploration of Dutch New Guinea, 1907-1936* (2001); and co-editor of *The Ok Tedi Settlement: Issues, Outcomes and Implications* (1997), *Fluid Ontologies: Myth, Ritual and Philosophy in the Highlands of Papua New Guinea* (1998), and *The Sweet Potato in Oceania: a Reappraisal* (2005).

Contributors

Stephanie Anderson is a Canberra-based independent scholar of French voyage, anthropological, and other literature.

Chris Ballard is a Fellow in Pacific and Asian History in the Research School of Pacific and Asian Studies at The Australian National University, Canberra.

Bronwen Douglas is a Senior Fellow in Pacific and Asian History in the Research School of Pacific and Asian Studies at The Australian National University, Canberra.

Helen Gardner is a Lecturer in History in the Faculty of Arts at Deakin University, Melbourne.

Vicki Luker is a Pacific historian and the Executive Editor of the *Journal of Pacific History* in the Research School of Pacific and Asian Studies at The Australian National University, Canberra.

Paul Turnbull is a Professor of History in the School of Arts at Griffith University, Brisbane.

Christine Weir is a Lecturer in History in the School of Social Sciences at the University of the South Pacific, Suva, Fiji.

Acknowledgements

Many debts are necessarily incurred in the course of such a long project. The editors particularly thank the contributors for the uniformly high quality of their chapters, their cheerful, tolerant responses to our editorial obsessions, and their patience over a much longer gestation period than planned. We thank Stephanie Anderson and Vicki Luker for outstanding research and editorial assistance respectively. We thank Noel Wendtham for her superb cover design.

We are grateful to the knowledgeable and helpful staff of the following libraries, museums, and archives: in Australia, The Australian National University Library, the Baillieu and Brownless Libraries at the University of Melbourne, the Matheson Library at Monash University, the Mitchell Library at the State Library of New South Wales, the National Library of Australia, and the State Library of Victoria; in France, the Archives nationales, the Bibliothèque du Musée de l'Homme, the Bibliothèque du Musée de la Marine, the Bibliothèque centrale du Muséum national d'Histoire naturelle, and the Bibliothèque nationale, all in Paris, the Ancienne Ecole de Médecine navale in La Rochelle, the Médiathèques in La Rochelle and Rochefort, the Musée des Beaux Arts in Chartres, the Muséums d'Histoire naturelle in Le Havre and La Rochelle, and the Service historique de la Défense, département Marine, in Vincennes, Rochefort, and Toulon; in the UK, the British Library, the British Museum, Cambridge University Library, the Library of the Linnean Society, and the National Maritime Museum. Particular thanks to Gabrielle Baglione, in Le Havre; to Yvonne Bouvier-Graux, Claude Stéfani, and Arnaud Thillier in Rochefort; and to Chantal de Gaye, Elise Patole-Edoumba, and Jean-Louis Mahe in La Rochelle. Paul Turnbull thanks the Council of the Royal College of Surgeons in London for permission to cite from manuscript material held in their Library.

We thank the following repositories for permission to reproduce images held in their collections: the David Rumsey Map Collection <http://www.davidrumsey.com> (Figure 1); the Service historique de la Défense, département Marine, Vincennes (Figures 8, 9, 12); the National Library of Australia, Canberra (Figures 3, 18, 19, 21, 22, 23, 24). We thank Bob Connolly and the Penguin Group for permission to reproduce a photograph to which they hold copyright (Figure 20).

Both editors enjoyed valuable opportunities to undertake research in Europe through the award of fellowships, visitorships, and research grants. Bronwen Douglas thanks the National Maritime Museum in Greenwich, UK, for a Caird Visiting Fellowship in 2001 and the Ecole des Hautes Etudes en Sciences Sociales (EHESS) for an appointment as *maître de conférence associé* at the Centre de Recherche et de Documentation sur l'Océanie (CREDO) in Marseille in 2007. Her research in France in 2004 was funded by a Getty Grant Program grant for a project on '*Tatau*/Tattoo: Embodied Art and Cultural Exchange, c. 1760-c. 2000', and in 2006-7 by an Australian Research Council Discovery grant for a project on 'European Naturalists and the Constitution of Human Difference in Oceania: Crosscultural Encounters and the Science of Race, 1768-1888'. Chris Ballard thanks the International Institute for Asian Studies, Amsterdam, for the award of an Exchange Fellowship in 1999; the Centre national de Recherche scientifique (France) for an appointment as *directeur de recherche* in CREDO in 1999-2000; and the EHESS for an appointment as *professeur invité* in 2001. His research in the UK in 2007 was funded by the ARC Discovery grant.

The editors thank the following colleagues for generous and incisive contributions to their particular chapters and during the course of the whole project: Alban Bensa, Claude Blanckaert, Peter Brown, Diana Carroll, John Cashmere, Elena Govor, Margaret Jolly, Gareth Knapman, Campbell Macknight, Andrew Pawley, Anton Ploeg, Anne Salmond, Martin Staum, Serge Tcherkézoff, and Nicholas Thomas. We are especially grateful to the lively critical stimulus provided by the participants in a postgraduate reading group on 'Encounters, Race, and the Construction of Human Difference in Oceania' held at The Australian National University in 2007, including Karen Fox, Hilary Howes, Sandra Manickam, Ashwin Raj, and Tiffany Shellam. Our greatest debts are to our families who have shared both the highs and the lows inseparable from a protracted project of research and writing while providing unswerving intellectual and emotional support. To Charles, Kirsty, Allie, and Andrew; and to Mem, Tessa, and Sebastian, this book is dedicated with much love and gratitude.

Introduction

Foreign Bodies in Oceania

Bronwen Douglas

In the five decades after World War II, a critical historical conjuncture — the defeat of Nazism, the Cold War, decolonization, the civil rights movements in North America and Australasia, and the anti-apartheid movement — authorized antiracism to the extent that the word 'race' itself, in its naturalized scientific sense of a broad, hereditary human grouping, became all but unsayable in public and academic discourses in both the West and the Soviet bloc. Biologists and anthropologists denied the physical or cultural reality of races and predicted the demise of the concept. Postcolonial scholars made hybridity a privileged metaphor and censored race from their vocabularies for fear of sustaining abhorrent racial theories or imputing racism to actually or formerly colonized people. Human variation was uncomfortably euphemized as ethnicity, identity, religion, or culture. Yet the notion that racial differences are materially true and determine the physical, intellectual, moral, or social qualities of identifiable groups has hardly been challenged in popular opinion or conservative politics across the globe, while many indigenous people have appropriated the word race as a weapon in their lexicons of identity and understand the euphemisms in racial terms.[1] With the Cold War finished but the ongoing legacies of racist regimes still evidently scarring the lives of victims and their descendants, with racial discrimination and persecution ongoing and racial scapegoating resurgent in the West, race has attracted renewed scholarly attention during the last decade or more and historians and philosophers are again charting the emergence, spread, illogic, and pernicious consequences of racialist thought.[2]

Notwithstanding this spirit of invigorated critical inquiry and some admirable scholarship on the history of race, anthropology, and geography,[3] general histories of race tend to be inadequately grounded in rigorous vernacular reading of the original works of Euro-American thinkers whose broad, labile gamut of positions on human differences is often collapsed under the homogenizing rubric of racism. There is a parallel dearth of systematic comparison of diverse national discourses on race.[4] In the twin contexts of these unexpected deficiencies in the comparative history of ideas and the near-total absence of detailed work on the history of race in Oceania as a broadly conceived region,[5] the essays in this collection open up important new terrains for critical historical inquiry — on the science of race, Oceanic studies, and the intersections of the two.

Strategies

Two striking elements of the idea of race are its slipperiness and the ontological realism it acquired during the nineteenth century, maintained in the face of fierce scientific and moral opposition during the late twentieth, and retained in conventional understandings virtually worldwide into the twenty-first. This volume challenges the naturalness of race by exposing its historicity and the tensions, incongruities, and fractures within or between shifting rival discourses on human similarity or difference. In the process, we probe the ambiguous conception of the modernist scientific notion of race in western Europe at the end of the eighteenth century; its subsequent normalization as an abstract system of knowledge, or raciology; its relationship to missionary and colonial praxis; and its instability, imprecision, and tenacity.

As historians of a potent and momentous concept, we treat ideas neither as purely abstract or discursive nor as a reflex of social relations and politics but as historically entangled with embodied human actions, including that of thinking — the word 'bodies' in the title is not mere rhetoric.[6] The persons and actions that primarily concern us are conceived in terms of a dynamic feedback loop linking metropoles with antipodes: savants rarely travelled but read, measured, dissected, thought, talked, wrote, and published; travellers, missionaries, and colonial naturalists or anthropologists observed, collected, recorded, and sometimes theorized in the light of prevailing ideas and their own interactions with indigenous people; and the products of these engagements fed novel concepts of human difference that both participated in and percolated into wider public spheres. By this logic, the idea of race was enmeshed in the interplay of unstable discourses and particular European experiences of encounters with non-European people, places, and things. Current ideas about human diversity were enacted and often transformed in such encounters which generated much of the evidence on which theorists relied to illustrate their deductions.

Our aim is not to explain racial thinking in causal terms but to convey an open-ended sense of the fertile, provisional, material transactions of persons, ideas, discourses, contexts, and their permutations, combinations, and performances. Spurning such an approach, the cultural geographer Kay Anderson chided me, along with George Stocking, Jr., Nancy Stepan, and other historians, for 'overgeneralisation' and for having hazarded 'no explanation' of the shift from Enlightenment humanism to nineteenth-century innatism. Yet this is a deliberate strategy, not an oversight. As an historian, I reject facile monocausal explanations such as Anderson's quite inadequate contention, based almost exclusively on a reading of anglophone literature, that 'race's founding' can be reduced to a '*crisis* of humanism' precipitated by British colonial encounters with Aboriginal '*intractability*'.[7] While we acknowledge that science is neither hermetic nor autonomous, we refuse to explain away the science of race as a simple effect of particular European discourses or social, political, or colonial circumstances. Contending that the interrelationships of science and society are not merely reflective, linearly causal, or even dialectical, we see the science of race and colonialism as parallel but porous domains of praxis, each with its own 'internal rhythm' and linked by complex, ambiguous intersections and exchanges.[8]

This grounded method for doing intellectual history requires detailed empirical ballast which in turn dictates a regional, rather than a global focus. Our regional focus on Oceania has both historical and pragmatic warrant: it acknowledges the considerable salience of indigenous Oceanian people in the natural history of man and the emergent science of race,[9] out of all proportion to their limited political, material, or demographic import to Europe; and it fits the research interests of the contributors. The term 'science of race' refers to systematic efforts made in various branches of natural history — particularly comparative anatomy, physiology, and zoology — to theorize physical differences between human groups as innate, morally and intellectually determinant, and possibly original. Such endeavours coalesced in the new disciplines of biology and anthropology which drew major stimulus from the rich stocks of information and objects repatriated from Oceania by scientific voyagers from the late 1760s.

Chronologically, we probe racial thinking in general and with specific relation to Oceania during a key era — the heyday of the scientific concept of race from its emergence in the second half of the eighteenth century until the outbreak of World War II. These two centuries encompassed important transitions in both global discourses and regional interactions. Globally, inchoate Enlightenment ideas about varieties within a common humanity metamorphosed into a ubiquitous but contested science of race which reified races as tangible markers of inherent somatic differences. Regionally, an uneven but steady contextual shift saw residence or settlement overlap and finally displace voyages as the dominant setting for European engagements with and knowledge of Oceanian people. The first of these transitions is the major theme of Part One; while the second weaves through Parts Two to Five.

Naming spaces

We apply 'Oceania' historically to the vast insular zone stretching from the Hawaiian Islands in the north, to Indonesia in the west, coastal Australia and Aotearoa New Zealand in the south, and Easter Island in the east. This extended sense reinstates the cartographic vision of the French geographers and naturalists who invented the term and transcends its restriction to the Pacific Islands in much later anglophone usage, including recent strategic appropriations by indigenous intellectuals concerned to negotiate postcolonial identities.[10] As originally conceived, Oceania embraced the Asian/Indian/Malay Archipelago or East Indies (the island of Borneo, modern Indonesia, Timor-Leste, Singapore, and the Philippines), New Guinea (modern Papua New Guinea and the Indonesian provinces of Papua and West Papua), New Holland (mainland Australia), Van Diemen's Land (Tasmania), New Zealand (Aotearoa), and the island groups of the Pacific Ocean (soon to be distributed between Melanesia, Micronesia, and Polynesia). The two centuries spanned by this volume comprise only a small, recent, mostly colonial fraction of the more or less immense length of human occupation of these places, estimated by archaeologists to range from as much as 65,000 years in Australia (and presumably earlier in Island Southeast Asia) to fewer than 800 years in Aotearoa.[11]

In 1804, Edme Mentelle (1730-1815) and Conrad Malte-Brun (1775-1826) coined the name *Océanique*, 'Oceanica', as a more precise label for 'this fifth part of the world usually grouped under the generic name of *Terres australes*', or 'southern lands'. The French term had pluralized *Terra Australis incognita*, the fifth continent of cartographic imagination since the early sixteenth century.[12] In 1756, the *littérateur* Charles de Brosses (1709-1777) proposed a geographic tripartition of this 'unknown southern world'. *Polynésie* (from Greek *polloi*, 'many') denoted 'everything in the vast Pacific Ocean' and encompassed what are now Polynesia, Micronesia, and much of Island Melanesia. *Australasie* (from Latin *australis*, 'southern') was located 'in the Indian Ocean to the south of Asia' and lumped hypothetical vast unknown lands together with actual places seen by voyagers in New Guinea, New Holland, Van Diemen's Land, New Zealand, and Espiritu Santo (in modern Vanuatu). *Magellanique* — a synonym for *Terra Australis* in earlier cartography — was for Brosses a purely speculative land mass stretching to the south of South America.[13] Mentelle and Malte-Brun retained only *Polynésie* from Brosses's nomenclature but, whereas Brosses had made it an umbrella label for the 'multiplicity of islands' in the Pacific Ocean generally, they contracted it to what would become Polynesia and Micronesia and substituted *Océanique* for the regional whole. In 1815, Adrien-Hubert Brué (1786-1832) in turn amended *Océanique* to *Océanie*, 'Oceania' (Figure 1).[14] In 1832, the navigator-naturalist Jules-Sébastien-César Dumont d'Urville (1790-1842) lent his considerable empirical authority to the name and broad geographic span of *Océanie* and in the process initiated the distribution of the Pacific Islands and their inhabitants between Melanesia, Polynesia, and Micronesia (Figure 2). Dumont d'Urville's terminology was formally adopted by the French Navy and popularized by his rival classifier Grégoire Louis Domeny de Rienzi (1789-1843), author of the highly derivative but widely-read *Océanie ou cinquième partie du monde*, 'Oceania or Fifth Part of the World' (1836-8).[15]

Figure 1: Adrien-Hubert Brué, 'Océanie ou cinquième partie du monde comprenant l'Archipel d'Asie, l'Australasie, la Polynésie, &.ª ... 1814'.[16]

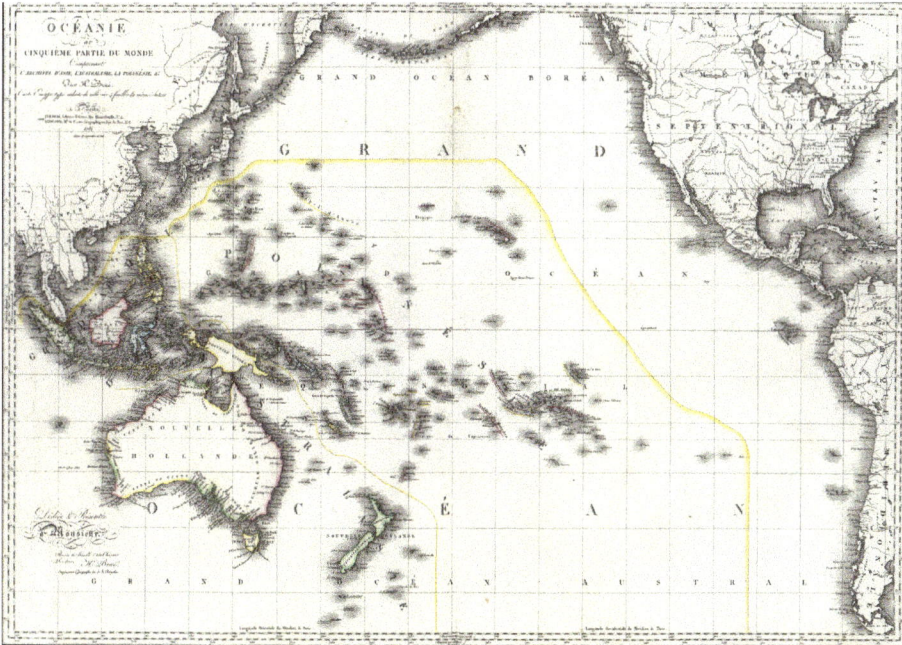

Engraving. David Rumsey Map Collection. Fulton, MD: Cartography Associates.

'Oceanica' evidently entered English in the 1820s via a translation of Malte-Brun's *Universal Geography* (1825) and was borrowed in the 1840s by two distinguished anglophone writers. The American philologist and ethnologist Horatio Hale (1817-1896), a member of the United States Exploring Expedition to the Pacific in 1838-42, made it his general label for all the land 'between the coasts of Asia and America', including New Holland and the 'East Indian Archipelago' (1846:3). And the British ethnologist James Cowles Prichard (1786-1848) found it the logical name for 'all the insulated lands that have been discovered in the Austral Seas', as far as and including Madagascar. A decade earlier, Prichard had occasionally used the phrases 'Oceanic race', 'nation', or 'tribes' but at that time limited 'Oceania' to 'the remote groupes' of Pacific Islands — a usage derived from the idiosyncratic racial taxonomy published by the French naval pharmacist and naturalist René-Primevère Lesson (1794-1849) following his voyage round the world on the *Coquille* in 1822-25. Lesson had restricted '*Océanie* properly speaking' to what is now called Polynesia and applied what might have been an early Portuguese usage of *Polynésie* to denominate the 'Asian archipelagoes', including New Guinea.[17] By contrast, British Evangelical missionaries who proselytized in the Pacific Islands from 1797 resisted the new French geographical labels until late in the nineteenth century but retained Brosses's ocean-wide span for Polynesia, only splitting 'Western' from 'Eastern'

Polynesia in the late 1830s in anticipation of their imminent encounter with a 'decidedly distinct', 'negro race' in the islands west of Fiji.[18]

Figure 2: Ambroise Tardieu, 'Carte pour l'intelligence du mémoire de M. le capitaine d'Urville sur les îles du grand océan (Océanie)'.[19]

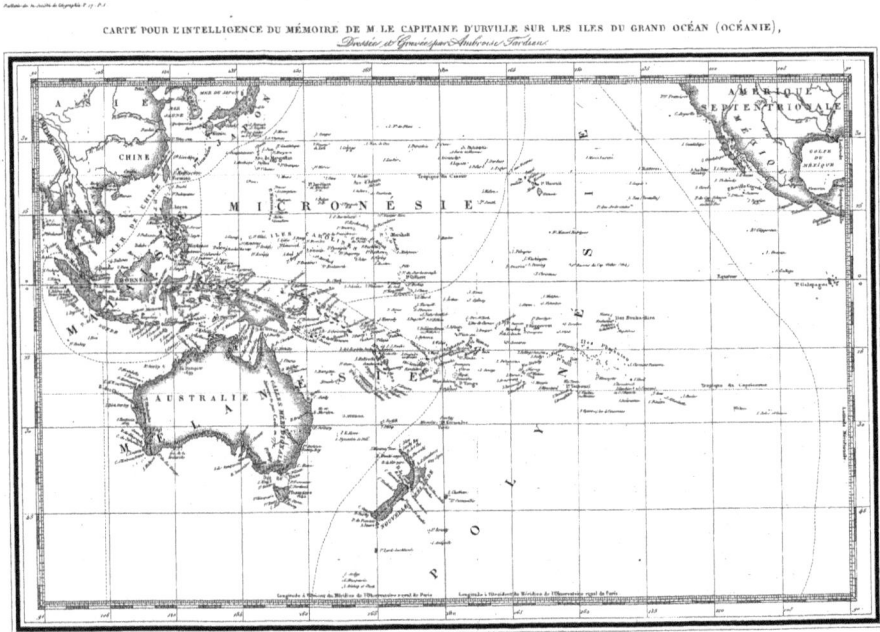

Engraving. Photograph B. Douglas.

Classifying people

From the outset, *Océanie* was internally racialized, with skin colour and physical organization the key differentiae in the elaboration of region-wide racial taxonomies. Mentelle and Malte-Brun located the 'very beautiful', 'copper-coloured', *'Polynesian race'* in what are now Polynesia and Micronesia and assigned it 'common origin' with 'the Malays of Asia'. They sharply differentiated 'the Polynesians' from the 'black race, that we can call *Oceanic Negroes'*, which inhabited New Guinea, Van Diemen's Land, and what is now Island Melanesia, and from a probable 'distinct third race' in New Holland which they ranked 'only a single degree above the brute' and likened to 'the apes'. Malte-Brun reasoned that the 'tanned' and the 'black' races must issue from 'two stocks as dissimilar in physiognomy as they are in language, namely, the *Malays* or yellow Oceanians, and the *Oceanic Negroes'*.[20]

In 1825, the French soldier and biologist Jean-Baptiste-Geneviève-Marcellin Bory de Saint-Vincent (1778-1846) took the radical step of dividing the human genus into fifteen separate *espèces*, 'species'. He called his seventh *espèce*

'Neptunian' and divided it between three *races*: 'Malay'; 'Oceanic' (the present-day Polynesians); and *Papou*, 'Papuan',[21] a 'hybrid' product of the alliance of Neptunians and 'Negroes of Oceanica'. The *Papous* were 'the most truly savage of all Men' along with Bory's eighth *espèce*, named 'Australasian' and mostly comprising mainland Aborigines. Australasians were 'the most brutish of Men', 'totally foreign to the social state', 'misshapen', and with 'the most deplorable facial resemblance' to mandrills. Bory's penultimate *espèce* reconfigured the Negroes of Oceanica as *Mélaniens*, a term derived from Greek *melas*, 'black', referring explicitly to skin colour. This species included the inhabitants of Van Diemen's Land ('timid, stupid, idle'), most of what is now Melanesia ('warlike and anthropophagous to the highest degree'), and remote areas of the larger islands of the Malay Archipelago ('hideous Men').[22]

Bory drew effusively for this part of his taxonomy on two key voyage texts: Lesson's contributions to the *Zoologie* of the *Coquille* expedition; and the *Zoologie* of the *Uranie* voyage (1817-20) produced by the naval surgeon-naturalists Jean-René Constant Quoy (1790-1869) and Joseph-Paul Gaimard (1793-1858) — Bory used 'Oceanic' in Lesson's restricted sense and owed his concept of hybridized *Papous* to Quoy and Gaimard.[23] Lesson (1829), a more ambitious classifier than most of his naval colleagues, divided 'the various Oceanians' (here using the term in its broad sense) into a tripartite racial hierarchy on the basis of physical organization, customs, presumed origins, and gross corporeal affinities. His '1st race', 'Hindu-Caucasic', derived from the Indian subcontinent and was divided between a 'Malay branch' and an 'Oceanian' one (present-day Polynesians) which he thought physically 'superior' to other South Sea Islanders. His '2nd race', 'Mongolic', was located in what is now Micronesia. His '3rd race', 'Black', was split into two branches: the 'Caffro-Madagascan' comprised a *Papou* variety inhabiting the New Guinea coast, nearby islands, and present-day Island Melanesia and a 'Tasmanian' variety in Van Diemen's Land; while the *Alfourous* occupied New Holland ('Australians') and the interior of New Guinea and some islands of the Malay Archipelago ('*Endamênes*').[24] Neither *Papou* nor *Alfourou* was a new term. In the early sixteenth century, *Papua* was a local toponym for islands to the west of New Guinea which Portuguese and Spanish travellers extended to the 'black' inhabitants of those islands and the New Guinea mainland. From the late eighteenth century, it was often generalized to 'black' Oceanian people as a whole. So-called *Alfourous* (*Alfours*, *Alfoërs*, *Haraforas*, etc.) were a recurrent, if elusive presence in Portuguese, Spanish, Dutch, French, and British colonial imaginaries from the sixteenth to the twentieth centuries.[25]

Dumont d'Urville's (1832) ethnological classification is more streamlined than these convoluted schemas, though no less racialized. He divided the inhabitants of Oceania into 'two distinct races' on the basis of skin colour, physical appearance, language, political institutions, religion, and reception of Europeans.

Dumont d'Urville reworked Bory's term *Mélanien* into *Mélanésien*, 'Melanesian', as his general name for the 'black Oceanian race' which he found 'disagreeable' and 'generally very inferior' to the 'copper-coloured race' of 'Polynesians' and 'Micronesians' and to the 'Malays'. The 'Australians' and the 'Tasmanians' were at the base of this racial hierarchy as 'the primitive and natural state of the Melanesian race'.[26] The racial implications of Dumont d'Urville's cartography were taken for granted in 1834 by Charles Monin (18?-1880) whose map of 'Océanie' overlaid the 'division adopted by the geographers' into Polynesia, Australasia, and the Indian Archipelago with Dumont d'Urville's 'division by race of men' (Figures 3, 3a). By 1830, few Euro-Americans would have disputed Dumont d'Urville's presumption of the material reality of discrete, physically defined, differentially endowed human races, though the origins, import, and future implications of racial distinctions were bitterly contested. His racial nomenclature for Oceania was quickly adopted in France but was viewed ambivalently by many anglophone writers. The American Hale (1846:3-116) fully embraced it and lauded the 'propriety' of correlating geographical 'departments' with 'the character of their inhabitants'. In mid-century, the Anglican Bishop of New Zealand, George Augustus Selwyn (1809-1878), appropriated Dumont d'Urville's neologism to name the Melanesian Mission, his peripatetic evangelistic enterprise in the southwest Pacific. Selwyn sometimes also used the term as a linguistic and racial label but, unlike the Frenchman, did so non-pejoratively, maintaining 'that civilization is a mere name, and that religion is the only real ground of difference between the various races of mankind'.[27] Robert Henry Codrington (1830-1922), a subsequent head of the Melanesian Mission, used Melanesian and Polynesian as anthropological labels but limited Melanesian to the island groups east and southeast of New Guinea. He too refused the idea of racial hierarchy. Prichard, in contrast, rejected Dumont d'Urville's wording — Melanesian lacked 'etymological accuracy' and should be replaced by 'Kelænonesian' — but rehearsed his invidious racial discrimination: 'the black races in Oceanica' were 'very different from' and 'very inferior to the Malayo-Polynesians'.[28]

Figure 3: Charles V. Monin, *Océanie: divisions de l'Océanie*.[29]

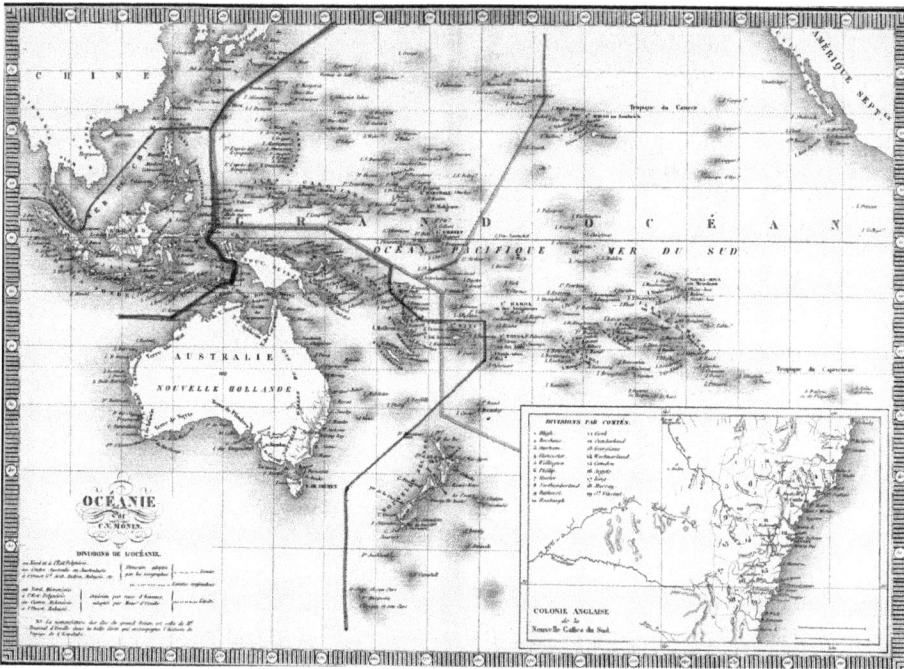

Engraving. MAP T 913/2. Canberra: National Library of Australia.

Figure 3a: Charles V. Monin, *Océanie: divisions de l'Océanie*, detail.[30]

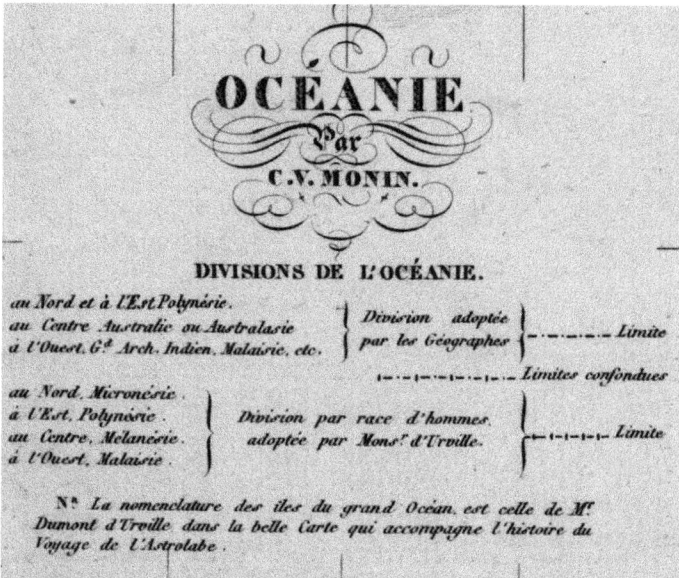

Engraving. MAP T 913/2. Canberra: National Library of Australia.

For much of the nineteenth century, English racial terminologies for Oceanian people were more varied and ambiguous than French, due in part to differing emphases in the respective fields of inquiry. In Britain, the science of man had strongly philanthropic roots and drew much empirical sustenance from missionary ethnography.[31] In France, the science of race was a highly deductive outgrowth of biology and physical anthropology, fed by the work of travelling naturalists.[32] Yet, notwithstanding principled humanitarian antipathy to the dehumanizing tendencies of the science of race, English writings on man were steadily infiltrated by racial logic and language. The authors of works on Oceania, including missionaries, routinely differentiated the 'black' 'Polynesian negro' from the 'brown' or 'copper-coloured' 'proper Polynesian', or the 'Papuan' race from the 'Malayo-Polynesian' race, before normalizing varieties of Dumont d'Urville's binary system late in the century.[33]

Oceania

Océanie retained both its breadth and its racial connotations in French usage well into the twentieth century.[34] By this stage, 'Oceania' was fairly common in English and just as racialized despite its narrower geographic span (see note 10). In 1920, the Foreign Office handbook on *British Possessions in Oceania* differentiated Pacific Islanders along explicitly social evolutionist racial lines: Solomon Islanders were 'a Melanesian race, still largely in a state of barbarism' and 'naked savages scarcely beyond the head-hunting stage of development'; whereas Tongans were 'a branch of the Polynesian race', 'a highly advanced native race who have accepted Christianity'.[35] By the 1970s, with the public discrediting of racial language, the regional name had shed overt intimations of race in both French and English. In French, *Océanie* had contracted in conformity with the international geopolitical norm that puts the Malay Archipelago in Asia and divides Asia from Oceania along the arbitrary colonial border which cuts the island of New Guinea in two.[36]

Recuperation of the broader early conception of Oceania suits our ethical, political, and intellectual interests. Ethically, we seek to expose the old racial implications of the term to rigorous historical critique. Politically, an inclusive construction of Oceania unsettles the unquestioned realism of the postcolonial national and ethnic boundaries that were inherited from colonial divisions and are further reinscribed in the partitioning of academic research. Historically, our terminology acknowledges farflung cultural and linguistic affinities, notably between Austronesian-speaking groups, and the trajectories of settlement and other human movements in the region, including those of Europeans, before the congealing of colonial borders in the late nineteenth century. At least until the 1880s, the indigenous inhabitants of New Holland/Australia and Van Diemen's Land/Tasmania were usually compared, classified, and ranked within the same regional frame as people labelled Malays, Polynesians, Micronesians, Melanesians,

Oceanic Negroes, or Papuans. And Oceania loomed large in its own right in the history of racial thinking: Oceanian experience and examples were central to the biologization of the idea of race from the late eighteenth century (see Chapters Two and Three); racial comparisons within Oceania and case studies from the region, especially Aboriginal Australia, figured prominently in the nineteenth-century appropriation of anthropology by the science of race and in qualified humanitarian opposition to the union (see Chapters Two, Four, Five, Six, and Seven); and the region contributed to science's rejection of race from the mid-twentieth century, notwithstanding entrenched popular beliefs and vocabularies and the naturalization of Dumont d'Urville's racial categories in modern indigenous usages.[37]

Foreign bodies

Apart from signalling historical particularity and embodiment, our use of the term 'foreign bodies' is deliberately ambiguous and ironic. As foreign bodies in Oceanian contexts, European and other travellers, missionaries, or colonizers were received unpredictably, sometimes with joy and hospitality but also with indifference, ambivalence, fear, rejection, or hostility. Indigenous reception helped shape the attitudes, reactions, and representations of visitors who in turn impinged to a greater or lesser extent on local patterns of action, relationship, and understanding. As foreign bodies in European representations, comparisons, classifications, and collections, indigenous Oceanian people were usually objectified and measured as specimens. Ultimately encompassed by colonial empires, indigenous bodies became colonial subjects and were often alienated from their own places — rendered foreign — especially in settler colonies.

It is nonetheless important to resist the distanced binary perspective which represents imperial and colonial encounters as the asymmetric opposition of discrete homogeneous communities, one local and subordinate, the other foreign and dominant.[38] Close attention to particular past situations, always messy and multiplex, reveals overlapping alliances between local people and foreigners whose respective social and cultural groupings intersected ambiguously and fractured internally along lines of gender, age, vocation, place, interest, and rank, class, or status. Moreover, the foreigners in such encounters were often not Europeans but other Oceanian people — travellers, labourers, missionaries, native police, health workers, other colonial appointees, and so forth. One product of indigenous liaisons with foreigners was the engendering of significant populations of mixed ancestry, further complicating the quixotic colonial quest for racial purity (see Chapters One and Eight).

Notwithstanding these caveats, this volume is not per se a history of encounters in Oceania but a history of the idea of race with specific reference to that region. Our major concern, with varying relative emphasis, is the entanglement of discourse and experience with respect to race. Experience was grounded in encounters, where racial ideas and representations were enacted, reworked, or forged, but the level of generality at which the collection is necessarily pitched means that particular embodied encounters figure only fleetingly as examples.[39] Our core themes are variety, flux, ambiguity, contestation, and recursion in the concept of race as well as in the exemplary representations and appropriations of indigenous Oceanian people and their bodies made by savants and scientists, field naturalists and collectors, colonial officials and humanitarians, settlers and missionaries. Our wide thematic net thus traces the threads of scientific conceptions of race into political, philanthropic, and public domains. We position race not only in relation to biological and anthropological discourses but also colonial and government policies, popular stereotypes, and equivocal humanitarian engagements with the idea of race and its science. We foreground ideological fractures and national, class, and personal variations which rendered European racial ideas and representations anything but homogeneous or consistent. But we also chart the ongoing, if now largely illegitimate appeal of the race concept, its chameleon capacity to take on the colouring of the time and the place, and its propensity to recur in the face of the most determined efforts to invalidate or extirpate it.

The chapters

Parts One and Two of this book set the global, regional, and empirical scenes for the remainder of the volume and constitute an original contribution to the history of ideas. In two substantial chapters of very different focal lengths, Bronwen Douglas investigates comparatively the formulation of the modernist concept of race in Germany and France; the scientific consolidation of racial theory in France, Britain, and the United States from the mid-eighteenth century to about 1880; transnational flows of ideas about human origins, unity or diversity, and racial mixing; and the relationships of theory to evidence derived in a particular field. Chapter One is a history of a European idea. By synthesizing a wide range of contemporary materials, it shows how the biologization of an older, genealogical conception of race in western Europe at the end of the eighteenth century enabled starker differentiations between essentialized extended human groups and paved the way for a normal science of race spanning a broad range of moral and theoretical positions. This remarkably tenacious paradigmatic set was not dislodged until the mid-twentieth century and its fallout endures worldwide.[40] Chapter Two particularizes the history of race in the light of the prolific empirical legacy of scientific voyaging in Oceania, the growing force of the taxonomic impulse, and the recurrent tension between global theoretical systems and regional facts. Through a focus on the interrelationships of selected savants and travelling naturalists, of deductive and empirical knowledge, this chapter probes the reciprocal significance of metropolitan discourses and Oceanic field experience for competing schools of the hardening science of race, as the orthodox doctrine of a single human species steadily lost ground to the mounting conceivability of polygeny — the belief in plural human origins or multiple species.

In Chapter Three, Chris Ballard addresses the middle phase of the irregular trajectory from voyaging to residence to colonial settlement as the primary conduit for the collection and deployment of information about indigenous Oceanian people. With particular reference to New Guinea, he maps a transition in heuristic authority between the 1820s and 1870: from distanced early colonial observers in the Malay or Indian Archipelago, whose imagined cartographies of human difference rested on haphazard temporal and spatial contrasts between the 'brown' Malay race and the 'Oceanic Negroes' or Papuans, to a new mid-nineteenth-century model of the terrestrial natural scientist engaged in longterm field observation under broad colonial aegis, embodied in the figure of Alfred Russel Wallace. Wallace, championing the scientific method, insisted on direct visual contact and the presence of the observer. Yet his concern for the correct identification of boundaries for human, as well as zoological distributions both presumed and prefigured key debates on the origins of pure racial types. The chimeric ideal of racial purity became a focal concept through an increasing emphasis on the 'problem' of racial mixing between Malay and Papuan.

Part Three takes the science of race into colonial settings, with specific attention to the importance of knowledge about Aboriginal Australian bodies, both living and dead, in the developing disciplines of anthropology in Britain and France; and to the negative implications for Aboriginal people of hardening conceptions of race. In Chapter Four, Paul Turnbull takes issue with the conventional narrative that attributes scientific lust for Aboriginal anatomical specimens solely to Darwinians anxious to confirm the evolution of humanity by speciation. He shows that Darwinians and their opponents, metropolitans and colonials, all engaged in bitter competition to acquire Aboriginal bodily remains for the contrasting knowledge about human racial differences and racial extinction presumed to inhere in them; and that such professional conflicts helped in practice to confirm the centrality of race in colonial attitudes and strategies towards indigenous Australians. In Chapter Five, Stephanie Anderson makes a single episode — an actual encounter between three Aborigines and several French anthropologists in Paris in 1885 — a synecdoche for the discursive colonization of Aboriginal Australians and Tasmanians by French raciology. However, she is alert both to ambiguities in the encounter and its representation and to tensions in the wider discourse between physicalist and ethnographic approaches. The Australians were objectified as characteristic specimens of a supposedly inferior, autochthonous racial type and yet traces of their individual personalities, capabilities, and emotional state punctuated the scientists' bleak, anthropometrical descriptions. So too, the bewildering physical and cultural variety apparent in ethnographic reports of actual Aboriginal people defied simplistic premises about racial homogeneity or racial purity and introduced doubt and contradiction to raciological analysis, problematizing its core assumption of natural racial hierarchy and ultimately the concept of race itself.

Part Four introduces new complexity into this story of uncertainty and rifts in nineteenth-century scientific discourses on race by extending the inquiry into the early twentieth century and addressing a striking lacuna in many histories of racial thinking — the ambivalent relationships between British Evangelical humanism and the science of race, ranging across a spectrum from antagonism, to compromise, to collaboration. In Chapter Six, Helen Gardner tracks a series of nineteenth-century debates in Britain and colonial Australia over the universal presence or racially selective absence of the human capacity for religious belief and for becoming Christian. Initially contested as evidence for human unity or plural origins, by late in the century the purported existence or lack of the 'faculty of faith' — particularly among Aboriginal Australians — was taken by competing strands of evolutionist anthropology as a sign of the stage of psychic development reached by different races. Such evolutionist arguments provoked both opposition and qualified adherence among Evangelical missionaries who had lived and worked with indigenous communities in Oceania. In Chapter Seven, Christine Weir provides another variant on the core themes of normalization, fracture, and recursion with respect to race by mapping entangled rival discourses — religious or secular, scientific or public — on human unity and difference in the late nineteenth and early twentieth centuries. In key texts by Evangelical missionaries, naturalized racial terminology and social evolutionist assumptions jostled with the humanizing imprint of personal acquaintance with individual Pacific Islanders and with Christian distrust of the concepts of natural racial hierarchy or the absolute separation of races. In the aftermath of World War I, interpersonal experience in the mission field informed an emerging humanist internationalism which confronted the strident biological determinism of white supremacist, 'world eugenics' rhetoric emanating from the United States. In Australia, a parallel contest between paternalist internationalism and hardline colonial self-interest developed in the course of debates about Australia's League of Nations' mandate over former German New Guinea.

Part Five recapitulates the linked themes of racial purity, miscegenation, and hybridity, transposed to pragmatic colonial and national settings in Oceania which exemplify the ambiguous flows between abstract racial theorizing, popular race pride or anxieties about racial integrity, and colonial praxis. In Chapter Eight, Vicki Luker concludes the volume with a comparative investigation into a colonial puzzle — the markedly discrepant attitudes to the 'half-caste' expressed in diverse settings in the South Pacific during the interwar period. Emphasizing contexts over theory, she probes the varied pragmatic import of latitude and relative chronology, sexualized racial ambivalence about miscegenation and half-castes, and institutional or environmental imperatives. She shows clearly that, if the science of race did not necessarily impinge directly on popular consciousness or colonial policy,[41] its eclectic theories on hybridity and acclimatization were repeatedly invoked in divergent positions taken on racial assimilation or racial purity in the new nations of Australia and New Zealand or in the colonies of Western Samoa and Fiji. Here, too, as in other settings discussed in this collection, the ambiguities of the idea of race itself and the deeply flawed logic of its science were patent, as were the tensions and fractures in the dissonant discourses that race at once infiltrated and informed.

References

Anderson, Kay. 2007. *Race and the Crisis of Humanism*. London and New York: Routledge.

Anderson, Warwick. 2000. The Possession of Kuru: Medical Science and Biocolonial Exchange. *Comparative Studies in Society and History* 42:713-44.

_____. 2002. *The Cultivation of Whiteness: Science, Health and Racial Destiny in Australia*. Carlton, VIC: Melbourne University Press.

Ballantyne, Tony, ed. 2004. *Science, Empire and the European Exploration of the Pacific*. Aldershot, Hants, UK, and Burlington, VT: Ashgate.

Ballard, Chris. 2001. Collecting Pygmies: the 'Tapiro' and the British Ornithologists' Union Expedition to Dutch New Guinea, 1910-1911. In *Hunting the Gatherers: Ethnographic Collectors, Agents and Agency in Melanesia, 1870s-1930s*, ed. Michael O'Hanlon and Robert L. Welsch, 127-54. New York and Oxford: Berghahn Books.

_____. 2006. Strange Alliance: Pygmies in the Colonial Imaginary. *World Archaeology* 38:133-51.

Bernasconi, Robert, ed. 2001a. *Concepts of Race in the Eighteenth Century*, 8 vols. Bristol, UK: Thoemmes.

_____. 2001b. *Race*. Malden, MA, and Oxford: Blackwell.

_____. 2002. *American Theories of Polygenesis*, 7 vols. Bristol, UK: Thoemmes.

_____. 2003. *Race and Anthropology*, 9 vols. Bristol, UK: Thoemmes.

_____. 2005. *Race, Hybridity, and Miscegenation*, 3 vols. Bristol, UK: Thoemmes.

Bernasconi, Robert, and Sybol Cook, ed. 2003. *Race and Racism in Continental Philosophy*. Bloomington: Indiana University Press.

Bibliothèque nationale de France. 2004. Domeny de Rienzi, Grégoire Louis (1789-1843). *Catalogue en ligne BP-OPALE PLUS* Notice no. FRBNF 13325735. Paris: Bibliothèque nationale de France. Accessed 16 December 2004, online <http://www.bnf.fr/pages/zNavigat/frame/catalog.htm>.

Blanckaert, Claude. 1988. On the Origins of French Ethnology. In *Bones, Bodies, Behavior: Essays on Biological Anthropology*, ed. George W. Stocking, Jr., 18-55. Madison: University of Wisconsin Press.

——. 2003a. Les conditions d'émergence de la science des races au début du XIXe siècle. In *L'idée de 'race' dans les sciences humaines et la littérature (XVIIIe et XIXe siècles)*, ed. Sarga Moussa, 133-49. Paris: L'Harmattan.

——. 2003b. Of Monstrous Métis? Hybridity, Fear of Miscegenation, and Patriotism from Buffon to Paul Broca. In *The Color of Liberty: Histories of Race in France*, ed. Sue Peabody and Tyler Stovall, 42-70. Durham, NC: Duke University Press.

——. 2006. 'Notre immortel naturaliste': Buffon, la science de l'homme et l'écriture de l'histoire. In *Buffon: de l'Homme*, ed. Michèle Duchet, 407-67. Paris: L'Harmattan.

Bory de Saint-Vincent, Jean-Baptiste-Geneviève-Marcellin. 1827 [1825]. *L'homme (homo): essai zoologique sur le genre humain*, 2 vols. 2nd edition. Paris: Rey et Gravier.

Brantlinger, Patrick. 2003. *Dark Vanishings: Discourse on the Extinction of Primitive Races, 1800-1930*. Ithaca, NY, and London: Cornell University Press.

Bravo, Michael T. 1996. Ethnological Encounters. In *Cultures of Natural History*, ed. N. Jardine, J.A. Secord, and E.C. Spary, 338-57. Cambridge: Cambridge University Press.

Bravo, Michael, and Sverker Sörlin, ed. 2002. *Narrating the Arctic: a Cultural History of Nordic Scientific Practices*. Canton, MA: Science History Publications.

[Brosses, Charles de]. 1756. *Histoire des navigations aux terres australes contenant ce que l'on sçait des mœurs & des productions des contrées découvertes jusqu'à ce jour ...*, 2 vols. Paris: Durand.

Brown, George. 1887. Papuans and Polynesians. *Journal of the Anthropological Institute of Great Britain and Ireland* 16:311-27.

——. 1910. *Melanesians and Polynesians: their Life-Histories Described and Compared*. London: Macmillan and Co.

Brué, Adrien-Hubert. 1816 [1814]. Océanie ou cinquième partie du monde, comprenant l'Archipel d'Asie, l'Australasie, la Polynésie, &.ª In *Grand atlas universel, ou collection de cartes encyprotypes, générales et détaillées des cinq parties du monde*, carte 36. Engraving. 2nd edition. Paris: Desray. David Rumsey Map Collection. Fulton, MD: Cartography Associates. Accessed 14 September 2007, online <http://www.davidrumsey.com/detail?id=1-1-25585-1040021&name=Oceanie>.

Caneva, Kenneth L. 1998. Objectivity, Relativism, and the Individual: a Role for a Post-Kuhnian History of Science. *Studies in History and Philosophy of Science* 29:327-44.

Codrington, R.H. 1881. Religious Beliefs and Practices in Melanesia. *Journal of the Royal Anthropological Institute* 10:261-316.

_____. 1891. *The Melanesians: Studies in their Anthropology and Folk-lore.* Oxford: Clarendon Press.

Copans, Jean, and Jean Jamin, ed. 1978. *Aux origines de l'anthropologie française: les mèmoires de la Société des observateurs de l'homme en l'an VII.* Paris: Le Sycomore.

Cowlishaw, Gillian K. 2000. Censoring Race in 'Post-colonial' Anthropology. *Critique of Anthropology* 20:101-23.

Dalrymple, Alexander. 1770-1. *An Historical Collection of the Several Voyages and Discoveries in the South Pacific Ocean*, 2 vols. London: J. Nourse, T. Payne and P. Elmsley.

Domeny de Rienzi, Grégoire Louis. 1836-8. *Océanie ou cinquième partie du monde: revue géographique et ethnographique de la Malaisie, de la Micronésie, de la Polynésie et de la Mélanésie, offrant les résultats des voyages et des découvertes de l'auteur et de ses devanciers, ainsi que ses nouvelles classifications et divisions de ces contrées*, 3 vols. Paris: Firmin Didot frères.

Douglas, Bronwen. 1999. Science and the Art of Representing 'Savages': Reading 'Race' in Text and Image in South Seas Voyage Literature. *History and Anthropology* 11:157-201.

_____. 2003. Seaborne Ethnography and the Natural History of Man. *Journal of Pacific History* 38:3-27.

_____. 2005. 'Cureous Figures': European Voyagers and *Tatau*/Tattoo in Polynesia, 1595-1800. In *Tattoo: Bodies, Art and Exchange in the Pacific and the West*, ed. Nicholas Thomas, Anna Cole, and Bronwen Douglas, 32-52. London and Durham, NC: Reaktion Books and Duke University Press.

_____. 2006. Slippery Word, Ambiguous Praxis: 'Race' and Late 18th-Century Voyagers in Oceania. *Journal of Pacific History* 41:1-29.

_____. 2007. The Lure of Texts and the Discipline of Praxis: Cross-Cultural History in a Post-Empirical World. *Humanities Research*, 14:11-30. Online <http://epress.anu.edu.au/hrj2007_citation.html>.

_____. 2008. Voyages, Encounters, and Agency in Oceania: Captain Cook and Indigenous People. *History Compass* 6 (3):712-37.

_____. n.d. Encountering Agency: Islanders, European Voyagers, and the Production of Race in Oceania. In *Changing Contexts — Shifting Meanings: Transformations of Cultural Traditions in Oceania*, ed. Elfriede Hermann. Honolulu: University of Hawai'i Press.

Dumont d'Urville, Jules-Sébastien-César. 1832. Sur les îles du Grand Océan. *Bulletin de la Société de Géographie* 17:1-21.

Duyker, Edward. 2003. *Citizen Labillardière: a Naturalist's Life in Revolution and Exploration (1755-1834)*. Carlton South, VIC: Miegunyah Press.

_____. 2006. *François Péron, an Impetuous Life: Naturalist and Voyager.* Carlton South, VIC: Miegunyah Press.

Eigen, Sara, and Mark Larrimore, ed. 2006. *The German Invention of Race.* Albany: State University of New York Press.

Eisler, William. 1995. *The Furthest Shore: Images of Terra Australis from the Middle Ages to Captain Cook*. Cambridge: Cambridge University Press.

Ellingson, Ter. 2001. *The Myth of the Noble Savage.* Berkeley: University of California Press.

Ellis, William. 1831 [1829]. *Polynesian Researches, During a Residence of Nearly Eight Years in the Society and Sandwich Islands*, 4 vols. 2nd edition. London: Fisher, Son, & Jackson.

Erskine, John Elphinstone. 1853. *Journal of a Cruise among the Islands of the Western Pacific ... in Her Majesty's Ship Havannah*. London: John Murray.

Fine, Oronce [Oronteus Finaeus]. 1531. *Nova, et Integra Universi Orbis Descriptio.* Woodcut. [Paris: Christian Wechel]. DL Q53/2. Sydney: Mitchell Library. Accessed 18 April 2008, online <http://www.nla.gov.au/exhibitions/southland/maps-1531_Fine.html>.

Fisher, Robin, and Hugh Johnston, ed. 1993. *From Maps to Metaphors: the Pacific World of George Vancouver*. Vancouver: UBC Press.

Frost, Alan. 1976. The Pacific Ocean: the Eighteenth Century's 'New World'. *Studies on Voltaire and the Eighteenth Century* 151-5:779-822.

Gardner, Helen Bethea. 2006. *Gathering for God: George Brown in Oceania.* Dunedin, NZ: University of Otago Press.

Gascoigne, John. 2007. The German Enlightenment and the Pacific. In *The Anthropology of the Enlightenment*, ed. Larry Wolff and Marco Cipolloni, 141-71.Stanford, CA: Stanford University Press.

Gelpke, J.H.F. Sollewijn. 1993. On the Origin of the Name Papua. *Bijdragen Tot de Taal-, Land-, en Volkenkunde* 149:318-32.

Goos, Pieter. 1668 [1666]. *The Sea-Atlas or the Watter-World, Wherein are described all the Sea Coasts of the Knowne World ...* Amsterdam: Pieter Goos.

Gould, Stephen Jay. 1996 [1981]. *The Mismeasure of Man.* 2nd edition. New York: Norton.

Great Britain, Foreign Office. 1920. *British Possessions in Oceania.* London: HM Stationery Office.

Hale, Horatio. 1846. *United States Exploring Expedition: during the years 1838, 1839, 1840, 1841, 1842, under the Command of Charles Wilkes, U.S.N.,* vol. 6. *Ethnography and Philology.* Philadelphia: Lea & Blanchard.

Hall, Catherine. 2002. *Civilising Subjects: Colony and Metropole in the English Imagination, 1830-1867.* Chicago and London: University of Chicago Press.

Hannaford, Ivan. 1996. *Race: the History of an Idea in the West.* Washington, DC, and Baltimore, MD: Woodrow Wilson Center Press and Johns Hopkins University Press.

Harrison, Faye V. 1995. The Persistent Power of 'Race' in the Cultural and Political Economy of Racism. *Annual Review of Anthropology* 24:47-74.

Hau'ofa, Epeli. 1993. Our Sea of Islands. In *A New Oceania: Rediscovering Our Sea of Islands*, ed. Eric Waddell, Vijay Naidu, and Epeli Hau'ofa, 2-16. Suva, Fiji: School of Social and Economic Development, University of the South Pacific.

————. 1998. The Ocean in Us. *Contemporary Pacific* 10:392-410.

Herbert, Christopher. 1991. *Culture and Anomie: Ethnographic Imagination in the Nineteenth Century.* Chicago: University of Chicago Press.

Higham, Thomas, Atholl Anderson, and Chris Jacomb. 1999. Dating the First New Zealanders: the Chronology of Wairau Bar. *Antiquity* 73 (280):420-7.

Hilliard, David. 1978. *God's Gentlemen: a History of the Melanesian Mission, 1849-1942.* St Lucia: University of Queensland Press.

Home, R.W., ed. 1988. *Australian Science in the Making*. Cambridge: Cambridge University Press.

Inglis, John. 1887. *In the New Hebrides: Reminiscences of Missionary Life and Work, Especially on the Island of Aneityum, from 1850 till 1877*. London: Thomas Nelson and Sons.

Jolly, Margaret. 2001. Imagining Oceania: Indigenous and Foreign Representations of a Sea of Islands. In *Framing the Pacific in the 21ˢᵗ Century: Co-existence and Friction*, ed. Daizaburo Yui and Yasua Endo, 29-48. Tokyo: Center for Pacific and American Studies, University of Tokyo.

————. 2007. Imagining Oceania: Indigenous and Foreign Representations of a Sea of Islands. *Contemporary Pacific* 19:508-45.

Jones, Rhys. 1988. Images of Natural Man. In *Baudin in Australian Waters: the Artwork of the French Voyage of Discovery to the Southern Lands 1800-1804*, ed. Jacqueline Bonnemains, Elliott Forsyth, and Bernard Smith, 35-64. Melbourne: Oxford University Press.

Kaiwar, Vasant, and Sucheta Mazumdar, ed. 2003. *Essays on Race, Orient, Nation*. Durham, NC: Duke University Press.

Kidd, Colin. 2006. *The Forging of Races: Race and Scripture in the Protestant Atlantic World, 1600-2000*. Cambridge: Cambridge University Press.

Kohn, Marek. 1996 [1995]. *The Race Gallery: the Return of Racial Science*. London: Vintage.

Kuhn, Thomas S. 1970 [1962]. *The Structure of Scientific Revolutions*. 2nd edition. Chicago: University of Chicago Press.

Lesson, René-Primevère. 1829 [1826]. Mémoire sur les races humaines répandues sur les îles du Grand-Océan, et considérées sous les divers rapports physiologiques, naturels et moraux. In *Voyage médical autour du monde, exécuté sur la corvette du roi La Coquille … pendant les années 1822, 1823, 1824 et 1825 …*, 153-228. Paris: Roret.

Lesson, René-Primevère, and Prosper Garnot. 1826-30. *Voyage autour du monde … sur la corvette de Sa Majesté, La Coquille, pendant les années 1822, 1823, 1824 et 1825 … par L.I. Duperrey. Zoologie*, 2 vols. Paris: Arthus Bertrand.

Liebersohn, Harry. 2006. *The Travelers' World: Europe to the Pacific*. Cambridge, MA: Harvard University Press.

Lincoln, Margarette, ed. 1998. *Science and Exploration in the Pacific: European Voyages to the Southern Oceans in the Eighteenth Century*. Woodbridge, Suffolk: Boydell Press in association with the National Maritime Museum.

Littlefield, Alice, Leonard Lieberman, and Larry T. Reynolds. 1982. Redefining Race: the Potential Demise of a Concept in Physical Anthropology. *Current Anthropology* 23:641-55.

McGregor, Russell. 1997. *Imagined Destinies: Aboriginal Australians and the Doomed Race Theory, 1880-1939.* Carlton, VIC.: Melbourne University Press.

Mackay, David. 1999. Myth, Science, and Experience in the British Construction of the Pacific. In *Voyages and Beaches: Pacific Encounters, 1769-1840*, ed. Alex Calder, Jonathan Lamb, and Bridget Orr, 100-13. Honolulu: University of Hawai'i Press.

MacLeod, Roy, and Philip F. Rehbock, ed. 1988. *Nature in its Greatest Extent: Western Science in the Pacific.* Honolulu, University of Hawaii Press.

————. 1994. *Darwin's Laboratory: Evolutionary Theory and Natural History in the Pacific.* Honolulu: University of Hawaii Press.

Malik, Kenan. 1996. *The Meaning of Race: Race, History and Culture in Western Society.* Basinstoke, Hampshire, UK: Palgrave.

Malte-Brun, Conrad. 1803. Géographie genérale, mathématique et physique. In Edme Mentelle and Conrad Malte Brun, *Géographie mathématique, physique et politique de toutes les parties du monde ...,* vol. 1, 151-552. Paris: H. Tardieu et Laporte.

————. 1810. *Précis de la geographie universelle, ou description de toutes les parties du monde, sur un plan nouveau, d'après les grandes divisions naturelles du globe,* vol. 1, *Histoire de la géographie.* Paris: F. Buisson.

————. 1813. *Précis de la geographie universelle, ou description de toutes les parties du monde, sur un plan nouveau, d'après les grandes divisions naturelles du globe ...,* vol. 4, *Description de l'Inde, de l'Océanique, et de l'Afrique septentrionale.* Paris: Fr. Buisson.

————. 1825. *Universal Geography, or a Description of all the Parts of the World, on a New Plan, according to the Great Natural Divisions of the Globe ...,* tr. unknown, vol. 3, *Containing the Description of India and Oceanica.* Boston: Wells and Lilly.

Marshall, P.J., and Glyndwr Williams. 1982. *The Great Map of Mankind: British Perceptions of the World in the Age of Enlightenment.* London: J.M. Dent & Sons.

Meijer, Miriam Claude. 1999. *Race and Aesthetics in the Anthropology of Petrus Camper (1722-1789).* Amsterdam-Atlanta, GA: Editions Rodopi.

Mentelle, Edme, and Conrad Malte Brun. 1804. *Géographie mathématique, physique et politique de toutes les parties du monde ...,* vol. 12, *Contenant la suite de l'Asie et les Terres Océaniques ou la cinquième partie du monde*. Paris: Henry Tardieu et Laporte.

Mercator, Gerard. 1587. *Orbis Terrae Compendiosa Descriptio* ... Engraving. Duysburghi Clivorum: Typis Aeneis. ZM2 100a/1587/1. Sydney: Mitchell Library. Accessed 20 April 2008, online <http://image.sl.nsw.gov.au/cgi-bin/ebindshow.pl?doc=crux/a127;seq=10>.

Monin, Charles V. 1834. *Océanie: divisions de l'Océanie*. Paris: no publisher. Engraving. MAP T 913/2. Canberra: National Library of Australia. Accessed 27 February 2008, online <http://www.nla.gov.au/apps/cdview?pi=nla.map-t913-2-e>.

Montagu, Ashley. 1997 [1942]. *Man's Most Dangerous Myth: the Fallacy of Race*. 6th edition. Walnut Creek, CA: AltaMira Press.

Moussa, Sarga, ed. 2003. *L'idée de 'race' dans les sciences humaines et la littérature (XVIIIe-XIXe siècles)*. Paris: L'Harmattan.

Murray, A.W. 1863. *Missions in Western Polynesia: Being Historical Sketches of these Missions, from their Commencement in 1839 to the Present Time*. London: John Snow.

_____. 1874. *Wonders in the Western Isles: Being a Narrative of the Commencement and Progress of Mission Work in Western Polynesia*. London: Yates and Alexander.

Nordman, Daniel. 2006. Les sciences historiques et géographiques dans l'exploration scientifique de l'Algérie (vers 1840-vers 1860). In *Géographies plurielles: les sciences géographiques au moment de l'émergence des sciences humaines (1750-1850)*, ed. Hélène Blais et Isabelle Laboulais, 235-53. Paris: L'Harmattan.

Nouveau petit Larousse illustré: dictionnaire encyclopédique. 1926. Paris: Librairie Larousse.

O'Gorman, Edmundo. 1961. *The Invention of America: an Inquiry into the Historical Nature of the New World and the Meaning of its History*. Bloomington: Indiana University Press.

Ortelius, Abraham. 1592 [1589]. Maris Pacifici, (quod vulgó Mar del Zur) .... In *Theatrum Orbis Terrarum*. 4th edition. Antwerp: Plantjin. Engraving. MAP NK 1528. Canberra: National Library of Australia. Accessed 16 April 2008, online <http://nla.gov.au/nla.map-nk1528>.

Oxford English Dictionary. 2008. Draft 3rd edition. Oxford: Oxford University Press. Online <http://dictionary.oed.com>.

Peabody, Sue, and Tyler Stovall, ed. 2003. *The Color of Liberty: Histories of Race in France*. Durham, NC: Duke University Press.

Petit Larousse illustré. 1977. Paris: Librairie Larousse.

Prichard, James Cowles. 1836-47. *Researches into the Physical History of Mankind,* 5 vols. 3rd edition. London: Sherwood, Gilbert, and Piper.

_____. 1843. *The Natural History of Man: Comprising Inquiries into the Modifying Influence of Physical and Moral Agencies on the Different Tribes of the Human Family.* London: H. Baillière.

Quoy, Jean-René Constant, and Joseph-Paul Gaimard. 1824. De l'homme: observations sur la constitution physique des Papous. In *Voyage autour du monde ... exécuté sur les corvettes de S.M.* l'Uranie *et* la Physicienne, *pendant les années 1817, 1818, 1819 et 1820 ... Zoologie,* 1-11. Paris: Pillet aîné.

Raj, Kapil. 2000. 18th-Century Pacific Voyages of Discovery, 'Big Science', and the Shaping of an European Scientific and Technological Culture. *History and Technology* 17:79-98.

Renneville, Marc. 1996. Un terrain phrénologique dans le grand océan (autour du voyage de Dumoutier sur *L'Astrolabe* en 1837-1840). In *Le terrain des sciences humaines: instructions et enquêtes (XVIIIᵉ-XXᵉ siècle),* ed. Claude Blanckaert, 89-138. Paris: L'Harmattan.

Richard, Hélène. 1986. *Une grande expédition scientifique au temps de la Révolution française: le voyage de d'Entrecasteaux à la recherche de La Pérouse.* Paris: CTHS.

Robertson, H.A. 1902. *Erromanga the Martyr Isle,* ed. John Fraser. London: Hodder and Stoughton.

Sanz, Carlos. 1973. *Australia su descubrimiento y denominación: con la reproducción facsimil del memorial número 8 de Quirós en español original, y en las diversas traducciones contemporáneas.* Madrid: Dirección General de Relaciones Culturales, Ministerio de Asuntos Exteriores.

Schaffer, Simon. 2007. 'On Seeing Me Write': Inscription Devices in the South Seas. *Representations* 97:90-122.

Schiebinger, Londa. 2004 [1993]. *Nature's Body: Gender in the Making of Modern Science.* 2nd edition. New Brunswick, NJ: Rutgers University Press.

Selwyn, George Augustus. 1842-67. Letters from the Bishop of New Zealand. 1842-1867. In Letters from the Bishop of New Zealand, and Others, vol. 1. TS, Auckland: Library of the Auckland Institute and Museum. Microfilm, Canberra: Division of Pacific and Asian History, Australian National University.

Serres, Etienne-Renaud-Augustin, et al. 1841. Rapport sur les résultats scientifiques du voyage de circumnavigation de *l'Astrolabe* et de *la Zélée*. *Compte rendu des séances de l'Académie des Sciences* 13:643-59.

Sivasundaram, Sujit. 2005. *Nature and the Godly Empire: Science and Evangelical Mission in the Pacific, 1795-1850*. Cambridge: Cambridge University Press.

Smith, Bernard. 1969 [1960]. *European Vision and the South Pacific 1768-1850: a Study in the History of Art and Ideas*. Oxford: Oxford University Press.

_____. 1992. *Imagining the Pacific: in the Wake of the Cook Voyages*. Carlton, VIC: Melbourne University Press at the Miegunyah Press.

Spriggs, Matthew, Sue O'Connor, and Peter Veth. 2006. The Aru Islands in Perspective: a General Introduction. In *The Archaeology of the Aru Islands, Eastern Indonesia*, ed. S. O'Connor, M. Spriggs, and P. Veth, 1-23. Canberra: ANU E Press. Accessed 5 June 2008, online <http://epress.anu.edu.au/terra_australis/ta22/pdf/ch01.pdf>.

Staum, Martin S. 2003. *Labeling People: French Scholars on Society, Race, and Empire, 1815-1848*. Montreal & Kingston: McGill-Queen's University Press.

Stepan, Nancy. 1982. *The Idea of Race in Science: Great Britain 1800-1960*. London: Macmillan.

Stocking, George W., Jr. 1968. *Race, Culture and Evolution: Essays in the History of Anthropology*. New York: Free Press.

_____. 1973. From Chronology to Ethnology: James Cowles Prichard and British Anthropology 1800-1850. In James Cowles Prichard, *Researches into the Physical History of Man*, ed. George W. Stocking, Jr., ix-cx. Chicago: University of Chicago Press.

_____. 1987. *Victorian Anthropology*. New York: Free Press.

_____, ed. 1988. *Bones, Bodies, Behavior: Essays on Biological Anthropology*. Madison: University of Wisconsin Press.

Stoler, Ann Laura. 1995. *Race and the Education of Desire: Foucault's* History of Sexuality *and the Colonial Order of Things*. Durham, NC: Duke University Press.

_____. 2002. *Carnal Knowledge and Imperial Power: Race and the Intimate in Colonial Rule*. Berkeley: University of California Press.

Stoler, Ann Laura, and Frederick Cooper. 1997. Between Metropole and Colony: Rethinking a Research Agenda. In *Tensions of Empire: Colonial Cultures in a Bourgeois World*, ed. Frederick Cooper and Ann Laura Stoler, 1-56. Berkeley: University of California Press.

Thomas, Nicholas. 1989. The Force of Ethnology: Origins and Significance of the Melanesia/Polynesia Division. *Current Anthropology* 30:27-41.

_____. 1994. *Colonialism's Culture: Anthropology, Travel and Government.* Cambridge: Polity Press.

_____. 1996. 'On the Varieties of the Human Species': Forster's Comparative Ethnology. In Johann Reinhold Forster, *Observations Made During a Voyage Round the World*, ed. Nicholas Thomas, Harriet Guest, and Michael Dettelbach, xxiii-xl. Honolulu: University of Hawaii Press.

_____. 1997. *In Oceania: Visions, Artifacts, Histories.* Durham, NC: Duke University Press.

_____. 2002. Dumont d'Urville's Anthropology. In *Lure of the Southern Seas: the Voyages of Dumont d'Urville 1826-1840*, ed. Susan Hunt, Martin Terry, and Nicholas Thomas, 53-66. Sydney: Historic Houses Trust of New South Wales.

Todorov, Tzvetan. 1989. *Nous et les autres: la réflexion française sur la diversité humaine.* Paris: Editions du Seuil.

Turnbull, Paul. 1998. 'Outlawed Subjects': the Procurement and Scientific Uses of Australian Aboriginal Heads, ca. 1803-1835. *Eighteenth-Century Life* 22:156-71.

_____. 2001. 'Rare Work Amongst the Professors': the Capture of Indigenous Skulls Within Phrenological Knowledge in Early Colonial Australia. In *Body Trade: Captivity, Cannibalism and Colonialism in the Pacific*, ed. Barbara Creed and Jeanette Hoorn, 3-23. New York and Annandale, NSW: Routledge and Pluto Press.

Turner, George. 1861. *Nineteen Years in Polynesia: Missionary Life, Travels, and Researches in the Islands of the Pacific.* London: John Snow.

Vanuatu, Tourism Office. 2006. National Flag and Emblem of Vanuatu. *Vanuatu Islands*. Port Vila: Vanuatu Tourism Office and Government of Vanuatu. Accessed 21 August 2006, online <http://www.vanuatutourism.com/vanuatu/export/sites/VTO/en/resources/flag_emblem.html>.

Vetter, Jeremy. 2006. Wallace's *Other* Line: Human Biogeography and Field Practice in the Eastern Colonial Tropics. *Journal of the History of Biology* 39:89-123.

Waddell, Eric, Vijay Naidu, and Epeli Hau'ofa, ed. *A New Oceania: Rediscovering Our Sea of Islands.* Suva, Fiji: School of Social and Economic Development, University of the South Pacific.

Wheeler, Roxann. 2000. *The Complexion of Race: Categories of Difference in Eighteenth-Century British Culture*. Philadelphia: University of Pennsylvania Press.

Williams, Glyndwr. 1979. Seamen and Philosophers in the South Seas in the Age of Captain Cook. *Mariner's Mirror* 65:3-22.

Williams, John. 1837. *A Narrative of Missionary Enterprises in the South Sea Islands: with Remarks upon the Natural History of the Islands, Origin, Languages, Traditions, and Usages of the Inhabitants*. London: John Snow.

Wilson, Kathleen. 2003. *The Island Race: Englishness, Empire and Gender in the Eighteenth Century*. London: Routledge.

Wroth, Lawrence C. 1944. The Early Cartography of the Pacific. *Papers of the Bibliographical Society of America* 38 (2):87-268.

Young, Robert M. 1977. Science *Is* Social Relations. *Radical Science Journal* 5 (1977):65-129.

Zimmerman, Andrew. 2001. *Anthropology and Antihumanism in Imperial Germany*. Chicago: University of Chicago Press.

Notes

[1] On these themes, see Cowlishaw 2000; Gould 1996; Harrison 1995; Kaiwar and Mazumdar 2003; Kohn 1996; Littlefield, Lieberman, and Reynolds 1982; Malik 1996; Montagu 1997.

[2] A sample of books on aspects of the history of race published or republished during this period includes Bernasconi 2001b; Bernasconi and Cook 2003; Brantlinger 2003; Eigen and Larrimore 2006; Ellingson 2001; Gould 1996; Hall 2002; Hannaford 1996; Kidd 2006; Meijer 1999; Montagu 1997; Moussa 2003; Peabody and Stovall 2003; Schiebinger 2004; Staum 2003; Stoler 1995, 2002; Wheeler 2000; Wilson 2003; Zimmerman 2001; see also Bernasconi's valuable facsimile editions of key eighteenth- and nineteenth-century texts on race (2001a, 2002, 2003, 2005).

[3] See especially the work of Claude Blanckaert (1988, 2003a, 2003b, 2006) and George W. Stocking, Jr. (1968, 1973, 1987, 1988) and recent studies of the significance of field encounters for the human sciences by historians of geography (e.g., Bravo 1996; Bravo and Sörlin 2002; Nordman 2006).

[4] See, e.g., Anderson 2007; Brantlinger 2003; Schiebinger 2004; Todorov 1989. Though these works have their virtues, the authors have in different ways sacrificed a precise, discriminative, comparative reading of contemporary texts to derivative analysis of an overarching discourse, presumed deductively to determine or explain aspects of racial thinking. On the other hand, while Nancy Stepan's (1982) pioneer general history of the science of race in Britain is sufficiently empirical and often insightful, it is also marred by inaccuracies of reading and interpretation.

[5] Bernard Smith's groundbreaking studies (1969, 1992) traced the genesis of racial thinking with respect to Australia and the Pacific Islands while Nicholas Thomas (1989; 1996; 1997:133-55; 2002) wrote brief but perceptive histories of the racial classification of Pacific Islanders. See also several recent histories of race in Australia (Anderson 2002; Anderson 2007; McGregor 1997); and incidental references to racial ideas in works on the science or the art of particular voyages in the region (Copans and Jamin 1978; Duyker 2003, 2006; Fisher and Johnston 1993; Jones 1988; Liebersohn 2006; Richard 1986; Stocking 1968:13-41).

[6] Caneva 1998; cf. Young 1977.

[7] Anderson 2007:22-4, 67, 109-12, 197-202, original emphasis. Anderson's only access to my thinking and sole reference to my work are to an unpublished conference paper — an ancestral version of the first two chapters of this collection.

[8] The phrase is Claude Blanckaert's (2003:43); see also Kohn 1996:2-3; Stepan 1982:xiv-xvi.

[9] See also Anderson 2007; Copans and Jamin 1978; Frost 1976:810-22; Marshall and Williams 1982; Smith 1969; Williams 1979. There is growing scholarly interest in the significance of Oceanic field experience in the construction of scientific knowledge generally (e.g., Anderson 2000; Ballantyne 2004; Gascoigne 2007; Home 1988; Liebersohn 2006; Lincoln 1998; Mackay 1999; MacLeod and Rehbock 1988, 1994; Raj 2000; Renneville 1996; Schaffer 2007; Staum 2003; Vetter 2006).

[10] For the limited geographic span of Oceania in English usages, see Great Britain Foreign Office 1920; and *Oxford English Dictionary* 2008 which defines the word thus: 'Oceania' — '(A collective name for) the islands and island-groups of the Pacific Ocean and its adjacent seas, including Melanesia, Micronesia, and Polynesia, and *sometimes also* Australasia and the Malay archipelago' (my emphasis). The most notable indigenous reclaimant of this restricted sense of Oceania is Epeli Hau'ofa (1993:8) for whom the term signified 'a sea of islands with their inhabitants' (see also Hau'ofa 1998; Waddell, Naidu, and Hau'ofa 1993; Jolly 2001, 2007). Hau'ofa (1998:403-4) explicitly excluded the Philippines and Indonesia from Oceania because they 'are adjacent to the Asian mainland' and because they 'do not have oceanic cultures'.

[11] Higham, Anderson, and Jacomb 1999:426; Spriggs, O'Connor, and Veth 2006:9-10.

[12] Eisler 1995:12-54; Mentelle and Malte-Brun 1804:357-63. With 'America' designated the *quarta pars*, 'fourth part', of the globe and its fourth 'continent' (O'Gorman 1961:117-33, 167-8), any imagined southern land must henceforth logically have been the fifth part or fifth continent. The designation 'fifth part of the world' appears on the title page of the first Latin translation (1612) of a memorial to the King of Spain by Pedro Fernández de Quirós (1563?-1615) who in 1595 and 1606 had crossed the *Mar del Sur*, 'South Sea', from Peru on two voyages of exploration, colonization, and evangelism. However, the phrase 'fifth part' is not used in Quirós's original Spanish text of 1610 which refers to the 'hidden' southern part as comprising 'a quarter of all the globe' (Sanz 1973:37-8, 83).

[13] [Brosses] 1756, I:77-80. See, e.g., the map by Abraham Ortelius (1527-1598) in which 'Terra Australis, or Magellanica, not yet revealed' encompasses much of the southern portion of the globe (Ortelius 1592). The classical theory that a large land mass must exist in the southern hemisphere to counterbalance those in the north was enthusiastically revived by Renaissance cartographers (Wroth 1944:163-74). The French mathematician Oronce Fine (1494-1555) first used the term 'Terra Australis', annotated as 'recently discovered, but not yet fully known', in his world map of 1531. In 1569, the Flemish cartographer Gerard Mercator (1512-1594) famously promoted the idea of a vast 'southern continental region' (Eisler 1995:37-9) and he added the label 'Terra Australis' to his world map of 1587 with the note: 'Some call this southern continent the Magellanic region after its discoverer'. Eight decades later, the Dutch cartographer Pieter Goos (c. 1616-1675) treated sceptically the 'cal[l] for a fifth part of the world Terra Australis or Magellanica' and left blank the far southern portion of his world map (1668:[7], map 1). Yet most cartographers and geographers, including Brosses and the Scottish hydrographer Alexander Dalrymple (1737-1808), clung to a hopeful belief in the necessary existence of an 'immense' southern continent as a 'counterweight' to the great northern land masses until definitively proven wrong by James Cook ([Brosses] 1856, I:13-16; Dalrymple 1770-1, I:xxii-xxx).

[14] Brué 1816; Mentelle and Malte-Brun 1804:362-3, 463-4.

[15] Dumont d'Urville 1832; Serres et al. 1841:652. Dumont d'Urville commanded the expedition of the *Astrolabe* to the Pacific in 1826-29 and circumnavigated the globe twice — as first lieutenant under Louis-Isidore Duperrey (1786-1865) on the *Coquille* (1822-25) and in command of the *Astrolabe* and the *Zélée* (1837-40). Domeny de Rienzi (1836-8, I:1-3) claimed wide experience in western Oceania acquired during 'five voyages' as an independent traveller, particularly in the Malay Archipelago, but was reputedly an 'illusionist, creator of a fantasmagoric autobiography' (Bibliothèque nationale de France 2004).

[16] 'Oceania or fifth part of the world including the Asian Archipelago, Australasia, Polynesia, etc... 1814' (Brué 1816).

[17] Lesson and Garnot 1826-30, I:2, note 1; Lesson 1829:156-65, 216-17, note 1; Malte-Brun 1810:495; 1813:229; Prichard 1837-46, I:xviii, xix, 251, 255, 298; V:1-3; 1843:326.

[18] Williams 1837:7-8, 503-4; see also Brown 1887:320; Inglis 1887:4; Murray 1863, 1874; Turner 1861.

[19] 'Map illustrating the memoir of Captain d'Urville on the islands of the Great Ocean' (Dumont d'Urville 1832: frontispiece).

[20] Malte-Brun 1803:548; 1813:228, 244; Mentelle and Malte-Brun 1804:474, 577, 612, 620, original emphasis.

[21] Since the French term *Papou* or *Papoua* does not always translate exactly into English 'Papuan', I retain the French forms as used and indicate their particular import.

[22] Bory de Saint-Vincent 1827, I:82, 94-7, 273-318, 297, 306, 318-28; II:104-13.

[23] Bory de Saint-Vincent 1827, I:84, 99-101, 299, 304-6, 308-18; II, 108; Quoy and Gaimard 1824; Lesson and Garnot 1826-30.

[24] Lesson 1829:157, 168, 202-5.

[25] Ballard 2006; Gelpke 1993:326-30; see Chapters Two (Douglas) and Three (Ballard), this volume.

[26] Dumont d'Urville 1832:6, 11, 14-15.

[27] Hilliard 1978:12-13, 23; Selwyn to his father, 15 Sep. 1849, in Selwyn 1842-67:216-19, 225-7, 230.

[28] Codrington 1881:261; 1891; Prichard 1836-47, V:4, 212-13, 282, 283.

[29] 'Oceania: divisions of Oceania' (Monin 1834).

[30] Monin 1834.

[31] Gardner 2006:105-27; Herbert 1991:155-203; Sivasundaram 2005; Stocking 1987:8-109; see Chapters Six (Gardner) and Seven (Weir), this volume.

[32] Moussa 2003; Staum 2003; see Chapters Two (Douglas) and Five (Anderson), this volume.

[33] E.g., Brown 1887:312, 320; 1910; Ellis 1831, I:78-9; Erskine 1853:2, 4, 13, 241; Inglis 1887:5; Robertson 1902:1; Williams 1837:503-4, 512. See also Gardner 2006:114-20; Kidd 2006:121-67.

[34] See, e.g., *Nouveau petit Larousse illustré* 1926:1571-2.

[35] Great Britain Foreign Office 1920:37, 38, 120.

[36] *Petit Larousse illustré* 1977:1569.

[37] E.g., according to the exegesis of the colour symbolism of the Vanuatu national flag on the official web site of the Vanuatu Tourism Office (2006), the colour black symbolizes 'Melanesia and the Melanesian race'.

[38] See Stoler and Cooper 1997; Thomas 1994.

[39] For detailed correlations of episodes in the history of racial thinking with the ethnohistory of particular encounters in Oceania, see Ballard 2001, 2006; Douglas 1999, 2003, 2005, 2006, 2007, 2008, n.d.; Turnbull 1998, 2001.

[40] I use the terms 'paradigm' and 'normal science' in Thomas Kuhn's (1970) sense of a broad conceptual framework shared by a disciplinary community of scientists and reified as dogma.

[41] See also Anderson 2002:3-4.

Part One

Emergence: Thinking the
Science of Race, 1750-1880

Chapter One

Climate to Crania: science and the racialization of human difference

Bronwen Douglas

In letters written to a friend in 1790 and 1791, the young, German-trained French comparative anatomist Georges Cuvier (1769-1832) took vigorous humanist exception to recent 'stupid' German claims about the supposedly innate deficiencies of 'the negro'.[1] It was 'ridiculous', he expostulated, to explain the 'intellectual faculties' in terms of differences in the anatomy of the brain and the nerves; and it was immoral to justify slavery on the grounds that Negroes were 'less intelligent' when their 'imbecility' was likely to be due to 'lack of civilization and we have given them our vices'. Cuvier's judgment drew heavily on personal experience: his own African servant was 'intelligent', freedom-loving, disciplined, literate, 'never drunk', and always good-humoured. Skin colour, he argued, was a product of relative exposure to sunlight.[2] A decade later, however, Cuvier (1978:173-4) was 'no longer in doubt' that the 'races of the human species' were characterized by systematic anatomical differences which probably determined their 'moral and intellectual faculties'; moreover, 'experience' seemed to confirm the racial nexus between mental 'perfection' and physical 'beauty'.

The intellectual somersault of this renowned savant epitomizes the theme of this chapter which sets a broad scene for the volume as a whole. From a brief semantic history of 'race' in several western European languages, I trace the genesis of the modernist biological conception of the term and its normalization by comparative anatomists, geographers, naturalists, and anthropologists between 1750 and 1880. The chapter title — 'climate to crania' — and the introductory anecdote condense a major discursive shift associated with the altered meaning of race: the metamorphosis of prevailing Enlightenment ideas about externally induced variation within an essentially similar humanity into a science of race that reified human difference as permanent, hereditary, and innately somatic. The discussion pivots initially on the varied disputes over human unity or diversity and monogeny or polygeny which engrossed the science of man in Britain and France. The resolution or supersession of these debates with the application of evolutionist theory to man shaped the particular national trajectories taken by the discipline of anthropology for the rest of the century and beyond.

Slippery word

According to the *Oxford English Dictionary* (2008, hereinafter *OED*), the etymology of the English term 'race' and its European cognates is 'uncertain and disputed'.[3] The *OED* derives race ultimately from Italian *razza*, via French *race*, and the semantic history of the English term is entangled with continental meanings. Dictionary definitions say nothing *per se* about a word's history and inevitably lag well behind embryonic usages. But inclusion in a dictionary does register the prior normalization of a meaning. The *OED*'s earliest citations date from the sixteenth century when, with reference to man, the concrete noun race signified a family, a kindred, or the posterity of a common ancestor, as in the 'race & stocke of Abraham' (1570). More generally, it meant a 'tribe, nation, or people regarded as of common stock', as in 'the Englishe race' (1572), or served as a synecdoche for humanity, as in 'the humane race' (1580).

The primary connotations of consanguinity and shared origin or descent are patent in the several translations of *une race*, 'a race', in an early French-Latin dictionary — they include *familia* ('house', 'family'); *gentilitas* ('kindred'); *genus* ('birth'); *sanguis* ('blood', 'descendant'); and *stirps* ('stock', 'stem', 'root', 'offspring').[4] The first French dictionary (Nicot 1606:533-4) explains that *race* 'signifies origin [*extraction*]', as in 'man, horse, dog, and other animal of good or bad race' or 'a noble race and house'. The *OED* cites parallel English usages from half a century earlier. This semantic conflation of a race with family breeding served to fortify the prerogatives of nobility over populace.[5] The first edition of *Le dictionnaire de l'Académie françoise* (1694, II:364) defines *race* as 'progeny [*lignée*], lineage [*lignage*], origin, all those who come from a single [noble] family'. Applied to domestic animals, it connoted Latin *species*, 'sort', 'kind', 'species'.[6] This suite of usages hardly varies up to the fifth edition of the *Dictionnaire de l'Académie* (1798, II:407) and recurs in the sixth (1835, II:553). The genealogical definition given for the English term race by Samuel Johnson (1709-1784) was similarly unchanged between the first edition of his *Dictionary of the English Language* (1756) and the revised eleventh edition (1799), published more than a decade after the lexicographer's death. But *race*/race were minor words in French and English before the late eighteenth century while their German equivalent *Race* or *Rasse* was a recent borrowing from French and rarely used (Forster 1786:159).

Importantly, however, the sixth edition of the *Dictionnaire de l'Académie* (1835, II:553) also gives an extended signified for *race*: 'a multitude of men who originate from the same country, and resemble each other by facial traits, by external form. *The Caucasian race. The Mongol race. The Malay race*'. The *OED* likewise cites late eighteenth-century and subsequent uses of race to mean 'any of the major groupings of mankind, having in common distinct physical features or having a similar ethnic background'. These emergent meanings are lexical confirmation of a series of important shifts in the linguistic and ideological significance of race in western Europe from the mid-eighteenth century as naturalists appropriated the term to serve novel taxonomic ends.[7] The word's dominant scientific sense became narrowly biological while the permeable humoral body of classical conception solidified into the bones, nerves, flesh, and skin of the measurable, dissectible anatomical body (Wheeler 2000:26-7).

Changing connotations

The biologization of race was preceded by significant extension of its older genealogical referents as some writers extrapolated the term to label extensive populations. They included the French physician and Asian traveller François Bernier (1620-1688), the German mathematician and philosopher Gottfried Wilhelm Leibniz (1646-1716), the French mathematician, astronomer, and biologist Pierre-Louis Moreau de Maupertuis (1698-1759), the Anglo-Irish writer, poet, and physician Oliver Goldsmith (1730?-1774), and the French naturalist Georges-Louis Leclerc, comte de Buffon (1707-1788),[8] whose expanded use of the term 'Lapp race' (Sami) provoked some disapproval.[9] In these extended usages, race was usually a concrete noun more or less interchangeable with 'tribe', 'nation', 'people', 'variety', 'class', 'kind', or 'species'. Leibniz used the word rarely but defined it relationally as 'generational series', *genealogy*.[10] Race was applied to Oceania in this fluid sense by the French *littérateur* Charles de Brosses (1709-1777), a friend of Buffon, and by the German naturalists Johann Reinhold Forster (1729-1798) and his son Georg (1754-1794), who sailed with James Cook (1728-1779) on his second Oceanic voyage of 1772-75.[11]

As subdivisions of a single human species, varieties or races were distinguished by physical criteria, especially skin colour, in addition to language, religion, customs, and supposed level of 'civility'. In practice, the venerable, widely-held tenet that all people shared a common origin and were essentially alike was in serious tension with pervasive distaste for non-whites and non-Christians. Following the overseas expansion of Europe and growing involvement in the west African slave trade from the mid-fifteenth century, a set of purportedly 'Negro' characteristics had become Europe's negative standard for the description and comparison of human beings. Nonetheless, prevailing Christian or neoclassical cosmologies generally ascribed both physical appearance and degree of civilized development to the transient effects of climate, other external conditions, history, or way of life, more than to heredity, and in principle espoused a universal potential for salvation or progress towards the civilized state.[12]

The changed and charged import of the concept race in the early nineteenth century is commonly seen by historians of ideas as a by-product of the abstract taxonomic method instituted from the 1730s by the Swedish botanist Carl

Linnaeus (von Linné) (1707-1778). By this argument, Linnaeus 'blurred' the frontier separating man from animals by classifying both within the same 'natural system' and thereby 'brought to light new differences between men'.[13] In the tenth edition of *Systema Naturae* (1758:5-24), he classed all known human geographical varieties within the single species *Homo sapiens* but included *Homo*, 'Man', within the 'Animal Kingdom' as the first genus in the mammalian order of primates, alongside *Simia*, 'Ape'. This failure to isolate man from the rest of creation and from the anthropoid apes in particular threatened the dogma of the singularity of mankind and outraged conventional opinions. In the monumental *Histoire naturelle, générale et particulière* (1749-89), Linnaeus's great rival Buffon criticized abstraction and classification alike: he transformed the abstract category *espèce*, 'species', by insisting on its 'real existence' and material historical continuity as a 'constant succession of similar individuals who reproduce themselves'; and he refused to position man in formal taxonomic relationship with animals. But by encompassing humanity within 'natural history', he eventually naturalized man as a physical species distinguished from animals only by the fragile criteria of speech and reason.[14]

Tzvetan Todorov (1989:126) damned Buffon for espousing 'the racialist theory in its entirety' but the charge is scarcely applicable to the haphazard, ambiguous use of *race* in Buffon's long essay on 'Varieties in the human species' (1749, III:371-530). He first systematically applied *race* to human beings in a much later *Supplément* to the *Histoire naturelle*, but with the broad connotation of 'resemblance' rather than direct filiation. He justified his earlier use of the phrase 'the Lapp race' by differentiating 'the word race in the most extended sense' from its 'narrow' (genealogical) meaning, synonymous with *nation*. An extreme climate had produced such 'resemblance' between all people living north of the Arctic Circle, whatever their 'first origin', that they had become 'a single identical race' though they were 'not of the same nation'. Juxtaposing two major signifieds of the French term *espèce* ('kind'/'species') and identifying *race* with the vaguer common sense, he concluded that these polar people were 'a single, similar kind of men [*espèce d'hommes*], that is, a single race different from all the others in the human species [*espèce humaine*]'.[15] The apparent biological modernity of this formulation is deceptive since Buffon continued to assert that the 'great differences between men depend on the diversity of climate'. In this conception, the *variétés*, *races*, or *espèces d'hommes* of the single *espèce humaine* remained flexible, theoretically reversible products of climatic variety and other external influences and were neither innately organic nor immutable.[16]

Though Maupertuis (1745:153-60) rarely used the word *race* in his short biological treatise *Vénus physique*, he proposed a prescient epigenetic theory of reproduction which made human physical diversity primarily the product of internal hereditary processes rather than the external 'influence' of climate and diet. By contrast, there is no hint of a biological account of race formation in Buffon's original essay which attributes the characteristic physical differences 'of the various peoples' to the impact of climate, food, and lifestyle but does not seek to explain why. From 1753, Buffon gradually enunciated a theory of the organic alteration of species through degeneration triggered by external conditions but he only applied these emerging ideas to human beings in the mid-1760s, when he argued that the quality of food channels 'the influence of the land' to alter man's 'internal form'. Perpetuated 'by generation' — but reversible in principle in a restored favourable environment — such organic changes 'became the general and constant characters in which we recognize the different races and even nations which compose the human genus'.[17] Still later, Buffon (1778:248) qualified his thesis of human degeneration with the proposition that the process of becoming civilized could itself enable and sustain organic improvement in man through better nutrition and 'plentiful reproduction'.

In Britain, Goldsmith (1774, II:212-42) avowedly synthesized Linnaeus and Buffon by distilling a formal classification of mankind into 'six distinct varieties', labelled geographically as the 'polar' race, 'the Tartar race', 'the southern Asiatics', 'the Negroes of Africa', 'the inhabitants of America', and 'the Europeans'. This explicit identification of discrete racial 'classes' flew in the face of Buffon's refusal to indulge in human taxonomy but in most respects Goldsmith's propositions were slavishly, if simplistically Buffonian. He differentiated man mainly on the basis of the 'tincture of his skin' and explained these differences as 'degeneracy' from a 'beautiful' white original caused by 'varieties of climate, of nourishment, and custom'. And, like Buffon, he concluded that such 'accidental deformities' would probably disappear in the long run with a 'kinder climate, better nourishment, or more civilized manners'.

New imperatives: taxonomy and biology

The German comparative anatomist Johann Friedrich Blumenbach (1752-1840) was a pivotal figure in the taxonomic and biological turns in the natural history of man and literally inscribed the changing import of the concept of a race. The oft-asserted primary motives for his 'favourite anthropological studies' were to prove the singularity of man's place in the animal kingdom — 'poles apart from the Orangutang' — and establish the membership of all human beings within 'the same common species'. But he also insisted that the normal process of classifying 'the races and degenerations' of animals and plants be applied to 'the varieties of mankind that had emerged from its common original stock'.[18]

Accordingly, in the radically revised third edition of *De Generis Humani Varietate Nativa*, 'On the Natural Varieties of Mankind', Blumenbach (1795:284-7) formalized his long emergent classification of the 'five foremost varieties of mankind, one true species', and labelled them 'Caucasian', 'Mongolian', 'Ethiopian',

'American', and 'Malay' (Figure 4). Through the three Latin editions of this work (1775, 1781, 1795), the concrete nouns Blumenbach used most often to refer to units of collective human difference were *gens*, 'nation', 'race', 'people', and *varietas*, 'variety'. Neither connoted a race in the narrowly biological sense but whereas he saw *gens* as a real, 'natural division', *varietas* was a 'general division' in a taxonomy 'which we constituted'.[19] In the penultimate section of the third edition of *De Generis Humani*, Blumenbach (1795:114-283) drew extensively on empirical descriptions of actual *gens* to illustrate his deduction that collective human 'degeneration' or change — as indexed particularly in 'national differences in [skin] colour' — resulted from the operation of external physical causes on a single migrating human species rather than from an original plurality of species. In the final section (1795:284-322), he moved from a consideration of abstract *varietas*, 'diversity', 'variety', in the major elements of human physical appearance to the formal classification of human beings into a small number of theoretically concrete *varietas*, 'varieties'. At this point, the empirical noun *gens* almost disappears, to be largely replaced by two botanical metaphors, *stirps* and *stemma*, both connoting descent from an ancestral stock.[20]

Figure 4: Anon., 'Crania collectionis meae quina selectissima adumbrat, ad totidem generis humani varietatum principalium diversitatem demonstrandam: 1. *Tungusae*; 2. *Caribaei*; 3. Feminae juvenis *Georgianae*; 4. *O-taheitae*; 5. *Aethiopissae Guineensis*'.[21]

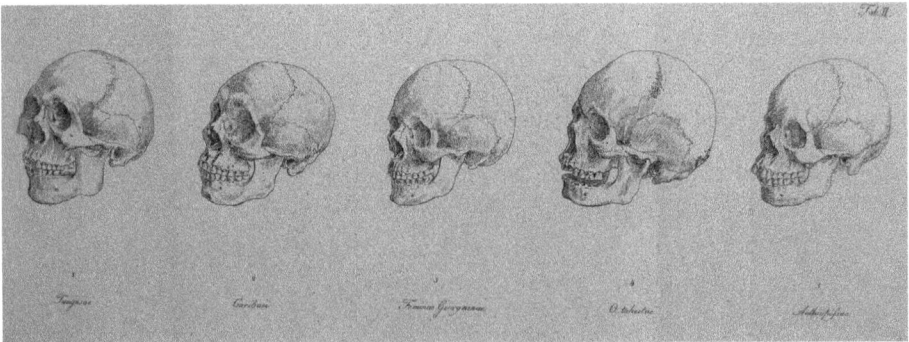

Engraving. Photograph B. Douglas.

The publication in 1798 of a German translation by Johann Gottfried Gruber (1774-1851) of the third edition of *De Generis Humani* was identified by Timothy Lenoir (1980:93) as a key moment in the articulation of Blumenbach's taxonomic lexicon and more generally in the biologization of the term race.[22] A close reading shows why. For much of the text, Gruber paralleled Blumenbach's Latin terminological mix and usually translated his concrete nouns *gens* and *varietas* respectively as *ein Volk*, 'a people', 'a nation', and *eine Varietät*, 'a variety'. *Stemma* and *stirps* are generally *ein Stamm*, 'a stock', 'a stem', but occasionally *eine Rasse* or *Race*, 'a race', always with reference to Blumenbach's problematic category of the Malay race — in these instances, the term had what Georg Forster called the 'undetermined' implication of a 'crowd' of people of 'idiosyncratic character' but 'unknown ancestry'.[23] Otherwise, *Rasse/Race* scarcely figure in the translation until the final section (1798:203-24). Here, *Varietät* is used initially for the taxonomic unit *varietas* but is abruptly supplanted by *Race* as the work climaxes in detailed characterization of Blumenbach's five *Abarten*, 'hereditary varieties', of mankind. The insertion of *Race* where the Latin text moves definitively into taxonomic mode was no mere whim but a deliberate semantic strategy by both author and translator, as Gruber (1798:259-61) made clear in a long appendix. In response to his own rhetorical complaint about the lack of a consistent classificatory vocabulary for the natural history of man, he lauded the precise *Natureintheilung*, 'natural classification', proposed by 'our great Kant'.

Gruber was alluding to a series of papers in which the German philosopher Immanuel Kant (1724-1804) had addressed a paradox at the core of natural history: the presence of radical, seemingly permanent physical diversity in a single human species with a common ancestral stock.[24] Kant's solution was to yoke teleology to genealogy in order to explain present human *Verschiedenheit*, 'variety' in the abstract, in terms of the triggering in different environments of pre-existent *Keime*, 'germs', or *Anlagen*, adaptive natural 'predispositions', within the single original *Menschenstamm*, 'human stock'. In the process, he formally differentiated *Racen*, 'races', from *Arten*, 'species', on the one hand, and from *Varietäten*, 'varieties', on the other: individuals of different races of the same *Stamm* could interbreed and produce fertile hybrid offspring, unlike those belonging to different species; while races, unlike varieties, 'remain constant over prolonged generation' when transplanted and could engender stable hybrids. Accordingly, a race was 'inevitably hereditary' and the demonstrated capacity to propagate a *Mittelschlag*, 'blended character', was a prime determinant of Kant's human classification.[25] This partial epigenetic theory differed from that of the mature Buffon in a crucial respect: for Kant, human races were structurally distinct because the original *Stamm* was predisposed to be permanently and irreversibly adaptive to different external conditions, making skin colour the paramount outward sign of 'natural' inner organic differences and capacities; whereas for Buffon, the human 'germ' was everywhere the same, degeneration was externally induced and theoretically reversible, and variations in skin, hair, and eye colour were 'superficial' products of 'the influence of climate only'.[26]

Lenoir (1980:92-5) linked Blumenbach's formal endorsement of Kant's biological terminology in 1798 to a recent metamorphosis in Blumenbach's thinking: his acknowledgment of reproductive criteria as critical signifiers of human diversity alongside his longstanding emphasis on morphology. In 1797, Blumenbach had modified his earlier insistence on external causes of morphological differences, especially in skin colour, by defining race along generative Kantian lines and invoking empirically the diagnostic significance of racial mixing: 'the word *race* indicates a character born of degeneration which necessarily and inevitably becomes hereditary through reproduction, as for example when whites engender mulattos with negroes, or métis with American indians'. He then acknowledged Kant as the first to identify heritability as the main 'difference between races and varieties'.[27] The imprint of Kantian terminology is patent in key changes between the 1790 and 1806 editions of Blumenbach's *Beyträge zur Naturgeschichte*, 'Contributions to Natural History'. In the first edition (1790:79-83), he briefly outlined but did not name the pentad of human 'varieties' that he had already sketched, also unnamed, in the second edition of *De Generis Humani* (1781:51-2), translating his own Latin phraseology directly into German as *fünf Spielarten*, 'five varieties/sports'.[28] The second edition of *Beyträge zur Naturgeschichte* (1806:55-66) includes a new section extolling the value of 'anthropological collections', notably Blumenbach's own, for an empirically based natural history of mankind. His unequalled assemblage of the 'skulls of foreign nations' rendered corporeal the paradox of human unity in diversity (that Kant's biology had resolved deductively): the collection displayed the 'identity of mankind as a whole' and the 'boundless transitions' linking its physical 'extremes'; but concurrently it provided 'proof of the natural division of the whole species into the five principal races [*Hauptrassen*]'. In the following section (1806:67-72), rehearsing his now named classification, he retained *Spielarten* as a general term for 'the varieties of mankind within its common original stock' but systematically substituted *Rassen* for *Spielarten* when referring to the particular divisions — his five *Hauptrassen* — suggested by his reading of the 'open book of nature'.

The insertion of *Race* or *Rasse* into Blumenbach's taxonomic vocabulary between 1795 and 1806, where he had previously used *Varietät* or *Spielart*, is a textual marker of the precipitation of a narrower, biological connotation of a race from a much older semantic slurry. It also signals the incipient normalization of hereditarian ideas of human difference in conjunction with new anatomical and physiological knowledge that challenged climatic and humoral explanations. In France, the altered usage slid easily into the technical lexicon of the natural history of man and the term race was duly redefined in the sixth edition of the *Dictionnaire de l'Académie* (1835). For instance, a prospectus for the shortlived Société des Observateurs de l'Homme issued in 1801 by the society's perpetual secretary and Cuvier's ally, the pedagogue and publicist Louis-François Jauffret (1770-1840), called for a 'methodical classification of the different races' grounded in a 'complete work on the comparative anatomy of peoples' (1978:74). On the cusp of this racialization of human difference, Cuvier exercised considerable practical influence in the emerging science of race, belying the relatively little he published on the subject.[29] If in the early 1790s he had refused to attribute supposed Negro shortcomings to their anatomy, by the end of the century

(1978:173-4), he had clearly imbibed Kant's and Blumenbach's reconfiguration of *Rassen* as organic and hereditary.

Cuvier's most authoritative pronouncement on human variation comprises a ten-page segment of his magnum opus *Le règne animal*, 'The Animal Kingdom' (1817a), concluding his discussion of the 'first order' of mammals, the '*Bimana* or Man'. He first sketched a standard four-stage Enlightenment theory of human progress:[30] 'man's development' was 'retarded' or 'advanced' at very different 'degrees' according to 'circumstances' such as climate, soil, and vegetation. But two ominous provisos qualified this universal schema and underwrote a rigid racial taxonomy: that the human species showed 'certain hereditary conformations which constitute what we call *races*'; and that 'intrinsic causes' appeared to 'halt the progress of certain races, even in the most favourable circumstances'. Earlier in the text, Cuvier had expressed strong doubt that all the characteristic differences between 'organized beings' could be produced 'by circumstances'. He now identified three 'eminently distinct' major human races characterized by congenital somatic features: the 'white, or Caucasic', ('to which we belong'), was typified by the 'beauty' of its 'oval head form'; the 'yellow, or Mongolic', by its 'prominent cheek bones', 'flat face', and 'narrow, slanting eyes'; and the 'negro, or Ethiopic' by its 'black' complexion, 'compressed skull', and 'squashed nose' while its 'projecting snout [*museau*] and thick lips put it visibly close to the apes'.[31] Faithful to the genre, the prose of these passages is purportedly scientific and definitive but nonetheless shot through with ill-disguised racialist presumptions. Yet the argument at this point follows logically from the seemingly objective principles of the science of animal 'organization' outlined in the book's introduction.[32] There, Cuvier had asserted a functional relationship between the extent of development of an animal's nervous system, the 'relative size of the brain', and its 'intelligence'. In conjunction, these factors determined the 'degree of animality', Cuvier's core criterion for the hierarchical grading of animals, implicit in his ranking of human races, and the ultimate source of the 'intrinsic causes' that allegedly stymied the 'progress of certain races' (Figlio 1976:24-5).

The novel signified of race as an hereditary natural category percolated more slowly into English, kept at bay by Evangelical philanthropic values — personified in the physician ethnologist James Cowles Prichard (1786-1848) — which retained ideological and moral ascendancy in the natural history of man in Britain until the mid-nineteenth century (Stocking 1973). The term race occurs relatively seldom in the first edition of Prichard's *Researches into the Physical History of Man(kind)* (1813) and more often in the second (1826), but in both is used in the loose eighteenth-century sense. The earlier text (1813:233-9) broadly differentiates 'savage' from 'civilized' but the logic of Prichard's speculative history of mankind made it 'probable' that the 'fairest races of white people in

Europe' were ultimately descended from 'Negroes'. Yet by 1850, the language applied by British humanitarians to non-whites, particularly Negroes and Aboriginal Australians, was often as racialized as that used earlier in the century by uncompromisingly physicalist French naturalists (Hall 1991, 2002). Prichard had rapidly shelved his early thesis that 'the primitive stock of men were Negroes'. In the third edition of *Researches* (1836-47), he reinscribed without comment the scurrilous racial terminology and discriminations of his (often French) sources and in the process essentialized the characters of certain races in very negative terms: 'the Australians', for example, were 'squalid', 'miserable hordes', 'repulsive', 'disgusting', and 'ferocious'. His conventional distaste for stereotyped Negro anatomy, muted in 1813, was now palpable: the corollary of 'black' skin and 'crisp' or 'woolly' hair was 'features of a corresponding ugliness'.[33]

In the earlier editions, the concept of races was sufficiently inconsequential to be left undefined but by the 1830s Prichard was prepared to naturalize 'those varieties in complexion, form, and habits, which distinguish from each other the several races of men'. The discursive dimensions of this shift are clear: the reification of human physical variation is manifest in the 'analogical' sections of the work which address 'the most strongly marked *anatomical diversities of human races*'; in contrast, qualifications, exceptions, and great diversity within races are ruling themes in the 'historical or ethnographical' sections which seek to delineate 'actual' changes in the 'physical characters' of nations or races.[34] The greater salience of the term race in the final edition of *Researches* parallels Prichard's increased resort to taxonomy and comparative anatomy. He had made little attempt to classify human groupings in the first edition but contextually identified a shifting set of descriptors with respect to 'varieties of form and colour': seven 'varieties of colour' but an indeterminate five 'Races' or varieties in the overall 'structure of the parts in which the variety of colour subsists'. At this stage, Prichard privileged colour as a more 'general' and more 'permanent' discrimination than 'peculiarities of figure'. In the second edition, he distributed 'the human family' into unnamed, geographically defined 'departments' marked at once by 'important physical diversities' and conversely by 'remarkable approximations to the characters prevalent in other tribes'. In the third edition, racial taxonomy and anatomy loomed larger still. Exhaustive comparison of 'the principal varieties of form and structure which distinguish the inhabitants of different countries' saw him identify seven 'classes of nations' which differed 'strikingly from each other' and were 'separated' by 'strongly marked lines', especially 'peculiar forms of the skull'.[35]

Yet Prichard always remained ambivalent about the racialization of human variation and at times tried to subvert the growing contemporary hegemony of the term race itself. His modern editor George Stocking, Jr. (1973:lxxi, lxxvi) argued that Prichard's nominalist distribution of human varieties into 'classes of nations' and his rejection of a higher level classification into a few racial types served to deny his classes 'the assurance of affinity [common descent] that alone would justify their designation as "races"'. There was surely an oppositional politics to Prichard's caveat, 'the various human races, if such exist'; to his consigning 'varieties' to 'the external and less essential parts' of 'the animal economy'; to his avowal of the 'common psychical nature' of mankind; and to his insistence that 'there are differences equally great, and even greater, between individuals and families of the same nation' as between different races.[36] In the end, Prichard was prepared to normalize races and embrace 'diversification and differentiation' in order to turn them against a greater peril — the increasingly fashionable doctrine of 'an original diversity of races'. By defining 'races' as 'properly successions of individuals propagated from any given stock' but insisting that the term not imply 'that such a progeny or stock has always possessed a particular character', he explicitly refuted 'writers on anthropology' who took for granted that racial distinctions were 'primordial' and transmitted in 'unbroken' succession. Such a race 'would be a species in the strict meaning of the word' — a position Prichard consistently rejected, as did most of his British colleagues until after 1850.[37]

That year, in *The Races of Men*, the Scottish anatomist Robert Knox (1791-1862) assailed the Prichardian creed and pronounced his notorious dictum: 'Race is everything: literature, science, art, in a word, civilization, depend on it'. The book was a collection of lectures delivered five years previously in provincial cities. At the time, Knox recalled, his views had been ignored by the London press; but since the outbreak of 'the war of race' in continental Europe — he meant the social and political upheavals of 1848 — the word race was in 'daily use' and his ideas had been appropriated by a 'leading journal'.[38] Prichard (1850:147) also noted the sudden 'importance in public attention' assumed by the 'subject of human races, and their division' within Europe. By 1860, the primacy of race in the vocabulary of human difference in Britain was consistent, prosaic, and empirical. For instance, the word persistently infiltrated the 1865 English translation by Thomas Bendyshe (1827-1886) of the third edition of Blumenbach's *De Generis Humani* (1795): *varietas* and *gens* are sometimes 'race'; adjectival inflections of *gens* are usually 'racial'; and even *stemma* and *stirps* are frequently 'race'.[39]

The biological notion of race emerged and gained potency in a complex historical conjuncture. Intellectually, the information about non-white people pouring into Europe from around the globe both enabled and seemed to require the demarcation of new scientific disciplines — notably biology and anthropology — which classed human beings as natural objects. Publicly, the escalation of European encounters with non-Europeans provoked fear and revulsion about supposed 'savages', not least in Oceania where several famous navigators met violent deaths at indigenous hands. Morally, the intensifying battle over slavery pushed abolitionists and defenders of slavery to adopt opposed scientific positions on the humanity or otherwise of Negroes. Imperially, a new phase of colonialism sought a philosophical basis for suppressing or governing indigenous people. Politically, revolution in France triggered dark imaginings about savages at home and abroad while its reactionary aftermath domesticated racial thinking by representing internal conflicts as the clash of a 'Gallic' third estate and a 'Germanic' nobility. By the mid-nineteenth century, the propensity to racialize local disputes had gripped much of Europe.[40]

Original unity and the paradox of human differences

In a single chapter, it is only possible to scratch the surface of the complex intersections whereby a novel meaning of race was normalized across a wide spectrum of western Europe discourses, as holistic, 'environmentalist' Enlightenment explanations for human variety and change lost ground to the differentiating physicalist agenda of biological determinism and taxonomy. I focus on the overlapping, recurrent tensions between ideas of human unity and diversity and between monogeny and polygeny, culminating in their partial resolution by evolutionist theory. These mobile, ambiguous relationships and the ideological conflicts, accommodations, transitions, and national variants they condense are illustrated by comparisons of key contributions to ongoing debates in France and Britain from the early nineteenth century to about 1880.

The period in question saw an emphatic shift in thinking about unity and diversity in the natural history of man, with belief in racial differences steadily outfacing the doctrine of human similitude. Anticipated in the semantic history of race, vocabularies of difference hardened, initially in Germany and France and somewhat later in Britain. As with changing usage of the word race, the relative emphasis on human unity or diversity is usefully mapped across the published corpus of several prolific, long-lived authors. The conundrum of diversity in unity dominates the writings on man of Buffon, who vigorously defended the orthodox position that all human beings belonged to a single species but eschewed classification while exhaustively cataloguing the ambiguous, mutable division of humanity into *variétés* or *races*. Blumenbach's lengthy intellectual effort to reconcile his belief in 'the identity of mankind as a whole' with the 'phenomena of corporeal diversity' was an ongoing preoccupation evident from his earliest work in Latin, which classifies mankind into four flexible *varietas*, to his later works in German which redefine varieties as five hereditary *Racen* or *Rassen*.[41] Prichard (1836-47, I:vii, 2, 9), too, always upheld the 'common parentage' and 'unity of species in all human races', despite 'the striking diversities in their aspect and manner of existence' which he spent forty years cataloguing anatomically and attempting to explain along historical or linguistic lines.[42]

In 1800, the French zoologist Etienne de Lacépède (1756-1825), who continued Buffon's *Histoire naturelle*, opened his zoology course at the Muséum national d'Histoire naturelle with a lecture on 'the races or principal varieties of the human species' whose original unity he took for granted. However, he invoked a kind of congealed late Buffonian biology to argue that at a very remote epoch, when climatic extremes were great enough to 'deform' the human body's 'most solid parts', there had been a radical organic differentiation of the human species into 'at least four races': 'Arab-Europeans', 'Mongols', 'Africans', and 'Hyperboreans'. He speculated that the Americas might originally have been occupied by a fifth, 'very distinct', 'truly aboriginal race'. The only Oceanian people to figure in this schema are 'the Malays' whom Lacépède thought were probably Mongols but might be descended from 'individuals of the European race', specifically Arabs or Phoenicians. They had ranged far beyond their place of origin in the Malacca (Malay) peninsula to settle New Holland, New Zealand, the Pacific Islands, and perhaps Peru. He also endorsed Buffon's argument that in 'very civilized countries', 'the art of man' could 'counterbalance the influence of climate'.[43] Two decades later, Lacépède (1821:383-94) revisited the theme of human diversity in a dictionary entry on 'Man'. The tone is markedly harsher and the terminology Cuvierian. Still 'alone in its genus', the human species was nonetheless divided by 'particular hereditary conformations, produced by constant general causes, which constitute distinct and permanent races'. Lacépède's 'great races' have shrunk to Cuvier's standard three — Caucasic, Mongol, and Negro or Ethiopic — which he sharply differentiated according to 'distinctive' physical characters, especially a marked divergence in facial angles.[44] He also identified several 'independent' lesser races. One was the Malays, whom he praised as 'active, audacious, intelligent' and positioned racially 'midway between the Mongols and the Negroes'. Another was 'the Papuans' of New Guinea, New Holland, and New Caledonia whom he vilified as 'the men least favoured by nature' and racialized as 'Asiatic representatives' of Africans but positioned even further from 'the Arab-European race' in physical conformation and their 'almost savage state'.

Notwithstanding his commitment to racial taxonomy and his adoption of a biological terminology to describe it, Blumenbach always insisted that any division of the single human species could only be 'arbitrary, and not at all clear-cut' because all 'national' somatic differences ran into each other 'by so many nuances' and 'imperceptible transitions'.[45] The earlier Lacépède (1800:7, 16-20, 30-1) allowed that the transition from the 'ignorance' of the 'semi-savage state' (epitomized in 'the African race') to the 'science', 'industry', 'ethics', 'sensibility', and 'reason' of civilization (epitomized in 'the Arab-European race') involved myriad 'insensible nuances' over an 'immense time'. But the idea of nuance is absent from Lacépède's later work and was evidently also lost on his Muséum colleague Cuvier who acknowledged human unity at the higher taxonomic levels but was noncommittal about the singularity of the human species.[46]

From Linnaeus to the early Lacépède, Enlightenment classifications mostly recognized the potential equality of all human beings in contradistinction to other animals and did not systematically rank the varieties or races into which the single human species was partitioned: such divisions were often taken to represent different stages along a unilinear trajectory of common human development from savagery to civility. But Cuvier's comparative anatomy entrenched racial inequality and hierarchy as immutable products of physical organization, notably the size of the brain as indexed by the crude gauge of the cranio-facial ratio: 'the more the brain grows, the more the skull that contains it increases in capacity; the more considerable it becomes in comparison with the face'. At the time — 1800 — the racial corollaries of his theory were still implicit but already damning: the area of a vertical section of 'the European' skull was 'almost four times that of the face'; the area of the face increased 'by about a fifth' in 'the negro', by 'only a tenth' in 'the calmuck' (Mongol), but by a 'slightly lesser proportion' in 'the *orang-outang*'.[47]

That same year, Cuvier (1978:171-3) instructed impending voyagers to seek empirical confirmation of the undoubtedly marked differences between the 'races of the human species' in certain key anatomical features: 'the proportion of the cranium to the face [cranio-facial ratio], the projection of the muzzle [facial angle], the breadth of the cheekbones, the shape of the eye-sockets'. These 'diverse structures', moreover, appeared to have significant 'influence' on the 'moral and intellectual faculties' of races. By 1817 (1817b:273), he was drawing an unequivocal nexus between the size of 'the skull and the brain' and a purported 'cruel law' (of nature) which had 'condemned to eternal inferiority the races with depressed and compressed skulls'. In *Le règne animal* (1817a, I:82, 94-5), Cuvier translated the 'distinctive' physical characters of his three major races into an explicit racial hierarchy expressed in an implicit history of racial progress or stasis: the Caucasic race was 'the most civilized' and 'generally dominated the others'; Mongolic civilization had 'always remained stationary'; while the component peoples of the Negro race had 'always remained barbarians'.

Cuvier's adamant biologism was reinscribed in Britain by the surgeon and comparative anatomist William Lawrence (1783-1867) whose 1818 lectures to the Royal College of Surgeons on the organic nature of life and the natural history of man provoked a storm of criticism when published the following year. His stated aims (1819:119) were 'to consider man as an object of zoology' and to explain 'the principal differences between the various races of mankind'. The perennial tension between human unity and diversity is patent in this book's incongruous mix of scientific logic with humanitarian or relativist gestures and a priori racial essentialism. Lawrence dedicated his work to Blumenbach; praised

Prichard; condemned slavery as 'revolting and antichristian'; proclaimed man's 'broad' distance from 'all other animals'; and asserted human specific unity: 'the various races' were only 'varieties of a single species'. Yet, (unlike Prichard), he refused on the grounds of inadequate 'data' to consider the question of whether all men 'descend from the same family' or to affirm 'that all the varieties of man have been produced from one and the same breed'. He maintained 'unequivocally' the structural approximation of 'the Negro' to 'the monkey'. He lionized Cuvier and echoed his position on the biological discreteness and differential endowments of races: 'comparison of the crania of the white and dark races' revealed 'the retreating forehead and the depressed vertex' of the 'dark varieties' which determined their 'moral and intellectual inferiority', 'limited' their 'natural capabilities' for civilization and Christianity, and ensured that 'Negroes' were 'every where, slaves to the race of nobler formation'.[48]

At the time in Britain, such racialist views no doubt struck popular chords but they were also widely denounced, in large part because they raised the spectre of heterodoxy emanating from France. Philanthropists and Evangelicals accused Lawrence of materialism — because he maintained that life and thought were purely organic — and of denying the equality of all men before God; Tories deplored his democratic politics; and the book was denied copyright and withdrawn from publication. This ensured its success since it circulated in numerous pirated editions for at least the next fifty years.[49] During this period, Lawrence's derivative but accessible synthesis of recent thinking about heredity and race formation was cited approvingly across the spectrum of the emerging British science of race: from Prichard, to the pioneer fieldworker, collector, and evolutionist Alfred Russel Wallace (1823-1914), to the anti-evolutionist, extreme racialist anthropologist James Hunt (1833-1869).[50]

Intimating polygeny

The teleological debate over human unity or racial diversity that convulsed the science of man after 1750 took its most extreme shape in the hostile opposition of the doctrines known from the mid-nineteenth century as 'monogeny' and 'polygeny'. Did all humanity comprise a single species with common ancestry (monogeny), as neoclassical cosmology assumed and the Church insisted? Or did the present existence of (apparently) morphologically distinct groups signify human descent from more than one independent set of ancestors (polygeny), as popular and scientific opinions increasingly maintained? Arguments for multiplicity flourished, especially in France and the United States, usually in tandem with harsh racial attitudes. These arguments in turn provoked vociferous defence of the orthodox position, especially in Britain where negative racial attitudes were nonetheless widespread.

Such debates were not entirely unprecedented. In the sixteenth and seventeenth centuries, scattered challenges to Biblical dogma on the unitary descent of man were repressed as heretical, notably that of the French deist Isaac de La Peyrère (1596-1676) who was forced to recant his theory of pre-Adamite creations (1655). An empirical case for inherent racial or specific differences between extended human groups was put by Bernier (1684:148 150) whose use of the term *race* is in some respects decidedly modern. In an anonymous article, he proposed a classification into 'four or five Species or Races of men whose difference is so notable' — and 'essential' or innate in the case of Africans — 'that it can justly serve as the basis for a new division of the Earth'. But this radical argument was largely ignored at the time and if Bernier anticipated the eighteenth-century natural history of man, he seemingly had little direct conceptual influence on its emergence.[51]

During the eighteenth century, a few sceptical philosophers — notably the Frenchman Voltaire (1694-1778) and the Scots David Hume (1711-1776) and Henry Home, Lord Kames (1696-1782) — contested the prevailing consensus on human unity by projecting the 'perceptible difference in the species of men inhabiting the four known parts of our world' back to nature's 'original' differentiation of plural human 'breeds' or 'species'.[52] The African slave trade, unsurprisingly, spawned polemical judgments on the matter by opponents and supporters alike. The naval surgeon John Atkins (1685-1757) served on the Guinea coast in the 1720s and was a strong critic of slavery, if no admirer of the 'Way of Living' and mental abilities of 'the Africans'. He nonetheless dismissed the capacity of climate to effect 'this remarkable division of Mankind into Blacks and Whites' and pronounced the opinion that 'White and Black must have descended of different Protoplasts', that they had '*ab origine*, sprung from different-coloured first Parents'. Atkins's scientific credentials render his (professedly 'a little Heterodox') verdict especially relevant to this study. In a notably venomous work, the Jamaica plantation owner, historian, and apologist for slavery Edward Long (1734-1813) opined that 'the White and the Negroe had not one common origin'. He concluded that 'the nature of these men, and their dissimilarity to the rest of mankind' proved that Negroes were 'a different species of the same *genus*'.[53] It was against the looming threat of such heterodoxy and the atrocities of Negro slavery that Buffon, Blumenbach, and Kant variously sought a scientific resolution to the problem of human diversity without fatal compromise to the established principle of the common origin of the single human species (Zammito 2006). Kant (2001:3, 12) did so pragmatically, invoking the principle of economy in explanation — why posit 'many local creations' and thereby 'unnecessarily duplicate the number of causes'? Blumenbach (1795:73) concurred but the issue for him was primarily ethical.

Phillip Sloan (1995:123, 133, 135) considered a 'slide into polygenism' to be a 'persistent implication' in Linnaean natural history from the tenth edition of *Systema Naturae* (1758) which posited more than one species of the genus *Homo*. In the 1780s, the German doctor and anatomist Samuel Thomas Soemmerring (1755-1830) — in a work dedicated to his friend Georg Forster — consigned 'the Moors' (Africans) to 'a lower echelon at the throne of mankind' and produced a catalogue of significant anatomical differences between Europeans and Negroes from which he inferred that 'the brain of a Negro is smaller' (1785:xi, 49-67). Blumenbach (1790:62-78) criticized the crude biological determinism of Soemmerring's movement from anatomy to intellect but Forster, who took a consistently morphological approach, professed admiration for this 'physiological and anatomical' proof for 'the corporeal difference of Negroes from Europeans'.[54] In graphic illustration of the liaison of ancient bigotry with a new biology, Forster brought the visual evidence of 'appearance' together with Soemmerring's anatomical argument to speculate that 'the Negro' might be 'a second human species' and 'an originally different stock' from 'white men'.

At the very end of the eighteenth century, the English surgeon and anatomist Charles White (1728-1813) argued for a 'gradation from the European man down to the ape' and located 'the African' much 'nearer to the ape'. He included an appendix of translations of lengthy extracts from Soemmerring's text. White challenged climatic or life style explanations for human variation and concluded that 'material differences in the corporeal organization', hair, and skin colour of 'various classes of mankind' proved that 'various species of men were originally created and separated, by marks sufficiently discriminative': 'the Negro, the American, some of the Asiatic tribes, and the European' were thus 'different species'.[55] White was arguably the earliest polygenist — though the term itself was well in the future — because he grounded his case systematically in comparative anatomy.[56] He was also the last British savant for nearly half a century to profess openly a belief in plural human species.

Origins, races, species

Donald Grayson (1983:140) pointed out that the hypothesis of polygenesis literally imputes separate origins to different human groups 'regardless of how those groups are treated taxonomically' — that is, without necessarily assigning them to distinct species. The reverse also applies: multiple species need not imply plural origins. Accordingly, Claude Blanckaert (1988:31) observed that 'polygenists implicitly identified race with species' and that, although the original unity of races 'remained always controversial', races were differentiated 'by the same triad of attributes that distinguishes "species": the resemblance, the descent, and the permanence of observable characteristics'. In the 1780s, Georg Forster seriously hypothesized the existence of more than one species of men, using species in the 'invariable' Linnaean sense, but as an anticlerical revolutionary he disparaged the question of origins as 'inexplicable'. Race, however, was a minor term in Forster's empirical vocabulary, positioned in 'tacit subordination' to species as an 'undetermined' synonym for variety. He vigorously rejected Kant's redefinition of races as environmentally determined but permanent and hereditary, on the grounds that indelibility was a character of species, not races.[57] Yet it was Kant's conceptual innovation that enabled the subsequent approximation of race and species. In the mid-nineteenth century, the polygenist entomologist Emile Blanchard (1819-1900) also took issue with '*races*' as a much used but 'ambiguous, even undetermined' word in science, adopted to 'avoid commitment on the importance attached to the differences observed' in the human genus. Yet he himself interchanged the terms *race* and *espèce* and insisted that 'the characters of the races perpetuate themselves from century to century without perceptible modification'.[58]

From 1800, some naturalists in France began to assert the plurality of human species. Buffon's disciple, the politically progressive military physician Julien-Joseph Virey (1775-1846), who had read White and whose own copious writings evidently reached a wide audience, divided the 'human genus' broadly into 'beautiful white' races and 'ugly brown and black' ones (1800, I:145). Sloan (1995:140-1, 151) argued that Virey's work synthesized central strands in eighteenth-century human science by combining Linnaean taxonomy and Buffonian historical geography in a 'fully naturalistic scenario' of man's ascent from the 'state of pure nature' to 'perfect civilization'. Virey nonetheless took serious issue with 'the immortal Buffon' in at least two ways: he represented races as 'primordial', 'permanent', 'hereditary', and resistant to the power of climate; and he hypothesized that 'the negro' — 'less human than the European' and 'close to simple animality' — could be considered a 'distinct species'.[59] In a much later elaboration of his thesis, Virey (1824, II:30) restricted 'permanence' in the face of external influences to specific characteristics and reconfigured races as merely 'variable modifications of a single, primordial species'.[60] The 'indelible perseverance of the physical and moral character of the negro' thereby justified Virey's division of the human genus into 'two distinct species', each comprising 'several principal races or stocks'. The species were unnamed but clearly ranked on the basis of markedly divergent facial angles and highly essentialized sets of opposed physical and moral traits, starting with skin colour. The four races of his '1st species' and the two of his '2nd' were labelled by colour and also ranked: he vaunted the 'white European race' as 'superior to all the others in physical and moral qualities' and positioned it 'at the head of the human genus', as 'no longer a simple animal'; he maligned the 'blackish' 'Papuans' of New Guinea, 'Australasia', and New Caledonia as being of characteristically 'diminished occipital capacity', 'the ugliest of men and the closest to the orang-outangs', while conceding that the latter 'belong to another genus'.[61] Reserving detailed calumny for 'the negro', whom he represented as naturally 'inferior and subjugated', with 'manifest' structural links to orangutans, Virey nonetheless condemned the slave trade and piously allowed that 'this race of men' might advance, with European help, 'to an honourable rank in the scale of perfectibility'.[62]

In the mid-1820s, at the further end of categorical amplification, the soldier-biologist Jean-Baptiste-Geneviève-Marcellin Bory de Saint-Vincent (1778-1846) and the physician, comparative anatomist, and physiologist Louis-Antoine Desmoulins (1796-1828) identified fifteen and sixteen separate human species respectively. In important other respects, though, their analyses are quite divergent. Bory de Saint-Vincent challenged Cuvier's contention that the human genus 'is unique in its order' by insisting that the genus *Orang*, composed of beings 'just like us', belonged 'naturally' to the same order as the genus *Homo*.[63] He then sharply divided the human genus, making physical structure and 'internal organization' his key determinants of the intellectual and moral limits of different 'species of Men' and combining them with skin colour as core criteria of specific differences. Predictably, his taxonomy was crowned by the 'more beautiful', 'Japhetic species', 'to which we belong'. The 'Negroes of Oceanica' or 'Melanians' comprised his 'next to last species' while the 'Hottentot species' — furthest from the Japhetic in 'appearance and anatomical characteristics', 'closest to the Orangs in the inferiority of its intellectual faculties' — purportedly marked 'the passage from the genus Man to the genera Orang and Gibbon, thus to the Apes'.[64] Yet, notwithstanding such clear intimations of ranking, both human and simian, Bory (1827a, II:128-9) denied hierarchical intent — he assigned 'no definitive position' for who 'would dare to raise one species above the others' or declare any 'incapable of emerging from the brutish state?' The disingenuousness of this seeming egalitarianism is evident in the flanking sentences which show the mutual complicity of class, national, and racial prejudices in his rhetoric: the Japhetic species owed its 'first rank' to the 'intellectual superiority of a few favoured men' while nine-tenths of the species were hardly more rational than the 'Hottentots' (Khoikhoi); 'beyond the Pyrenees', 'proud' Europeans had fallen 'to the level of New Caledonian savages' whereas Africans transplanted to Haiti had raised themselves 'to the sublime level of the Anglo-American'.

Desmoulins set out to refute both the Buffonian hypothesis that climate determined human 'physical characters' and its monogenist premise that present human occupation of the globe was a product of 'emigrations' by descendants of a single common ancestral stock. He argued instead for 'the invariability of forms', the 'original diversity of species', and the 'plurality of centres of creation'. His determining principle for the concept of species was the 'permanence of the type in the face of contrary influences' but in practice he treated species and race as synonymous. Species could change or new ones emerge only as a product of generation through racial mixing. Species and races were reified entities with constant physiological characters that determined intellect, morality, and behaviour.[65] However, unlike Bory, Desmoulins insisted on the 'infinite' anatomical distance separating 'the most perfect of the apes from the most imperfect of men'. Moreover, his racial adjudications were relatively benign apart from a residual distaste for Negroes and some native Americans and a tacit presumption of European superiority. He was remarkably positive, if patronizing, about the usually maligned 'Austro-Africans'. The 'Boschisman' (Bushmen or San) and 'Hottentot' races differed markedly from each other and from 'the Negroes'. The Hottentots were 'gentle, quiet, honest', but indolent, and 'much superior' to most Ethiopians in the level of civilization reached. Any identification of the Boschismans with the apes was 'absurd and false' on anatomical, moral, and intellectual grounds: they were 'lively', 'spiritual', energetic, 'ingenious', and, 'after the Caffres, the most moral and intelligent of the peoples of southern Africa'.[66] Desmoulins's work concludes with a catalogue of 'the species and the races of the human genus': this schematic series of essentialized physical descriptions is relatively dispassionate apart from the recurring negative stereotype of Negro features; moral and intellectual faculties are scarcely mentioned; and racial hierarchy is only implicit in the geographical ordering of species. The inhabitants of Oceania are classified as Species 11-14 under then standard labels: 'Malay or Oceanic'; 'Papuan'; 'Oceanian Negro'; and 'Australasian'.

After about 1800, most naturalists and anthropologists, whatever their theoretical and moral persuasions, subordinated historical conjecture about human origins to the physical description and classification of races or species and abandoned questions of racial genealogy to the avowedly historical disciplines of comparative philology and ethnology.[67] Desmoulins (1826:336-57), exceptionally, did address etymological and historical implications of his zoology. The Italian geographer Adriano Balbi (1782-1848) maintained that the systematic comparison and classification of languages — which he called *ethnographie* — was the only means to reveal the 'primitive origin' of the 'nations' now inhabiting the world but he accepted Desmoulins's innovatory insistence that a shared language in the present need not mean a common racial derivation. Formally committed to the conventional assumption that 'all men' stemmed from a 'single stock, subdivided only into varieties', Balbi nonetheless refused to 'adopt or reject' Desmoulins's 'system' of multiple human species. With respect to the 'Maritime World' of Oceania, Balbi's strongly racialized linguistic geography, gleaned largely from travellers' reports, differentiated a far-flung Malay 'family' of languages from a 'second branch' of unrelated non-Malay tongues designated 'Languages of the Oceanian Negroes'. Their speakers included 'the Australians' whom he disparaged as 'the most brutish savages of the globe' and as 'beings who seem to differ from the orang-outang only by the use of speech'.[68]

Ethnologie denoted a broad field of inquiry established in France in the 1830s by the physician William-Frédéric Edwards (1777-1842) whose blending of physiology, linguistics, and history, Blanckaert noted (1988:22), combined 'the physical idea of race and the cultural principle of "nationality"'. Edwards (1841) gave renewed impetus to the natural history of man but also confirmed the fixity of races as morphological types. Yet, despite Edwards's own polygenist leanings and the considerable influence of his raciology, the focus of *ethnologie* on the 'historic races' of Europe and on the interdependence of the moral and physical characteristics of races made it peripheral to the narrowly physicalist polygenism which controlled *anthropologie* in France during much of the second half of the nineteenth century.[69]

In Britain, the term ethnology was borrowed in the early 1840s as a retrospective label for the venerable Prichardian approach which continued to dominate the natural history of man for a decade after his death in 1848, in the face of serious challenges to its premises and methods. Strongly philanthropic in origin and institutional connections, ethnology was politically less heterogeneous and religiously more orthodox than *ethnologie*. Its fundamentally historical goal was to trace the differentiation of all the existing 'races of men' from a 'single stock', in particular through comparative philology.[70] In contrast, 'Anthropological' enemies of ethnology such as Hunt professed agnosticism on the 'profitless' question of 'Man's origin' but insisted on the specific or even generic division of humanity on physical, intellectual, and moral grounds, including the 'far more numerous' analogies 'between the Negro and apes than between the European and apes'.[71] The elision of origins — 'an Anglicized Hebrew myth' — and the conflation of race with species were patent in the definitions given by the polygenist Egyptologist George Gliddon (1809-1857) in 1857 to his neologisms 'monogenist' and 'polygenist': 'the doctrines of schools professing to sustain dogmatically the unity or the diversity of human races' (1857:402, 428-31).

The triumph of racial difference

The shift in attention from a teleological concern for origins to the measurement and classification of existing groups diminished the practical import of the ideological opposition of monogeny and polygeny, despite the huge rhetorical investment of both sides in the debate. Belief in original human unity coexisted more or less uneasily with perceptions of present diversity in the thinking of several of the savants discussed above, who endorsed the conventional position but with growing equivocation. Cuvier and most of his followers — who included Lawrence as well as several polygenists — evinced little concern for origins.[72] But they espoused the fixity of species, the inheritance of racial characteristics, the primacy of physical organization, and the diagnostic interconnectedness of cranial structure and intelligence as a key racial differentia.[73] In a reminder of

Lacépède, Cuvier (1812:105-6) posited an ancient — perhaps originary? — differentiation of 'the negroes' as the 'most degraded human race', closest in form to 'the brute', and without the 'intelligence' to achieve regular government or sustained knowledge. All the characters of this race, he asserted, showed 'clearly' that it had 'escaped the great catastrophe at another point from the Caucasic and Altaic [Mongol] races' and had 'perhaps' been separated from them long before it occurred. Cuvier's ambivalence about original human unity mirrored the reservations of the geographer Conrad Malte-Brun (1775-1826) about the 'orthodox doctrine', the '*system* of a common human origin', that he would 'neither refute nor confirm'. Balbi was similarly noncommittal with respect to Desmoulins's polygenist 'system'.[74] It was thus not merely politic for Bory de Saint-Vincent to dedicate his polygenist treatise *L'homme* to Cuvier, in whose 'footsteps' he claimed to tread, or inappropriate for him to acknowledge Malte-Brun as his precursor 'in distinguishing the species of Men ... under the designation of races'. Bory's functional set of specific differentiae and their pessimistic corollaries echoed Cuvier's racial criteria. Human species did 'not derive their differences from colour only' but were distinguished more by 'structure' and aspects of 'internal organization' which influenced 'the intellectual faculties' and determined 'the level of moral development each can reach'.[75]

Notwithstanding this broad community of racial assumptions, particularly evident in France, polygenists' taxonomies were in general more starkly racialized than those of monogenists because they typically classed some human species close to the apes while quarantining 'civilized man'/'the white man'/'the European' from this debasing association. White's work (1799) is an obvious case in point though that of Desmoulins (1826) is not. Virey (1824, III:460-3) refused absolutely to place 'this king of the globe' alongside 'the orang-outang' because the civilized European 'reigns' over all other beings in the creation, including 'the inferior races of his own species'. Not for him Bory's contemptuous denial of rationality to all but a favoured handful of Japhetic men. In Virey's view, an 'immense distance' separated a 'Hottentot Boschisman' from even a 'simple European peasant'. Therefore, although 'the ape' could not be grouped 'with us', the orangutan genus, in particular, was clearly 'not very far from the least perfect species of men'. Monogenists, in contrast, usually expressed their core premise of human psychic uniqueness by segregating the single human species as the sole genus of a separate order within the animal kingdom.

The number of species identified by polygenists and the degree of disparateness attributed to races by monogenists were key signifiers of the relative acrimony and rigidity of racial discriminations. Multiplication of species widened purported inequalities between groups and heightened scepticism about the improvability of some.[76] Thus, Bory de Saint-Vincent's hairsplitting taxonomy of numerous human species and his bracketing of the genus *Homo* with the genus *Orang* within the family or order of *Bimana* (see note 64) had invidious implications for certain groups that were not inherent in Cuvier's sweeping division of the human genus into three races isolated as *Bimana*. The systemic metonymy of Bory's ranking of the 'Hottentot species' as the generic 'passage' from man to orang was potentially more injurious — though no more insulting — than Cuvier's incidental analogy of 'negro' resemblance to 'the apes'. Yet assessing the relative obloquy of racialized language is problematic and perhaps futile since the ideological impact of Bory's entire 'zoological essay' on man was arguably outweighed by the 'veritable raciological synthesis' — Blanckaert's phrase — contained in Cuvier's cursory remarks about human races, made by a highly influential savant who rejected speculative 'system' and laid claim to the 'more solid edifice of facts and of induction'.[77] Cuvier's position was also paradoxical with respect to the 'minimally polygenist' Virey who posited two human species but represented the final race of his '1st species' — the 'Malay or Polynesic' — as close to the 'negro type', an 'intermediate nuance between the Mongols and the Negroes', and a 'bastard race' linked by 'diverse gradations' to the 'blackish' Papuans.[78] Such racial indeterminacy was normally an argument for human specific unity but Cuvier's formal adherence to this credo was vitiated by his insistence that races were 'eminently distinct'.

When human variation was judged to be confined within a single species, acknowledgement of the transposability and the internal diversity of races could have the reverse effect to multiplication of species — narrowing rather than widening divergence and attendant inequalities. From this perspective, the greater the perceived intraspecific variation, the stronger the case for a unified human species since apparently different races overlapped or blended and physical differences within races could exceed those between them, points made strongly by Prichard (1826, II:588-9): the 'character of one race passes into that of another' while sometimes 'the most different complexions, and the greatest diversities of figure, known to exist, are to be found among tribes which appear to belong to the same nation, or family of nations'. Contemporary contributors to the polemic on the unity of the human species were aware that 'the fractionating tendency', as Stocking put it (1973:lxxi-lxxii), produced 'monogenetic rather than polygenetic conclusions'. Lawrence (1819:502) maintained pragmatically that 'the very numerous gradations' in human appearance, form, and attributes were 'an almost insuperable objection to the notion of *specific difference*', since any might be attributed to 'original distinction of species', in which case 'the number of species would be overwhelming'.[79] Prichard (1826, II:588) insisted that there was 'no clearly traced and definite line which the tendency to variety or deviation cannot pass, and therefore, no specific distinction'. The English naturalist Charles Darwin (1809-1882) witnessed great human variation in the course of HMS *Beagle's* global surveying voyage of 1831-36. Years later (1871, I:225-6), he distilled that experience into a monogenist precept: 'the most weighty of all the arguments against treating the races of man as distinct species, is that they graduate into each other … and that it is hardly possible to discover clear distinctive characters between them'.

Yet by 1860, Prichardian ethnology and biblical monogeny had lost scientific credibility in Britain and been overshadowed by more naturalistic approaches to the science of man. A mostly polygenist, highly racialist group of Anthropologicals led by Hunt briefly seized the limelight but were in turn eclipsed by the dominant evolutionism of the next decade.[80] In the face of the growing credibility of polygeny, embattled monogenists normalized racial terminology and logic, as Prichard had steadily done from the 1820s. Lawrence, who had vigorously defended human specific unity in his 1818 lectures, reportedly admitted in 1856 that he was now 'convinced of the diversity of human origin'.[81] In France, polygenist belief in multiple human species was integral to the heavily anthropometric and craniological *anthropologie* practised under the leadership of the physician-anatomist Paul Broca (1824-1880), recent founder of the Société d'Anthropologie de Paris (Figure 5). Leading monogenist naturalists of the Muséum national d'Histoire naturelle, such as the comparative anatomist Etienne-Renaud-Augustin Serres (1786-1868), the zoologist Isidore Geoffroy Saint-Hilaire (1805-1861), and the anthropologist Armand de Quatrefages (1810-1892), co-existed uneasily with Broca'a institutional control of *anthropologie* by combining equivocal belief in original human unity with firm commitment to the scientific worth of craniometry and acceptance of the irreversibility, permanence, and inequality of races, regarded as biological types.[82]

In 1841, Serres had endorsed a significant gesture toward polygeny in presenting a special report of a commission of the Académie des Sciences on the anthropological collections made by the phrenologist Pierre-Marie Alexandre Dumoutier (1797-1871) during the recent global circumnavigation of Jules-Sébastien-César Dumont d'Urville (1790-1842). With respect to the contentious issue of the unity or plurality of human types, the report argues for a 'double character': the human species was 'unique' with respect to generation but definitely plural with respect to 'the hereditary transmission of characters'. By conceding that Aboriginal Australians might 'at a pinch' be seen as autochthonous, the commission left open the possibility of a separate origin for this allegedly 'most inferior' of Oceanian races. The members agreed with Dumont d'Urville (1832:15-16) that the 'black race' was the 'mother stock' of the 'primitive inhabitants' of the region who had been displaced by successive 'invasions' of 'more advanced' races. The supposed displacement process climaxed in the onset of vastly 'superior' European civilization and imminent racial 'fusion'. The report thus implies a teleological trajectory from a single human creation, to the very ancient differentiation of 'three primordial types', culminating in the prospect of ultimately renewed unity through colonialism and asymmetric racial crossing.

Since the final stage was still 'in full swing' in Oceania, the region exemplified the realization in practice of the universal scheme. Throughout the report, a compromised monogenism jostles with profound ambivalence about the 'black race' and a smug conviction that the European race 'dominates all the others by the superiority of its physical and moral characters'.[83]

Figure 5: [Alphonse] Vien, 'Le craniographe de M. Broca'.[84]

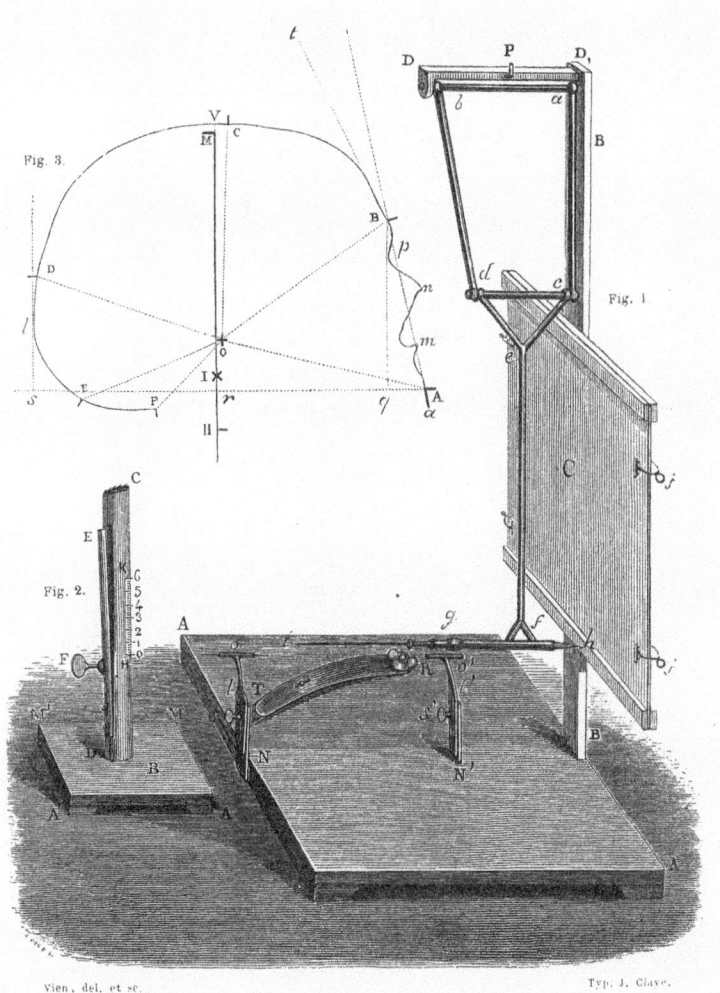

LE CRANIOGRAPHE DE M. BROCA.

Engraving. Photograph B. Douglas.

Two decades later, in a paper published posthumously, Geoffroy rejected Cuvier's authoritative ternary division of the human genus on the basis of skin colour but followed him by defining races as characteristic 'modifications of the species' and stressing 'constancy' in their 'hereditary transmission'. His threefold criteria for anthropological taxonomy show significant accommodations of polygenist and racialist thinking: the multiplicity of human races; their 'unequal' anatomical, physiological, and psychological value; and the importance of traits derived from the conformation of the head. Accordingly, he increased the number of races to twelve and nominated four as 'principal types' — the 'cardinal points of anthropology' — by adding 'the Hottentot type' to Cuvier's standard racial trinity of Caucasic, Mongolic, and Ethiopic.[85] Geoffroy's classification 'diametrically opposed' two of these types: the Caucasic — racially glorified as 'the most beautiful' with the 'highest intellectual faculties'; and the Hottentot — racially vilified as the 'inferior' and 'last term in the anthropological series', a branch so 'profoundly separated from the common trunk' as to compromise the 'tradition' of the *original unity* of the human genus.[86] These unsubstantiated assertions of 'relative superiority or inferiority' depended scientifically on the hoary Cuvierian measure of the cranio-facial ratio: the theory that the greater the development of the 'superior parts' (the skull and the brain), the higher the race; and that the greater the development of the 'inferior parts' (the sense organs and the jaws), the lower the race. The Caucasic had 'maximum cranial development' and was therefore 'superior'; the Hottentot had 'maximum facial development' and was therefore 'inferior'.[87]

Species, hybrids, synthesis

Defining a species

Before the publication of Darwin's *On the Origin of Species* (1859), the concept of species was given diverse, often ambiguous meanings depending on a shifting constellation of relative emphases: on reproductive or morphological criteria; history or taxonomy; environment or heredity; hybridization or racial purity; and transmutation or fixity. From Linnaeus to Darwin, definitions of species oscillated unsteadily between versions of fixism and transformism, often pivoted on the vexed question of racial crossing and its status in the unity or otherwise of the human species. Linnaeus initially professed what James Larson called a 'naive religious faith' that species were fixed, discrete products of the original creation of a 'single pair of all living beings'. Though this early conviction consistently informed Linnaeus's abstract taxonomic practice, from about 1760 the oft-reiterated dictum *nullae species novae*, 'no new species', vanished from his writings as he became convinced empirically that new plant species could emerge through cross-breeding — indeed, his contemporaries often branded him a transformist.[88]

Although Buffon paid lip service to the dominant contemporary dogma that species were original and eternal, he represented them in practice in secular historical terms as real, dynamic physical entities comprising 'similar individuals who reproduce themselves'. His mature formulation that animals might be reduced to 'a quite small number of families or principal stocks, from which it is not impossible that all the others have issued' through degeneration, acknowledged the problematic of transformation in altered environments. As with Kant (who, however, always insisted on the original permanance of races and species and rejected developmentalism), Buffon's breeding criterion for species membership — the capacity for 'constant reproduction' — qualified the strong morphological emphasis common to most taxonomists, foregrounded the question of hybrids, and served to validate his principled belief that all human beings belonged to 'a single same species' since, despite dramatic differences in appearance, they could all interbreed and produce fertile offspring.[89] While Blumenbach did not doubt human interfertility, he saw the 'principle sought from copulation' as 'uncertain' and 'not sufficient' to define the concept of a species or differentiate it from a variety. He resorted instead to the morphological criteria of '*analogy* and resemblance'. Blumenbach dismissed coupling between different species as rare and usually sterile but attributed some transformative potential to 'hybrid generation' between different varieties of the same species which produced offspring identical to neither parent but 'midway' in form between them.[90] Yet in his ultimate view, the *Umschaffung*, 'remodelling', of species over time signified only 'the great mutability in nature' which he attributed in turn 'to the benevolent, wise dispensation of the Creator'. Lenoir pointed out that Blumenbach was not an evolutionist because he did not posit 'a transformation of species by means of the acquisition of *new* characters', an impossibility in Kantian theoretical terms.[91]

Cuvier's immense institutional prestige in France no doubt enhanced the authority of his core premise of the integrity and fixity of species: a species comprised 'all the beings' with a common 'fixed' form, perpetuated 'by generation' and 'confined within quite narrow limits' that had remained intact and unchanged 'since the origin of things'. Nature, moreover, sought to prevent the alteration of species through mixing by ensuring their 'mutual aversion'.[92] He successfully discredited the transformist theories promulgated by his Muséum colleagues, the zoologists Jean-Baptiste de Monet de Lamarck (1744-1829) and Etienne Geoffroy Saint-Hilaire (1772-1844), the father of Isidore, who proposed materialist narratives about the transmutation over time of 'lower' into 'higher' organisms.[93] In Martin Rudwick's judgment (1997:179, note 4), Cuvier's refutation of Lamarck determined the direction of research on the question of species 'right up to the time of Darwin'.

In Britain, Lawrence endorsed Cuvier's twin dictums that species were 'constant and permanent'; and that uniformity was maintained 'by generation' and instinctive 'aversion to union with other species'. But unlike Cuvier, he sought to explain the formation of new races within the single human species, though he too was no evolutionist. He concluded that human diversity was not original but the 'result of subsequent variation' produced by the inheritance of 'native or congenital variety', rather than by the effect of 'external agencies' such as climate, nutrition, or mode of life. Such 'native variety' occurred spontaneously in individuals; or might in principle, on the model of plant and animal breeding, result from 'hybrid generation' between different varieties of the human species.[94] In his derivative way (the book was a published collection of lectures), Lawrence evidently owed the hypothesis of heritable variations to Prichard who had argued that 'connate variety' always tended 'to become hereditary and permanent in the race', though neither man could explain how the process worked.[95] In the first edition of *Researches* (1813), Prichard denied the capacity of 'external powers' to produce permanent human varieties. In the second (1826), he restated the dictum that all 'connate peculiarities of body' were hereditary but brought milieu back into his equation by outlining a 'law of adaptation' to 'particular local circumstances' to account for localized specific diversities within a genus and varieties within a species, including humanity.[96] Kentwood D. Wells (1971:346-8, 356) saw this tacit recognition of 'conservative aspects of natural selection' as an anticipation of Darwinian evolution though Prichard, like Lawrence, was not an evolutionist since he believed in the fixity of species and was oblivious to the 'creative role' of natural selection in the formation of new ones.

Buffon's breeding criterion had been unproblematically rehearsed by Cuvier: as a young man, he maintained that sexual union was 'the only certain and even infallible character' distinguishing a species; and as a mature savant he allowed that 'the human species appears unique, since all individuals can intermix without distinction, and produce fertile offspring'.[97] But, like Blumenbach, neither Prichard nor Lawrence thought the breeding criterion a sufficient rationale for human unity because of reported 'exceptions' to the 'supposed law' that cross-species hybrids were sterile. Prichard modified the classic norm by promoting the theoretical premise of 'instinctive repugnance' to the intermixture of species in the wild, with the twin corollary that 'there are no hybrid *races*' (said of plants) and that animals which propagate together 'frequently and habitually' in their natural state are of the same species. By analogical reasoning, since there was no 'invincible' repugnance between men and women of different races and since human 'mixed breeds' were invariably prolific and capable of engendering 'an entirely new and intermediate stock', they were 'not hybrid' and 'the several tribes of men are but varieties of the same species'.[98] Lawrence (1819:265-71) invoked Blumenbach's morphological criterion of 'analogy and probability' to draw the same conclusion on similar grounds.

Confronting hybrids

If Buffon's principle of 'continuous fecundity' within the human species was an article of faith for monogenists (Flourens 1850:167-9), a related postulate in their creed, also attributed to Buffon, gave greater scope for racialist cynicism. In 1849, Buffon speculated that some 'Tartars' were 'less ugly & whiter' than others because of intermixture with neighbouring 'European nations'; he later formalized the proposition that it would take only a couple of hundred years to 'wash the skin of a Negro' through 'mixing with the blood of the White' whereas climate alone would take many centuries to produce the same effect.[99] Early nineteenth-century monogenists reworked Buffon's idea as the principle that 'racial mixing' was ameliorative, at least for the allegedly inferior of the races involved. Prichard, unusually evenhanded, cited anecdotal instances of 'mixed breeds' who were physically superior to either European or indigenous components and made it a dictum, in response to the rising racial hysteria of the late 1840s, that the 'mixture of races' was often 'much more advantageous than their separation'. But Lawrence, relentlessly racialist, declared that 'contamination' by an admixture of 'black or red blood' would cause the 'intellectual and moral character' of Europeans to 'deteriorate', whereas 'an infusion of white blood' would 'improve and ennoble the qualities of the dark varieties'.[100] Improvement or degeneration thus became two sides of a single racialist coin.

Somewhat paradoxically, the early polygenists tended to be less doctrinaire than Cuvier, Lawrence, and Prichard about the fixity of species and more relaxed about racial crossing which provided their proof for the plurality of human species and their motor for specific change. In works published over more than two decades, Virey spanned a wide gamut of opinion, from empirical to essentialist, though his ambivalent words betray a hankering for the certainty of fixed species and racial purity. On the one hand, he did not doubt the fecundity of human hybrids but subverted Buffon's breeding criterion into an argument *against* human 'specific unity' on the pragmatic analogy that distinct but adjacent species of animals and plants commonly produced fertile offspring from 'adulterous mixings'. If such crossings could engender 'bastard, intermediary lineages able to propagate themselves continuously' (denied by monogenists), the 'formation of new species' was not theoretically impossible. On the other hand, since nature abhorred specific mixing and inspired universal 'repugnance' against it, species were 'essentially unalterable' in type.[101] Virey's ambivalence is patent in his discussion of 'mulattos'. He denigrated them as an 'ambiguous', perhaps unstable 'caste', a 'multitude of bastards' produced 'in the colonies' from the abuse of grossly unequal power relations between white men and female slaves. Yet he applauded their physical strength, agility, and vigour as proof of Buffon's supposed claim (endorsed by monogenists) that 'racial crossing improves individuals'.[102] Bory de Saint-Vincent (1827a, II:134-6) took for granted that human species, races, and varieties were 'naturally and constantly reproduced through innumerable mixtures' and that, as with domesticated animals, their 'characteristic limits' had 'partly disappeared'. Desmoulins (1826:158, 194-7) explicitly qualified his argument that it was 'the permanence of the type, in the face of contrary influences, which constitutes the species' with the proviso that altered or new species could emerge through 'generation', as products of 'the mixing, the fusion of heterogeneous peoples'.

Blanckaert (2003b:46-8) identified the 'status of racial crossbreedings' as the key site for conflict between monogenists and polygenists from about 1830 to 1860. A striking feature of such debates is the tendency for protagonists across the board to camouflage their a priori, value-ridden points of view as scientific and objective while recycling a limited stock of tenuous, circumstantial 'facts' as evidence for radically opposed positions (Stocking 1968:49). Another feature is the steady increment in racialization crosscutting the monogeny/polygeny fault line. Serres's report on Dumoutier's collections is a case in point. It splices nominal monogenism to a theory of physical, intellectual, and moral 'improvement' through racial crossing and gradual 'fusion', trumpeted as the creator's 'natural means' to restore human unity. Though egalitarian in theory, the process envisaged was profoundly 'unequal' in operation since the characters of the 'superior' race were said to 'predominate' in the offspring over those of the 'inferior'.[103] An identical vision for a monochromatic future, but without the egalitarian veneer and with overt advocacy of racial obliteration, was outlined by the polygenist surgeon-naturalist Jacques-Bernard Hombron (1798-1852), Dumoutier's colleague on Dumont d'Urville's final voyage of 1837-40 (1846:104-5): 'men will one day comprise only a single race; civilization will extend everywhere, and the inferior races and species will exist only in the archives of history'.

During these three decades, most polygenists took fundamentalist positions against the viability of human hybrids and in favour of morphological criteria for the constancy of species. The presumption of multiple human types enabled them to pervert the monogenists' analogical reasoning by appropriating the axioms of interspecific repugnance and continuous intraspecific fecundity to their own agenda. Notable amongst them were three men with close links to Dumont d'Urville's final voyage: the ships' surgeon-naturalists Hombron and Honoré Jacquinot (1814-1887) who invoked their wide global experience to authorize the individual volumes on 'man' and on 'anthropology' and 'human races' that they contributed to the co-authored *Zoologie* section of the official voyage publication; and Blanchard, a naturalist at the Muséum national d'Histoire naturelle, who wrote the *Anthropologie* volume based on Dumoutier's collections.[104] Hombron insisted that all species, including the 'several species of men', had been created for particular locales and were 'unchangeable'; that only parents of proximate species could produce fertile offspring; and that the lower a species was in the 'human series', the less its hybrid 'fruits' would share the physical and moral qualities of the 'more beautiful' parent. On these grounds, he damned the progeny of Chinese-Malay and Malay-Papuan unions as 'very disagreeable', 'very ugly', 'monstrous', and probably of limited fertility.[105] Jacquinot maintained the 'persistence and conservation' of the three 'unalterable' primitive types into which he divided the human genus and took a particularly hard line on human mixing. He denied the prospect of specific change through interbreeding and condemned interspecies sexual relations as a 'perversion of the generative impulse' which occurred in man only through the 'shameful exploitation' of female slaves. The products of such unions were 'abnormal, monstrous', and 'very limited' in fertility. They were almost unknown in New Holland. Jacquinot claimed to be 'the first' to signal the 'sterility' of interspecific human crossbreeds but admitted his lack of 'rigorous' statistical evidence: rather, it was a 'well-known fact' in the colonies and the 'impression' gained from his own 'general observation'.[106]

Nearly a decade later, Blanchard synthesized and modified the positions taken by Hombron and Jacquinot. He asserted with Hombron that many 'different species of men', comprising a 'natural genus', were created in the countries they still occupied and retained their characters indefinitely 'without perceptible alteration'. He agreed with Jacquinot that racial 'mixtures' were numerically insignificant 'relative to the mass' and rehearsed the theme of natural 'repugnance' against inter-specific coupling. Contra Prichard, the claim of repugnance became his proof that all human beings could not have issued from the same stock and that 'the racial instinct is innate in man's heart'. Blanchard, too, admitted the 'little true knowledge' so far available and leaned heavily on colonial rumour. He moderated Jacquinot's scepticism about durable human crossings: on the one hand, the hybrid products of 'the most different races in the human genus', such as 'whites and negroes', could not be perpetuated indefinitely 'without new mixings'; on the other, 'neighbouring peoples' of very similar races had undiminished interfecundity.[107] The attribution of differential fertility to human hybrids on racial grounds would be a cornerstone of subsequent debates and often became a critical issue in Europe's colonies.[108]

Before 1850, polygeny was primarily a continental and American doctrine with few acknowledged advocates in Britain. Even Knox, whose extreme racial and physical determinism and hard line on human hybrids were the equal of any French polygenist, did not profess literal poly*genesis* since he insisted on the 'evident' unity of man within 'one family, one origin'. However, this 'unity of the organization' was 'embryonic' or 'generic', 'not specific', and the 'one great natural family' of mankind comprised 'many distinct species'.[109] An institutional outsider, pessimistic and nihilistic, he preached an incongruous amalgam of uncompromising racialism with anticolonial political radicalism and nonprogressive developmentalism, synthesized by an idiosyncratic transcendental biology imbibed from Germany and France via the elder Geoffroy Saint-Hilaire.[110] Knox discerned 'remarkable' organic, mental, and moral differences between the 'races of men' while race was an 'all-pervading, unalterable, physical character', the prime determinant of human history and human character, 'individual, social, national'. Historically, at least, human races were 'permanent' and not interconvertible. Since 'species never mingle' due to 'innate dislike', human hybrids were 'a monstrosity of nature' which could not 'hold their ground' over more than two or three generations and hybrid races were non-existent, even in the case of 'closely affiliated' parents.[111]

Flatly rejecting the possibility of the slow, unilinear 'transmutation of species' or of 'successive perfectability', Knox argued that the only transmutation known to Nature was '*generic*, and not *specific*' and was as likely to be 'retrogressive' as 'progressive': 'the development, in time and place, of natural families and species already provided for in the structure of the embryo'. Thus, every human embryo embodied 'the type of all the races of men', past, present, and future.[112] This anti-transmutationist biology underwrote Knox's denial of 'all theories of human progress in time' and fuelled his profound racial and historical pessimism. He pronounced it likely that the 'dark races', (who included 'the Jewish, Coptic, and Gipsy races'), were 'doomed to destruction and extermination' by the 'inextinguishable hatred of races', the 'savage energy' of the 'fair races', and their own physical and psychological 'inferiority', since they could or would not 'progress' and were uncivilizable.[113] Yet, paradoxically, he also declared any successful colonization to be impossible due to the 'great physiological law' of 'continental influences' — the indirect but powerful influence of milieu, exemplified in the expulsion of the French from Haiti. By this law, which Knox claimed to have discovered, every race was naturally adapted only to its continent of origin: the white man was unable to 'colonize a tropical country' and no race could permanently seize 'any other continent than the one to which they are indigenous'. Thus, not only were races unalterable by 'metamorphosis' or 'intermarriage', but they could not be 'extinguished' by conquest, providing they still occupied 'the soil on which nature first placed them'.[114]

Darwinian synthesis

Though Knox was institutionally marginal in the science of man in Britain during his own lifetime, the extreme racialist views expounded during his provincial lecture tours evidently struck popular chords.[115] Moreover, as Evelleen Richards (1989:406-35) has shown, Knox's 'moral anatomy' was far from marginal to the hardening science of race in the 1860s and 1870s or to the well-known struggle for ideological control of anthropology between the Ethnological and Anthropological Societies of London. Not only was Knox acknowledged as the main theoretical inspiration of Hunt and his (mostly) scientifically disreputable, ultra-conservative Anthropological followers, but racial opinions congruent to Knox's were common intellectual currency, including amongst the (mostly) scientifically respectable, politically liberal or radical Darwinians.[116] Indeed, the application of natural selection to human groups — *the Preservation of Favoured Races in the Struggle for Life*, Darwin's subtitle (1859) — is inherently racialist, notwithstanding any associated philanthropic values.

Thus, the biologist and comparative anatomist Thomas Henry Huxley (1825-1895), who campaigned strongly for emancipation on moral grounds, maintained in 1865 in a popular polemical essay that, even when freed, 'our prognathous relative' lacked the natural intellect 'to compete successfully with his bigger-brained and smaller-jawed rival' or to attain 'the highest places in the hierarchy of civilisation' (1893:66). Wallace (1864:clxiv-clxv), the co-inventor of the concept of natural selection and an egalitarian utopian socialist,[117] contended in an address to the Anthropological Society that Europeans were intellectually, morally, and physically 'superior' to the 'low and mentally undeveloped populations' they had encountered in the Americas and the antipodes, whose 'inevitable extinction' he confidently predicted through the operation of Darwin's 'great law'. He partly recanted a few years later on the still highly ethnocentric grounds that natural selection could not explain certain key human physical and intellectual characteristics: even the 'lowest savages' might follow the European trajectory of 'gradual development' since their brains were 'so little inferior in size and complexity to that of the highest types (such as the average European)'.[118] Darwin himself was a passionate opponent of slavery who normally eschewed overtly racialist language and acknowledged his first-hand experience of the 'mental similarity' of the 'most distinct races of men'. But he did not doubt the reality of a human racial hierarchy or the certainty of displacement of 'the lower races'.[119] One notorious passage in *The Descent of Man* (1871:200-1) grafts the ancient idea of the 'organic chain' to the 'principle of evolution' to produce a chilling prognosis: the 'savage races' were positioned nearer to the 'anthropomorphous apes' than were the 'civilised races of man' who would before long 'exterminate and replace' both savages and anthropoids. By positing differential human racial affinity with apes — a position taken by most polygenists — Darwin violated the traditional monogenist concern to quarantine all humanity from categorical intimacy with animals.

Yet Hunt's (1866:327, 339) primary charge against the Darwinians was that they had reinstated the 'unity hypothesis' as a 'new form of monogenism'. Indeed, Wallace candidly explained to the Anthropological Society the Darwinian logic that 'if you do but go far back enough, you must come to a unity of origin', so that man must once have been 'a homogeneous race'. Huxley was more equivocal but reasoned pragmatically that even if the differences between human beings were 'specific', they were so small that it was 'altogether superfluous' to presume 'more than one primitive stock for all'. Darwin made much the same point.[120] At once historical and rigorously naturalist, environmentalist and hereditarian, his 'principles of evolution' rehabilitated human origins as a legitimate subject for secular, scientific inquiry, shorn of any lingering implications of scriptural authority, but left the question of the present singularity or plurality of the human species largely a matter of definition.[121] As early as 1845, in a private letter endorsing Prichard's and Lawrence's hypothesis of human variation through the propagation of spontaneous individual 'peculiarities', Wallace had remarked that a 'permanent peculiarity' owing nothing to 'external causes' was zoologically a 'distinction of species & not of mere variety': thus, 'the "Negro" the red Indian & the European' should be considered 'distinct species of the genus Homo'.[122] Both he and Huxley argued diplomatically that the theory of speciation through natural selection could 'harmonise', 'reconcile', and 'combine' the conflicting positions of the 'Monogenistic and Polygenistic schools'. Darwin, for his part, merely anticipated the 'silent and unobserved death' of the dispute with general acceptance of his theory and expressed 'indifference' about terminology: man might be equally be classed into races, species, or sub-species though he preferred the latter.[123] Huxley (1894:209) compromised with the term 'persistent modifications'.

Broca and the degrees of hybridity

Stocking read this contemporary British sensibility to the synthesizing potential of Darwinian theory as an 'institutional dialectic', largely brokered by Huxley and culminating in the emergence of the Royal Anthropological Institute in 1871 out of the bitter Ethnological/Anthropological conflict.[124] Stocking (1973:lxx) tartly remarked on the aptness of evolutionism as an intellectual circuit-breaker in this contest because it was 'at once monogenist and racist'. Blanckaert (1988:48) saw no such synthesis occurring in France where Broca's rigidly physicalist, harshly racialist, polygenist *anthropologie* held sway. The principal human 'types', Broca argued, must have been created separately because the 'anatomical characters' that differentiated them were 'hereditary and unalterable' and such 'profound' differences were totally at odds with the hypothesis of common origin. Throughout the 1860s, he retained the opinion that species were fixed but allowed for some modification through the 'durable' intermixture of 'neighbouring, but distinct' species.[125]

In a polemical synthesis on the 'thorny' question of human hybridity, Broca (1858-9, 1859-60) launched a concerted attack on earlier work across the discursive spectrum. He denounced polygenist racial purists such as Knox, the aristocratic French social thinker Arthur de Gobineau (1816-1882), and the American physician Josiah Clark Nott (1804-1873) for their pessimistic 'opinion' that racial crossing was inevitably degenerate and that no 'crossed race' could procreate independently. And he equally condemned the conclusion of monogenists like Prichard that there were no hybrid races because all human beings were uniformly prolific.[126] Broca instead built on the hypothesis outlined by the American polygenist physician-anatomist Samuel George Morton

(1799-1851) that differential 'disparity or affinity' between species resulted in 'degrees of hybridity': thus, the interbreeding of 'remote species of the same genus' produced no hybrids; 'allied species' produced infertile offspring; and 'proximate species' produced fertile progeny. Applying Morton's model to mankind, Nott then sharply differentiated the 'prolific' crossings of proximate human species such as Saxons and Celts from the supposed sterility or limited fertility of the offspring of unions between the 'most widely separated' species, such as Europeans and Negroes, Hottentots, or Australians.[127]

Broca used an exhaustive survey of hybridity in animals to invert the conceptual core of the monogenists' 'unitary' system — the premise that continuous fecundity at once defined the limits of a species and supplied proof of common origin. By showing that certain interspecific animal crossings could produce 'perfectly and indefinitely fertile' hybrids, he claimed backing by analogy for the polygenist doctrine of plural human species.[128] The second, more problematic part of his agenda was to demonstrate that not all human couplings were equally fertile, enabling him at once to defend the 'crossed races' of France against the racial purists' accusation of hybrid degeneration; and to distance the 'highest' races in the 'human series' from proximity to the 'most inferior'. Here, too, Broca worked by animal analogy, mapping a four-stage taxonomy of 'degrees of hybridity' according to the relative fecundity of first-generation hybrids: *agénésique*, 'quite infertile'; *dysgénésique*, 'almost entirely sterile'; *paragénésique*, 'partly fertile'; *eugénésique*, 'fully fertile'.[129] Transposed to humanity, this classification condensed his deductions that there were 'very varied' degrees of *homœogénésie*, 'sexual affinity', in the human genus, resulting in 'very unequal' degrees of hybridity; and that the 'more distant' the parent species, the more 'more defective' the hybrids. Given these premises, it is hardly surprising that Broca's scale of human hybridity spanned eugenesic unions between proximate European races; paragenesic unions of Europeans and Negroes; and purportedly dysgenesic unions between the 'two extremities of the human series' — the Anglo-Saxons, 'humanity's first race', and the Australians and Tasmanians, the 'two most inferior races'.[130] In marked contrast, the monogenist Quatrefages (1868-9) devoted much of his 1869 anthropology course at the Muséum to refuting polygenism on the grounds that crossings of the most 'distant' human groups, such as Tasmanians or New Hollanders with Europeans, could produce fertile, viable mixed races.

Broca's 'theoretical antihumanism' (Blanckaert 2003b:60) was cloaked in a cynical scientistic rhetoric and logic. A political radical and opponent of slavery, he at once acknowledged a 'vast hiatus' in the 'animal ladder' between the highest apes and 'inferior' human types but bracketed this 'profession of faith' with a priori assertions that the Negro was physically 'intermediary' between the European and the ape while the Australians and Tasmanians were 'nearest the brute'. He deplored the contamination of science by religion and politics and yet hypocritically defended polygenism on the prejudicial grounds that its doctrine was not 'humiliating' to 'inferior' races, unlike the monogenist attribution of racial inequality to divine curse or degeneration from original perfection.[131] Similarly, in advocating greater precision for the notoriously ambiguous term *race* (1859-60:608, 613), he differentiated its 'particular and exact' use to describe collections of physically similar individuals of plausible common descent (such as Arabs, Celts, Australians, *Papouas*), from its 'general and deceptive' application to classify a few broad 'natural groups' comprising all individuals with certain 'common characters' and some 'morphological affinity' (such as the Caucasic or Ethiopian races). The collection of characters common to such a group constituted its *type* but human types were 'fictive', 'ideal', heuristic 'abstractions' and should not be granted a 'real existence' as 'facts'. Yet, Broca himself used race haphazardly in both senses and consistently stands accused of reifying racial types.

The study of hybridity eventually impelled Broca to jettison entirely the 'classic' doctrine of the inalterability of species. In 1858, he had proposed hybridization as the sole motor for past specific change: actual species were permanent outcomes of 'fusions' and 'modifications' resulting from past 'crossings'. Agnostic about transmutation in 1866, he formally endorsed the principle of 'the evolution of organic forms' in 1870, echoing the celebrated quip that it was better to be 'an advanced ape than a degenerated Adam'.[132] Notwithstanding this conversion, Broca did not renounce polygenism and coined the term '*polygenic transformism*' to designate the principle — rather bizarrely attributed to Buffon (1766:358) — that living beings as evolving 'natural products' had 'multiple origins' and multiple 'primordial forms'.[133]

Topinard's synthesis

If Broca's formulation was more compromise than resolution with respect to the war over human origins and the challenge of evolutionism, a French synthesis of sorts was mooted by his self-avowed disciple and institutional successor, the physician-anthropologist Paul Topinard (1830-1911) whose first significant anthropological publications were detailed surveys of craniological or ethnographic materials on Aboriginal Tasmanians (1868) and Australians (1872).[134] Though no less committed than Broca to the paradigm of a highly physical *anthropologie* rooted firmly in morphology and comparative craniometry, Topinard was polygenist more by default than conviction. He reasoned (like Wallace) that, while the great human ideal types (Mongol, Australian, European, and Negro) undoubtedly had the 'morphological value of species', the vast expansion in the time span of human existence had rendered irrelevant the old controversy over origins — the question, he complained, left him cold, though he glimpsed, 'in a prodigiously distant past, a generic trunk common to all humanity'.[135] A convinced transformist, Topinard asserted French theoretical precedence by tracing evolution's intellectual genealogy directly from Lamarck to Darwin and reconfiguring transformism as historically the 'first' opposition to classic monogenism, more 'serious' than polygenism, rather than as the subsequent dialectical synthesis it looked like to the English.[136]

As ever, the question of interracial unions was pivotal in this new series of debates on the classificatory status of human diversity. Broca's contentious hypothesis of very unequal degrees of human hybridity was sceptically received by English Darwinians and quietly ignored by Topinard. Huxley and Darwin brought their usual pragmatic mix of emphatic naturalism and racialized philanthropy to the matter. Both rejected the extremist position that 'mixed breeds of mankind' were infertile or unviable and cited in evidence the Pitcairn Islanders, thriving progeny of English sailors and Tahitian women. Darwin refuted claims that Australian and Tasmanian women could not procreate with European men with the equally global assertion that 'the half-castes are killed by the pure blacks'. He concluded that the 'races of man' were 'not sufficiently distinct to co-exist without fusion'. Huxley admitted both his predisposition to expect some infertility between the 'extreme modifications' of humanity but lack of 'any satisfactory proof' of its reality.[137] Topinard sketched a classification of species parallel to Broca's: '*hostile*' (no fertile crossings), '*intermediate*' (no sustained posterity), and '*friendly*' (indefinitely fertile). But although he identified 'different degrees' of interracial fertility, 'the closest more, the more distant relatively less', Topinard nonetheless encompassed the entire human genus, Australians included, within the third category. He proposed racial crossing as the 'mechanism' that had at once produced 'the infinite diversity of present races' and ensured the survival of traces of purportedly extinct types, such as Tasmanians, in their hybrid descendants.[138]

Arguably, Topinard's most important contribution to his science was his attempt to specify and dereify the anthropological notion of *race*. In a detailed history of the concept (1879), he showed how the terms *race* and *espèce* were plucked from common usage to serve the abstract taxonomic needs of eighteenth-century naturalists and quickly concretized as real entities. But historians, ethnologists, and linguists confused matters by using *race* in an expanded 'public' sense, conflated with the social and political idea of *peuple*, 'people', in ignorance or defiance of the anthropological verity that *races* were physically determined constituents of *peuples*.[139] Thanks to countless migrations, crossings, and fusions over innumerable generations, there were no pure *races*, only *types*: assemblages of 'common characters' identified in *peuples* by observation or measurement and subject to the vicissitudes of the struggle for existence — fusion, absorption, disappearance, atavism. It was *peuples* large or small that anthropologists actually studied and the *type*, like the *race*, was an abstraction without 'indefinite permanence'.[140] Yet in the end, Topinard's demand for a more systematic terminology petered out in limp re-endorsement of his 'master', Broca's, partition of anthropology between the science of man in general and the science of human races, or ethnology, in particular; while Topinard's clarion call to dematerialize race as an idea, not a reality, came to grief on his own and his colleagues' inability to shake their conviction that 'the determination of race' was 'anthropology par excellence'.[141]

Residual monogeny and the spectre of extinction

In certain important respects, Darwin and Wallace's (1858) revolutionary concept of 'natural means of selection', its elaboration in Darwin's theory, and its application to man at once confirmed and required a sea change in the concept of species, in ideas about man's place in nature, and in explanations for human differences. Yet however novel Darwinism looked in Britain (though not in France), rupture is an insufficient metaphor for this intellectual transformation since its logic was also historically embedded in contemporary discourses. Moreover, Darwinian speculations on the origins of human diversity — dysteleology notwithstanding — recall in part certain earlier monogenist strategies to combat polygenist assaults on their doctrine by compromising with the racialization of anthropology. Wallace and Darwin both endeavoured to reconcile the premise of a unitary human origin with the seeming reality of 'those striking and constant peculiarities which mark the great divisions of mankind' by hypothesizing that 'the races of man diverged at an extremely remote epoch from their common progenitor' and thenceforth evolved differentially during the immensely long process of speciation.[142] Wallace's proposition that human races originated through the ancient operation of natural selection on the physical structure of a 'single homogeneous' primitive race (with the power of natural selection afterwards confined to man's 'mental and moral' character) is analogous to Lacépède's projection of the organic differentiation of very divergent races to a long-distant past when the impact of climate on the single original human species was much greater. So too, Serres's concept of 'three primordial types' had served tacitly to rationalize the premise of original unity with the alleged facts of actual racial difference and inequality.[143]

Wallace's conjectural history of human racial evolution culminates in a utopian scenario in which the 'inevitable extinction' and displacement of the 'lower and more degraded races' would produce a world 'again inhabited by a single homogeneous race, no individual of which will be inferior to the noblest specimens of existing humanity'. Darwin similarly anticipated a 'not very distant' future in which 'man in a more civilised state, as we may hope, than the Caucasian' would be separated from the remaining apes by a 'break' wider than the present one 'between the negro or Australian and the gorilla'. In his textbook on anthropology, Topinard evidently agreed. These evolutionist prognoses of a bleak future for all 'lower' — non-white — races resemble more the polygenist

Hombron's prediction of the obliteration of 'inferior races and species' than they do Serres's more optimistic forecast of the restoration of human unity through racial 'fusion'.[144] Yet elsewhere, Topinard proposed a variation on Serres's theme, envisaging 'plurality of races in the past and unity in the future' as a necessary outcome of endless crossings and extinctions. Theoretical future unity, however, would be limited by the 'influence of the milieus', an 'adjuvant cause' without effect on 'ancient, fixed types' but which would come into its own as a modifying force on 'types decomposing through crossings', thereby ensuring the persistence of diversity and the continued hybrid existence of otherwise extinct types.[145]

Recent scholarship has shown how 'extinction discourse' or 'doomed race theory' with respect to newly colonized dark-skinned autochthones developed from the late Enlightenment as a corollary of readings of Spanish colonial history, recent experience in North America and Oceania, and confidence in the necessity of progress. For most of two centuries, belief in the inevitable demise of 'inferior races' in the face of civilization served as an umbrella discourse transcending ideological differences within imperialism, notably between anthropologists, philanthropists, settlers, and administrators.[146] Humanitarian credence in the scenario and the tension thus engendered between philanthropic and scientific imperatives are patent in a paper 'On the Extinction of Human Races' read by Prichard (1840:168-70) to the British Association late in 1839. Deploring 'the extermination of the native tribes' with the onset of European colonization, he called on 'Christian nations' to make a serious effort to prevent 'these calamities'; yet he took racial 'destruction' for granted as the inevitable outcome of encounters between 'simple' tribes and 'the more civilized agricultural nations' — 'this seems to have been the case from the time when the first shepherd fell by the hand of the first tiller of the soil'. Accordingly, he focused 'philosophical' concern on the need for what would later be called salvage ethnography, 'to obtain much more extensive information than we now possess of their physical and moral characters'.

In contrast to Prichard, John Lort Stokes (1812-1885), a shipmate of Darwin on HMS *Beagle* and its commander during the latter part of that vessel's Australian survey voyage of 1837-43, challenged the widely-held opinion that an 'all-powerful law', confirmed by 'history', necessitated 'the depopulation of the countries we colonize'; he took serious issue with the humanitarian rationalization of 'extinction' as a 'mysterious dispensation of Providence' that left no part for philanthropy but 'to smooth, as it were, the pillow of an expiring people'; and he called for acknowledgement of 'moral responsibility on the part of the whites'. Yet, even though he had celebrated the 'sharp', 'intelligent', 'fine-looking' appearance of the half-caste offspring of Tasmanian women with foreign men that he had met in the Bass Strait Islands, Stokes too pronounced a specific elegy for the handful of Tasmanians still surviving on Flinders Island:

'Their destiny is accomplished'; 'all we can do is to soothe their declining years, to provide that they shall advance gently, surrounded by all the comforts of civilization, and by all the consolations of religion, to their inevitable doom; and to draw a great lesson from their melancholy history'.[147]

Conclusion

Semantically, this chapter has traced the crystallization by naturalists and anthropologists of an old genealogical term and an ancient mindset of widely shared European distaste for certain visible human characters into the scientific concept of a race. Initially a concrete denominator for essentialized human groups, it was ultimately systematized as an abstract noun condensing a total theoretical system, as in Knox's aphorism, 'Race is everything', and Blanchard's assertion that 'the instinct of race is innate in man's heart'.[148]

Discursively, the chapter has investigated a major transition hinged roughly on the passage from the eighteenth to the nineteenth century: the broad shift from the Enlightenment differentiation of universal stages of linear social development in the natural history of man to the hierarchical classification of discrete biological races by the science of race; and the parallel displacement of optimistic scenarios of general human progress by pessimism about the aptness of non-Europeans for civilization or even in some cases for survival. Though the case for discursive hiatus is compelling, it should obscure neither the significant continuities in European attitudes to non-white people over at least five hundred years nor the tenacity with which certain cardinal concepts and dispositions — among which race has been pre-eminent for the past two centuries — can and do metamorphose and recur across ideological spectrums. Moreover, by modern antiracist standards of verbal propriety, my metaphors of movement and transformation may seem irrelevant, with Enlightenment and nineteenth-century writers deemed equally guilty of racism: Buffon, Blumenbach, and Kant have each been portrayed as precursors of Anthropology's ambivalent complicity in the normalization of scientific racism.[149] Yet the blanket charge of racism is too blunt and anachronistic an instrument for most historians who want to discriminate precisely between discourses, ideologies, vocabularies, and authors and to understand them in contemporary terms. Such a perspective, for example, sharply differentiates Blumenbach's relativism, professed lack of anti-Negro prejudice, and insistence on the 'perfectibility' of 'our black brethren' from the diverse racial fundamentalisms of Cuvier, Lawrence, Knox, Hunt, Broca, or most of the polygenists.[150]

Intellectually, the chapter has tracked the tortuous trajectories by which climate and crania, environment and heredity, reproduction and morphology were opposed or interwoven as divergent relative emphases in hostile schools of anthropological explanation and were eventually fused in evolutionary theory.

The environmentalist monogenism of Buffon, Kant, and Prichard heavily emphasized reproductive criteria. Like them, Blumenbach also attributed human diversity to external stimuli but he only belatedly acknowledged reproduction as a key index of racial variation, in addition to cranial structure. Before 1850, most polygenists denied environmental influences on race formation in favour of a static morphological approach while Broca brought reproduction and morphology together in his work on hybridity and craniology. So too did his transformist disciple Topinard (1879:655) who admitted the 'action of the milieus' on races made unstable by the twin impact of the struggle for existence and crossbreeding. Darwinian synthesis conceived species, races, or 'persistent modifications' as labile products of very long-run adaptations to milieus, transmitted by generation, but remained heavily reliant on morphology and anthropometry. Thus Darwin (1871:231) remarked that the 'form' of every organic being 'depends on an infinitude of complex relations': the 'variations' which have 'arisen' and 'been preserved' in response to 'surrounding physical conditions', to rival 'surrounding organisms', and to 'inheritance from innumerable progenitors' whose forms had resulted from 'equally complex relations'. Huxley (1894:219), the comparative anatomist, insisted on the application of 'purely zoological methods' to man. All these strands ultimately came together in the new science of 'ecology' as conceived by the German evolutionary biologist Ernst Haeckel (1834-1919): the 'whole science of the relationships of the organism to the surrounding external world'.[151]

Feeding back and forth, to and from common usages, the biological idea of race underwrote the explosion of race pride in nineteenth-century Europe and the United States together with its negative corollary, the steady hardening of prejudice against racial difference. Such pride and prejudices — shared, theorized, and justified by scientists of race — had, by the end of the nineteenth century, become a key component of the ideological underpinning of Euro-American imperialism and the colonial domination it was extending over significant portions of the world.

References

Appel, Toby A. 1987. *The Cuvier-Geoffroy Debate: French Biology in the Decades Before Darwin*. Oxford: Oxford University Press.

Atkins, John. 1734. Appendix: Physical Observations on the Coast of Guiney. In *The Navy-Surgeon: or, a Practical System of Surgery*. London: Cæsar Ward and Richard Chandler.

_____. 1735. *A Voyage to Guinea, Brasil, and the West-Indies; in his Majesty's Ships, the* Swallow *and* Weymouth ... London: Cæsar Ward and Richard Chandler.

Balbi, Adrien. 1826a. *Atlas ethnographique du globe, ou classification des peuples anciens et modernes d'après leurs langues, précédé d'un discours sur l'utilité et l'importance de l'étude des langues appliquée à plusieurs branches des connaissances humaines* ... Paris: Rey et Gravier.

————. 1826b. *Introduction à l'Atlas ethnographique du globe, contenant un discours sur l'utilité et l'importance de l'étude des langues appliquée à plusieurs branches des connaissances humaines* ... Paris: Rey et Gravier.

Banks, Joseph. [1770-1820]. Foreign Correspondence. Manuscript. Add. MS 8094-8100. London: British Library.

Bernasconi, Robert. 2001a. Introduction. In *Concepts of Race in the Eighteenth Century*, ed. Robert Bernasconi, vol. 1, *Bernier, Linnaeus and Maupertuis*, vii-xiii. Bristol, UK: Thoemmes.

————. 2001b. Who Invented the Concept of Race? Kant's Role in the Enlightenment Construction of Race. In *Race*, ed. Robert Bernasconi, 11-36. Malden, MA, and Oxford: Blackwell.

————. 2006. Kant and Blumenbach's Polyps: a Neglected Chapter in the History of the Concept of Race. In *The German Invention of Race*, ed. Sara Eigen and Mark Larrimore, 73-90. Albany: State University of New York Press.

[Bernier, François]. 1684. Nouvelle division de la Terre, par les differentes Especes ou Races d'hommes qui l'habitent, envoyée par un fameux Voyageur à Monsieur * * * * * à peu près en ces termes. *Journal des Sçavans* 12:148-55.

Blanchard, Emile. 1854. *Voyage au pôle sud et dans l'Océanie sur les corvettes l'Astrolabe et la Zélée; exécuté ... pendant les années 1837-1838-1839-1840 sous le commandement de M. J. Dumont-d'Urville ... publié ... sous la direction supérieure de M. Jacquinot .... Anthropologie*. Paris: Gide et J. Baudry.

Blanckaert, Claude. 1988. On the Origins of French Ethnology: William Edwards and the Doctrine of Race. In *Bones, Bodies, Behavior: Essays on Biological Anthropology*, ed. George W. Stocking, Jr., 18-55. Madison: University of Wisconsin Press.

————. 1998. La naturalisation de l'homme de Linné à Darwin: archéologie du débat nature/culture. In *La culture est-elle naturelle? Histoire, épistémologie et applications récentes du concept de culture*, ed. Albert Ducros, Jacqueline Ducros, and Frédéric Joulian, 15-24. Paris: Editions Errance.

————. 2003a. Les conditions d'émergence de la science des races au début du XIXe siècle. In *L'idée de 'race' dans les sciences humaines et la littérature (XVIIIe et XIXe siècles)*, ed. Sarga Moussa, 133-49. Paris: l'Harmattan.

_____. 2003b. Of Monstrous Métis? Hybridity, Fear of Miscegenation, and Patriotism from Buffon to Paul Broca. In *The Color of Liberty: Histories of Race in France*, ed. Sue Peabody and Tyler Stovall, 42-70. Durham, NC: Duke University Press.

_____. 2006. 'Notre immortel naturaliste': Buffon, la science de l'homme et l'écriture de l'histoire. In *Buffon: de l'Homme*, ed. Michèle Duchet, 407-67. Paris: L'Harmattan.

Blumenbach, Johann Friedrich. 1775. *De Generis Humani Varietate Nativa*. Goettingae: Frid. Andr. Rosenbuschii.

_____. 1781. *De Generis Humani Varietate Nativa*. 2nd edition. Goettingae: Abr. Vandenhoek.

_____. 1789 [1781]. *Uber den Bildungstrieb*. 2nd edition. Góttingen: Johann Christian Dieterich.

_____. 1790. *Beyträge zur Naturgeschichte*, vol. 1. Göttingen: Johann Christian Dieterich.

_____. 1795. *De Generis Humani Varietate Nativa*. 3rd edition. Gottingae: Vandenhoek et Ruprecht.

_____. 1798 [1795]. *Über die natürlichen Verschiedenheiten im Menschengeschlechte*, tr. Johann Gottfried Gruber. Leipzig: Breitkopf und Härtel.

_____. 1803 [1799]. *Manuel d'histoire naturelle*, tr. François Artaud de Soulange, 2 vols. 6th edition. Metz and Paris: Collington and Levrault frères, Henriche, Lenormant.

_____. 1806. *Beyträge zur Naturgeschichte*, vol. 1. 2nd edition. Göttingen: Heinrich Dieterich.

_____. 1865 [1795]. On the Natural Variety of Mankind [3rd edition]. In *The Anthropological Treatises of Johann Friedrich Blumenbach*, tr. and ed. Thomas Bendyshe, 145-276. London: Longman, Green, Longman, Roberts, and Green for the Anthropological Society.

Bory de Saint-Vincent, Jean-Baptiste-Geneviève-Marcellin. 1822. Bimanes. In Jean-Baptiste-Geneviève-Marcellin Bory de Saint-Vincent, et al., *Dictionnaire classique d'histoire naturelle*, vol. 2, 319-20. Paris: Rey et Gravier; Baudouin frères.

_____. 1827a [1825]. *L'homme (homo): essai zoologique sur le genre humain*, 2 vols. 2nd edition. Paris: Rey et Gravier.

_____. 1827b. Orang. In Jean-Baptiste-Geneviève-Marcellin Bory de Saint-Vincent, et al., *Dictionnaire classique d'histoire naturelle*, vol. 12, 261-85. Paris: Rey et Gravier; Baudouin frères.

Boulle, Pierre H. 2003. François Bernier and the Origins of the Modern Concept of Race. In *The Color of Liberty: Histories of Race in France*, ed. Sue Peabody and Tyler Stovall, 11-27. Durham, NC: Duke University Press.

Bowler, Peter J. 1984. *Evolution: the History of an Idea*. Berkeley: University of California Press.

Brantlinger, Patrick. 2003. *Dark Vanishings: Discourse on the Extinction of Primitive Races, 1800-1930*. Ithaca, NY, and London: Cornell University Press.

Broberg, Gunnar. 1983. *Homo sapiens*: Linnaeus's Classification of Man. In *Linnaeus: the Man and his Work*, ed. Tore Frängsmyr, 156-94. Berkeley: University of California Press.

Broca, Paul. 1858-9. Mémoire sur l'hybridité en général, sur la distinction des espèces animales et sur les métis obtenus par le croisement du lièvre et du lapin. *Journal de la physiologie de l'homme et des animaux* 1:433-71, 684-729; 2:218-58, 345-96.

————. 1859-60. Des phénomènes d'hybridité dans le genre humain. *Journal de la physiologie de l'homme et des animaux* 2:601-25; 3:392-439.

————. 1860-3. Mémoire sur le craniographe et sur quelques-unes de ses applications communiqué à la Société d'Anthropologie dans les séances du 19 décembre 1861 et du 6 novembre 1862. *Mémoires de la Société d'Anthropologie de Paris* 1:349-78.

————. 1866. Discours sur l'homme et les animaux. *Bulletins de la Société d'Anthropologie de Paris*, 2ᵉ série 1:53-79.

————. 1870. Sur le transformisme. *Bulletins de la Société d'Anthropologie de Paris* 2ᵉ série, 5:168-239.

[Brosses, Charles de]. 1756. *Histoire des navigations aux terres australes contenant ce que l'on sçait des mœurs & des productions des contrées découvertes jusqu'à ce jour ...*, 2 vols. Paris: Durand.

Buffon, Georges-Louis Leclerc, comte de. 1749. Histoire naturelle de l'homme. In *Histoire naturelle, générale et particulière*, vol. 2, 427-603; vol. 3, 305-530. Paris: Imprimerie royale.

————. 1749-89. *Histoire naturelle, générale et particulière*, 36 vols. Paris: Imprimerie royale.

————. 1753. L'asne. In *Histoire naturelle, générale et particulière*, vol. 4 , 377-403. Paris: Imprimerie royale.

————. 1766. De la dégénération des animaux. In *Histoire naturelle, générale et particulière*, vol. 14, 311-74. Paris: Imprimerie royale.

_____. 1777. *Histoire naturelle, générale et particulière: supplément*, vol. 4, *Servant de suite à l'histoire naturelle de l'homme*. Paris: Imprimerie royale.

_____. 1778. Des époques de la nature. In *Histoire naturelle, générale et particulière: supplément*, vol. 5, 1-254. Paris: Imprimerie royale.

Bynum, William F. 1975. The Great Chain of Being after Forty Years: an Appraisal. *History of Science* 13:1-28.

Camper, Petrus. 1794 [1791]. *The Works of the Late Professor Camper on the Connexion Between the Science of Anatomy and the Arts of Drawing, Painting, Statuary, &c &c....*, tr. Thomas Cogan. London: C. Dilly.

Cunningham, Peter. 1828 [1827]. *Two Years in New South Wales: a Series of Letters, Comprising Sketches of the Actual State of Society in that Colony; of its Peculiar Advantages to Emigrants; of its Topography, Natural History, &c. &c.*, 2 vols. 3rd edition. London: Henry Colburn.

Cuvier, Georges. 1800-5. *Leçons d'anatomie comparée*, ed. C. Duméril and G.-L. Duvernoy. 5 vols. Paris: Baudouin; Genets jeune.

_____. 1812. Discours préliminaire. In *Recherches sur les ossemens fossiles de quadrupèdes, ou l'on rétablit les caractères de plusieurs espèces d'animaux que les révolutions du globe paroissent avoir détruites*, vol. 1, 1-116. Paris: Déterville.

_____. 1817a. *Le règne animal distribué d'après son organisation, pour servir de base à l'histoire naturelle des animaux et d'introduction à l'anatomie comparée*, 4 vols. Paris: Déterville.

_____. 1817b. Extrait d'observations faites sur le cadavre d'une femme connue à Paris et à Londres sous le nom de Vénus Hottentotte. *Mémoires du Muséum d'Histoire naturelle* 3:259-74.

_____. 1858. *Lettres de Georges Cuvier à C.M. Pfaff, sur l'histoire naturelle, la politique et la littérature, 1788-1792*, tr. [from German] Louis Marchant. Paris: V. Masson.

_____. 1978 [1857]. Note instructive sur les recherches à faire relativement aux différences anatomiques des diverses races d'hommes. In *Aux origines de l'anthropologie française: les mèmoires de la Société des Observateurs de l'Homme en l'an VIII*, ed. Jean Copans and Jean Jamin, 171-6. Paris: Le Sycomore.

Cuvier, Georges, et al. 1807. Rapport sur un ouvrage manuscrit de M. André, ci-devant connu sous le nom de P. Chrysologue de Gy, lequel ouvrage est intitulé *Théorie de la surface actuelle de la terre*, par MM. Hauy, Lelièvre, et Cuvier, rapporteur. *Mémoires de la Classe des Sciences mathématiques et physiques de l'Institut national de France*, premier semestre:128-45.

Darwin, Charles. 1839. *Narrative of the Surveying Voyages of His Majesty's Ships Adventure and Beagle, between the Years 1826 and 1836, Describing their Examination of the Southern Shores of South America, and the Beagle's Circumnavigation of the Globe*, vol. 3, *Journal and Remarks, 1832-1836*. London: Henry Colburn.

————. 1859. *On the Origin of Species by Means of Natural Selection: or the Preservation of Favoured Races in the Struggle for Life*. London: John Murray.

————. 1871. *The Descent of Man, and Selection in Relation to Sex*, 2 vols. London: John Murray.

————. 1882 [1871]. *The Descent of Man, and Selection in Relation to Sex*. 2nd edition. London: John Murray.

————. 1958. *The Autobiography of Charles Darwin 1809-1882 with Original Omissions Restored*, ed. Nora Barlow. London: Collins.

Darwin, Charles, and Alfred Russel Wallace. 1858. On the Tendency of Species to Form Varieties; and on the Perpetuation of Varieties and Species by Natural Means of Selection. *Journal of the Proceedings of the Linnean Society of London. Zoology* 3:45-62.

Desmoulins, Antoine. 1826. *Histoire naturelle des races humaines du nord-est de l'Europe, de l'Asie boréale et orientale et de l'Afrique australe, d'après des recherches spéciales d'antiquités, de physiologie, d'anatomie et de zoologie, appliquée à la recherche des origines des anciens peuples, à la science étymologique, à la critique de l'histoire, etc.,...* Paris: Méquignon-Marvis.

Dictionnaire de l'Académie françoise, revu, corrigé et augmenté par l'Académie elle-même. 1798. 2 vols. 5th edition. Paris: J.J. Smits.

Dictionnaire de l'Académie française. 1835. 2 vols. 6th edition. Paris: Firmin Didot frères.

————. 1878. 2 vols. 7th edition. Paris: Firmin-Didot.

————. 1932-5. 2 vols. 8th edition. Paris: Hachette. Online <http://www.lib.uchicago.edu/efts/ARTFL/projects/dicos/ACADEMIE/HUITIEME>.

Douglas, Bronwen. 2005. Notes on 'Race' and the Biologisation of Human Difference. *Journal of Pacific History* 40:331-8.

Dover, Cedric. 1951. Race. *Man* 51 (April 1951):55-6.

Dumont d'Urville, Jules-Sébastien-César. 1832. Sur les îles du grand océan. *Bulletin de la Société de Géographie* 17:1-21.

Duvernay-Bolens, Jacqueline. 1995. L'homme zoologique: races et racisme chez les naturalistes de la première moitié du XIXᵉ siècle. *L'Homme* 35 (133):9-32.

Eddy, J.H., Jr. 1984. Buffon, Organic Alterations, and Man. In *Studies in History of Biology*, vol. 7, ed. William Coleman and Camille Limoges, 1-45. Baltimore: Johns Hopkins University Press.

Edwards, William-Frédéric. 1841 [1829]. *Des caractères physiologiques des races humaines considérés dans leurs rapports avec l'histoire: lettre à M. Amédée Thierry, auteur de l'*Histoire des Gaulois. Paris: Dondey-Dupré.

Ellingson, Ter. 2001. *The Myth of the Noble Savage*. Berkeley: University of California Press.

Estienne, Robert. 1539. *Dictionaire Francoislatin, contenant les motz & manieres de parler Francois, tournez en Latin*. Paris: Imprimerie de Robert Estienne.

Eze, Emmanuel Chukwudi. 1995. The Color of Reason: the Idea of 'Race' in Kant's Anthropology. In *Anthropology and the German Enlightenment: Perspectives on Humanity,* ed. Katherine M. Faull, 200–41. Lewisburg, PA: Bucknell University Press.

Farber, Paul L. 1972. Buffon and the Concept of Species. *Journal of the History of Ideas* 5:259-84.

Fausto-Sterling, Anne. 1995. Gender, Race, and Nation: the Comparative Anatomy of 'Hottentot' Women in Europe, 1815-1817. In *Deviant Bodies: Critical Perspectives on Difference in Science and Popular Culture*, ed. Jennifer Terry and Jacqueline Urla, 19-48. Bloomington and Indianapolis: Indiana University Press.

Fenves, Peter. 2006. What 'Progresses' has Race-Theory Made Since the Times of Leibniz and Wolff? In *The German Invention of Race*, ed. Sara Eigen and Mark Larrimore, 11-22. Albany: State University of New York Press.

Féraud, Jean-François. 1787-8. *Dictionnaire critique, de la langue française*, 3 vols. Marseille: Jean Mossy.

Figlio, Karl M. 1976. The Metaphor of Organization: an Historiographical Perspective on the Bio-medical Sciences of the Early Nineteenth Century. *History of Science* 14:17-53.

Flourens, Pierre. 1850 [1844]. *Histoire des travaux et des idées de Buffon*. 2nd edition. Paris: L. Hachette.

Forster, Georg [George]. 1777. *A Voyage Round the World in His Britannic Majesty's Sloop, Resolution …*, 2 vols. London: B. White, J. Robson, P. Elmsly, and G. Robinson.

Forster, Georg. 1786. Noch etwas über die Menschenrassen. *Teutsche Merkur* October 1786:57-86; November 1786:150-66.

Forster, Johann Reinhold [John Reinold]. 1778. *Observations made during a Voyage Round the World, on Physical Geography, Natural History, and Ethic Philosophy.* London: G. Robinson.

Gailey, Christine Ward. 1996. Politics, Colonialism, and the Mutable Color of Pacific Islanders. In *Race and Other Misadventures: Essays in Honor of Ashley Montagu in his Ninetieth Year,* ed. Larry T. Reynolds and Leonard Lieberman, 36-49. Dix Hills, NY: General Hall, Inc.

Garnot, Prosper. 1836. Homme, *Homo.* In *Dictionnaire pittoresque d'histoire naturelle ...,* ed. Félix Edouard Guérin-Méneville, vol. 4, 6-16. Paris: Bureau de souscription.

Geoffroy Saint-Hilaire, Etienne. 1833. Quatrième mémoire, lu à l'Académie royale des sciences, le 28 mai 1831, sur le degré d'influence du monde ambiant pour modifier les formes animales; question intéressant l'origine des espèces téléosauriennes et successivement celle des animaux de l'époque actuelle. *Mémoires de l'Académie royale des sciences de l'Institut de France* 12:63-92.

Geoffroy Saint-Hilaire, Isidore. 1828. Quadrumane. In Jean-Baptiste-Geneviève-Marcellin Bory de Saint-Vincent, et al., *Dictionnaire classique d'histoire naturelle,* vol. 14, 402. Paris: Rey et Gravier; Baudouin frères.

————. 1829. Singes. In Jean-Baptiste-Geneviève-Marcellin Bory de Saint-Vincent, et al., *Dictionnaire classique d'histoire naturelle,* vol. 15, 441-9. Paris: Rey et Gravier; Baudouin frères.

————. 1860-3. Sur la classification anthropologique et particulièrement sur les types principaux du genre humain. *Mémoires de la Société d'Anthropologie de Paris* 1:125-44.

Glass, Bentley. 1960. Eighteenth-Century Concepts of the Origin of Species. *Proceedings of the American Philosophical Society* 104:227-34.

Gliddon, George Robins. 1857. The Monogenists and the Polygenists: Being an Exposition of the Doctrines of Schools Professing to Sustain Dogmatically the Unity or the Diversity of Human Races; with an Inquiry into the Antiquity of Mankind upon Earth, Viewed Chronologically, Historically, and Palæontologically. In *Indigenous Races of the Earth; or, New Chapters of Ethnological Inquiry ...,* ed. Josiah Clark Nott and George Robins Gliddon, 402-602. Philadelphia and London: J.B. Lippincott and Trübner.

Gobineau, Arthur de. 1884 [1853-5]. *Essai sur l'inégalité des races humaines,* 2 vols. 2nd edition. Paris: Firmin-Didot.

Goldsmith, Oliver. 1774. *An History of the Earth, and Animated Nature*, 8 vols. London: J. Nourse.

Gould, Stephen Jay. 1994. The Geometer of Race. *Discover* 15 (11):64-9.

Grayson, Donald K. 1983. *The Establishment of Human Antiquity*. New York: Academic Press

Greene, John C. 1954. Some Early Speculations on the Origin of Human Races. *American Anthropologist*, n.s. 56:31-41.

Gruber, Johann Gottfried. 1798. Vorerinnerung. In Johann Friedrich Blumenbach, *Über die natürlichen Verschiedenheiten im Menschengeschlechte*, tr. Johann Gottfried Gruber, 227-88. Leipzig: Breitkopf und Härtel.

Haeckel, Ernst. 1866. *Generelle Morphologie der Organismen: allgemeine Grundzüge der organischen Formen-Wissenschaft, mechanisch begründet durch die von Charles Darwin reformirte Descendenz-Theorie*, 2 vols. Berlin: G. Reimer.

Hall, Catherine. 1991. Missionary Stories: Gender and Ethnicity in England in the 1830s and 1840s. In *Cultural Studies*, ed. Lawrence Grossberg, Cary Nelson, and Paula A. Treichler, 240-76. New York and London: Routledge.

_____. 2002. *Civilising Subjects: Colony and Metropole in the English Imagination, 1830-1867*. Chicago and London: University of Chicago Press.

Haller, John S. 1970. The Species Problem: Nineteenth-Century Concepts of Racial Inferiority in the Origin of Man Controversy. *American Anthropologist*, n.s. 72:1319-29.

Hombron, Jacques-Bernard. 1846. *De l'homme dans ses rapports avec la création*, vol. 1, Jacques-Bernard Hombron and Honoré Jacquinot, *Voyage au Pôle Sud et dans l'Océanie sur les corvettes l'Astrolabe et la Zélée ... pendant les années 1837-1838-1839-1840, sous le commandement de M. J. Dumont-d'Urville ... publié ... sous la direction supérieure de M. Jacquinot ... Zoologie*. Paris: Gide.

Hombron, Jacques-Bernard, and Honoré Jacquinot. 1846-54. *Voyage au pôle sud et dans l'Océanie sur les corvettes l'Astrolabe et la Zélée ... pendant les années 1837-1838-1839-1840, sous le commandement de M. J. Dumont-d'Urville ... publié ... sous la direction supérieure de M. Jacquinot ... Zoologie*, 5 vols. Paris: Gide.

Hörstadius, Sven. 1974. Linnaeus, Animals and Man. *Biological Journal of the Linnean Society* 6:269-75.

Hudson, Nicholas. 1996. From 'Nation' to 'Race': the Origin of Racial Classification in Eighteenth-Century Thought. *Eighteenth-Century Studies* 29:247-64.

Hume, David. 1987 [1777]. *Essays Moral, Political, and Literary*, ed. Eugene F. Miller. Indianapolis, IN: Liberty Classics. Accessed 13 June 2007, online <http://olldownload.libertyfund.org/EBooks/Hume_0059.pdf>.

Hunt, James. 1863a. Introductory Address on the Study of Anthropology, Delivered Before the Anthropological Society of London, February 24th, 1863. *Anthropological Review* 1:1-20.

_____. 1863b. On the Physical and Mental Characters of the Negro. *Anthropological Review* 1:386-91.

_____. 1864a. *On the Negro's Place in Nature*. London: Trubner, for the Anthropological Society of London.

_____. 1864b. On the Negro's Place in Nature. *Anthropological Review* 2:xv-lvi.

_____. 1866. On the Application of the Principle of Natural Selection to Anthropology, in Reply to Views Advocated by Some of Mr. Darwin's Disciples. *Anthropological Review* 4:320-40.

_____. 1867. The President's Address. *Anthropological Review* 5:xliv-lxx.

_____. 1868. On the Origin of the Anthropological Review and its Connection with the Anthropological Society. *Anthropological Review* 6:431-42.

Huxley, Thomas Henry. 1893 [1865]. Emancipation — Black and White. In *Collected Essays*, vol. 3, *Science and Education*, 66-75. London: Macmillan.

_____. 1894 [1865]. On the Methods and Results of Ethnology. In *Collected Essays*, vol. 7, *Man's Place in Nature and Other Anthropological Essays*, 209-52. London: Macmillan.

Jacquinot, Honoré. 1846. *Considérations générales sur l'anthropologie suivies d'observations sur les races humaines de l'Amérique méridionale et de l'Océanie*, vol. 2, Jacques-Bernard Hombron and Honoré Jacquinot, *Voyage au Pôle Sud et dans l'Océanie sur les corvettes l'Astrolabe et la Zélée … pendant les années 1837-1838-1839-1840, sous le commandement de M. J. Dumont-d'Urville … publié … sous la direction supérieure de M. Jacquinot … Zoologie*. Paris: Gide.

Jauffret, Louis-François. 1978 [1909]. Introduction aux mémoires de la Société des Observateurs de l'Homme. In *Aux origines de l'anthropologie française: les mèmoires de la Société des observateurs de l'homme en l'an VIII*, ed. Jean Copans and Jean Jamin, 71-85. Paris: Le Sycomore.

Johnson, Samuel. 1756. *A Dictionary of the English Language in which the Words are Deduced from their Originals, Explained in their Different Meanings, and Authorized by the Names of the Writers in whose Works they are*

Found, 2 vols. London: J. Knapton, C. Hitch, and L. Hawes, A. Millar, R. and J. Dodsley, and M. and T. Longman.

_____. 1799. *A Dictionary of the English Language in which the Words are Deduced from their Originals, Explained in their Different Meanings, and Authorized by the Names of the Writers in whose Works they are Found*, 2 vols. 11th edition. London: J. Johnson, et al.

Jones, Greta. 2002. Alfred Russel Wallace, Robert Owen and the Theory of Natural Selection. *British Journal for the History of Science* 35:73-96.

[Kames, Henry Home, Lord]. 1774. *Sketches of the History of Man*, 2 vols. Edinburgh and London: W. Creech and W. Strahan and T. Cadell.

Kant, Immanuel. 1777. Von den verschiedenen Racen der Menschen. In *Der Philosoph für die Welt*, ed. Johann Jacob Engel, vol. 2, 125-64. Leipzig: Dyk.

_____. 1785. Bestimmung des Begriffs einer Menschenrace. *Berlinische Monatsschrift* 6:390-417.

_____. 1788. Ueber den Gebrauch teleologischer Principien in der Philosophie. *Teutsche Merkur* January 1788:36-52; February 1788:107-36.

_____. 2001 [1775]. *Von den verschiedenen Racen der Menschen zur Ankundigung der Vorlesungen der physische Geographie im Sommerhalbenjahre 1775*. Königsberg: G.E. Hartung. In *Concepts of Race in the Eighteenth Century*, ed. Robert Bernasconi, vol. 3, *Kant and Forster*. Bristol, UK: Thoemmes.

Kidd, Colin. 2006. *The Forging of Races: Race and Scripture in the Protestant Atlantic World, 1600-2000*. Cambridge: Cambridge University Press.

Knox, Robert. 1850. *The Races of Men: a Fragment*. Philadelphia: Lea and Blanchard.

_____. 1855a. Some Remarks on the Aztecque and Bosjieman Children, now Being Exhibited in London, and on the Races to which they are Presumed to Belong. *Lancet* 65:357-60.

_____. 1855b. Introduction to Inquiries into the Philosophy of Zoology. *Lancet* 65:625-7.

_____. 1855c. Contributions to the Philosophy of Zoology, with Special Reference to the Natural History of Man. *Lancet* 66:24-6, 45-6, 68-71, 162-4, 186-8, 216-18.

_____. 1862 [1850]. *The Races of Men: a Philosophical Enquiry into the Influence of Race over the Destinies of Nations*. 2nd edition. London: Henry Renshaw.

Lacépède, Étienne de. 1800. *Discours d'ouverture du cours de zoologie de l'an IX: sur l'histoire des races ou principales variétés de l'espèce humaine.* [Paris]: Plassan.

————. 1821. Homme. In Frédéric Cuvier, et al., *Dictionnaire des sciences naturelles ... Par plusieurs professeurs du Jardin du Roi, et des principales écoles de Paris,* vol. 21, 323-409. Strasbourg and Paris: F. G. Levrault and Le Normant.

Lagier, Raphaël. 2004. *Les races humaines selon Kant.* Paris: Presses Universitaires de France.

Lamarck, Jean-Baptiste de Monet de. 1907 [1800-6]. *Discours d'ouverture [des cours de zoologie donnés dans le Muséum d'histoire naturelle] (an VIII, an X, an XI et 1806).* Lille, France: L. Danel.

[La Peyrère, Isaac de]. 1655. *Praeadamitae: sive exercitatio super versibus duodecimo, decimotertio et decimoquarto capitis quinti Epistolae D. Pauli ad Romanos, quibus inducuntur primi homines ante Adamum conditi.* [Amsterdam]: no publisher.

Larson, James L. 1968. The Species Concept of Linnaeus. *Isis* 59:291-9.

Lawrence, William. 1819. *Lectures on Physiology, Zoology, and the Natural History of Man, Delivered at the Royal College of Surgeons.* London: J. Callow.

Le dictionnaire de l'Académie françoise, dedié au roy. 1694. 2 vols. Paris: Veuve de Jean Baptiste Coignard et Jean Baptiste Coignard.

Leibniz, Gottfried Wilhelm von. 1718a. Lettre de Mr. Leibniz à Mr. Sparvenfeld [1697]. In *Otium Hanoveranum, sive, Miscellanea ...,* ed. Joachim Friedrich Feller, 32-9. Lipsiae: Johann Christiani Martini.

————. 1718b. [*Nova terra divisio* per diversas hominum species]. In *Otium Hanoveranum, sive, Miscellanea ... ,* ed. Joachim Friedrich Feller, 158-60. Lipsiae: Johann Christiani Martini.

Lenoir, Timothy. 1980. Kant, Blumenbach, and Vital Materialism in German Biology. *Isis* 71:77-108.

Lesson, René-Primevère. 1839. *Voyage autour du monde entrepris par ordre du gouvernement sur la corvette la Coquille,* 2 vols. Paris: R. Pourrat frères.

Lewis, Charlton T., and Charles Short. 1879. *A Latin Dictionary.* Oxford: Clarendon Press. Online <http://www.perseus.tufts.edu/cgi-bin/resolveform?lang=Latin>.

Liebersohn, Harry. 2006. *The Travelers' World: Europe to the Pacific.* Cambridge, MA: Harvard University Press.

Linnaeus, Carolus [Carl von Linné]. 1758. *Systema Naturæ,* vol. 1, *Regnum Animale.* 10th edition. Holmiæ: Laurentii Salvii.

[Long, Edward]. 1774. *The History of Jamaica: or, General Survey of the Antient and Modern State of that Island ...*, 3 vols. London: T. Lowndes.

MacGillivray, John. 1852. *Narrative of the Voyage of H.M.S. Rattlesnake, Commanded by the Late Captain Owen Stanley, R.N., F.R.S. &c., during the Years 1846-1850. Including Discoveries and Surveys in New Guinea, the Louisiade Archipelago, etc....*, 2 vols. London: T. and W. Boone.

McGregor, Russell. 1997. *Imagined Destinies: Aboriginal Australians and the Doomed Race Theory, 1880-1939*. Carlton, VIC.: Melbourne University Press.

McKinney, H. Lewis. 1969. Wallace's Earliest Observations on Evolution: 28 December 1845. *Isis* 60:370-3.

Malte-Brun, Conrad. 1803. Géographie genérale, mathématique et physique. In Edme Mentelle and Conrad Malte Brun, *Géographie mathématique, physique et politique de toutes les parties du monde ...*, vol. 1, 151-552. Paris: Henry Tardieu et Laporte.

Maupertuis, Pierre-Louis Moreau de. 1845. *Vénus physique.* [No place: no publisher].

Meijer, Miriam Claude. 1999. *Race and Aesthetics in the Anthropology of Petrus Camper (1722-1789)*. Amsterdam-Atlanta, GA: Editions Rodopi.

Meiners, Christoph. 1785. *Grundriss der Geschichte der Menschheit*. Lemgo: Meyer.

Mentelle, Edme, and Conrad Malte Brun. 1804. *Géographie mathématique, physique et politique de toutes les parties du monde: rédigée d'après ce qui a été publié d'exact et de nouveau par les géographes, les naturalistes, les voyageurs et les auteurs de statistique des nations les plus éclairées*, vol. 12. Paris: Henry Tardieu et Laporte.

Morton, Samuel George. 1850-1. Some Remarks on the Value of the Word *Species* in Zoology. *Proceedings of the Academy of Natural Sciences of Philadelphia* 5:81-2.

Nicot, Jean. 1606. *Thresor de la langue francoyse, tant ancienne que moderne ...* Paris: David Douceur.

Nott, Josiah Clark. 1855 [1854]. Hybridity of Animals, Viewed in Connection with the Natural History of Mankind. In Josiah Clark Nott and George Robins Gliddon, *Types of Mankind: or, Ethnological Researches, Based upon the Ancient Monuments, Paintings, Sculptures, and Crania of Races, and upon their Natural, Geographical, Philological, and Biblical History ...*, 372-410. 7th edition. Philadelphia and London; Lippincott, Grambo and Trübner.

Oxford English Dictionary. 2008. Draft 3rd edition. Oxford: Oxford University Press. Online <http://dictionary.oed.com>.

Prichard, James Cowles. 1813. *Researches into the Physical History of Man*. London: John and Arthur Arch.

_____. 1826. *Researches into the Physical History of Mankind*, 2 vols. 2nd edition. London: John and Arthur Arch.

_____. 1836-47. *Researches into the Physical History of Mankind*, 5 vols. 3rd edition. London: Sherwood, Gilbert, and Piper.

_____. 1840. On the Extinction of Human Races. *Edinburgh New Philosophical Journal* 28:166-70.

_____. 1843. *The Natural History of Man: Comprising Inquiries into the Modifying Influence of Physical and Moral Agencies on the Different Tribes of the Human Family*. London: H. Baillière.

_____. 1848. On the Relations of Ethnology to Other Branches of Knowledge. *Journal of the Ethnological Society of London* 1:301-29.

_____. 1850. Anniversary Address for 1848, to the Ethnological Society of London on the Recent Progress of Ethnology. *Journal of the Ethnological Society of London* 2:119-49.

_____. 1851 [1849]. Ethnology. In *A Manual of Scientific Enquiry: Prepared for the Use of Officers in Her Majesty's Navy; and Travellers in General*, ed. John F.W. Herschel, 438-55. London: John Murray.

Quatrefages, Armand de. 1867-8. Muséum d'histoire naturelle. Anthropologie. Cours de M. de Quatrefages. *Revue des cours scientifiques de la France et de l'étranger* 5:366-9, 431-8, 450-5, 495-503, 510-18, 528-36, 544-50, 559-64, 579-84, 592-600, 621-31, 655-63, 685-96, 707-12, 720-8, 730-44, 751-60.

_____. 1868-9. Muséum d'histoire naturelle. Anthropologie. Cours de M. de Quatrefages. *Revue des cours scientifiques de la France et de l'étranger* 6:85-9, 122-8, 184-9, 201-6, 219-24, 235-40, 266-72.

_____. 1870. Discussion sur le transformisme. *Bulletins de la Société d'Anthropologie de Paris* 2e série, 5:156-7, 239-42.

Quatrefages, Armand de, and Ernest-Théodore Hamy. 1882. *Crania ethnica: les crânes des races humaines, décrits et figurés d'après les collections du Muséum d'histoire naturelle de Paris, de la Société d'anthropologie de Paris et les principales collections de la France et de l'étranger*, 2 vols. Paris: J. B. Baillière et fils.

Quoy, Jean-René Constant, and Joseph-Paul Gaimard. 1830. De l'homme. In *Voyage de découvertes de l'Astrolabe … pendant les années 1826-1827-1828-1829 … Zoologie*, vol. 1, 15-59. Paris: J. Tastu.

Richards, Evelleen. 1989. The 'Moral Anatomy' of Robert Knox: the Interplay between Biological and Social Thought in Victorian Scientific Naturalism. *Journal of the History of Biology* 22:372-436.

Richelet, Pierre. 1732. *Dictionnaire de la langue françoise, ancienne et moderne*, 2 vols. Amsterdam: aux depens de la Compagnie.

Rudwick, Martin J.S. 1997. *Georges Cuvier, Fossil Bones, and Geological Catastrophes: New Translations & Interpretations of the Primary Texts*. Chicago: University of Chicago Press.

Schwartz, Joel. 1984. Darwin, Wallace, and the *Descent of Man*. *Journal of the History of Biology* 17:271-89.

Serres, Etienne-Renaud-Augustin, et al. 1841. Rapport sur les résultats scientifiques du voyage de circumnavigation de *l'Astrolabe* et de *la Zélée*. *Compte rendu des séances de l'Académie des Sciences* 13:643-59.

Sloan, Phillip R. 1979. Buffon, German Biology, and the Historical Interpretation of Biological Species. *British Journal for the History of Science* 12:109-53.

———. 1995. The Gaze of Natural History. In *Inventing Human Science: Eighteenth-Century Domains*, ed. Christopher Fox, Roy Porter, and Robert Wokler, 112-51. Berkeley: University of California Press.

———. 2002. Preforming the Categories: Eighteenth-Century Generation Theory and the Biological Roots of Kant's A Priori. *Journal of the History of Philosophy* 40:229-53.

Soemmerring, Samuel Thomas. 1784. *Uber die körperliche Verschiedenheit des Mohren vom Europaer*. Mainz: [no publisher].

———. 1785. *Über die körperliche Verschiedenheit des Negers vom Europäer*. 2nd edition. Frankfurt and Mainz: Varrentrapp, Sohn und Wenner.

———. 1799. Detached Passages, Selected from Professor Soemmering's Essay on the Comparative Anatomy of the Negro and European, tr. Dr Holme. In Charles White, *An Account of the Regular Gradation in Man, and in Different Animals and Vegetables; and from the Former to the Latter*, cxxxix-clxvi. London: C. Dilly.

Stauffer, Robert C. 1957. Haeckel, Darwin, and Ecology. *Quarterly Review of Biology* 32:138-44.

Staum, Martin S. 1996. *Minerva's Message: Stabilizing the French Revolution*. Montreal and Kingston: McGill-Queen's University Press.

_____. 2000. Paris Ethnology and the Perfectibility of 'Races'. *Canadian Journal of History* 35:454-72.

_____. 2003. *Labeling People: French Scholars on Society, Race, and Empire, 1815-1848*. Montreal and Kingston: McGill-Queen's University Press.

Stepan, Nancy. 1982. *The Idea of Race in Science: Great Britain 1800-1960*. London: Macmillan.

Stocking, George W., Jr. 1968. *Race, Culture and Evolution: Essays in the History of Anthropology*. New York: Free Press.

_____. 1971. What's in a Name? The Origins of the Royal Anthropological Institute (1837-71). *Man*, n.s. 6:369-90.

_____. 1973. From Chronology to Ethnology: James Cowles Prichard and British Anthropology 1800-1850. In James Cowles Prichard, *Researches into the Physical History of Man*, ed. George W. Stocking, Jr., ix-cx. Chicago: University of Chicago Press.

_____. 1987. *Victorian Anthropology*. New York: Free Press.

Stokes, John Lort. 1846. *Discoveries in Australia; with an Account of the Coasts and Rivers Explored and Surveyed During the Voyage of H.M.S. Beagle, in the Years 1837-38-39-40-41-42-43 ...*, 2 vols. London: T. and W. Boone.

Strack, Thomas. 1996. Philosophical Anthropology on the Eve of Biological Determinism: Immanuel Kant and Georg Forster on the Moral Qualities and Biological Characteristics of the Human Race. *Central European History* 29:285-308.

Strzelecki, Paul Edmund de. 1845. *Physical Description of New South Wales and Van Diemen's Land: Accompanied by a Geological Map, Sections and Diagrams, and Figures of the Organic Remains*. London: Longman, Brown, Green, and Longmans.

Stuurman, Siep. 2000. François Bernier and the Invention of Racial Classification. *History Workshop Journal* 50:1-21.

Todorov, Tzvetan. 1989. *Nous et les autres: la réflexion française sur la diversité humaine*. Paris: Seuil.

Topinard, Paul. 1868. Etude sur les Tasmaniens. *Mémoires de la Société d'Anthropologie de Paris* 3:307-29.

_____. 1872. Sur les races indigènes de l'Australie. *Bulletins de la Société d'Anthropologie de Paris*, 2ᵉ série 7:211-327.

_____. 1875. Sur les métis australiens. *Bulletins de la Société d'Anthropologie de Paris*, 2ᵉ série 10:227-40.

_____. 1876. *L'anthropologie*. Paris: C. Reinwald.

_____. 1879. De la notion de race en anthropologie. *Revue d'Anthropologie* 2ᵉ série, 2:589-660.

Trevor, J.C. 1951. Race. *Man* 51 (April 1951):56.

Venturino, Diego. 2003. Race et histoire: le paradigme nobiliaire de la distinction sociale au début du XVIIIᵉ siècle. In *L'idée de 'race' dans les sciences humaines et la littérature (XVIIIᵉ et XIXᵉ siècles)*, ed. Sarga Moussa, 19-38. Paris: L'Harmattan.

Virey, Julien-Joseph. 1800. *Histoire naturelle du genre humain, ou recherches sur ses principaux fondemens physiques et moraux …*, 2 vols. Paris: F. Dufart.

_____. 1803. Homme. In *Nouveau dictionnaire d'histoire naturelle*, vol. 11, 99-317. Paris: Déterville.

_____. 1817a. Espèce. In *Nouveau dictionnaire d'histoire naturelle*, vol. 10, 441-68. New revised edition. Paris: Déterville.

_____. 1817b. Homme, Homo. In *Nouveau dictionnaire d'histoire naturelle*, vol. 15, 1-255. New revised edition. Paris: Déterville.

_____. 1817c. Homme. In *Dictionaire des sciences médicales*, vol. 21, 191-344. Paris: C.L.F. Panckoucke.

_____. 1824. *Histoire naturelle du genre humain*, 3 vols. 2nd edition. Paris: Crochard.

Voltaire. 1829 [1769]. *Essay sur les mœurs et l'esprit des nations*, 4 vols. In *œuvres de Voltaire*, ed. Adrien-Jean-Quentin Beuchot, vols 15-18. Paris: Werdet et Lequien fils.

Wallace, Alfred Russel. 1845. Letter to Henry Walter Bates, 28 December 1845. Wallace Online Transcription. WP 1/3/17. London: Natural History Museum. Accessed 13 June 2007, online <http://www.nhm.ac.uk/nature-online/collections-at-the-museum/wallace-collection/transcript.jsp?itemID=57&theme=Evolution>.

_____. 1864. The Origin of Human Races and the Antiquity of Man Deduced from the Theory of 'Natural Selection'. *Journal of the Anthropological Society of London* 2:clviii-clxxxvii.

_____. 1867. Mr. Wallace on Natural Selection Applied to Anthropology. *Anthropological Review* 5:103-5.

[Wallace, Alfred Russel]. 1869. Sir Charles Lyell on Geological Climates and the Origin of Species. *Quarterly Review* April 1869:359-94.

Wells, Kentwood D. 1971. Sir William Lawrence (1783-1867): a Study of Pre-Darwinian Ideas on Heredity and Variation. *Journal of the History of Biology* 4:319-61.

Wheeler, Roxann. 2000. *The Complexion of Race: Categories of Difference in Eighteenth-Century British Culture*. Philadelphia: University of Pennsylvania Press.

White, Charles. 1799. *An Account of the Regular Gradation in Man, and in Different Animals and Vegetables; and from the Former to the Latter*. London: C. Dilly.

Williams, Raymond. 1983 [1976]. *Keywords: a Vocabulary of Culture and Society*. Rev. ed. New York: Oxford University Press.

Zammito, John H. 2006. Policing Polygeneticism in Germany, 1775: (Kames,) Kant, and Blumenbach. In *The German Invention of Race*, ed. Sara Eigen and Mark Larrimore, 35-54. Albany: State University of New York Press.

Notes

[1] The works in question were by Soemmerring (1784, 1785) and Meiners (1785).

[2] Cuvier to Pfaff, 31 December 1790 and 19 February 1791, in Cuvier 1858:201-3, 215-16. See also Blanckaert 2003a:147-8; Stocking 1968:35.

[3] For discussions of the problematic etymology of race see, e.g., Boulle 2003; Dover 1951; Hudson 1996:247-8; Topinard 1879; Trevor 1951; Williams 1983:248.

[4] Estienne 1539:411. Latin-English translations are based on Lewis and Short 1879.

[5] Blanckaert 1988:25; Boulle 2003:12-13; Venturino 2003.

[6] Richelet 1732, II:536.

[7] Bernasconi 2001a; Blanckaert 1988:24-34; 2003a; Douglas 2005; Duvernay-Bolens 1995:10; Hudson 1996; Stocking 1968:35-41; Topinard 1879; Williams 1983:248-9.

[8] [Bernier] 1684; Buffon 1749, III:371-530; Goldsmith 1774, II:213-31; Leibniz 1718a:37-8; 1718b; Maupertuis 1745.

[9] Buffon 1749, III:379; 1777:455-63.

[10] Leibniz [1677-86], quoted in Fenves 2006:13, original emphasis.

[11] E.g., [Brosses] 1756, I:17, 80; II:348, 376, 378-9; Forster 1777, II:226-31; Forster 1778:276-9; see Chapter Two (Douglas), this volume.

[12] Blanckaert 2003a:138; Stocking 1968:35-8; Venturino 2003:31.

[13] Duvernay-Bolens 1995:9-10, 12-13, 25; see also Broberg 1983; Sloan 1995:121-6; cf. Blanckaert 1998:17-20.

[14] Buffon 1749, II:437-44; 1753:386; Eddy 1984:4-12, 39; Farber 1972; Sloan 1995:128-33, 135-9.

[15] Buffon 1777:462-3, 478-80, 484. The contemporary dictionary of Jean-François Féraud (1725-1807) defines *espèce*, first, as a term in logic meaning 'What is below the genus and contains several individuals below itself'; and, second, as *sorte*, 'kind', 'type' (1787-8, II:148).

[16] Buffon 1749, III:371-9, 523-4, 530; 1766:313; 1777:462; see also Blanckaert 2003a:135-8; 2006:458-61; Douglas 2005; Eddy 1984:31, 38; cf. Hudson 1996:253-5; Sloan 1995:135.

[17] Buffon 1749, III:446-8, 526; 1766:313-16; see also Eddy 1984:12-39.

[18] Blumenbach to Banks, 24 January 1797, in Banks [1770-1820]: 8098/314; Blumenbach 1795:322; 1806:50, 68-9.

[19] Blumenbach 1775:60; 1795:167. Latin *gens*, 'that which belongs together by birth or descent', literally means 'clan' and has a strong connotation of common origin when used in its extended sense of 'a race, nation, people'.

[20] *Stemma* literally means 'garland (hung upon an ancestral image)' and by extension 'pedigree, genealogical tree'; *stirps* literally means 'stock, stem, stalk' and, by extension to human beings, 'stock, race, family, lineage'.

[21] 'Five very select skulls from my collection, to demonstrate the equivalent number of the principal varieties of mankind: 1. Tungun [Mongolian]; 2. Caribbean [American]; 3. young female Georgian [Caucasian]; 4. Tahitian [Malay]; 5. Ethiopian of Guinea [Ethiopian]' (Blumenbach 1795:324-6; plate 2).

[22] The translation received Blumenbach's input and approval (Blumenbach 1798:xii).

[23] Blumenbach 1795:121, 303, 320; 1798:94-5, 213, 223; Forster 1786:159-60. As early as 1793, Blumenbach had privately applied the English term race in this indefinite sense to the Pacific Islanders (Blumenbach to Banks, 1 November 1793, in Banks [1770-1820]: 8098/116-17); see Chapter Two (Douglas), this volume.

[24] Kant first explicitly addressed in print the question of *den verschiedenen Racen der Menschen*, 'the diverse races of men', in 1775, in a prospectus for a summer course on physical geography (2001). A revised version was published in 1777 and subsequent articles on the theme followed in 1785 and 1788. For the wider philosophical and ideological settings of these papers, see also Bernasconi 2001b, 2006; Greene 1954:36-9; Lagier 2004; Lenoir 1980:90-5; Liebersohn 2006:197-208; Sloan 1979:125-37; 2002:238-41; Strack 1996:290-9; Zammito 2006:36-43.

[25] Kant 1777:125-32, 156-60; 1785:404, 407-8; 2001:2-4, 6-12.

[26] Buffon 1766:311, 313-14; Kant 1777:139-64; 1785:394-5, 402-17; see also Blanckaert 2003a:142-6; Eze 1995:214-19; Greene 1954:36-8; Lenoir 1980:87-92.

[27] Blumenbach 1803, I:29, original emphasis. This passage first appeared in the fifth edition of the *Handbuch der Naturgeschichte*, 'Manual of Natural History' (1797), which I have not seen. My rendition is from François Artaud de Soulange's French translation of the 1799 sixth edition which, he said, was produced 'under the eyes' of Blumenbach who reviewed the manuscript (Blumenbach 1803, I:xvi). Lenoir (1980:83-96) saw Blumenbach's acceptance of reproductive criteria as a symptom of the steady theoretical convergence since the late 1780s of his signature concept of the *Bildungstrieb*, 'formative force' — 'the agent responsible for organic structure', conceived as a 'Newtonian force' — with Kant's equally teleological idea of the *Stamm* and its *Anlagen* as the generative source of different races. This meeting of minds paralleled the shift by both men from preformationist to epigenetic theories of generation. Blumenbach described the *Bildungstrieb* or *nisus formativus* as linking the 'two principles which explain the nature of organic bodies, the physico-mechanical with the *teleological*' (1789; 1795:82-8, original emphasis; see also Sloan 2002:246-53).

[28] In *Beyträge zur Naturgeschichte*, Blumenbach mostly preferred *Spielart* to *Varietät* but they were clearly synonyms, both used to translate Latin *varietas*, 'a variety'.

[29] Blanckaert 2003a:145-9; Figlio 1976:23-8, 35-9; Stocking 1968:29-39.

[30] See Staum 1996:26-7.

[31] Cuvier 1817a, I:18-19, 91-100, original emphasis. According to the *Dictionnaire de l'Académie française* (1835), the term *museau*, 'muzzle', 'snout', referred specifically to 'the dog and some other animals' and was sometimes 'popularly' extended to people, 'but only with contempt or in jest'. It was routinely applied to certain people by the science of race.

[32] Cuvier 1817a, I:16, 30-56. Karl Figlio (1976:21, 33-5) pointed to the metaphor of 'organization' as 'the central concept of life sciences' in the early nineteenth century, to comparative anatomy as 'the science of organization' and its 'methodological partner', and to Cuvier's seminal position 'at the centre of comparative anatomical thought'.

[33] Prichard 1813:233; 1836-47, I:xix, 2, 257, 284-97; V:285.

[34] Prichard 1836-47, I:1, 110-11; V:547, original emphasis. E.g., Prichard (1836-47, I:284-97) allowed that his 'physical history of the different tribes' of Africa would reveal that 'the features of the Negro races' were less 'widely diffused in so strongly marked a degree' than was implied by his anatomical discussion.

[35] Prichard 1813:15-25, 166-7; 1826, II:589; 1836-47, I:246-7.

[36] Prichard 1836-47, I:4, 113, 216, 304, 358, 376.

[37] Prichard 1836-47, I:vii, 109; Stocking 1973:lxxi.

[38] Knox 1850:7, 13, 22-4.

[39] E.g., *generis humani varietatum principalium*, 'principal varieties of mankind', as 'principal human races'; *hominum gentes et nationes multifarias*, 'the peoples and the multifarious nations of men', as 'the races and the multifarious nations of men'; *varietates craniorum gentilitiae*, 'national varieties of skulls', as 'racial varieties of skulls'; *hominum stemmata*, 'human stocks', as 'races of men'; *pulcherrimam hominum stirpem*, 'most beautiful human stock', as 'most beautiful race of men' (Blumenbach 1795:1, 65, 114-283, 303, 324; 1865:162, 163, 188, 207-63, 269).

[40] Blanckaert 1988:25, 29; Stocking 1968:36-8; Venturino 2003:20-2.

[41] Blumenbach 1775:41-2; 1795:73; 1798:208; 1806:60, 67-9; Buffon 1749, III:529-30.

[42] See Chapter Two (Douglas), this volume.

[43] Lacépède 1800:2, 7, 14, 22-4, 27-9.

[44] In the late eighteenth century, the Dutch anatomist and artist Petrus Camper (1722-1789), a founder of craniometry, had proposed that the 'lines which mark the countenance, with their different angles' could be systematically measured and compared to provide an aesthetic diagnostic of characteristic 'difference' in 'national physiognomy'. The resultant 'facial angle' was that formed on a profiled head between a horizontal line drawn from the bottom of the nose to the opening of the ear and the 'facial line' drawn from the upper lip to the forehead along the nasal bone. Camper published his measurements of 'an assemblage of craniums' with results ranging from angles of 58° for an orangutan to 100° for an idealized Greek image; his living human range was from 70° for a Negro to 80° for a European. Camper himself argued ardently for the singularity and the unity of 'the whole human race' and dismissed as merely 'superficial' and 'amusing' the 'striking resemblance' that his juxtapositions seemingly displayed 'between the race of Monkies and of Blacks' (1794:1, 9, 32-44, 50). However, others were less scrupulous — notably the Englishman Charles White (1799) — and the facial angle or its derivatives became staples in subsequent racial mensuration and differentiation. See also Meijer 1999.

[45] Blumenbach 1775:40-1; 1795:308, 322; 1803, I:73; 1806:68-9.

[46] Cuvier (1817a, I:81, 94) proclaimed: 'Man forms only one genus, and that genus is unique in its order'. However, he was more circumspect about asserting human specific unity, prefacing his definition of races as 'hereditary conformations' with the qualification: 'Although the human species appears unique …'.

[47] Cuvier 1800-5, II:2-15. Cuvier's cranio-facial ratio incorporated and elaborated Camper's equally crude comparative measure of the facial angle (see note 44).

[48] Lawrence 1819:iii-iv, 31-5, 126-7, 245-6, 271, 300, 341, 363, 481, 500-1, 516, 555.

[49] Bynum 1975:8-14; Ellingson 2001:250-1; Lawrence 1819:1-16; Stepan 1982:11; Wells 1971:321-2, 330-6, 359-60; see also Chapter Six (Gardner), this volume.

[50] Ellingson 2001:250-1; Hunt 1868:432; Prichard 1826, I:vi; 1836-47, I:vii; Wallace 1845; Wells 1971:336-51.

[51] Boulle 2003:20; Stuurman 2000:2, 12-16. In a letter written in 1697, Leibniz (1718a:37-8) mentioned 'a certain traveller [who] had divided men into certain tribes, races, or classes', evidently an allusion to Bernier. But in implied qualification of this position, Leibniz affirmed his own belief in essential human unity: 'this does not mean that all men, who inhabit this globe, are not all of a single race, which has been altered by different climates'. Blumenbach (1795:296) acknowledged the anonymous author of the 1694 article simply as the first to divide 'mankind into varieties'.

[52] In 1753, in a notorious footnote to a new edition of his essay 'Of national characters', Hume (1987:262-3, cf. 98) declared 'the negroes, and … all the other species of men (for there are four or five different kinds) to be naturally inferior to the whites' as a result of 'an original distinction' made by nature 'betwixt these breeds of men'. In 1769, Voltaire (1829, I:7) maintained that the 'prodigious' physical differences between Negroes and 'the other species of men' were 'inherent' and could not be explained in conventional climatic terms. Kames (1774, I:37) also rejected Buffonian climatic determinism and argued: 'were all men of one species, there never could have existed, without a miracle, different kinds, such as exist at present'.

[53] Atkins 1734:18-21, 23-4; 1735:39, 176-9; [Long] 1774, II:356, original emphasis.

[54] Forster 1786:76-7, 163-5; Sloan 1979:131-4. See also Strack 1996:302-5, 303, note 69.

[55] Soemmerring 1799; White 1799: 56, 67, 83, 98, 125, 134.

[56] I thank Claude Blanckaert for this insight (pers. com., 23 May 2006; see also Blanckaert 1988:31).

[57] Forster 1786:79-80, 86, 157, 158-60, 161-5.

[58] Blanchard 1854:18-19, 30, 213.

[59] Virey 1800, I:86, 87, 124, 138, 145, 189, 413.

[60] However, Virey did not consistently maintain the distinction between species and races since he also claimed that certain races — notably the Jews — maintained 'permanent characters, an indelible type' (1824, I:435; see Blanckaert 1988:30-1). Between the first and second editions of his *Histoire naturelle du genre humain*, 'Natural History of the Human Genus', Virey had refined his thesis on human specific

differences in the course of lengthy entries on 'Man' published in several dictionaries of natural history or the medical sciences (1803:217-65; 1817b:142-98; 1817c:244-73).

[61] Virey 1824, I:431, 436-8, 439, 452; II:17-18, 22, 30-195, 30-1, 106-7; III, 460. Virey sometimes used the term *orang-outang* in the generic sense of 'ape' but his phrase 'the true orang-outang' referred to a particular animal genus, positioned 'closest' to the human genus and comprising two species: Linnaeus's *simia satyrus* (the modern genus *Pongo*, the orangutan of Malaysia and Indonesia) and his *simia troglodytes* (the modern genus *Pan*, the African chimpanzee) (Virey 1824, III:428, 448-92, 508). See Broberg 1983:179-93 on the troubled history of the nomenclature of the great apes generally and the orangutan in particular during the eighteenth century.

[62] Virey 1824, I:431; II:30-195, 106-7; III:460-3.

[63] Bory de Saint-Vincent 1822; 1827a, I:1-5; 1827b; Cuvier 1817a, I:81.

[64] Bory de Saint-Vincent 1827a, I:72, 82, 103-5; II:104, 113, 124. Like White's (1799) notion of 'gradation', Bory's concept of 'passage' (1827a, I:14-15) reinscribed the classical notion of the 'great chain of being' in support of a polygenist agenda (see Bynum 1975:12-22; Stepan 1982:6-19). Unlike Bory, most contemporary French naturalists, including the polygenist Desmoulins (1826:189), more or less followed Cuvier who, (himself following Blumenbach and rejecting global application of the 'so called scale of beings' as 'erroneous'), isolated man within the order *Bimana*, the first of the class *Mammalia*, and positioned the genera *Orang* and *Gibbon* in the family *Simia*, 'Ape', as the first of the *Quadrumana*, the second order of *Mammalia* (Cuvier 1817a, I:xx-xxi, 70-104; Geoffroy Saint-Hilaire 1828, 1829). In a dictionary entry on 'Orang' , Bory (1827b:262-4, 268-81) elaborated his zoological taxonomy by coupling the genus *Orang* with the human genus as the 'first' 'tribe' of the family *Bimana* of the order *Anthropomorpha* — thus reinstating a term that Linnaeus had used originally and relabelled *Primates* in 1758. Though 'notably inferior' to orangs in physical organization and intelligence, the genus *Gibbon* was 'still quite close' to man and constituted the 'second tribe' of *Bimana*. The families *Singe* and *Lémurien* completed the order. Bory's genus *Orang*, like Virey's, comprised two species: the African chimpanzee and the southeast Asian orangutan.

[65] Desmoulins 1826:4-7, 158, 194-7, 219, 294-5, 335; see also Blanckaert 1988:27, 31-3.

[66] Desmoulins 1826:189, 299-300, 304-8, 312-17.

[67] Blanckaert 1988; 2003a:146-7.

[68] Balbi 1826a:XXIV; 1826b:xxi, lxxx-lxxxii, 61, 231.

[69] Blanckaert 1988:34-49; Staum 2000; see below and Chapter Five (Anderson), this volume.

[70] Prichard 1836-47, I:2; 1848; 1851; Staum 2003:125-57; Stocking 1973; 1987:48-53, 239-46. 'The history of nations, termed ethnology', wrote Prichard in a late work (1843:132-3), 'must be mainly founded on the relations of their languages'.

[71] Hunt 1863a:9-10, 17; 1863b:386-7; 1864a; 1864b:liii, lv; 1867:lvii, lxvi. On the one hand, Hunt (1866:321, 327; 1867:lvii, lxvi) refused to 'give any preference to the various theories of man's origin'; on the other, he maintained that 'there were at present several distinct species, if not genera, of man'. He nonetheless found the polygenist hypothesis 'the most reasonable', if 'of no great scientific value', and railed against the renewed 'monogenism' of the Darwinians: to allow the 'diversity of existing species of man', he warned, did not necessarily mean belief in 'diversity of origin'.

[72] In 1790, for instance, Cuvier had privately questioned the usefulness of the naturalists' definition of a species as 'the entire posterity of the first couple created by God', on the grounds that it was now impossible to 'recover the thread of that genealogy' (Cuvier to Pfaff, 22-23 August 1790, in Cuvier 1858:178-9). See also Rudwick 1997:260-1.

[73] Fausto-Sterling 1995:27-8; Stocking 1968:39.

[74] Balbi 1826:lxxx-lxxxi; Malte-Brun 1803:540; Mentelle and Malte-Brun 1804:377, original emphasis.

[75] Bory de Saint-Vincent 1827a, I:[i], 72, 94.

[76] Duvernay-Bolens 1995:14-15, 20-5; Staum 2003:119.

[77] Blanckaert 2003a:148; Cuvier et al. 1807:135, 137.

[78] Blanckaert 1988:31; Virey 1824, I:437, 500, 511.

[79] Original emphasis.

[80] Ellingson 2001:248-323; Stocking 1971; 1987:246-57; see also Chapter Four (Turnbull), this volume.

[81] Stocking 1973:lxx, lxxvi; 1987:66. In an important recent work, the historian Colin Kidd (2006:122) put a convincing case that 'white racial self-confidence' was underpinned by 'persistent and troubling

religious doubts, to which the problem of racial diversity itself contributed' and that 'race turns out to have been a significant … feature in the wider ecology of religious crisis'.

[82] Blanckaert 1988:45; Staum 2000:462-5; see also Chapter Five (Anderson), this volume. Geoffroy Saint-Hilaire held the chair in the Zoology of Mammals and Birds at the Muséum from 1841-61; Serres was the inaugural holder of the chair in the Anatomy and Natural History of Man from 1839-55 and was succeeded by Quatrefages who held the chair, renamed Anthropology, until 1892. Both men were avowedly naturalists first and anthropologists second (Quatrefages 1867-8:366). Quatrefages was co-author of a monumental global survey of 'ethnic skulls' (Quatrefages and Hamy 1882).

[83] Serres et al. 1841:645, 648, 649-50, 653-4, 655, 656-7.

[84] 'Mr Broca's craniograph' (Broca 1860-3: pl. 7).

[85] Geoffroy Saint-Hilaire 1860-3:127-8, 131-3, 137, 141, 143.

[86] Original emphasis.

[87] Geoffroy Saint-Hilaire 1860-3:132, 137, 139-40, 143.

[88] Larson 1968:291-2, 296-9; see also Hörstadius 1974:274-5.

[89] Buffon 1753:377-91; 1766:358; Kant 1785, 1788, 2001:2-4; see also Blanckaert 2003b:44-8; Farber 1972:262-5, 275-84; Glass 1960:227-32; Quatrefages 1870:240-1; Sloan 2002:244-50.

[90] Blumenbach 1795:66-71, 85-8, 98-102; 1803, I:27-31.

[91] Blumenbach 1790:23-31; Lenoir 1980:93-5, original emphasis.

[92] Cuvier 1812:76; 1817a, I:19-20.

[93] Appel 1987; Bynum 1975:20-1; Geoffroy Saint-Hilaire 1833; Lamarck 1907; Rudwick 1997:82-3, 168, 179, 253, 260-4; Cuvier 1812:58, 73-5; 1817a, I:xx-xxi.

[94] Lawrence 1819:260-2, 268, 293-4, 297, 303-4, 502-3, 510, 515-49; Wells 1971:323-5, 329.

[95] Lawrence 1819:127, 515; Prichard 1813:25, 194-5, 198; Wells 1971:355-60.

[96] Prichard 1813:204, 231-2; 1826, II:537, 558-83.

[97] Cuvier to Pfaff, 22-23 August 1790, in Cuvier 1858:179; 1817a, I:94.

[98] Prichard 1826, I:95-8, 126-8; 1836-47, I:147, 150; 1843:11-26, my emphasis.

[99] Buffon 1749, III:382-4; 1766:313.

[100] Lawrence 1819:296, 300; Prichard 1826, I:127; 1836-47, I:148-50; 1850:147.

[101] Virey 1800, I:412; 1817a:458-9; 1817c:244, 267-8.

[102] Virey 1824, II:183-5, 192-5.

[103] Serres et al. 1841:645-50, 655, 657.

[104] Blanchard 1854:7-13; Hombron 1846:272; Hombron and Jacquinot 1846-54; Jacquinot 1846:5. See also Blanckaert 2003b:49-50; Staum 2003:115-17; Chapter Two (Douglas), this volume.

[105] Hombron 1846:76-8, 85, 104, 275-84, 301, 302, 395.

[106] Jacquinot 1846:36, 90-104. His claim to precedence was ill-founded as the belief that 'Mulattos' were 'of the mule-kind, and not so capable of producing from one another as from a commerce with a distinct White or Black' ([Long] 1774, II:335) had been commonplace in literature on the West Indies and the American South at least since the eighteenth century (Nott 1855:397-8).

[107] Blanchard 1854:19, 30, 31-6.

[108] See Chapter Eight (Luker), this volume.

[109] Knox 1850:145-7, 296-8, 301; 1855a:357-8.

[110] Knox 1850; 1855a, b, c; 1862; Richards 1989.

[111] Knox 1850:9-23, 52, 66-7, 107, 145, 298; 1855a:358; 1855b:626.

[112] Knox 1850:297; 1855b:627, original emphasis; 1855c:25-6, 45; Richards 1989:400.

[113] Knox 1850:28, 145-91, 300-6; Richards 1989:404.

[114] Knox 1850:88, 178, 319, note 10; 1855a:357-8.

[115] Knox 1850:22-5; Stocking 1971:374; 1987:65-6.

[116] Ellingson 2001:248-323; Stocking 1971; 1987:238-73; see Chapter Four (Turnbull), this volume.

[117] Darwin and Wallace 1858; Jones 2002; Schwartz 1984.

[118] On the earlier occasion, Wallace was perhaps pandering to the racial extremism of some Anthropological Society members since the later paper — a review of the work of the geologist Charles

Lyell (1797-1875) published in the Tory *Quarterly Review* — is racially more temperate, if also generally more snide (1869:391-2): natural selection 'could only have endowed the savage with a brain a little superior to that of an ape, whereas he actually possesses one but very little inferior to that of the average members of our learned societies'.

[119] Darwin 1839:25-8; 1871, I:34, 169, 232, 238-40; 1882, I:181-92; 1958:73-4.

[120] Darwin 1871, I:229; Huxley 1894:248; Wallace 1864:clxvi, clxxxiv; 1867:103.

[121] Darwin 1871, I:233-6; Wallace 1867:103.

[122] Wallace 1845: folio 1, 3-4; see also McKinney 1969.

[123] Darwin 1871, I:228-9, 235; Huxley 1894:242, 248; Wallace 1864:clviii-clix, clxvi, clxxxiv.

[124] Stocking 1971:384-6; 1987:269-73.

[125] Broca 1858-9:434, 451-71, 684-728. In 1858, Broca (1858-9:440) condensed his current position on the fixity of species in the 'short formula' that 'species no longer change, because they have already done so as much as they can'.

[126] Broca 1858-9:434; 1859-60:601-3, 614-16; Gobineau 1884, I:24; Knox 1850:107; Nott 1855:407; Prichard 1843:12-13. Blanckaert (2003b:51-3, 57-63) lucidly summarized Broca's contributions to mid-nineteenth-century debates on human hybridity.

[127] Morton 1850-1:82; Nott 1855:376, 397-8. Blanckaert (2003b:56-8) saw the renewed emphasis on gradation as yet another reincarnation of the 'great chain of being' (Bynum 1975). In this vein, Broca's prose is peppered with terms like 'ladder', 'degrees', and 'series' (e.g., 1858-9:716, 218; 1859-60:412, 616, 620).

[128] Broca 1858-9:727-8, 218-58, 345-96; 1859-60:428, 433-4.

[129] Broca 1858-9:237-8; 1859-60:618-25, 412.

[130] Broca 1858-9:232-3; 1859-60:616-25, 392-429. Broca's (1859-60:412-13) seemingly authoritative relegation of Australians and Tasmanians to the negative extreme of the 'human series', as 'absolutely incorrigible savages', cited only three works by men with significant Australian experience — a naval surgeon, a naturalist, and a geologist (Cunningham 1828; MacGillivray 1852; Strzelecki 1845); plus a handful of scientific publications by French naval naturalists who had fleetingly visited Australia or Tasmania in the course of scientific voyages (Garnot 1836; Jacquinot 1846; Lesson 1839; Quoy and Gaimard 1830).

[131] Broca 1858-9:716; 1859-60:414, 435-9.

[132] Broca 1858-9:435-41; 1866:62; 1870:169-70, 193-218. The author of the epigram was the Swiss comparative anatomist René-Edouard Claparède (1832-1871).

[133] Broca 1870:190-3, original emphasis; see also Chapter Four (Turnbull), this volume.

[134] See Chapter Five (Anderson), this volume. Topinard succeeded Broca as director of the Ecole d'Anthropologie and as secretary-general of the Société d'Anthropologie de Paris.

[135] Topinard 1876; 1879:599, 603, 613-14, 627, 633-42, 655, 659. See also Blanckaert 1988:48; Chapter Five (Anderson), this volume.

[136] Topinard 1876:15, 547-64; 1879:600-3, 612. He defined Darwinism as '*Natural selection through the struggle for existence, applied to Lamarck's transformism*' (1876:550, original emphasis).

[137] Darwin 1871, I:215, 220-6; Huxley 1894:219-24, 234, 240-2, 252.

[138] Topinard 1875; 1879:599, 613-14, 645-7, 652, original emphasis.

[139] Topinard 1879:589-600, 612-28.

[140] Topinard 1879:631-3, 642-3, 648, 651, 657.

[141] Topinard 1876:2-9; 1879:589, 660.

[142] Darwin 1871, I:229-35; Wallace 1864:clxv-clxvi.

[143] Lacépède 1800:22-4; Serres et al. 1841:645-6; Wallace 1864:clxiii-clxvi, clxxxiv. See also Haller 1970; Stocking 1987:146-50; Richards 1989:406-35; Wells 1971:336-51.

[144] Darwin 1871, I:201; Hombron 1846:104-5; Serres et al. 1841:647-50, 655-7; Topinard 1876:435-8, 557-9; Wallace 1864:clxiv-clxv, clxix; 1867.

[145] Topinard 1875:235-6; 1879:596, 645-8, 652-5, 657-8.

[146] See especially Brantlinger 2003; McGregor 1997. See also Chapters Two (Douglas) and Four (Turnbull), this volume.

[147] Stokes 1846, I:263-4; II:450-1, 463-4, 470.

[148] Blanchard 1854:32; Knox 1850:7.

[149] Eze 1995:237; Gailey 1996:37; Gould 1994; Sloan 1995:148, note 79; Todorov 1989;126. See also Blanckaert 2003a:133-4; Bowler 1984:87-8.

[150] Blumenbach 1795:178, 289; 1806:73-97.

[151] Haeckel 1866, II:286-7; Stauffer 1957:140-1.

Part Two

Experience: the Science of
Race and Oceania, 1750-1869

Chapter Two

'*Novus Orbis Australis*':[1] Oceania in the science of race, 1750-1850

Bronwen Douglas

In December 1828, the leading comparative anatomist Georges Cuvier (1769-1832) made a triumphalist presidential address (1829) to the annual general assembly of the Société de Géographie in Paris. He reminded his audience of the recent 'conquests of geography' which had revealed to the world the 'greatly varied tribes and countless islands' that the Ocean had thus far 'rendered unknown to the rest of humanity'. Cuvier's 'conquests' were not merely topographical: 'our voyagers' in Oceania were 'philosophers and naturalists, no less than astronomers and surveyors'. They collected the 'products' of lands visited, studied the 'languages and customs' of the inhabitants, and enriched 'our museums, grammars and lexicons' as much as 'our atlases and maps'. 'Saved for science' in archives, natural history collections, and lavishly illustrated publications, this copious legacy of the classic era of scientific voyaging between 1766 and 1840 propelled Oceania to the empirical forefront of European knowledge — not least in the natural history of man and the nascent discipline of anthropology which made prime subject matter of the descriptions, portraits, plaster busts, human bodily remains, and artefacts repatriated by antipodean travellers and residents.

History can be a potent antidote to the spurious aura of reality and permanence that infects reified concepts. This chapter and the previous one dislodge the realism of 'race' by historicizing it but do so from different perspectives. Whereas the first chapter is a wide-ranging intellectual history of the invention of the modernist concept of race and the normalization of its science, the present chapter is grounded in a regional subset of the field materials on which theorists drew to illustrate their deductions about human diversity.[2] I consider anthropological deployment of Oceanian examples by a variety of metropolitan thinkers but direct the most sustained attention to works by four major figures who each professed belief in the unity of the single human species and claimed to favour 'facts' and 'induction' over 'system'. They are Cuvier; the French naturalist Georges-Louis Leclerc, comte de Buffon (1707-1788); the German comparative anatomist and pioneer anthropologist Johann Friedrich Blumenbach (1752-1840); and the British physician-ethnologist James Cowles Prichard (1786-1848).[3] These men reasoned in historical or taxonomic terms and from varied ideological perspectives: they debated human relationships to animals and the classification and ranking of human variation; they pondered the origins and development of what the new disciplines of anthropology and ethnology regarded as separate races or even separate species; while their conception and use of the idea of races spanned shifting contemporary spectrums of learned opinion and argument, from humanist to racialist, environmentalist to innatist, holistic to segregative, 'monogenist' to 'polygenist'.[4]

Bridging the global abstractions of such savants and the empirical specificity of voyagers' or residents' narratives were the regional anthropological taxonomies and speculative histories proposed by naturalists who had travelled widely in Oceania as members of scientific naval expeditions. Such men brought general theoretical precepts and a classifying mindset to bear on transient, often confronting personal experience of encounters with actual indigenous people.[5] Aside from the work of the Germans Johann Reinhold Forster (1729-1798) and his son Georg (1754-1794) who sailed with James Cook (1728-1779) on his second voyage of 1772-75, much of the early anthropology of Oceania published before 1850 was produced by French naturalists who are a primary focus of this chapter.[6] François Péron (1775-1810) was a zoologist on the Australian voyage of Nicolas Baudin (1754-1803) in 1800-04. The navigator-naturalist Jules-Sébastien-César Dumont d'Urville (1790-1842) undertook three voyages to Oceania between 1822 and 1840, the last two as commander. The naval medical officers Jean-René Constant Quoy (1790-1869) and Joseph-Paul Gaimard (1793-1858) served also as naturalists with Louis de Freycinet (1779-1842) in 1817-20 and with Dumont d'Urville in 1826-29; their colleague Prosper Garnot (1794-1838) and the pharmacist René-Primevère Lesson (1794-1849) did so with Louis-Isidore Duperrey (1786-1865) and Dumont d'Urville in 1822-25; while the surgeon-naturalists Jacques-Bernard Hombron (1798-1852) and Honoré Jacquinot (1814-1887) accompanied Dumont d'Urville in 1837-40, together with the phrenologist Pierre-Marie Alexandre Dumoutier (1797-1871).

By probing the relationships between anthropological systems and Oceanic facts and the interplay of deductive and inductive modes of knowing, this chapter illustrates the reciprocal significance of discourse and experience, taxonomy and history for different camps of the burgeoning science of race.

Buffon and Dampier — 'great variety of Savages'

The emergence of an embryonic biological concept of race in the 1770s has been ascribed to both the 'natural system' of Carl Linnaeus (1707-1778) and the rival 'natural history' of Buffon.[7] Most naturalists on eighteenth-century voyages to Oceania followed Linnaean taxonomic principles but the region does not figure in his terse classification of *Homo sapiens* into four geographically defined varieties (1758:20-2). Unlike Linnaeus, Buffon (1749a) segregated man from the other animals as a unique species while his exhaustive geographical survey of 'Varieties in the Human Species' (1749b, III:371-530) drew heavily on travellers' narratives. The shortage of such material on Oceania limited his discussion of the people of that region and dictated significant reliance on the perspicacious writings of the late seventeenth-century English voyager William Dampier (1652-1715). However, in his later *Supplément* (1777:539-55), Buffon addressed in detail the descriptions of the 'South Sea Islanders' and the 'inhabitants of the Austral lands' published in recent explorers' accounts and in the compendium of voyage texts dating from the sixteenth century assembled by his friend Charles de Brosses (1709-1777), the French *littérateur* and president of the Burgundian *parlement*. Brosses's work (1756) included a speculative program for discovery, commerce, and settlement in the *Terres australes*, 'Austral lands', that helped inspire the great French and British circumnavigations of the 1860s.[8]

Buffon's essay on man has often been interpreted as a methodical classification of humanity into varieties or races: Blumenbach and Charles Darwin (1809-1882) said he had listed six; the historian of anthropology Michèle Duchet discerned a 'spectral analysis of the human species' into 'four principal *races*'.[9] Such readings are overly categorical since Buffon avoided systematic labelling or formal taxonomy. Rather, the bulk of the work describes the myriad 'nuances' of the multiple 'kinds', 'varieties', 'races', 'nations', or 'peoples' known to him within the single human species.[10] Slotted into this painstaking catalogue between 'the inhabitants of the kingdoms of Pégu and Aracan' (in what is now Myanmar) and the 'peoples of the Indian peninsula' is a sixteen-page segment discussing the inhabitants of the Malay Archipelago, some western Pacific Islands, New Guinea, and New Holland (mainland Australia).[11] The section concludes with Buffon's reflection that the inhabitants of Formosa and the Marianas Islands 'seem to form a separate race different from all those nearby' while the *Papous* and other Islanders from around New Guinea were 'true blacks and resemble those of Africa'.[12] With hindsight, these remarks might be seen to anticipate the later racial differentiation of Micronesians and Melanesians.

Yet this anachronistic reading misconstrues both Dampier and Buffon. There is no classificatory sub-text to Dampier's ethnocentric descriptions of the 'great variety of Savages' he had seen on his voyages. There is only comparison rather than implied categorical opposition between the 'Indians' he met in present-day Micronesia, the Philippines, and Indonesia and the 'Negroes' he encountered along the New Guinea coasts. He regarded *both* as savages with the human potential to become civilized through commerce, though he clearly took relative Negro inferiority for granted. These fairly evenhanded assessments are in sharp contrast to his very negative published impressions of the inhabitants of the west coast of New Holland whose indifference to material inducement led him to question their capacity to become civilized.[13] This was an early statement of a commonplace nexus drawn by Europeans between lifestyle, material desires, and alleged lack of perfectibility, very often to the detriment of Aboriginal Australians.

It is equally inappropriate to attribute methodical binary intent to Buffon, notwithstanding his presumption of an overarching human division into 'the white race' and 'the race of the blacks', his vaunting of 'the most white', his absolute denigration of Negroes, and his paraphrase of Dampier's harsh words about the people of New Holland.[14] At this point, Buffon later claimed (1777:462, 478), he had sometimes used *race* with the 'extended sense' of 'resemblance' rather than in its 'narrow' genealogical sense. But in practice, his a priori dichotomy of white and black races repeatedly dissolved into overlapping 'varieties' and 'nuances'. The 'descriptions' of Dampier and other travellers provided his evidence 'that the islands and coasts of the [east] Indian Ocean are peopled by men very different from each other' — 'Indians', 'Chinese', 'Europeans', 'true blacks', and others. It was the multiplicity of actual human 'differences' which most impressed Buffon and which he correlated exhaustively with climate, geography, and lifestyle to produce a broadly humanist conclusion: that 'humankind is not composed of essentially different species' but that present diversity was entirely the product of the lengthy operation of (in principle reversible) 'external and accidental causes' on what was 'originally only a single species of men'.[15] His subsequent reading of recent voyagers' texts on the South Sea Islanders and the people of New Holland only confirmed this judgment (1777:555): 'the great differences' — the main human 'varieties' — were 'dependent entirely on the influence of climate' and specifically on 'temperature'. Temperature determined not only 'the colour of men' but also their nutrition which served as a 'second cause' with profound effects on the (biological) 'nature' of human beings. Here, Buffon was alluding to the theory of environmentally generated, organic, but still theoretically reversible degeneration of species that informed his work on the natural history of man from the 1760s.[16]

Brosses and the Forsters — 'two great varieties'

Dampier was acknowledged as an authoritative precursor by the scientific voyagers of the later eighteenth century,[17] most of whom were no more interested in classifying human beings than he had been. The earliest systematic classification of the inhabitants of Oceania was the joint product of Georg Forster and his father Reinhold (1778:ii), self-styled purveyors of 'facts' over 'systems formed in the closet'. In a post-voyage treatise, Reinhold Forster proposed his well-known identification of 'two great varieties of people in the South Seas', one 'more fair' and the other 'blacker'; both seen 'living in the same climate, or nearly so'. This formal binary division of Pacific humanity had been anticipated empirically in Georg Forster's narrative of the voyage which differentiated the Malakulans of what is now north Vanuatu as 'a race totally distinct' in 'form', 'language', and 'manners' from the 'lighter-coloured nation' he had seen in the eastern and central Pacific and in New Zealand (Aotearoa). He speculatively aligned the Malakulans with the 'black race' earlier reported in and around New Guinea and wondered whether 'some other tribes' might be 'a mixture of both races'.[18]

Similar lexical imprecision with respect to the word race is evident in Reinhold Forster's further hypotheses that 'each of the above two races of men, is again divided into several varieties, which form the gradations towards the other race'; that these 'two different tribes' might stem from 'two different races of men', probably 'the two distinct [East] Indian tribes'; and that the 'five races' of the 'fairer' tribe were 'really descended from the same original nation'. His subsequent ruminations on settlement and 'the origin of ranks' in the highly stratified societies of Tahiti, the Society Islands, and Tonga made local differences in skin colour the main ground for supposing that a 'successive' migration of 'ancient Malays' had supplanted 'the aboriginal black race' of 'cannibals' whom he equated with 'the tribe of the Papuas', 'people from New-Guinea, and its neighbourhood', and those he had seen in the New Hebrides (now Vanuatu). Purportedly 'subdued' by their 'more polished and more civilized conquerors', these imagined black aborigines became 'the lowest rank' in Forster's reflections on people he had actually encountered in the eastern and central Pacific Islands. A parallel argument was put by the French navigator Jean-François de Galaup de La Pérouse (1741-1788) to explain the differences between 'two very distinct races' he thought he saw in Upolu, Samoa, in 1787.[19]

At issue here are two modes of thinking about human differences which often intersect but are inappropriately conflated:[20] one, emergent in the late-eighteenth century, is taxonomic and incidentally historical; the other is an older, deeply anti-Negro conjectural history of inevitable displacement of black-skinned autochthones by more civilized, lighter-skinned immigrants. The second, but not the first, was applied to Oceania by Brosses, though he was by no means its inventor. The Spanish navigator Pedro Fernández de Quirós (c. 1563-1615), who had twice traversed the *Mar del Sur*, 'South Sea', at the turn of the sixteenth century, proposed an early version. He recalled that in Luzon, in the Philippines, there were 'black men' who were said to be 'the aborigines' but who had been driven into remote 'corners' by invading 'Moors and other Indians'. Quirós hypothesized that these 'persecuted' people had sought and found new places to settle in New Guinea, the Solomon Islands, and eventually Santa Cruz where he himself saw 'black' inhabitants in 1595.[21] A century and a half later, Brosses prefigured Reinhold Forster, La Pérouse, and numerous others in plotting a displacement narrative to account for a supposed 'difference in the human species [*l'espèce humaine*]' within the same climatic zone — an anomaly in Buffonian terms. Brosses's conjectural history represented 'the native inhabitants of

Australasie' as an 'old race' of 'frizzy-haired blacks', identical to 'the African negroes', and like them among the 'first inhabitants of the torrid zone'. They were 'a more brutish and savage kind of men [*espèce d'hommes*]' than 'foreign colonies of Malay peoples' who had driven them from 'their possessions in Asia' and gradually 'destroyed the race' — as the Spanish did to the Americans. The blacks retained sole possession only of remote '*Virgin* countries', such as New Holland and other 'unknown Austral lands', though Brosses refused 'to believe that any kind of men is totally uncivilizable'.[22] His geographical division of the *Terres australes* into *Polynésie*, *Australasie*, and *Magellanique* did not extend to systematic classification of the 'many different peoples' of this 'fifth part of the world' and it is anachronistic to recast it as anticipating subsequent dual ethnological or racial categories.[23] But the teleological presumption of racial dispersal and destruction would haunt the subsequent project of racial taxonomy in Oceania.

Notwithstanding the invidious implications of Reinhold Forster's speculative racial history and chromatic differentiation of Pacific Islanders, his term race was evidently interchangeable with variety, tribe, and nation. A Lutheran pastor, he was committed on scriptural grounds to the conventional position '*that all mankind, though ever so much varied*' is '*of one species*' and '*descended from one couple*'; he did not doubt that all varieties were 'only accidental'; and, like Brosses, he allowed a universal human potential to 'progress' towards 'civilization' or 'degenerate' towards 'animality'.[24] Moreover, his flexible rankings of particular groups of Islanders were contingent on perceived indigenous behaviour and appearance rather than predetermined by biology.[25] Yet as a naturalist, Forster sought to bolster scripture with science by explaining the 'evident difference' between the 'two great tribes' he had seen. Convinced that 'climate alone' could not produce 'any material alteration' in man except over the very long run, he hypothesized that they must be 'descended from two different races of men' and thus were products of 'a different round of climates, food, and customs'. In his narrative, Georg Forster professed agnosticism as to the 'general and powerful influence of climates' on human variation, thereby anticipating his subsequent heterodoxy on the question of human specific unity.[26]

A decade later, in an article on *Menschenrassen*, 'human races', Georg Forster (1786:64-6) dichotomized the South Sea Islanders in far harsher terms — 'these two so conspicuously different peoples', the one 'beautiful' and 'light brown', the other 'ugly blacks'. In this essay and another of similar date extolling Cook as discoverer (1985b), Forster invoked the inductive authority of his experience as global circumnavigator to lambast the teleological reasoning, deductive logic, and taxonomic terminology of his fellow-German, the philosopher Immanuel Kant (1724-1804), who had theorized human *Racen*, 'races', as permanent, hereditary divisions of a single human species with common ancestry.[27] A fervent advocate for the 'clear-sighted and reliable empiricist' over the 'biased systematizer', Forster rejected both taxonomy and historical speculation on the 'inexplicable' question of human origins, including Kant's presumption of original unity, arguing instead for 'the most subtle nuances' within holistic, immensely complex observable nature.[28] The term *Rasse*, he argued, was 'thus far undetermined' but was 'synonymous' with *Varietät*, 'variety', which was 'changeable' and 'accidental'. Voyagers only applied *Rasse* to South Sea Islanders when they were 'uncomfortable' with *Varietät* so that *Rasse* should only imply a 'crowd' of people of 'idiosyncratic character and unknown ancestry', such as the *Papuaner*, 'Papuans', and the 'black islanders of the Southern Seas incidentally related to them'. To this point, Forster's explication of *Rasse* was consistent with ambiguous eighteenth-century usages: in its gesture to Buffon's 'extended sense'; and in its echo of Reinhold Forster's equation of 'races or varieties' and conviction that 'all varieties are only accidental'.[29]

Notwithstanding his empirical credentials and fundamental disagreement with Kant, Forster was no less enmeshed in Eurocentric logic, morality, and aesthetics than the armchair philosopher. The anthropological reflections of both men attest to a shared late Enlightenment faith in progress, reason, and the 'pre-eminence of our civilized society', though both condemned its excesses.[30] Kant took for granted the 'greater perfectibility' of the white race and argued that a *Volk*, 'people', who were content to be static — such as the Pacific Islanders described by Forster — must be held back by a 'natural predisposition' and were superfluous to general human advance: 'the world would lose nothing, if Tahiti goes under'.[31] Forster was more equivocal, less consistent, but equally ethnocentric. On the one hand, he allowed a common human capacity for progress: 'the New Hollanders' (whom he had not seen) were the 'most wretched' of all the 'races' which might 'claim to be called human'; yet they were on 'a path to civilization'; and he hoped that European colonial example might stimulate their evident 'skill and capability'.[32] On the other hand, the abstract figure of 'the Negro in Guinea' was his extreme negative signifier. Convinced of the reality of marked anatomical differences between Europeans and Africans, Forster queried how both could be engendered by 'the same father'; he regarded sexual relations between blacks and whites with 'aversion and abhorrence'; and he pronounced that in structure 'the Negro visibly corresponds far more closely to the monkey genus than the white man'. The New Hollanders — though reportedly 'black' of skin and 'frizzy and woolly' of hair — looked less 'unpleasant' and were presumably more human because they lacked the simian facial features of his Negro stereotype. In a major deviation from the ethos of essential human similitude professed by his father, Buffon, and Kant and at odds (at least in theory) with his own egalitarian revolutionary politics, Forster hypothesized that 'the Negro' might be 'a second human species' — a position

Kant rejected as extraneous and immoral but a portent of the commonplace polygenism of the nineteenth century.[33]

Yet Forster also acknowledged that an 'ape-like man' is 'no ape' and that whites and blacks were 'closely related'. He rationalized his insinuation of multiple human species in humanitarian terms with the quixotic hope that the strategy of 'separating the Negro from white men as an originally different stock' might encourage whites to assume their paternal duties towards blacks and develop in them 'the sacred spark of reason'. And he reasserted the premise of human specific unity in his essay on Cook whose voyages, Forster claimed, had shown that 'human nature', though it varied with climate, was everywhere '*specifically the same*' in 'organization', 'instincts', and 'the course of its development'.[34]

Blumenbach — 'this remarkable variety'

The critical redefinition of race as a permanent inherited characteristic, the biologization of the concept, and its formal taxonomic differentiation from the categories species and variety were given coherent expression in a series of papers published between 1775 and 1788 by Kant and were concretized from the late 1790s by Blumenbach. Though a pioneer in making the conformation of the skull the key signifier of racial diversity which demanded scientific classification, Blumenbach was also sharply alert to the tension between his ethical insistence on the established doctrine of human unity and the fissive implications of taxonomy or rigid physical distinction of human groups.[35] His anthropological vocabulary was always more systematic than Buffon's but it remained versatile through the three Latin editions of *De Generis Humani Varietate Nativa*, 'On the Natural Varieties of Mankind' (1775, 1781, 1795), and only began to harden along racial lines in works published in German at the end of the century (1798, 1806).[36]

Particularly in the four decades after 1766, scientific voyaging in Oceania supplied much of the empirical material on which comparative human anatomy and the nascent science of anthropology fed.[37] This section and part of the next probe the considerable significance of representations and anatomical specimens of Oceanian people in the articulation of Blumenbach's racial thinking. The footnotes to his anthropological writings draw heavily on travel literature, especially accounts of the recent expeditions to the South Seas. In the index to the 1865 English translation of his major works (Bendyshe 1865), no traveller scores more references than do four men with strong Oceanic credentials: Joseph Banks (1743-1820), the chief naturalist on Cook's first Pacific voyage of 1768-71 and President of the Royal Society from 1778; John Hawkesworth (1715?-1773), editor of the first published narrative of Cook's first voyage; and the two Forsters. Blumenbach was an assiduous correspondent, friend, and collaborator of Banks over more than thirty years. He corresponded with both Forsters and was related by marriage to the son. Blumenbach personally set up and developed the fine Cook-Forster ethnographic collection still held in the Institut für Ethnologie at the University of Göttingen and regularly used it for illustrative purposes in his classes on natural history.[38]

It was precisely the uneven advent of novel materials from *'novus orbis australis'*, 'the new southern world', that forced Blumenbach to expand and modify his initial quadripartite classification of mankind. In the first edition of *De Generis Humani* (1775:41), he had located the second of four geographically defined varieties — comprising 'dark men, with flattened noses' — in southern Asia and the Austral lands and islands. By the second edition (1781:52), the desire to be 'more consonant with nature' saw Blumenbach identify a fifth human variety spread between the island groups immediately beyond mainland Asia, which were inhabited by 'men of a uniformly very dark colour, with broad nose, and thick hair', and 'the Pacific archipelago' which Reinhold Forster had further subdivided into 'two Tribes'. Forster's dual classification of South Sea Islanders was thus firmly inscribed in metropolitan scholarly awareness within three years of its publication. By 1793, in a letter written in English to Banks, Blumenbach naturalized Forster's 'two Tribes' as 'the two principal Races which constitute this remarkable variety in the 5th. part of the world': the '<u>black</u> race' and the '<u>brown</u> one'.[39] By 1795, he had further refined his classification of human varieties and named them 'Caucasian', 'Mongolian', 'Ethiopian', 'American', and 'Malay'. Citing Banks (via Hawkesworth) as his earliest authority, he justified the final name on the linguistic grounds that 'this variety of men' mostly spoke Malay. He did not weight the varieties equally but positioned the Malay as transitional between Caucasian and Ethiopian — between the purportedly original 'medial variety of mankind' and one of the 'two extremes' (see Figure 4, Chapter 1). Far-flung and very diverse, the Malay variety served as Blumenbach's prime illustration of 'insensible transition' within and between his pentad of varieties and supplied the final proof confirming his core argument for assigning *'all the varieties of men thus far known to one and the same* species'. In 1799, again referring specifically to the 'Malay race', he summarized his theory of the formation of human races by the 'degeneration' (meaning 'change') of a migrating 'common stock': the degree of deviation from the white 'primitive figure of the intermediate race' towards the extremes was relative to the 'stronger or longer influence of different climates and other causes' on the 'peoples' dispersed around the world. Thus, whereas the 'extreme' form of the Ethiopian race occurred 'under the burning sky of Africa', this race ran into the Malay race in the 'much milder air' of New Holland and the New Hebrides.[40]

The tension between the rival imperatives of human unity, racial diversity, and the taxonomic impulse is an undercurrent in Blumenbach's discussion of the Malay variety in his 1795 text but it is patent by 1806 in the equivalent section of the second edition of *Beyträge zur Naturgeschichte*, 'Contributions to Natural History'. In the earlier work, Blumenbach (1795:319-21) used a series of inductive shifts to distil an internal subdivision of the Malay variety from published voyage narratives. He first observed that Malay speakers themselves varied so greatly in 'beauty and other bodily attributes' that the Tahitians had been divided into 'two different stocks': one 'pale' and European-like in facial features, the other very like 'Mulattos'. He cited two authorities in footnotes: the Frenchman Louis-Antoine de Bougainville (1729-1814) who had circumnavigated the globe in 1766-69 and whose own term '*races*' Blumenbach added in parenthesis; and the Portuguese-born Spaniard Quirós who, claimed Blumenbach, had 'carefully distinguished the variety of men inhabiting the Pacific Islands' by saying that some were 'white' while comparing others to 'Mulattos' and others again to 'Ethiopians'. Thus, the second Tahitian 'stock' resembled Islanders further west in the Pacific Ocean, while the inhabitants of the New Hebrides 'gradually' approached the Papuans and New Hollanders, who themselves merged imperceptibly with the 'Ethiopian variety', so that they might 'not unfittingly' be classed with them.

In appropriating voyagers' descriptions of Oceanian people to his classificatory agenda, Blumenbach succumbed to the common historical snare of anachronism, projecting backwards on to earlier representations the seeming realism of his own reifications.[41] Bougainville's published *Voyage* — though not his shipboard journal (1977) — did note marked physical differences between two culturally uniform *races* seen in Tahiti and between Tahitians and 'black men' seen further west. Yet he, like his English translator Reinhold Forster, used race in its multivalent eighteenth-century sense.[42] Quirós reported a finely discriminated continuum of skin and hair colour and considerable local variety in people he had seen and heard about in both the eastern and western Pacific Islands. However, he did not 'compare' some to the Ethiopians, as Blumenbach thought, deceived by the mistranslation into English by the Scottish hydrographer, Alexander Dalrymple (1737-1808), of Quirós's Spanish adjective *loros*, 'dark brown', as the noun 'negroes'.[43] Quirós could not have conceived and Bougainville did not propose a systematic physical typology of Oceanic humanity. Their labels and descriptive terms, though often derogatory and anti-Negro, were conventional, comparative, or experiential rather than regionally categorical (Douglas 2006:10-13). Quirós attributed no specific geographic, racial, or moral coordinates to the human 'differences' he discerned which interested him mainly as supposed signs of the 'vicinity of better governed people' and the occurrence of 'great commerce and communication' — as they would also interest the mid-eighteenth-century compilers of collections of South Sea voyage texts, Brosses and Dalrymple.[44]

However a priori, the sequential logic enunciated in 1795 shows the morphological criteria of '*analogy* and resemblance' — Blumenbach's terms — at work in his taxonomic practice.[45] Thus far, his occasional, ambiguous usage of the term race and its synonyms tribe, variety, and stock signal the relative lexical insignificance of race, its instability, and its ongoing contemporary genealogical connotations. But in the new edition of *Beyträge zur Naturgeschichte* revised in the light of Kant's biological conception of races (1806:72), Blumenbach reconfigured 'the black Papus ['Papuans'] at New Holland, etc.' as a *Volk* whose 'more or less striking formation' distinguished them from the 'brown' Pacific Islanders so that they had become a 'separate' *Unterarten*, 'subspecies', of the Malay *Rasse*. There is no such passage in the first edition of this work (1790:83). The reformulation, invoking organic difference more than analogy and nuance, brought Blumenbach nearer to the position recently put by the French geographers Edme Mentelle (1730-1815) and Conrad Malte-Brun (1775-1826) who had pioneered the explicit racial division of Pacific Islanders into copper-coloured 'Polynesians' and black '*Oceanic Negroes*'. In the process, they challenged Blumenbach's placement of the New Hollanders within the 'Malay race' on the grounds that he had himself acknowledged their characteristic physical similarity to the 'Ethiopian or African race': his 'system', they sneered, was thus undermined by his own data.[46] The advent of racial taxonomy with respect to Oceania and the dilution (by Blumenbach) or shelving (by Mentelle and Malte-Brun) of the concept of 'insensible transition' between varieties are textual markers of a hardening in prevailing discourses on human differences and the biologization of the vocabulary available for their description and classification.

Collecting races

Late eighteenth-century developments in comparative osteology anticipated the growing significance attached to the conformation of the skull by an embryonic anthropology, initially for its own sake (as with Blumenbach) and before long as signifier of the size of the brain (as with Cuvier). Cuvier (1817b:270, 273) neatly encapsulated the diagnostic transition from aesthetics to anatomy in association with a shift in the terminology of human difference: the head was 'the most sure means of distinction' between races because it had been 'better studied' and was 'the basis on which we have always classed nations'; 'today', though, 'we distinguish the races by the skeleton of the head'. The transitional phase is manifest in an official *Mémoire* addressed by the French Académie des Sciences in 1785 to the savants about to embark with La Pérouse on his voyage round the world. The memoir counsels voyagers to extend the 'comparison' of diverse human varieties — a Buffonian innovation[47] — beyond the usual limits of the 'external characters' of colour, stature, and form and instead undertake 'anatomical researches' into 'internal' variations in the 'form of the bones of the head'. To this end, they should try to obtain the head and hyoid bones of a representative corpse from every 'nation' which obviously differed in facial or head shape from those of the 'temperate countries of Europe' — this last phrase alluded to the climatic theory of collective human difference also primarily associated with Buffon.[48]

Blumenbach (1795:198) insisted on the importance of 'careful anatomical investigation of genuine skulls of different nations' in the study of human variety because the skull had structural primacy as 'the firm and stable foundation of the head'. A single specimen (1806:60, 70) — 'my beautiful head of a young Georgian female' (see Figure 4, Chapter 1) — determined his highly ethnocentric verdict on 'the really most beautiful form of skull' and became his metonym for the 'Caucasian race' who, 'according to the European conception of beauty', were the 'most cultivated of men'. It is clear from his correspondence with Banks that the empirical force of particular skulls and portraits was subordinate to his presumptions about what was 'truly national & characteristical'.[49] Blumenbach, though, never jettisoned his early attribution of 'almost all' the cranial diversity in 'different peoples' to their 'mode of life' and to 'art'.[50]

For exotic skulls and portraits, Blumenbach (1795:v-xlii) owed a major debt to Banks whom he acknowledged fulsomely in the third edition of *De Generis Humani*. A collection of Blumenbach's correspondence with Banks held at the British Library begins with a letter written in French in 1787 outlining Blumenbach's longterm project 'to assemble a collection of skulls of the diverse varieties of the human species' and asking for help in obtaining 'one of these crania of your South Sea islanders'; or 'at least a plaster copy'; 'or a drawing'; 'or just a silhouette'. Banks could not currently oblige with an actual skull but replied that had 'exhorted the Captain & will do the surgeon' of HMS *Bounty*, which was bound for Tahiti, 'to collect cranie for me wherever he touches'. Blumenbach subsequently lamented the 'unhappy fate' of the *Bounty* as a 'loss' for his own 'particular interest' as well as 'for humanity itself'. In 1793 and 1794, Banks's 'generousity' enabled Blumenbach to complete two full sets each of 'Five very choice examples of the principal varieties of mankind' by adding two long-promised 'sculls of both the two principal Races' of the South Seas to an earlier gift of a 'pretious Caribean skull', an exemplar of Blumenbach's American variety (see Figure 4, Chapter 1). The two new skulls were those of an Aboriginal man from New Holland and of a Tahitian woman procured by William Bligh (1754-1817) on his second voyage to Tahiti in search of breadfruit. The forthcoming 'new very much improved edition' of *De Generis Humani* would, Blumenbach told Banks, 'receive his most interesting ornament by a description of this exceeding rare Tahitian cranium'. A further Aboriginal skull was forthcoming from Banks in 1799.[51]

Cuvier reworked the assumption of savants such as Blumenbach that the major purpose of cranial structure was to provide the solid base for surface facial appearance. He upheld the primacy of the 'bony head' as the 'first base' in comparative anatomy, and by extension the science of race, because it signified the size of the brain and hence the degree of 'intelligence': 'in all mammals, the brain is moulded in the cavity of the skull, which it fills exactly; so that knowledge of the bony part tells us at least about the external form of the brain'; 'intelligence, insofar as it can be observed, is in constant proportion to the relative size of the brain'.[52]

In 1800, on behalf of the Institut impérial, Cuvier composed an 'Instructive Note' (1978) for impending voyagers, notably the naturalists about to depart for Australian waters with Baudin, and particularly Péron, a medical student and self-styled 'anthropologist' appointed to the expedition at Cuvier's request as zoologist 'specially charged' with comparative anatomy.[53] The anatomical agenda of the 'Note' resembles that of the Académie's *Mémoire* of 1785 but its rationale, tone, and terminology are significantly altered. Cuvier took for granted the anatomical 'differences that characterize the races of the human species' and signalled his emerging racial theory that would attribute the 'moral and intellectual faculties' of entire races to systematic cranial variation. He identified three 'great races of the old continent' — 'caucasic' ('white'), 'mongolic' ('yellow'), and 'ethiopic' ('negro') — and allowed the possibility of three others: one in the polar regions ('brown'), one in the Americas ('red'), and one in the South Sea Islands and New Holland, which 'varies from yellow to black'. The remainder of the text outlines a practical program for the voyage anthropologist whose main duty was to fill the gaps in knowledge about humanity, especially of the 'Papous' of New Guinea, 'who have long been regarded as Negroes', and the inhabitants of most of New Holland, the South Sea Islands, and the Strait of Magellan. 'Anatomical specimens', principally of the 'bony head', were the key to establishing the 'physical and moral' characters of each race. They must be systematically assembled in conjunction with 'numerous true portraits' and 'thoughtful, careful observations made on the spot' — unlike the purportedly unreliable descriptions and ethnocentric drawings made by previous voyagers. In practice, the great difficulty of procuring skulls would increase the importance of 'rigorous' portraits made with 'geometric precision'. Cuvier thereupon outlined strict standards for empirical racial portraiture and collecting that a generation of French voyage artists and naturalists in Oceania would endeavour to follow.

In the event, the artists on Baudin's voyage of 1800-04, Nicolas-Martin Petit (1777-1804) and Charles-Alexandre Lesueur (1778-1846), produced a wonderful series of portraits and ethnographic drawings of indigenous people in Timor, Van Diemen's Land, New Holland, and the Cape of Good Hope — the 'most exact of this genre so far known', claimed Péron.[54] However, the overall anthropological legacy of the voyage was mixed, notwithstanding Cuvier's lavish official praise for Péron's research on the 'various peoples' encountered (Cuvier et al. 1806). The experience of 'difficult and perilous' encounters with 'fierce men' in Van Diemen's Land led Péron, author of most of the official voyage narrative, to endorse the bleak opinion that 'men of nature' whose character was 'not yet softened' by civilization were 'wicked' and could not be 'mistrusted' too much.[55] He had embarked on his travels professing a qualified primitivist idealism for the 'robust majesty of natural man'; but believing, with Cuvier, that 'moral sensibility' depended largely on 'physical organization'; and hypothesizing that physical and moral 'perfection' were inversely related.[56] During the voyage, he conducted a series of experiments to test the relative physical strength of different races using a dynamometer recently developed by Edme Regnier to compare the strength of various men and draught animals (Figure 6). In Péron's narrative, the very dubious results of these tests become 'precious' proof of a 'gradation of the social state'. The 'very remarkable weakness' of the 'savages' of Van Diemen's Land consigned them to the 'last degree'. Those of New Holland, apparently not much stronger and 'hardly more civilized', ranked only slightly higher. The next three 'degrees' were assigned in principle to the New Guineans, the New Zealanders, and the Pacific Islanders whom Péron had not seen or tested. He allotted the sixth 'rung' to the 'inhabitants' of Timor and the Moluccas who, despite their 'fairly advanced state of civilization', were 'much weaker' than the English and the French and (presumably) ranked much lower.[57]

Experience and experiment thus conjoined to qualify Péron's pre-voyage abstract enthusiasm for natural man and make him a passionate advocate for the physical, as well as the moral superiority of the civilized. To this end, his narrative causally links 'physical constitution' with 'social organization' or its supposed 'absence': the alleged physical 'weakness' and 'structural flaw' (excessively thin extremities) of the inhabitants of Van Diemen's Land resulted from the deficient diet and life-style of 'the savage state' itself; an improved 'social state' would promote 'abundance' and transform them physically.[58] At this point, Péron's ideological agenda required a social explanation and he merely toyed with the idea that the structural flaw might be inherent — the result of idiosyncratic 'physical organization'.[59] This constraint vanished later in the text when he made a zoological argument for 'the absolute difference of the races' in Van Diemen's Land and New Holland and added a footnote promising subsequent proof that the former 'differ *essentially* from all other known peoples'.[60] The phrase arguably implies discrete autochthonous origin, a radical but by no means unthinkable concept for the time given recent publication of the polygenist treatises of the English surgeon and anatomist Charles White (1728-1813) and the French military physician Julien-Joseph Virey (1775-1846).[61] Péron went on to challenge climatic explanations for human variation: the darker skin colour and 'frizzy' rather than 'straight' hair of the Van Diemen's Landers — 'singular anomalies' given the much colder conditions in which they lived — proved 'the imperfection of our systems on the communications of peoples, their transmigrations, and the influence of climate on man'.[62]

Figure 6: Anon., 'Développement du dynamomètre de Cit[en]. Regnier'.[63]

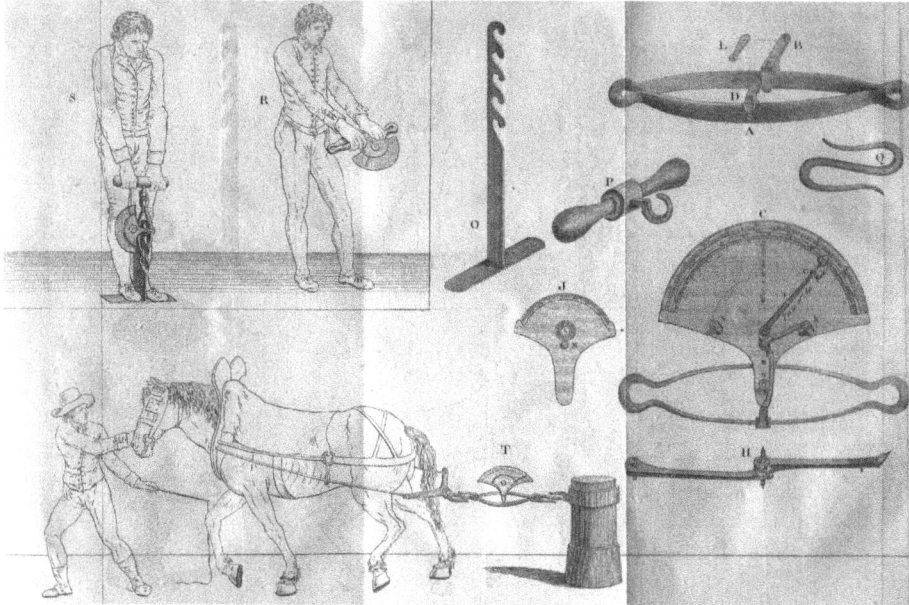

Engraving. Photograph B. Douglas.

Péron died young with two projected racial studies unrealized: a 'particular history of the peoples of Van Diemen's Land' and a comparative philosophical history of the 'relationship of the physical and the moral' in the various human races.[64] His voyage narrative nonetheless not only provided empirical sustenance for increasingly negative attitudes towards the indigenous people of Van Diemen's Land and New Holland, both in the metropoles and within the Australian colonies,[65] but put Péron along with Cuvier in the theoretical vanguard of biological, anthropometric, and racialist tendencies in the science of man. Indeed, modern historians see Péron as a forerunner of the 'medicalized' physical anthropology dominant in France in the second half of the nineteenth century.[66]

Cuvier wrote relatively little on man but was a central figure in the emerging discipline of anthropology over more than three decades, not least because, as a perpetual secretary in the Institut de France, he acted as selector, instructor, and zoological commentator in relation to the naturalists on scientific voyages, notably those to Oceania. As with Baudin's expedition, traces of his patronage are scattered through the chain of official instructions and commentaries and echoed in the writings of the naturalists on the Restoration voyages of Freycinet, Duperrey, and Dumont d'Urville.[67] All professed allegiance to the principles and 'general order' of the taxonomic system developed in Cuvier's 'classic' work on comparative anatomy, *Le règne animal*, 'The Animal Kingdom' (1817a); all took as given his claim for the primacy of physical organization; all endorsed his tripartite classification of 'white', 'yellow', and 'negro' races — 'the most simple', according to Garnot, 'which separates the human species into three great divisions with strongly contrasting characteristics'.[68] Cuvier's personal dividend from Oceanic voyaging was privileged access to a wealth of antipodean zoological specimens which helped him ground his science of comparative anatomy and cement his reputation as the pre-eminent taxonomist of his generation.[69] He assured Quoy that he would content himself with 'your leftovers' and 'religiously conserve' the naturalist's manuscripts and drawings for Quoy to publish himself. However, Quoy later commented privately that Cuvier was not always scrupulous about giving voyagers credit for their discoveries.[70]

Towards autochthony

From the first Portuguese and Spanish contacts with the Moluccas, the Philippines, and New Guinea in the early sixteenth century, diversity was a recurrent theme in descriptions of Oceanian people. By the late eighteenth century, the kaleidoscope of skin and hair colour seen in the Pacific Islands by Quirós had settled into the paradox of Forster's 'two great varieties'. On the one hand, it was recognized that cognate language communities — now called Austronesian — were scattered across the vast area from Madagascar to the Malay Archipelago and the furthest Pacific Islands. The Dutch scholar Adriaan Reelant (1676-1718) had discerned this striking linguistic affinity early in the century by comparing published wordlists; Banks established it empirically; the East India Company employee and orientalist philologist William Marsden (1754-1836) confirmed it; and Reinhold Forster joined language to physical form as taxonomic criteria, noting 'a very remarkable similarity' between words spoken by the 'fair tribe' of South Sea Islanders and 'some' Malays. On the other hand, the groups comprising his 'blacker' variety supposedly spoke 'wholly different', mutually unrelated languages despite physical and behavioural commonalities.[71] The New Hollanders, whom Forster had not seen, were reportedly 'totally different' in appearance, 'customs', and language from both varieties of South Sea Islanders though Georg Forster later allowed that physical and moral parallels between the New Hollanders and nearby 'black' Islanders might suggest 'a certain relationship' or even a common origin, despite very different languages and life styles.[72]

For several decades, Reinhold Forster's classification of South Sea Islanders, or one resembling it, was rehearsed in much the same humanist spirit by voyagers and savants alike.[73] Signs of significant divergence from this relatively generous, optimistic ethos emerged around the turn of the century as certain naturalists and geographers redeployed Forster's categories to serve altered agendas. In a drastic departure from orthodoxy, Virey (1800, I:135-8) drew on travellers' narratives to classify the 'human genus' into five or six 'primordial races' split between two 'distinct species'. His first species included the 'reddish-brown Malay tribes' who were widely dispersed but analogous in 'form, colour, customs, and mother tongue'. The 'Negro or Ethiopian' comprised a second species distributed between two stocks: one, 'more or less black', peopled much of Africa, the 'land of the Papous', and New Guinea; the second, 'blackish olive' in colour, encompassed the 'Hottentots' and the inhabitants of New Holland, New Caledonia, and the New Hebrides whom Virey characterized venomously as 'excessively stupid and brutish' with a 'vile' face, 'elongated like an ape's muzzle', and a 'squashed nose'. The major differences dividing the human genus, he asserted (1800, I:166, 415-19), were 'radical', 'indelible', and 'endemic' to physical organization which was itself largely immune to the 'superficial' influence of climate and other external conditions.

The longstanding concern of geographers to demarcate and denominate the 'parts' and the 'great natural divisions' of the physical globe had usually encompassed current knowledge and speculation about its human inhabitants, as with Brosses. However, later authors not only proposed new geographic nomenclatures for the fifth part of the world but evinced a novel preoccupation to map and classify human types, entangled with emerging ideas of race as innate and permanent.[74] A key figure in this process was Malte-Brun who dismantled Brosses's geography and categorized the region's inhabitants into races: 'black' Oceanic Negroes and 'tanned' or 'copper-coloured' Polynesians. Replacing *Terres australes* with *Océanique*, 'Oceanica', he and Mentelle jettisoned *Australasie* and contracted *Polynésie* to label '*two* Polynesias', separated 'naturally' by the equator and soon to be called Micronesia and Polynesia. Noncommittal about the orthodox '*system* of a common human origin' and unwilling to accept Reinhold Forster's argument that the South Sea Islands must have been populated from the west, in the teeth of prevailing winds and currents, they hypothesized that the 'race called *Malay*' might be 'native' to the Pacific Ocean.[75] A few years later, Malte-Brun formally partitioned *Océanique* into western (Malay Archipelago), eastern (Polynesia), and central segments occupied by races emergent from two 'very distinct' physical and linguistic stocks: the Malays 'or yellow Oceanians' and the Oceanic Negroes. The central region, comprising New Holland, Van Diemen's Land, New Guinea, and the large archipelagoes immediately to the east, contained the 'most substantial remnants' of the Oceanic Negro race. They were, he suggested, echoing his earlier intimation of an independent islands origin for the Malays, probably 'originary to this part of the world'. Indeed, the differences between the Van Diemen's Landers, the New Caledonians and the *Papous* were such that he was 'uncertain' whether they were descendants of 'a common stock' or whether each race had originated *in situ*.[76] As with Péron's ruminations on the 'essential' difference of the inhabitants of Van Diemen's Land from 'all other known peoples', such insinuations of autochthony signalled the growing conceivability of the hitherto heterodox idea that the diversity of human races was fundamental, innate, and possibly original rather than an ambiguous product of interbreeding or the degeneration of a single species triggered by migration to new environments.

Naval naturalists and racial taxonomy in Oceania

Péron's proposed socio-physical hierarchy was explicitly racial but the relatively limited geographical span of his voyage made regional racial classification largely irrelevant to his narrative. Indeed — except with respect to New Holland and Van Diemen's Land where Europeans were ensconced after 1788 and 1803, respectively, and Tahiti where missionaries settled in 1797 — the knowledge base readily available for such an enterprise did not grow significantly between Cook's last voyage and the resumption of scientific voyaging by France in 1817 after the long hiatus of Empire and war. Cuvier's (1817a, I:94-100) brief catalogue of the 'varieties of the human species', published that year, was both exiguous and indecisive about the 'handsome' Malays, who included the South Sea Islanders, and the 'frizzy-haired', 'black', 'negroid', 'extremely barbarous' *Papous*. He complained of insufficient information to identify either with one of his three great races but thought the *Papous* might be 'negroes who had long ago strayed across the Indian Ocean'.

Péron's successors as naturalists on the French Restoration voyages were all serving naval officers, in keeping with a new policy instituted from 1817 to circumvent the conflicts with civilian scientific personnel that had plagued Baudin's voyage. Henceforth, only naval medical officers instructed in natural history would be formally appointed as naturalists on scientific voyages though other officers also contributed, most notably Dumont d'Urville.[77] Several turned their hand to regional taxonomy of the human populations they had encountered, observed, and studied. The shifts and ambiguities in voyage naturalists' representations and classifications of indigenous Oceanian people after 1817 provide another index of congealing racial presumptions in the science of man. However, the influx of new empirical knowledge only complicated the difficulties of trying to match received theoretical systems with fleeting observations of baffling human variation or ambiguous affinities and the ambivalent experience of unpredictable local behaviour.

The first of the new breed of professional surgeon-naturalists were Quoy and Gaimard who served with Freycinet on the *Uranie* in 1817-20.[78] They co-produced the official *Zoologie* volume and plates of the voyage (1824a, 1824b), though Quoy seems to have drafted much of the text. Only eleven of 712 pages and two of 96 plates were devoted to 'Man', in the shape of a brief scientific paper on the 'physical constitution of the Papous'.[79] The authors' primary concern for the skull as 'the bony envelope' for the organs of intelligence recalls Cuvier's earlier instructions to Péron. Though descriptive rather than taxonomic, the paper reveals the uneasy liaison of an a priori racial system and recalcitrant facts. *Papou* was a vexed and ambiguous category.[80] From the early sixteenth century, Portuguese and Spaniards had extended the local toponym *Papua* to refer to the 'black' inhabitants of the 'Papuan Islands' and the nearby New Guinea mainland (now in Indonesia); Blumenbach and Cuvier 'generalized' *Papus/Papous* to denominate 'black' Oceanian people collectively; so did Freycinet, Quoy and Gaimard's commander.[81] But the naturalists themselves limited *Papou* to certain people they had seen in Waigeo and neighbouring islands and sharpened the term's racial import by differentiating them from the similarly coloured 'race' inhabiting New Guinea itself, said to be 'true Negroes'. The *Papous* posed a racial conundrum for Quoy and Gaimard who could not work out their 'distinctive characters'. They reasoned that racial 'mixing' in a dense cluster of islands must have produced such a 'multitude of nuances' that it was hard to determine the components: in physiognomy and hair, the *Papous* seemed 'to occupy the middle ground' between Malays and Negroes; their skull form was close to the Malays; and their facial angle corresponded to that of Europeans.[82]

Two engraved plates of skulls of *Papous* plundered from indigenous graves illustrate Quoy and Gaimard's text (Figure 7). They had submitted them 'for examination' to the German physiologist Franz Joseph Gall (1758-1828), founder of the science of the cerebral localization of mental faculties known as phrenology. Gall's influence on Quoy and Gaimard's paper clearly outstripped that of their patron Cuvier, a professional enemy of Gall, and drew a sceptical response from the editors of the *Nouvelles annales des voyages* — one of whom was Malte-Brun — which published the earliest version of the paper in 1823.[83] The authors' confident summary of the 'moral and intellectual faculties' of the *Papous* shows how readily phrenological terminology could slide into conventional racial essentialism (1824c:9-11): they had innate 'dispositions to theft'; a 'destructive instinct' so strong as to produce a 'penchant for murder' and the presumption of cannibalism; and a 'tendency to superstition'. Yet the paper's optimistic conclusion — entirely missing from the first published version — is a paradoxical reminder that phrenology could offer a radical technology for personal and racial improvement:[84] the *Papous* were 'wrongly considered by clever naturalists to be close to the Apes';[85] they were 'capable of education'; and they only needed 'to exercise and develop their intellectual faculties in order to hold a distinguished rank among the numerous varieties of the human species'.

Figure 7: Jean Louis Denis Coutant after Antoine Chazal, 'Crânes de Papous'.[86]

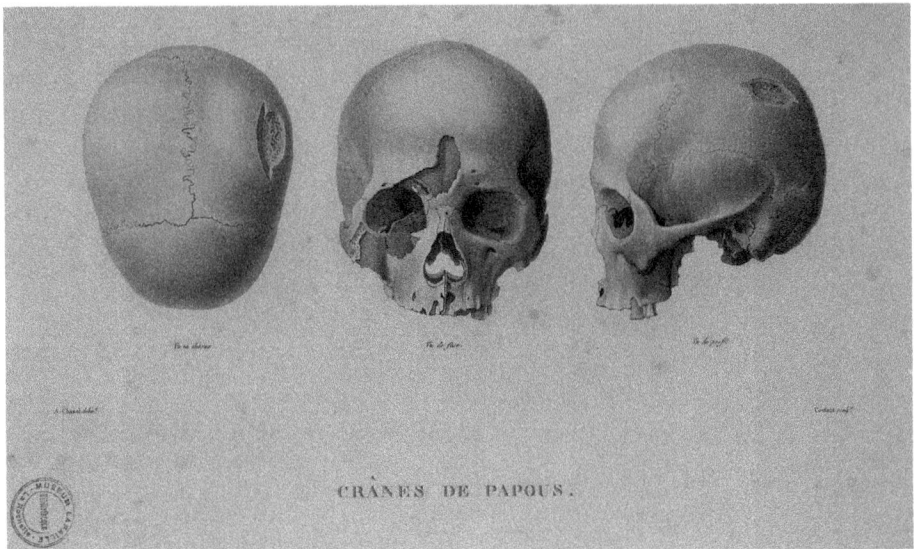

CRÂNES DE PAPOUS.

Engraving. Photograph B. Douglas.

The racial taxonomy of Oceania gained new momentum from the early 1820s when the recently formed Société de Géographie in Paris offered one of its annual prizes for a memoir on the 'differences and similarities' between the 'various peoples' of the region. Garnot, Lesson, and Dumont d'Urville, who had ranged widely across Oceania with Duperrey on the voyage of the *Coquille* (1822-25),[87] all tackled the theme following their return to France but it seems that no entry was actually considered and the prize eventually lapsed in 1830 without award.[88] These works were self-consciously enunciated in the discourse of an emerging professional science of race by men whose primary vocation was medical, or naval, or both, but who aspired to convert their empirical authority into scientific credibility by reading papers to scientific societies and publishing in their journals (Staum 2003). Like Malte-Brun and following Cuvier, all three men used the term *race* in a modernist biological sense. Their racial pronouncements were at best patronizing, partial, and essentialist and at worst scurrilous. The physicalism and racialism of their scientific agenda are patent in Lesson's (1826:110) published advice to his younger brother — about to sail for Oceania as Dumont d'Urville's assistant surgeon — to try to advance Cuvier's 'wise works in comparative anatomy' by procuring indigenous skeletons: their 'very characteristic facial type' would enable anatomists to draw 'new conclusions from skeletal structure in order to throw light on the races'.

Garnot's first effort (1826-30) was a global classification of 'the human races' along 'simple' Cuvierian lines. In the process, he differentiated an 'Oceanic branch' of the 'yellow race', occupying most of the South Sea Islands, from a generalized

Papou branch of the 'black race' located in the western Pacific Islands, New Guinea, Van Diemen's Land, and New Holland. The 'Oceanians' were typified in the 'well-built' Tahitians whose facial angle was 'as open as that of the Europeans'; the *Papous* were 'in a way a hybrid variety' characterized by a much more oblique facial angle than Tahitians; those inhabiting New Holland had an even narrower facial angle and were 'without doubt the most hideous peoples known'.[89] An expanded version of the memoir published in a dictionary of natural history concludes with six engraved plates, four of which deploy images of Oceanian people to typify the 'Mongolic' and 'Ethiopic' races.[90] In a companion piece on the 'Negro', focussing on 'the Negro of New Holland', Garnot (1837:628-30) abandoned the term *Papou* and reconstituted the 'black race' of Oceania as a 'frightful'-looking branch of the 'Negro race'. A 'very different' physical organization 'from ours' meant that Negroes in general were 'inferior' to the 'yellow and white races' while some were 'uncivilizable' — notably in New South Wales where their organization was 'closest to the Baboons'.

The pharmacist Lesson, who became chief surgeon when Garnot was forced by illness to quit the voyage at Port Jackson, published a far more elaborate regional racial classification.[91] In contrast to Garnot's broad brush, Lesson proposed a convoluted schema that lauded the 'Hindu-Caucasic' Oceanians (modern Polynesians) as 'superior' to all other South Sea Islanders in 'beauty' and bodily conformation and split the 'black race' into two branches distributed between four varieties: the *Papouas* or modern Melanesians; the 'Tasmanians' of Van Diemen's Land; the *Endamênes* of the interior of New Guinea and some large Malay islands; and, at the base of the hierarchy, the 'Australians' of New Holland. He represented all 'these negroes' as intellectually and morally deficient but the 'austral Negroes' of New Holland — whom he had only seen demoralized by disease, expropriation, and alcohol in colonized areas around Port Jackson — as sunk in especially 'profound ignorance, great misery, and a sort of moral brutalization'.[92]

In Lesson's work, as in Quoy and Gaimard's, the anomalous appearance and conformation of certain so-called *Papous* confounded a presumptive racial system and induced tortuous logic and muddled rhetoric. In his contemporary shipboard journal, Lesson confidently assigned 'the natives' of Buka, north of Bougainville, to the 'race of the *Papous*' on the basis of the 'characteristic' small facial features and bouffant hairstyles of six men fleetingly encountered at sea (Figure 8). In nearby New Ireland, where the vessel anchored for ten days, he described meeting a 'negro race' with 'woolly' hair worn in braids who closely resembled the Africans of Guinea but 'differ much' from their *Papou* 'neighbours' in Buka (Figure 9).[93] He restated the case for radical difference in a letter sent from Port Jackson to the editor of an official publication (1825:326): the New Irelanders were of 'negro race' and in physical constitution 'quite opposite' to the *Papous*.

Figure 8: Jules-Louis Le Jeune, 'Papou de L'Ile ~~Bougainville~~ Bouca' [1823].[94]

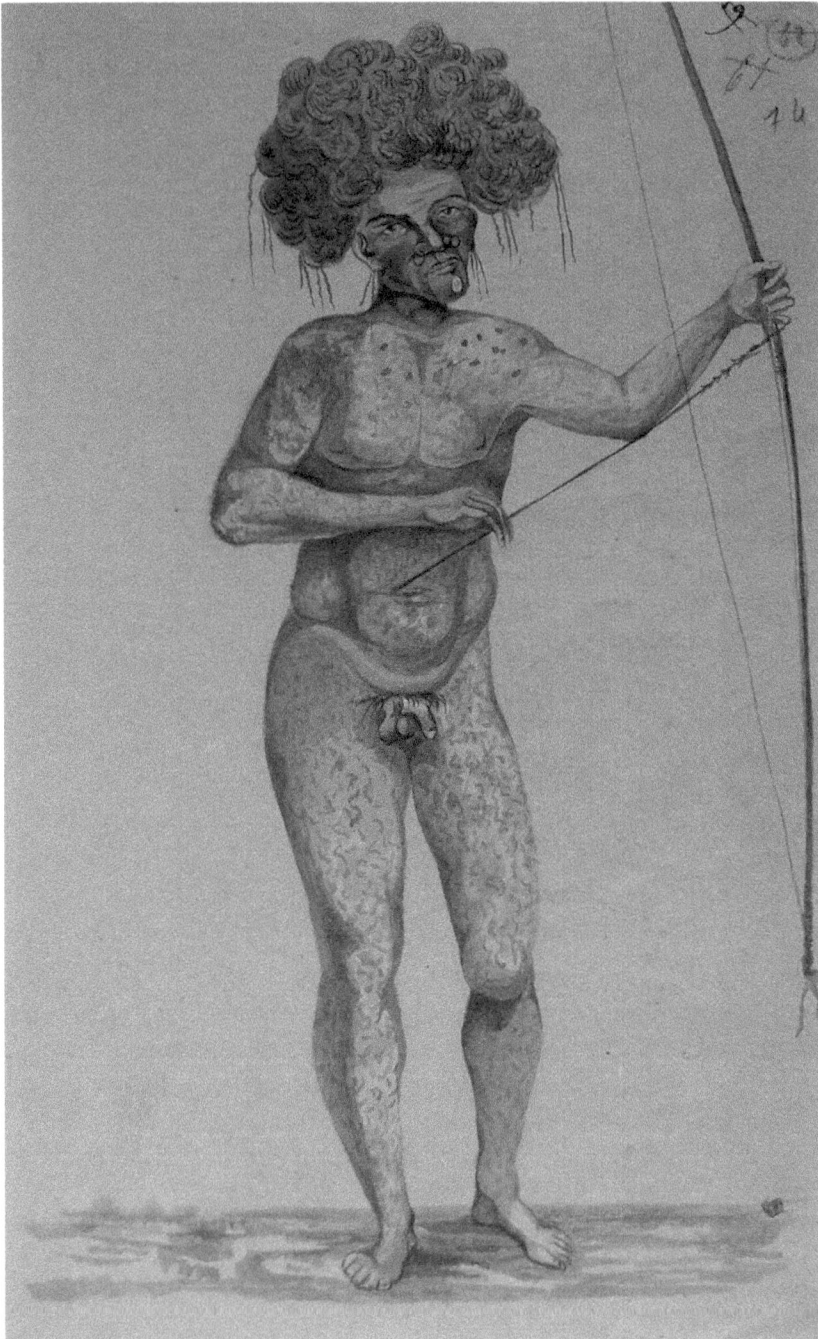

Pen and wash drawing. SH 356. Vincennes, France: Service historique de la Défense, département Marine.
Photograph B. Douglas.

Figure 9: Jules-Louis Le Jeune, 'n^{elle} Irlande' [1823].[95]

Pen and wash drawing. SH 356. Vincennes, France: Service historique de la Défense, département Marine. Photograph B. Douglas.

Yet Lesson evidently thought better of his initial impression since, in his journal, the phrase 'differ *much*' is crossed out and replaced with 'differ *little*'.[96] The confusion is compounded in his formal racial taxonomy by shifts between narrow and more generalized meanings of the term *Papous/Papouas* (1829:200-7): between Quoy and Gaimard's specialized sense of 'Negro-Malay' hybrids living on the 'frontiers' of the Malay islands and along the northwest coast of New Guinea; and a broader signification to designate 'negroes' inhabiting the New Guinea littoral and the island groups as far east as Fiji — that is, the modern Island Melanesians. Eventually, in a belatedly published narrative of the voyage (1839, II:13, 35, 56), Lesson conflated the once 'opposite' Bukans and New Irelanders as 'Papouas', 'negroes', or 'Papoua negroes'. Yet this usage was less inclusive than Cuvier's and Garnot's blanket labelling of all 'black' Oceanians as *Papous* since Lesson (1829:200-25) consistently differentiated *Papouas* from the 'negro' *Alfourous* or *Endamênes* supposedly 'aboriginal' to inland New Guinea and to New Holland.

Dumont d'Urville's journal (1822-5) of his voyage as first lieutenant of the *Coquille* remains unpublished but in the year before he left again for Oceania in 1826, in command of the *Astrolabe*, he wrote an unfinished manuscript ([1826]) addressing the essay prize questions. In the process, he split the inhabitants of Oceania into 'three great divisions which seem the most natural': first, 'Australians', 'Blacks', or 'Melanians' ('from the dark colour of their skin');[97] second, 'peoples of Tonga', the 'true Polynesians', 'adherents of taboo'; and third, 'Carolines'. The 'Malay race properly speaking' at this stage remained outside the classification but the manuscript anticipated in all but names Dumont d'Urville's classic tripartition of Pacific Islanders into Melanesians, Polynesians, and Micronesians.

Quoy and Gaimard served as naturalists on Dumont d'Urville's expedition which crisscrossed western Oceania in 1826-29 and they again co-produced the *Zoologie* section (1830-4) of the official voyage publication.[98] Quoy began this work with a short treatise locating man in Oceania 'in his zoological relationships' as first among mammals.[99] Explicitly taxonomic, he lauded Forster's 'natural' divisions of Oceanian people but reconfigured them as 'two pronounced types', 'the *black* race and the *yellow* race'. For Quoy, as for Cuvier and most contemporary naturalists, the primary races were ontologically real and 'very distinct': the differences between them were innate and based in physical organization whereas the differences between the varieties of those races were 'only nuances' produced by external 'modifiers' such as climate, soil, and 'habits'. Since the 'two principal types' of Oceanian people were unmistakable, the anthropological task of the anatomically trained naturalist was to 'grasp the varieties'.[100] Accordingly, Quoy devoted the bulk of his chapter 'On Man' to differentiating each race into the varieties known personally to him and

Gaimard.[101] This empirical section incorporates long extracts from Quoy's shipboard journal, producing marked tension in the text between his deductive system and circumstantial anecdotes: between a reductive, purportedly objective, but fundamentally racialized theoretical schema and contingent details about the haphazard, idiosyncratic behaviour and appearance of actual human beings.[102]

Though mainly concerned to catalogue the 'physical characters' distinguishing the admired 'yellow race' (the future Polynesians and Micronesians) from the vilified 'blacks' (the future Melanesians and Australians), Quoy discerned 'no less fundamental distinctions' in 'morals' and 'habits'. He dichotomized responses to Europeans in what would become enduring racial stereotypes: the yellow race welcomed voyagers with trade and women whereas the blacks were isolated, warlike, suspicious, and 'excessively jealous of their women'. These 'defining characters' ensured that one race, with European help, would take 'great strides towards civilization' while the other, 'refusing all contact', would 'stagnate'.[103] In manuscript notes for his chapter (n.d.a), Quoy drew an explicit, Cuvierian causal linkage between the physical and the moral by attributing intellect and morality to biology: the 'progress' of the 'negro race', he maintained, was thwarted by an 'obstacle in its organization' which ensured its 'inferiority' and could only be overcome by racial crossing. This grim prognosis is at odds with the catholic optimism of Quoy and Gaimard's earlier text (1824c:2, 11) which allows the *Papous* the capacity for intellectual advance; attributes the 'miserable' condition of people seen at Shark Bay in western New Holland to 'a soil of the most frightful poverty' which had stymied their 'development and perfection'; and asserts their common humanity, since their 'state' was 'still far' from brutish. In dramatic contrast, Quoy's later chapter represents the New Hollanders as barely human — 'a very distinct and one of the most degraded' varieties of the black race — and as possibly a separate species.[104] This shift in tone and outlook between the 1824 and 1830 texts attests both to a hardening in learned European opinion on human differences in the interval between the voyages and to the authors' more intense and fraught experience of indigenous behaviour on the second.

In 1832, Quoy's commander Dumont d'Urville published a seminal paper synthesizing a quadripartite regional geography and a dual racial classification from the works of his predecessors and his own wide-ranging travels.[105] Spatially, he divided Oceania into four 'principal divisions': Polynesia, Micronesia, Malaysia, and Melanesia. Like Quoy, Dumont d'Urville claimed to be heir to the 'simple and lucid system of the immortal Forster' but appropriated it to serve a starkly racialized anthropology. He reconfigured Forster's labile varieties into two 'truly distinct races': a 'copper-coloured' race of 'conquerors' had come from the west to destroy, expel, or co-exist and intermix with a 'black race' who were 'the true natives' or at least the first occupants of the region. He distributed the copper-coloured race between 'Polynesians' and 'Micronesians'; replaced Melanian with the neologism 'Melanesian' to name 'the black Oceanian race'; and consigned the 'Australians' and the 'Tasmanians' to the 'last degree' of his human hierarchy as 'the primitive and natural state of the Melanesian race' which was 'only a branch of the black race of Africa'. He adjudged Melanesians to be 'hideous' in appearance, 'limited' in languages and institutions, and 'generally very inferior' to the copper-coloured race in dispositions and intelligence, except where they had been improved by frequent communications and racial intermixture with Polynesians, as in Fiji. But he saved his most persistent obloquy for the Australians and Tasmanians who were 'probably the most limited, the most stupid of all beings and those essentially closest to the unreasoning brute'.[106] Not only did Dumont d'Urville (1832:15-20) reinscribe the conjectural narrative of ancient racial migration and displacement proposed by Brosses and Forster but, like Quoy, he reworked it as modern history and colonial necessity: 'organic differences' in the 'intellectual faculties' of races determined a 'law of nature' that the black 'must obey' the others or 'disappear' while the white 'must dominate'.

Dumont d'Urville's racial taxonomy was more concise and economical than his colleagues' long-winded efforts but actual human idiosyncrasy and diversity threatened the integrity of his categories and challenged his racial preconceptions. Again (1832:17-18), the *Papous* were notable culprits. Like Quoy and Gaimard, he confined them to 'a very small part' of the coasts of west New Guinea and neighbouring islands which he had personally visited and distinguished them from the 'true Melanesians' populating most of New Guinea and the island groups to the east. However, he postulated migration rather than hybridity to solve the mystery of the *Papous'* affinities and origins: they might be just 'a handsome variety of the Melanesian race' but more likely were relatively 'recent' arrivals from as far afield as Madagascar. A candid passage reveals the aesthetic and discursive power of racial stereotypes, particularly the disagreeable spectre of the Negro and its Oceanic metonym. In Celebes (now Sulawesi in Indonesia), Dumont d'Urville heard that the inhabitants of the interior were *Alfourous*, a term which 'instantly' brought to mind the blackness, 'frizzy hair', and 'flat nose' of the 'true Melanesians'. 'Astonished' when they turned out in the flesh to resemble figures he had seen in Tahiti, Tonga, and New Zealand, he duly installed Celebes as a likely 'cradle' of the Polynesian race.

Despite such anomalies, Dumont d'Urville's elegant racial classification of Oceania ultimately prevailed and became, with minor modifications, the standard international terminology. Eventually, shorn of his brutally negative caricature of Melanesians — though not of its racial connotations — it was naturalized in modern indigenous usages by Pacific Islanders themselves.

Morality, science, and the lure of polygeny

By the late eighteenth century, many naturalists and philosophers were uncomfortable with the biblical credo of human descent from a single couple even if they avowed, with Buffon (1749b, III:530), that 'there was originally only a single species of men'. A few eminent savants like the Frenchman Voltaire (1694-1778) and the Scot David Hume (1711-1776) flirted with the notion of multiple origins.[107] Kant proclaimed an end to the 'hitherto obligatory accepted interpretation of world history as mystical salvation history' and duly proposed a rational, scientific justification for human unity. Prichard, too, insisted that 'all mankind constitute but one race or proceed from a single family' but denied 'religious predilections' and claimed to rest his case on 'distinct and independent grounds', including the supposition, attributed to Linnaeus, that every species was created 'in a single stock; probably a single pair'.[108] Among voyage naturalists, Philibert Commerson (1727-1773), who sailed with Bougainville in the 1760s, asserted that 'only a mythologist' could explain how the 'very distinct races of men' could be the issue of 'a common stock' and speculated that 'our good Tahitians', whom he idealized, might be autochthonous. Georg Forster also mocked the 'hypothesis of one single couple' as 'mythology', 'unknowable', and no less problematic than the 'assumption' of human descent from 'several original stocks' emergent in 'different parts of the world'.[109]

The writings of nineteenth-century naturalists on Oceanian people are punctuated by signs of both the growing scientific and demotic appeal of polygeny and the countervailing moral and political inertia exerted by the established doctrine, especially over conventional genres. In a popular work, Dumont d'Urville's protagonist flirts with the notion of 'the Australian' as 'half-man, half-brute', condemned to 'perish entirely' because he lacked 'the conditions of amalgamation which might create, like elsewhere, a class of half-breeds'. In his racial taxonomy, directed to a scientific audience, Dumont d'Urville was noncommittal as to whether the three major human races might belong to 'different or successive creations or formations'. Yet, in reprinting this memoir in his official voyage narrative — a very conventional genre — he added a footnote endorsing the orthodox 'opinion' that all races derived from the 'same primitive stock'.[110] Lesson's memoir on the races of Oceania (1829:156) likewise acknowledged in passing the 'fundamental premise, that man constitutes only a single species'. But in a later general work on natural history (1847:14-15), he at once maintained that 'the human species is one and indivisible'; insisted that the existence of 'numerous and very diversified' permanent races was 'palpable' and that 'we cannot mistake the real and profound characters of race'; but refused to speculate whether racial diversity was originally created or a product of externally induced 'degeneration'.

Quoy's strategic vacillations on the issue of human unity pepper his texts. His manuscript journal of the *Uranie* voyage (1817-20:[ii]) is prefaced by this highminded but evidently sincere statement of intent, indicating his belief at the time in the common humanity of 'the natives' he expected to meet: 'I swear here that I prefer to lose my life than to keep it by killing unfortunates who are barbarians only for want of judgment or civilization'. In keeping with this avowal, his and Gaimard's chapter 'On Man' in the *Zoologie* of the voyage (1824c) shows traces of an environmentalist, albeit ambivalent humanism. Yet Quoy's equivalent chapter in their *Zoologie* of the *Astrolabe* voyage (1830) is much altered in tone. Here, he refused to 'engage in conjecture' on the 'origin' of 'the species [*espèce*] which inhabits New Holland' though the term *espèce* was loaded in the context. He admitted as much in a handwritten marginal comment on a personal copy of the volume: 'here I am not too clear. I apparently had in mind the unity of the human species, *in which I do not believe*'. At the time, however, either he, Gaimard, or their editors were evidently unprepared to dispute the doctrine openly: the published text sticks consistently to the term *race* whereas Quoy's manuscript draft interchanges *espèce* and *race*, suggesting conflation of the concepts in principle but conscious editorial avoidance of controversial terminology. In a much later manuscript, Quoy took the plurality of human species as given, significantly with reference to the New Hollanders who were always among the populations most likely to be relegated to other or less than fully human status: the handful of 'naked savages' seen 'wandering like animals in search of their food' at Shark Bay in 1818 were 'truly the most degraded *species* in the world, occupying the last echelon of humanity' — a notably less generous estimation than in his 1824 text.[111] Taken together, such equivocations and about-turns register both a widening acceptance by French naval naturalists of the radical notion of multiple human species, if not separate origins, and their anxious efforts to accommodate the frequently incommensurate demands of intellectual fashion and moral conformity, epitomized respectively in their scientific and naval vocations.

By the mid-nineteenth century, polygenist thinking was pervasive in anthropology in France. Restoration-era constraints on its expression in officially sanctioned literature had receded and professed monogenists were often ambiguously complicit in the by now dominant racial agenda.[112] These patterns were already evident in the voluminous body of scientific material on the people of Oceania generated by Dumont d'Urville's final voyage of 1837-40. The works in question were produced by the phrenologist Dumoutier, who believed in a single human species, and the variously polygenist naturalists Hombron, Jacquinot, and Emile Blanchard (1819-1900), who did not.[113]

Dumoutier promoted the key phrenological principles of individuality and the equal mental potential of all human beings while his novel method of casting *moulages*, plaster busts, from living indigenous subjects demanded personal intimacy with likely models and patient negotiation to obtain cooperation from them or their governors (Figures 10 and 11).[114] Yet his mostly unpublished writings on the voyage (1837-40) show a striking disjunction between theory and unsettling experience: expressed humanist values jar with conventional racial essentialism and deeply ambivalent reactions to Oceanian people, especially when they acted in independent or threatening fashion or reminded him of Negroes. Though his phrenological investigations suggested significant differences in the cerebral development of various Oceanian populations, he clearly did not see such variation as innately organic since 'the organization of the brain is the same in all men'. Instead, like the later Buffon, he represented organic differences as the indirect product of external influences — climate, 'the social state', 'the mode of existence', and ancient histories of migration by 'conquering strangers' who successively displaced and dispersed the 'two primitive black races' which, he thought, were probably 'original to the torrid zone' and doomed to 'nonexistence'. One was 'a particular race' which inhabited most of New Holland, was positioned 'at the lowest degree of civilization', and spoke many different languages that 'resemble no dialect of any other human race'.[115] Here, too, an insinuation of autochthony prefigured a whiff of polygeny and the spectre of racial extinction.

Dumoutier's theoretical commitment to ideals of human unity and general improvability jostled in his writings with complacent conviction of European superiority and deep ambivalence about 'primitive black races'. However, few such uncertainties troubled the volumes produced by his surrogate Blanchard or his fellow voyager Hombron. Blanchard asserted that the human genus 'comprises several species'; that they were necessarily 'created in the very countries where we observe them today'; and that there must therefore have been 'a considerable number of original stocks'. Races were permanent while their 'physical' characters were primary, 'rigorously determined', and coincident with their 'moral and intellectual' characters.[116] There was direct correlation between European physical characters and the greatest 'volume of intelligence' but no 'equality' between men since those whose heads were 'contracted on top and in front and elongated behind' and whose jaw bones 'projected' — such as the '*Papous*', 'the Australians and Tasmanians', and 'the Negroes of Africa' — were bereft of 'genius or even talent, in the European sense'.[117] On the basis of Dumoutier's skull collection, Blanchard distinguished six 'very distinct types' in Oceania, arranged in a hierarchy of relative physical and moral 'superiority' and 'inferiority'. The 'Malay type', though 'very imperfect' compared to the European, ranked highest and was 'greatly superior' to the Micronesian who in turn had 'the advantage' over the Polynesian. The skulls of the *Papous* closely resembled the Polynesian type but were 'more degraded'. Dismissing Quoy and Gaimard's portrayal of *Papous* as 'Negro-Malay metis' and citing Prichard in support, Blanchard made them the 'true natives' of the lands they occupied from New Guinea to Fiji, a discrete race positioned at 'one of the last degrees of human civilization'. The Australians and Tasmanians were anthropologically 'at the last rank among men', along with the Negroes of Africa, and lacked any 'trace of civilization' or capacity to achieve it.[118]

Hombron's treatise 'On Man' is a prolix, idiosyncratic effort to reconcile polygeny with divine creation. It is profoundly racialized: the 'several species of men' had separate local creations, were distinguished by 'intelligence', and were grouped into 'three natural families'. The 'family of blacks' belonged 'to the primitive human creations' and continued to occupy 'the most arid and inaccessible' places where their 'conquerors' had not bothered to follow them; the 'copper-coloured' family, which included the eastern Oceanians or Polynesians, emerged subsequently; the 'great white family' was created last as the 'logical consequence of the union of matter and intelligence' to form the link between 'man occupying the last echelons of the human series, and the supreme intelligence'.[119] However, the rival treatise by Hombron's young medical colleague Jacquinot (1846:36, 375-6) — on 'anthropology' and 'the human races of south America and Oceania' — is a useful reminder that extreme racialism was not a necessary corollary of polygeny and that personal impressions could flout racial preconceptions. An avowed believer that the human genus comprised 'three distinct species', he nonetheless denied the standard representation of 'the black races of Oceania as brutish nomadic tribes, lacking industry and intelligence'. The stereotype hardly applied even to the 'most brutish tribes' of New Holland, whose 'miserable state' resulted largely from the 'sterility of the soil', while in other parts of the country they had shown themselves to be 'intelligent' and as educable as the children of English settlers. The 'Melanians' (Melanesians), he claimed, 'cede nothing to the Polynesians and even surpass them sometimes', especially in 'industry'; conversely, in 'ferocity and perfidy', the Polynesians yielded nothing to the Melanians, as the first navigators had found to their cost.

Figure 10: [J.-B.?] Léveillé after photograph by [Louis-Auguste?] Bisson of Pierre-Marie Alexandre Dumoutier, 'Ma-Pou-Ma-Hanga. Native de l'Ile de Manga-Réva, Archipel Gambier (Polynésie)' (1846).[120]

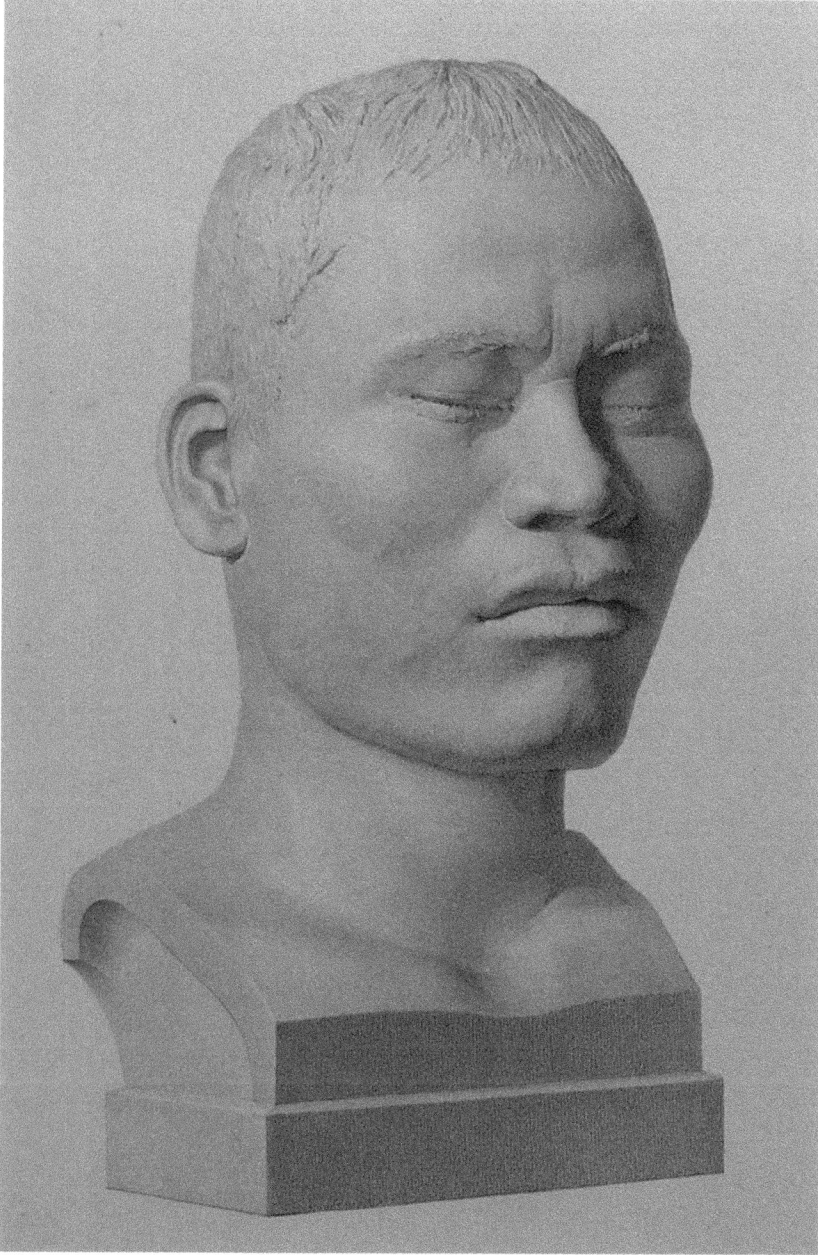

Lithographed photograph of plaster bust. Photograph B. Douglas.

Figure 11: [J.-B.?] Léveillé after photograph by [Louis-Auguste?] Bisson of Pierre-Marie Alexandre Dumoutier, 'Guenney. Natif de Port-Sorelle, (Comté de Dévon), Côte-Nord de la terre de Van Diemen (Mélanésie)' (1846).[121]

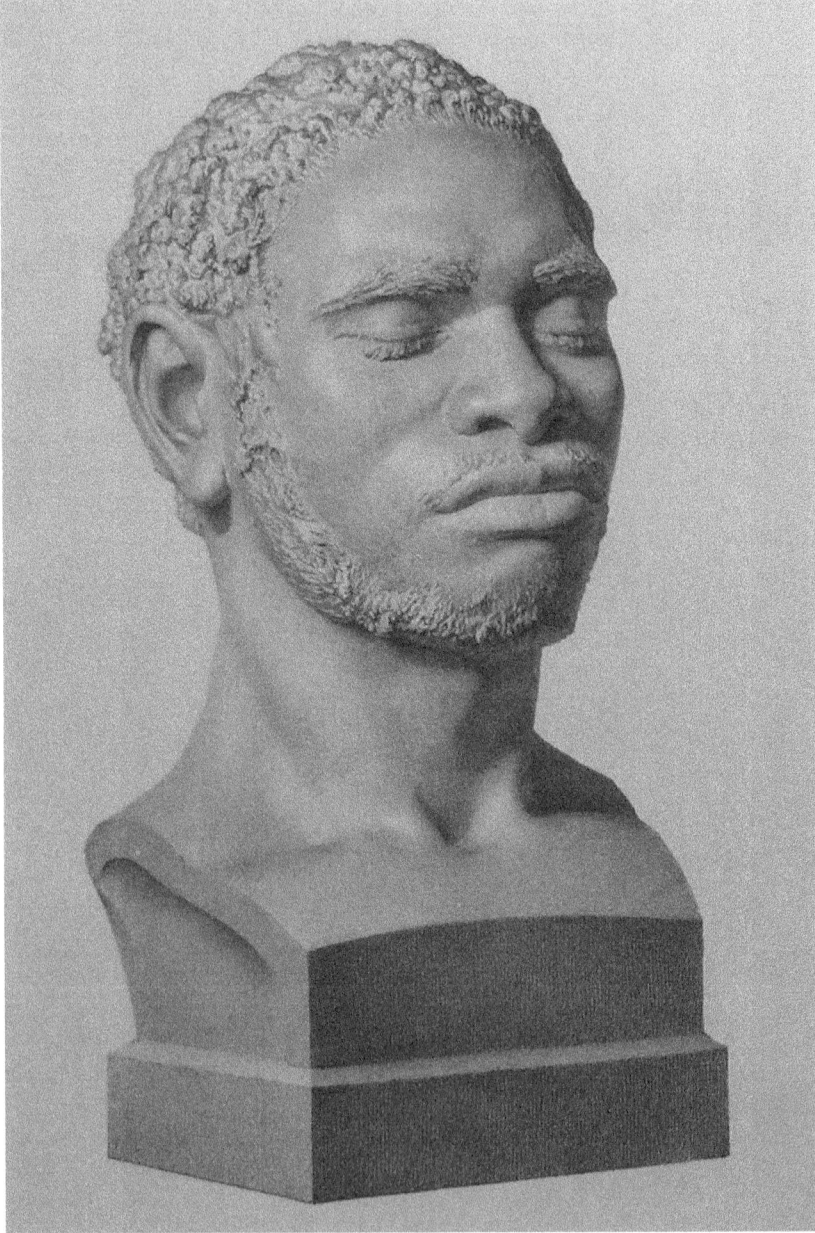

Lithographed photograph of plaster bust. Photograph B. Douglas.

Prichard — 'one original'; 'three principal groupes'

Meanwhile, in natural history in Britain, the threat of uncompromising physicalism or proto-polygenist heterodoxy emanating mainly from France was partly repulsed until the mid-nineteenth century by the ideological dominance of Evangelical humanitarianism.[122] Evangelical attitudes to 'pagans' were more bleak and rigid than had been the optimistic Christian humanism of Reinhold Forster and other Enlightenment Reformed Protestants such as Blumenbach, but British Evangelicals shared their fervent commitment to the biblical doctrine of human unity. In Britain before 1850, the science of man was strongly comparative and linguistic, befitting a longstanding philanthropic bent and the label 'ethnology' that it bore in the 1840s. Both values owed much to the influence of Prichard, a devout Anglican of Quaker origins, a follower of Blumenbach, and doyen of British ethnologists for more than thirty years until his death in 1848 (Stocking 1973; 1987:48-53). Prichard was nonetheless not immune to the infiltration of racialized logic and vocabulary into mainstream discourses: by mid-century, physical differences and their supposed moral corollaries were racially definitive for most western Europeans, including humanitarians.[123]

Prichard's work bears a marked antipodean imprint. George Stocking, Jr. (1973:xxxv), who edited a modern reprinting of the first edition of *Researches into the Physical History of Man* (1813),[124] stressed his particular debt to the Cook voyage literature. In this edition, Prichard accorded an axial interpretive position to 'the South-Sea and Indian Islanders' who, he supposed, were 'all propagated from one original' but were 'divided into two principal classes': one, 'Eastern Negroes or Papuas', were 'savages' and probably 'aborigines'; the other, unnamed, inhabited the islands of modern Polynesia and Micronesia and the Malay Archipelago, were 'more civilized', and resembled Europeans. In a long empirical section, these Oceanian people served as primary evidence for his then startling but shortlived thesis that 'the primitive stock of men were Negroes' and that the 'evolution of white varieties in black races of men', via the 'effects of Cultivation or Civilization', was a universal 'process of Nature'. Invoking the particular authority of William Anderson (?1748-78), surgeon-naturalist on Cook's second and third voyages, Prichard argued that the South Sea Islanders, broadly conceived to embrace the Papuas and the New Hollanders, were all 'branches of one stock' but provided 'a fair example of the greatest diversity of the human species, depending on the condition of society, and on the mode of life' rather than 'the influence of climate'.[125]

The glut of information pouring into Europe about non-white people globally meant exponential growth in the length of subsequent editions of *Researches* but a steady decline in the relative empirical significance of Oceania. Yet, in the two-volume second edition, Prichard (1826, I:365-468) continued to foreground the region as the world's most prolific source of 'facts' on the physical history of mankind. He now split its 'races of men' into three 'classes': the 'black or swarthy' Papuas had 'woolly hair', remained 'barbarous and unimproved', and occupied New Guinea, the islands as far eastward as Fiji, parts of the Malay Archipelago, and Van Diemen's Land; the 'fairer and less barbarous' Polynesians inhabited modern Polynesia and Micronesia and much of the Malay Archipelago; while the 'Haraforas' or 'Alfoërs' (Alfourous) were 'black', 'extremely barbarous', had 'straight or lank hair', were 'indigenous' to the Malay Archipelago, and occupied New Holland. However, Prichard (1826, I:480-3) ultimately qualified this differentiating agenda by allowing that the Papuan and Polynesian races had some 'remarkable characters in common', notably in language and skull conformation.

Even in the five-volume third edition (1836-47), the 'Oceanic races' retain significant heuristic value, though Prichard no longer considered them 'one stock' but separated them into three 'remarkably' different 'principal groupes'. Only the far-flung 'Malayo-Polynesian tribes' comprised a 'particular race or family of nations' and were relatively 'civilised', though the 'lower class' had 'approximated towards the character of the savage races' through the 'agency of the climate'. His two remaining groups together comprised the 'black races' of 'Kelænonesia' but were related only through 'uncertain' Asian origin and some behavioural and physical 'resemblance'. The 'Pelagian or Oceanic Negroes' were physically very diverse and 'very inferior' to the Malayo-Polynesians in 'arts and civilisation'. The 'Alfourous' or Australians had a 'peculiar' head shape and no linguistic affinity to the other Oceanic races. These races continued collectively to exemplify 'almost every physical variety of the human species' but were now mobilized in support of a standard climatic-environmental causal theory as putative products of 'the agency of climate and physical influences' on a single migrating species — a position Prichard had first adopted in 1826.[126]

Oceanic voyage literature remains prominent in the third edition, especially that addressing the racial conundrum of the Papuas. An exhaustive survey of writings on the subject in French and English prompted Prichard to make them 'a particular division' of the Oceanic Negroes, 'a genuine and peculiar' race limited to New Guinea, New Britain, New Ireland, and the Solomons and differentiated both from the 'mixed people' of Waigeo and nearby islands and from the Fijians who, 'though a black race', exceeded the 'more civilised and fairer' Tongans in 'vigour and enterprise'. In the Preface to this edition, Prichard complained of the prevalence of the doctrine of 'an original diversity of races' in recent treatises — 'even' by Cuvier — and in works by 'the most celebrated scientific travellers', including navigators and naturalists on recent French expeditions to Oceania. This was an allusion to Dumont d'Urville, Lesson, and Quoy and Gaimard whose writings Prichard nonetheless reproduced verbatim or paraphrased despite disavowing their purported racial theories. His ongoing obsession with the threat to human unity posed by polygeny presumably sensitized him to their prevarications on the issue, since neither they nor Cuvier openly professed belief in plural human origins.[127]

The grand design of Prichard's magnum opus remained unchanged over more than thirty years: he set himself with extraordinary industry and persistence to prove the orthodoxy that human physical differences arose 'from the variation of one primitive type' and that 'all the races of men are of one species', thus refuting the polygenist heresy that such differences were original or 'permanent and therefore specific characters'.[128] There are nonetheless clear shifts in language, tone, and emphasis from the first to the third editions. Though he consistently avoided systematic taxonomy of the human populations of Oceania, Prichard's division into classes became steadily more racialized. The 1813 text hinges on a broad, historically mutable distinction between savage and civilized while the epithets applied to so-called savages are mostly descriptive and fairly detached. In contrast, the third edition normalizes invidious racial terminology and discriminations: the 'black races in Oceanic Negroland' were 'ferocious and sullen, of savage and menacing aspect'; their 'physical characters' were 'very different from those of the agile, graceful, and comparatively fair Polynesians'; they included some which 'exceed in ugliness the most ill-favoured brood of the African forests, whom they rival in the sooty blackness of their complexion'. Even more disturbing than Prichard's by now conventionally racialized language is the intimation of racial displacement in his conjectural history of the Oceanic 'nations': the black races were the 'aborigines' of Kelænonesia, its 'immemorial and primitive inhabitants' who had spread across the 'austral islands' long before the arrival of the Malayo-Polynesians and were, by implication, exterminated, conquered, or dispersed inland by them.[129]

Conclusion

The wider discursive setting of this and the previous chapter is one of entrenched but embattled holism under siege from emerging innatist conceptions of human difference that increasingly blurred into attributions of racial autochthony and polygenism. As the ontological reality of races firmed during the first half of the nineteenth century, polygeny became more and more conceivable and acquired fugitive appeal even for some professed monogenists. Taken broadly, the century after 1750 saw a steady hardening in the vocabulary and the science of race, though the positions adopted by individual savants and voyage naturalists were neither straightforward nor consistent.

The chapter correlates the emergence of a normal science of race with the asymmetric interplay of two overlapping modes of knowing, one global and deductive, the other regional and empirical. Metropolitan savants deployed travellers' accounts of Oceanians as evidence in support of abstract classifications of human varieties, races, or species. Voyage naturalists constructed regional anthropological taxonomies by bringing global theories to bear on their own ambiguous encounters with particular Oceanians. In both cases, the taxonomic project objectified and dehumanized actual indigenous people as racial types. Yet, whereas the imprint of encounters was all but effaced in most universal racial systems, voyagers' classificatory efforts were always vulnerable to the mismatch of theory and praxis — the challenge of trying to cram personal experience of a highly varied mix of human physical features, lifestyles, and behaviours into neat racial pigeonholes. This recurrent tension between systems and facts is epitomized in the tortuous attempts by travelling French naturalists to identify and classify the *Papous* or Papuans, culminating in Prichard's late, racially ambivalent attempt to resolve the taxonomic muddle by further complicating it. Prichardian ethnology, allergic to system and heavily reliant on historical detail, would ultimately choke on the surfeit of idiosyncrasy disclosed in the burgeoning empirical literature on exotic people worldwide.

Universal and regional racial taxonomies alike were often bracketed with historical conjecture about racial origins and movements. Anticipated by Reinhold Forster, taken for granted by Cuvier and his disciples, implied by Prichard, the strategic yoking of history and taxonomy became a standard rhetorical ploy as the natural history of man transmogrified into the science of race and a new era of energetic European colonialism blossomed. With respect to Oceania, such histories usually involved speculation about autochthony and migration culminating in racial displacement or extirpation along lines spelled out by Brosses. Reinhold Forster derived his 'two distinct races' in the South Seas from the hypothetical conquest of 'aboriginal black tribes' by 'fairer', *'more civilized'* Malay immigrants. In the nineteenth century, a just-so story of the inexorable displacement of primitive blacks by lighter-skinned, *racially superior* invaders developed powerful momentum. Dumont d'Urville's dual typology climaxed in the lethal 'law of nature' that 'the black must obey' the white and yellow races, 'or disappear'.[130] Even British Evangelicals — who long battled to reconcile their dogma that all humanity was equal in the sight of God and equally susceptible to salvation with what seemed to be compelling evidence of the division and unequal endowments of races — explained the peopling of Oceania by two 'decidedly distinct' races in terms of the supplanting of the 'most ancient tribe' of Oceanic Negroes by 'fairer' Polynesians.[131]

More sinister was the slippage from conjectural history to modern prognosis. The purported inevitability of the displacement of inferior by superior races was taken to justify colonial expropriation of indigenous lands and was brutally enacted in the settler colonies of Australia, Aotearoa New Zealand, and Kanaky New Caledonia. Still worse, widely-held preconceptions about innate racial characters and inexorable racial displacement intersected with colonial fears and desires to promote a discourse of racial stagnation or extinction with respect to certain Oceanian people, notably but not exclusively Aboriginal Tasmanians and Australians.[132] Whereas Enlightenment thinkers such as Buffon, Brosses, Blumenbach, and the Forsters had presumed a universal human aptitude to become civilized, their more pessimistic nineteenth-century successors tended to believe, with Cuvier (1817a, I:94), that 'intrinsic causes' retarded the 'progress of certain races' and found their views confirmed in antipodean experience. In a paper read to the Philosophical Society of Australia in 1822, Barron Field (1786-1846), the judge of the Supreme Court of New South Wales, assigned the 'degenerate Ethiopian character' to 'the Australians' on the basis of 'the skull, the genius, the habits'. He inferred by analogy that they would 'never be civilized', that 'experience is every day fulfilling the reasoning', and that 'our colonization', however benevolent, was likely to produce the eventual 'decay or extermination' of this 'simple race' (1825:196-7, 224-8). Following a visit to Hobart Town in 1827, Dumont d'Urville (1830-3, V:96) predicted that 'the Tasmanian, and later the Australian, incapable of ever being civilized, will end up disappearing entirely' in the face of European invasion, as so many native American and other 'savage peoples' had before them. Even more portentous, after meeting a party of 'black aborigines' near Sydney in 1836, Darwin (1839:519-20) lamented the 'mysterious agency' which appeared to dictate that 'wherever the European has trod, death seems to pursue the aboriginal'. The future theoretical and practical import of this grim, if inaccurate prophecy can scarcely be overestimated.

References

Agnew, Vanessa. 2003. Pacific Island Encounters and the German Invention of Race. In *Islands in History and Representation*, ed. Rod Edmond and Vanessa Smith, 81-94. London: Routledge.

Anderson, Warwick. 2002. *The Cultivation of Whiteness: Science, Health and Racial Destiny in Australia*. Carlton, VIC: Melbourne University Press.

Anon. 1825. Programmes des prix. *Bulletin de la Société de Géographie* 3:209-16.

Anon. 1830. Séance du 19 mars 1830. *Bulletin de la Société de Géographie* 13:173-4.

Arago, François, et al. 1821. Rapport fait à l'Académie des Sciences, le lundi 23 avril 1821, sur le voyage autour du monde de la corvette l'*Uranie*, commandée par M. de Freycinet. *Annales de Chimie et de Physique* 16:389-427.

Banks, Joseph. [1770-1820]. Foreign Correspondence. Manuscript. Add. MS 8094-8100. London: British Library.

_____. 1962. *The* Endeavour *Journal of Joseph Banks 1768-1771*, ed. J.C. Beaglehole, 2 vols. Sydney: Public Library of N.S.W. with Angus and Robertson.

Beer, Gillian. 1996. Travelling the Other Way. In *Cultures of Natural History*, ed. N. Jardine, J.A. Secord and E.C. Spary, 322-37. Cambridge: Cambridge University Press.

Bendyshe, Thomas. 1865. Index of Authors. In *The Anthropological Treatises of Johann Friedrich Blumenbach*, tr. and ed. Thomas Bendyshe, 399-406. London: Longman, Green, Longman, Roberts, & Green for the Anthropological Society.

Bernasconi, Robert. 2001. Introduction. In *Concepts of Race in the Eighteenth Century*, ed. Robert Bernasconi, vol. 1, *Bernier, Linnaeus and Maupertuis*, vii-xiii. Bristol, UK: Thoemmes Press.

Blanchard, Emile. 1854. *Voyage au pôle sud et dans l'Océanie sur les corvettes l'Astrolabe et la Zélée; exécuté ... pendant les années 1837-1838-1839-1840 sous le commandement de M. J. Dumont-d'Urville ... publié ... sous la direction supérieure de M. Jacquinot .... Anthropologie.* Paris: Gide et J. Baudry.

Blanckaert, Claude. 1988. On the Origins of French Ethnology. In *Bones, Bodies, Behavior: Essays on Biological Anthropology*, ed. George W. Stocking, Jr., 18-55. Madison: University of Wisconsin Press.

_____. 2003. Les conditions d'émergence de la science des races au début du XIXe siècle. In *L'idée de 'race' dans les sciences humaines et la littérature (XVIIIe et XIXe siècles)*, ed. Sarga Moussa, 133-49. Paris: L'Harmattan.

_____. 2006. 'Notre immortel naturaliste': Buffon, la science de l'homme et l'écriture de l'histoire. In *Buffon: de l'Homme*, ed. Michèle Duchet, 407-67. Paris: L'Harmattan.

Blumenbach, Johann Friedrich. 1775. *De Generis Humani Varietate Nativa.* Goettingae: Frid. Andr. Rosenbuschii.

_____. 1781. *De Generis Humani Varietate Nativa.* 2nd edition. Goettingae: Abr. Vandenhoek.

_____. 1790. *Beyträge zur Naturgeschichte*, vol. 1. Göttingen: Johann Christian Dieterich.

_____. 1795. *De Generis Humani Varietate Nativa.* 3rd edition. Gottingae: Vandenhoek et Ruprecht.

_____. 1798 [1795]. *Über die natürlichen Verschiedenheiten im Menschengeschlechte*, tr. Johann Gottfried Gruber. Leipzig: Breitkopf und Härtel.

_____. 1803 [1799]. *Manuel d'histoire naturelle*, tr. François Artaud de Soulange, 2 vols. 6th edition. Metz and Paris: Collington and Levrault frères, Henriche, Lenormant.

_____. 1806. *Beyträge zur Naturgeschichte*, vol. 1. 2nd edition. Göttingen: Heinrich Dieterich.

Bodi, Leslie. 1959. Georg Forster: the 'Pacific Expert' of Eighteenth-Century Germany. *Historical Studies Australia and New Zealand* 8:345-63.

Bonnemains, Jacqueline. 1988. Note on the Zoological Items (Sections 66 to 80). In *Baudin in Australian Waters: the Artwork of the French Voyage of Discovery to the Southern Lands 1800-1804*, ed. Jacqueline Bonnemains, Elliott Forsyth, and Bernard Smith, 181. Melbourne: Oxford University Press.

Bonnemains, Jacqueline, Elliott Forsyth, and Bernard Smith, ed. 1988. *Baudin in Australian Waters: the Artwork of the French Voyage of Discovery to the Southern Lands 1800-1804*. Melbourne: Oxford University Press.

Bory de Saint-Vincent, Jean-Baptiste-Geneviève-Marcellin. 1827 [1825]. *L'homme (homo): essai zoologique sur le genre humain*, 2 vols. 2nd edition. Paris: Rey et Gravier.

[Bougainville, Louis-Antoine de]. 1771. *Voyage autour du monde par la frégate du roi la Boudeuse et la flûte l'Etoile en 1766, 1767, 1768 & 1769*. Paris: Saillant & Nyon.

Bougainville, Louis-Antoine de. 1977. Journal de Bougainville, commandant de la *Boudeuse*. In *Bougainville et ses compagnons autour du monde 1766-1769*, ed. Etienne Taillemite, vol. 1, 141-497. Paris: Imprimerie nationale.

Brantlinger, Patrick. 2003. *Dark Vanishings: Discourse on the Extinction of Primitive Races, 1800-1930*. Ithaca, NY, and London: Cornell University Press.

Bravo, Michael T. 1996. Ethnological Encounters. In *Cultures of Natural History*, ed. N. Jardine, J.A. Secord and E.C. Spary, 338-57. Cambridge: Cambridge University Press.

Bravo, Michael, and Sverker Sörlin, ed. 2002. *Narrating the Arctic: a Cultural History of Nordic Scientific Practices*. Canton, MA: Science History Publications.

[Brosses, Charles de]. 1756. *Histoire des navigations aux terres australes contenant ce que l'on sçait des mœurs & des productions des contrées découvertes jusqu'à ce jour ...*, 2 vols. Paris: Durand.

Buffon, Georges-Louis Leclerc, comte de. 1749a. Premier discours: de la manière d'étudier & de traiter l'histoire naturalle. In *Histoire naturelle, générale et particulière*, vol. 1, 3-62. Paris: Imprimerie royale.

_____. 1749b. Histoire naturelle de l'homme. In *Histoire naturelle, générale et particulière*, vol. 2, 427-603; vol. 3, 305-530. Paris: Imprimerie royale.

_____. 1749-67. *Histoire naturelle, générale et particulière*, 15 vols. Paris: Imprimerie royale.

_____. 1777. *Histoire naturelle, générale et particulière: Supplément*, vol. 4, *Servant de suite à l'histoire naturelle de l'homme.* Paris: Imprimerie royale.

_____. 1778. Des époques de la nature. In *Histoire naturelle, générale et particulière: supplément*, vol. 5, 1-254. Paris: Imprimerie royale.

Burney, James. 1803-17. *A Chronological History of the Discoveries in the South Seas or Pacific Ocean*, 5 vols. London: Luke Hansard.

Bynum, William F. 1975. The Great Chain of Being after Forty Years: an Appraisal. *History of Science* 13:1-28.

Chamisso, Adelbert von. 1821. Bemerkungen und Ansichten … von dem Naturforscher der Expedition. In Otto von Kotzebue, *Entdeckungs-Reise in die Sud-See und nach der Berings-Strasse zur Erforschung einer nordöstlichen Durchfahrt: Unternommen in den Jahren 1815, 1816, 1817 und 1818 …*, vol. 3. Weimar: Gebrüder Hoffmann.

_____. 1986 [1821, 1836]. *A Voyage Around the World with the Romanzov Exploring Expedition in the Years 1815-1818 in the Brig* Rurik, *Captain Otto von Kotzebue*, tr. and ed. Henry Kratz. Honolulu: University of Hawaii Press.

Commerson, Philibert. n.d. Post scriptum sur l'isle dela nouvelle Cythere ou Tayti. Par M. Commerson docteur en medecine embarqué sur la fregate du Roy la Boudeuse commandée par M. De Bougainville. Manuscript. MS 1927. Paris: Muséum national d'Histoire naturelle.

Cook, James. 1955. *The Journals of Captain James Cook on his Voyages of Discovery*, ed. J.C. Beaglehole, vol. 1, *The Voyage of the* Endeavour *1768-1771*. Cambridge: Hakluyt Society.

Cook, James, and James King. 1784. *A Voyage to the Pacific Ocean. Undertaken by the Command of his Majesty, for Making Discoveries in the Northern Hemisphere … in the Years 1776, 1777, 1778, 1779, and 1780*, [ed. John Douglas], 3 vols. London: G. Nicol and T. Cadell.

Copans, Jean, and Jean Jamin. 1978. Présentation: de la filiation déviée à l'oubli des origines. In *Aux origines de l'anthropologie française: les mèmoires de la Société des Observateurs de l'Homme en l'an VIII*, ed. Jean Copans and Jean Jamin, 23-67. Paris: Le Sycomore.

Cuvier, Georges. 1800-5. *Leçons d'anatomie comparée*, ed. C. Duméril and G.-L. Duvernoy, 5 vols. Paris: Baudouin; Genets jeune.

_____. 1817a. *Le règne animal distribué d'après son organisation, pour servir de base à l'histoire naturelle des animaux et d'introduction à l'anatomie comparée*, 4 vols. Paris: Déterville.

_____. 1817b. Extrait d'observations faites sur le cadavre d'une femme connue à Paris et à Londres sous le nom de Vénus Hottentotte. *Mémoires du Muséum d'Histoire naturelle* 3:259-74.

_____. 1825. Rapport ... sur la zoologie [de l'expédition de *la Coquille*] ... lu, le 18 juillet [1825], à l'Académie des sciences. *Journal des voyages, découvertes et navigations modernes, ou archives géographiques du XIXe siècle* 27:175-88.

_____. 1829. Discours prononcé par M. le baron Cuvier, à l'Assemblée générale annuelle du 5 décembre 1828. *Bulletin de la Société de géographie* 11:29-32.

_____. 1829-30 [1817]. *Le règne animal distribué d'après son organisation, pour servir de base à l'histoire naturelle des animaux et d'introduction à l'anatomie comparée*, 5 vols. 2nd edition. Paris: Déterville.

_____. 1830. Rapport fait à l'Académie royale des sciences par M. le Bon Cuvier, dans la séance du 26 octobre 1829, sur les collections zoologiques provenant de l'expédition de l'*Astrolabe*, commandée par M. d'Urville. *Annales maritimes et coloniales* part 2, vol. 1:104-12.

_____. 1978 [1857]. Note instructive sur les recherches à faire relativement aux différences anatomiques des diverses races d'hommes. In *Aux origines de l'anthropologie française: les mèmoires de la Société des Observateurs de l'Homme en l'an VIII*, ed. Jean Copans and Jean Jamin, 171-6. Paris: Le Sycomore.

Cuvier, Georges, et al. 1806. Rapport [à l'Institut national, Classe des Sciences physiques et mathématiques,] sur les travaux de Mr. Peron, l'un des naturalistes de la dernière expédition de découvertes et sur ceux de M. Le Sueur, l'un des dessinateurs attachés à la même expédition, Paris, le 12 juin 1806. Manuscript. BB4 996. Vincennes, France: Service historique de la Défense, département Marine.

_____. 1807. Rapport sur un ouvrage manuscrit de M. André, ci-devant connu sous le nom de P. Chrysologue de Gy, lequel ouvrage est intitulé *Théorie de la surface actuelle de la terre*, par MM. Hauy, Lelièvre, et Cuvier, rapporteur. *Mémoires de la Classe des Sciences mathématiques et physiques de l'Institut national de France*, premier semestre:128-45.

Dalrymple, Alexander. 1770-1. *An Historical Collection of the Several Voyages and Discoveries in the South Pacific Ocean*, 2 vols. London: J. Nourse, T. Payne, and P. Elmsley.

Dampier, William. 1697. *A New Voyage Round the World* ... London: James Knapton.

_____. 1699. *Voyages and Descriptions*, vol. 2. London: James Knapton.

_____. 1703. *A Voyage to New-Holland, &c. In the Year, 1699*, vol. 3. London: James Knapton.

_____. 1709. *A Continuation of a Voyage to New-Holland, &c. In the Year 1699*, vol 3, part 2. London: James Knapton.

Darwin, Charles. 1839. *Narrative of the Surveying Voyages of His Majesty's Ships Adventure and Beagle, between the Years 1826 and 1836, Describing their Examination of the Southern Shores of South America, and the Beagle's Circumnavigation of the Globe*, vol. 3, *Journal and Remarks, 1832-1836*. London: Henry Colburn.

_____. 1871. *The Descent of Man, and Selection in Relation to Sex*, 2 vols. London: John Murray.

Deleuze, Joseph-Philippe-François. 1816. Eloge historique de François Péron. In François Péron and Louis de Freycinet, *Voyage de découvertes aux terres australes ... sur les corvettes le Géographe, le Naturaliste, et la goëlette le Casuarina, pendant les années 1800, 1801, 1802, 1803 et 1804. Historique*. vol 2, Appendice, 434-57. Paris: Imprimerie royale.

Douglas, Bronwen. 1999a. Art as Ethno-historical Text: Science, Representation and Indigenous Presence in Eighteenth and Nineteenth Century Oceanic Voyage Literature. In *Double Vision: Art Histories and Colonial Histories in the Pacific*, ed. Nicholas Thomas and Diane Losche, 65-99. Cambridge: Cambridge University Press.

_____. 1999b. Science and the Art of Representing 'Savages': Reading 'Race' in Text and Image in South Seas Voyage Literature. *History and Anthropology* 11:157-201.

_____. 2001. Comment on John Edward Terrell, Kevin M. Kelly, and Paul Rainbird, Foregone Conclusions? In Search of 'Austronesians' and 'Papuans'. *Current Anthropology* 42:111-12.

_____. 2003. Seaborne Ethnography and the Natural History of Man. *Journal of Pacific History* 38:3-27.

_____. 2005. Notes on 'Race' and the Biologisation of Human Difference. *Journal of Pacific History* 40:331-8.

_____. 2006. Slippery Word, Ambiguous Praxis: 'Race' and Late 18th-Century Voyagers in Oceania. *Journal of Pacific History* 41:1-29.

_____. n.d. Encountering Agency: Islanders, European Voyagers, and the Production of Race in Oceania. In *Changing Contexts — Shifting Meanings:*

Transformations of Cultural Traditions in Oceania, ed. Elfriede Hermann. Honolulu: University of Hawai'i Press.

Duchet, Michèle. 1995 [1971]. *Anthropologie et histoire au siècle des lumières*. 2nd edition. Paris: Albin Michel.

Dumont d'Urville, Jules-Sébastien-César. 1822-5. Journal d'un voyage autour du monde entrepris sur la Corvette de S.M. la Coquille sous les ordres de Mr. Duperrey Lieutenant de vaisseau. Manuscript. MS 1602. Paris: Muséum national d'Histoire naturelle.

_____. [1826]. [Sur les peuples de l'Océanie]. Manuscript. 7GG2 30 (2). Vincennes, France: Service historique de la Défense, département Marine.

_____. 1830-3. *Voyage de la corvette l'Astrolabe exécuté ... pendant les années 1826-1827-1828-1829 ... Histoire du voyage*, 5 vols. Paris: J. Tastu.

_____. 1832. Sur les îles du grand océan. *Bulletin de la Société de Géographie* 17:1-21.

_____. 1834-5. *Voyage pittoresque autour du monde: resumé général des voyages de découvertes ...*, 2 vols. Paris: L. Tenré & Henri Dupuy.

Dumoutier, Pierre-Marie Alexandre. 1837-40. Journal de son voyage à bord de l'Astrolabe. Manuscript. MS 72. Paris: Musée de l'Homme.

_____. [1838-40]. Moulages. Plaster busts. Paris: Laboratoire d'anthropologie biologique, Musée de l'Homme.

_____. 1843. *Notice phrénologique et ethnologique sur les naturels de l'Archipel Nouka-Hiva (Iles Marquises)*. Paris: Fain et Thunot.

_____. n.d. [Notes sur les peuples à l'état sauvage]. In Pierre-Marie Alexandre Dumoutier, [Notes et rapports sur l'homme], 89-90. Manuscript. MS 73. Paris: Musée de l'Homme.

[Dumoutier, Pierre-Marie Alexandre]. 1846. *Voyage au pôle sud et dans l'Océanie sur les corvettes l'Astrolabe et la Zélée ... pendant les années 1837-1838-1839-1840 sous le commandement de M. J. Dumont-d'Urville ... publié ... sous la direction supérieure de M. Jacquinot ... Atlas anthropologique*. Paris: Gide.

Dunmore, John. 1965-9. *French Explorers in the Pacific*, 2 vols. Oxford: Clarendon Press.

Ellis, William. 1829. *Polynesian Researches During a Residence of Nearly Six Years in the South Sea Islands ...* London: Fisher, Son, & Jackson.

_____. 1831 [1829]. *Polynesian Researches, During a Residence of Nearly Eight Years in the Society and Sandwich Islands*, 4 vols. 2nd edition. London: Fisher, Son, & Jackson.

Entrecasteaux, Joseph Antoine Bruni d'. 1808. *Voyage de Dentrecasteaux envoyé à la recherche de La Pérouse ...*, ed. Elisabeth-Paul-Edouard de Rossel, 2 vols. Paris: Imprimerie impériale.

Eze, Emmanuel Chukwudi. 1995. The Color of Reason: the Idea of 'Race' in Kant's Anthropology. In *Anthropology and the German Enlightenment: Perspectives on Humanity,* ed. Katherine M. Faull, 200–41. Lewisburg, PA: Bucknell University Press.

Field, Barron. 1825. On the Aborigines of New Holland and Van Diemen's Land. In *Geographical Memoirs on New South Wales; by Various Hands ...*, ed. Barron Field, 192-229. London: John Murray.

Forster, Georg [George]. 1777. *A Voyage Round the World in His Britannic Majesty's Sloop, Resolution,... During the Years 1772, 3, 4, and 5.* 2 vols. London: B. White, J. Robson, P. Elmsly, and G. Robinson.

Forster, Georg. 1786. Noch etwas über die Menschenrassen. *Teutsche Merkur* October 1786:57-86; November 1786:150-66.

————. 1985a [1787]. Neuholland und die brittische Colonie in Botany-Bay. In *Georg Forsters Werke: Sämtliche Schriften, Tagebücher, Briefe*, vol. 5, *Kleine Schriften zur Völker- und Länderkunde*, ed. Horst Fiedler, et al., 161-80. Berlin: Akademie-Verlag.

————. 1985b [1787]. Cook, der Entdecker. In *Georg Forsters Werke: Sämtliche Schriften, Tagebücher, Briefe*, vol. 5, *Kleine Schriften zur Völker- und Länderkunde*, ed. Horst Fiedler, et al., 191-302. Berlin: Akademie-Verlag.

Forster, Johann Reinhold [John Reinold]. 1778. *Observations Made During a Voyage Round the World, on Physical Geography, Natural History, and Ethic Philosophy* ... London: G. Robinson.

Forster, Johann Reinhold. 1982. *The* Resolution *Journal of Johann Reinhold Forster 1772-1775*, ed. Michael E. Hoare, 4 vols. London: Hakluyt Society.

France, Marine nationale. 1796-1815. Expédition du capitaine de vaisseau Baudin dans les mers australes. Manuscripts. BB4 995-7. Vincennes, France: Service historique de la Défense, département Marine.

Freycinet, Louis de. 1825-39. *Voyage autour du monde,... exécuté sur les corvettes de S.M.* l'Uranie *et la* Physicienne, *pendant les années 1817, 1818, 1819 et 1820 ... Historique,* 3 vols. Paris: Pillet aîné.

Gall, Franz Joseph, and Johann Gaspar Spurzheim. 1809. *Recherches sur le système nerveux en général, et sur celui du cerveau en particulier: mémoire présenté à l'Institut de France, le 14 mars 1808, suivi d'observations sur le rapport qui en a été fait à cette compagnie par ses commissaires.* Paris: F. Schoell, H. Nicolle.

_____. 1810-19. *Anatomie et physiologie du système nerveux en général, et du cerveau en particulier, avec des observations sur la possibilité de reconnoître plusieurs dispositions intellectuelles et morales de l'homme et des animaux, par la configuration de leurs têtes*, 4 vols. Paris: F. Schoell.

Gardner, Helen Bethea. 2006. *Gathering for God: George Brown in Oceania*. Dunedin, NZ: University of Otago Press.

Garnot, Prosper. 1826-30. Mémoire sur les races humaines. In René-Primevère Lesson and Prosper Garnot, *Voyage autour du monde ... sur la corvette de Sa Majesté, La Coquille, pendant les années 1822, 1823, 1824 et 1825 ... Zoologie*, vol. 1, 507-22. Paris: Arthus Bertrand.

_____. 1836. Homme, *Homo*. In *Dictionnaire pittoresque d'histoire naturelle ...*, ed. Félix Edouard Guérin-Méneville, vol. 4, 6-16. Paris: Bureau de souscription.

_____. 1837. Nègre. In *Dictionnaire pittoresque d'histoire naturelle ...*, ed. Félix Edouard Guérin-Méneville, vol. 5, 628-32. Paris: Bureau de souscription.

Gascoigne, John. 2007. The German Enlightenment and the Pacific. In *The Anthropology of the Enlightenment*, ed. Larry Wolff and Marco Cipolloni, 141-71. Stanford, CA: Stanford University Press.

Gelpke, J.H.F. Sollewijn. 1993. On the Origin of the Name Papua. *Bijdragen tot de Taal-, Land- en Volkenkunde* 149:318-32.

Gomsu, Joseph. 2002. Langue et littérature en-deçà et au-delà de la nation: amour du particulier et cosmopolitisme chez Georg Forster. *TRANS: Internet-Zeitschrift für Kulturwissenschaften* 11. Accessed 24 February 2007, online <http://www.inst.at/trans/11Nr/gomsu11.htm>.

[Greatheed, Samuel]. 1799. Preliminary Discourse: Containing a Geographical and Historical Account of the Islands Where Missionaries have Settled, and of Others with Which They are Connected. In [James Wilson], *A Missionary Voyage to the Southern Pacific Ocean, Performed in the Years 1796, 1797, 1798, in the Ship Duff ...*, i-lxxxviii. London: T. Chapman.

Hale, Horatio. 1846. *United States Exploring Expedition: during the years 1838, 1839, 1840, 1841, 1842, under the Command of Charles Wilkes, U.S.N.*, vol. 6. *Ethnography and Philology*. Philadelphia: Lea & Blanchard.

Hall, Catherine. 2002. *Civilising Subjects: Metropole and Colony in the English Imagination, 1830-1867*. Chicago and London: University of Chicago Press.

Hamy, Ernest-Théodore. 1906. Notes intimes sur Georges Cuvier rédigées en 1836 par le Dr Quoy pour son ami J. Desjardins, de Maurice. *Archives de Médecine Navale* 86:455-75.

Herbert, Christopher. 1991. *Culture and Anomie: Ethnographic Imagination in the Nineteenth Century*. Chicago: University of Chicago Press.

Herder, Johann Gottfried. 1812 [1784-91]. *Ideen zur Philosophie des Geschichte der Menschheit*, 2 vols. Leipzig: Johann Friedrich Hartsnoch.

Hombron, Jacques-Bernard. 1846. *De l'homme dans ses rapports avec la création*, vol. 1, Jacques-Bernard Hombron and Honoré Jacquinot, *Voyage au Pôle Sud et dans l'Océanie sur les corvettes l'Astrolabe et la Zélée ... pendant les années 1837-1838-1839-1840, sous le commandement de M. J. Dumont-d'Urville ... publié ... sous la direction supérieure de M. Jacquinot ... Zoologie*. Paris: Gide.

Hombron, Jacques-Bernard, and Honoré Jacquinot. 1846-54. *Voyage au pôle sud et dans l'Océanie sur les corvettes l'Astrolabe et la Zélée ... pendant les années 1837-1838-1839-1840, sous le commandement de M. J. Dumont-d'Urville ... publié ... sous la direction supérieure de M. Jacquinot ... Zoologie*, 5 vols. Paris: Gide.

Jacquinot, Honoré. 1846. *Considérations générales sur l'anthropologie suivies d'observations sur les races humaines de l'Amérique méridionale et de l'Océanie*, vol. 2, Jacques-Bernard Hombron and Honoré Jacquinot, *Voyage au Pôle Sud et dans l'Océanie sur les corvettes l'Astrolabe et la Zélée ... pendant les années 1837-1838-1839-1840, sous le commandement de M. J. Dumont-d'Urville ... publié ... sous la direction supérieure de M. Jacquinot ... Zoologie*. Paris: Gide.

Jones, Rhys. 1988. Images of Natural Man. In *Baudin in Australian Waters: the Artwork of the French Voyage of Discovery to the Southern Lands 1800-1804*, ed. Jacqueline Bonnemains, Elliott Forsyth and Bernard Smith, 35-64. Melbourne: Oxford University Press.

Kant, Immanuel. 1785. Bestimmung des Begriffs einer Menschenrace. *Berlinische Monatsschrift* 6:390-417.

————. 2001 [1775]. *Von den verschiedenen Racen der Menschen zur Ankundigung der Vorlesungen der physischen Geographie im Sommerhalbenjahre 1775*. Königsberg: G.E. Hartung. In *Concepts of Race in the Eighteenth Century*, ed. Robert Bernasconi, vol. 3, *Kant and Forster*. Bristol, UK: Thoemmes.

Kelly, Celsus, tr. and ed. 1966. *La Austrialia del Espíritu Santo: the Journal of Fray Martín de Munilla O.F.M. and Other Documents Relating to the Voyage of Pedro Fernández de Quirós to the South Seas (1605-1606) and the Franciscan Missionary Plan (1617-1627)*, 2 vols. Cambridge: Hakluyt Society.

Kidd, Colin. 2006. *The Forging of Races: Race and Scripture in the Protestant Atlantic World, 1600-2000*. Cambridge: Cambridge University Press.

Lagier, Raphaël. 2004. *Les races humaines selon Kant*. Paris: Presses Universitaires de France.

Langsdorff, Georg Heinrich von. 1812. *Bemerkungen auf einer Reise um die Welt in den Jahren 1803 bis 1807*, 2 vols. Frankfurt am Mayn: Friedrich Wilmans.

[La Pérouse, Jean-François de Galaup de]. 1797. *Voyage de la Pérouse autour du monde, publié conformément au décret du 22 avril 1791*, ed. Louis-Antoine Milet-Mureau, 4 vols. Paris: Imprimerie de la République.

Le Jeune, Jules-Louis. [1822-5]. Voyage autour du monde sur la Corvette La Coquille ... Folio album of drawings. SH 356. Vincennes, France: Service historique de la Défense, département Marine.

Lesson, René-Primevère. 1823-4. [Voyage de la Coquille], 2 vols. Manuscript. MS 1793. Paris: Muséum national d'Histoire naturelle.

_____. 1825. [Lettre à] A.M. Bajot, Port-Jackson (Nouvelle-Galles du S.), le 30 janvier 1824. *Annales maritimes et coloniales* part 2:322-31.

_____. 1826. Lettre à un jeune naturaliste partant pour un voyage autour du monde. *Journal des voyages, découvertes et navigations modernes, ou archives géographiques du XIXe siècle* 29:101-10.

_____. 1829 [1826]. Mémoire sur les races humaines répandues sur les îles du Grand-Océan, et considérées sous les divers rapports physiologiques, naturels et moraux. In *Voyage médical autour du monde, exécuté sur la corvette du roi* La Coquille ... *pendant les années 1822, 1823, 1824 et 1825* ..., 153-225. Paris: Roret.

_____. 1839. *Voyage autour du monde entrepris par ordre du gouvernement sur la corvette la Coquille*, 2 vols. Paris: R. Pourrat frères.

_____. 1847. *Description de mammifères et d'oiseaux récemment découverts, précédée d'un tableau sur les races humaines*. Paris: Lévêque.

Lesson, René-Primevère, and Prosper Garnot. 1826-30. *Voyage autour du monde* ... *sur la corvette de Sa Majesté, La Coquille, pendant les années 1822, 1823, 1824 et 1825* ... *Zoologie*, 2 vols. Paris: Arthus Bertrand.

Lesueur, Charles-Alexandre, and Nicolas-Martin Petit. [1807]. *Voyage de découvertes aux terres australes exécuté par ordre de S.M. l'Empereur et Roi. Partie Historique. Atlas.* [Paris: Imprimerie impériale].

_____. 1824. *Voyage de découvertes aux terres australes. Historique. Atlas.* 2nd edition. Paris: Arthus Bertrand.

Lewis, Charlton T., and Charles Short. 1879. *A Latin Dictionary*. Oxford: Clarendon Press. Online <http://www.perseus.tufts.edu/cgi-bin/resolveform?lang=Latin>.

Liebersohn, Harry. 2006. *The Travelers' World: Europe to the Pacific*. Cambridge, MA: Harvard University Press.

Linnaeus, Carolus [Carl von Linné]. 1758. *Systema Naturae*, vol. 1, *Regnum Animale*. 10th edition. Holmiae: Laurentii Salvii.

McGregor, Russell. 1997. *Imagined Destinies: Aboriginal Australians and the Doomed Race Theory, 1880-1939*. Carlton, VIC.: Melbourne University Press.

Malte-Brun, Conrad. 1803. Géographie genérale, mathématique et physique. In Edme Mentelle and Conrad Malte Brun, *Géographie mathématique, physique et politique de toutes les parties du monde ...*, vol. 1, 151-552. Paris: H. Tardieu et Laporte.

_____. 1810a. *Précis de la géographie universelle, ou description de toutes les parties du monde, sur un plan nouveau, d'après les grandes divisions naturelles du globe ... Collection de cartes géographiques*. Paris: François Buisson.

_____. 1810b. *Précis de la géographie universelle, ou description de toutes les parties du monde, sur un plan nouveau, d'après les grandes divisions naturelles du globe ...*, vol. 1, *Histoire de la géographie*. Paris: F. Buisson.

_____. 1810c. *Précis de la géographie universelle, ou description de toutes les parties du monde, sur un plan nouveau, d'après les grandes divisions naturelles du globe ...*, vol. 2, *Théorie générale de la géographie*. Paris: F. Buisson.

_____. 1813. *Précis de la géographie universelle, ou description de toutes les parties du monde, sur un plan nouveau, d'après les grandes divisions naturelles du globe ...*, vol. 4, *Description de l'Inde, de l'Océanique, et de l'Afrique septentrionale*. Paris: Fr. Buisson.

Marsden, William. 1782. Remarks on the Sumatran Languages ... In a Letter to Sir Joseph Banks, Bart. President of the Royal Society [21 February 1881]. *Archaeologia: or, Miscellaneous Tracts Relating to Antiquity* 6:154-8.

Marx, K.F.H. 1865 [1840]. Life of Blumenbach. In *The Anthropological Treatises of Johann Friedrich Blumenbach*, tr. and ed. Thomas Bendyshe, 1-45. London: Longman, Green, Longman, Roberts & Green for the Anthropological Society.

Maupertuis, Pierre-Louis Moreau de. 1768 [1752]. Lettre sur le progrès des sciences. In *Œuvres de Maupertuis*, vol. 2, 375-431. New revised edition. Lyon: Jean-Marie Bruyset.

Mentelle, Edme, and Conrad Malte Brun. 1804. *Géographie mathématique, physique et politique de toutes les parties du monde ...*, vol. 12, *Contenant la suite de l'Asie et les Terres Océaniques ou la cinquième partie du monde.* Paris: Henry Tardieu et Laporte.

Montagu, Ashley. 1997 [1942]. *Man's Most Dangerous Myth: the Fallacy of Race.* 6th edition. Walnut Creek, CA: AltaMira Press.

Ollivier, Isabel. 1988. Pierre-Adolphe Lesson, Surgeon-Naturalist: a Misfit in a Successful System. In *Nature in its Greatest Extent: Western Science in the Pacific,* ed. Roy MacLeod and Philip F. Rehbock, 45-64. Honolulu: University of Hawaii Press.

Péron, François. 1809. *A Voyage of Discovery to the Southern Hemisphere, Performed by Order of the Emperor Napoleon during the Years 1801, 1802, 1803, and 1804,* tr. unknown. London: Richard Phillips.

_____. 1978 [1913]. Observations sur l'anthropologie, ou l'histoire naturelle de l'homme, la nécessité de s'occuper de l'avancement de cette science, et l'importance de l'admission sur la flotte du capitaine Baudin d'un ou de plusieurs naturalistes, spécialement chargés des recherches à faire sur ce sujet. In *Aux origines de l'anthropologie française: les mèmoires de la Société des Observateurs de l'Homme en l'an VIII,* ed. Jean Copans and Jean Jamin, 177-85. Paris: Le Sycomore.

[Péron, François]. n.d. [Sur les résultats généraux de l'expédition]. Manuscript. Dossier 22078. Le Havre, France: Collection Lesueur, Muséum d'Histoire naturelle du Havre.

Péron, François, and Louis de Freycinet. 1807-16. *Voyage de découvertes aux terres australes ... sur les corvettes le Géographe, le Naturaliste, et la goëlette le Casuarina, pendant les années 1800, 1801, 1802, 1803 et 1804. Historique.* 2 vols. Paris: Imprimerie impériale/Imprimerie royale.

Pinkerton, John. 1802. *Modern Geography: a Description of the Empires, Kingdoms, States, and Colonies; with the Oceans, Seas, and Isles; in all Parts of the World ...,* 2 vols. London: T. Cadell Jun. and W. Davies and T.N. Longman and O. Rees.

Prichard, James Cowles. 1813. *Researches into the Physical History of Man.* London: John and Arthur Arch.

_____. 1826. *Researches into the Physical History of Mankind,* 2 vols. 2nd edition. London: John and Arthur Arch.

_____. 1836-47. *Researches into the Physical History of Mankind,* 5 vols. 3rd edition. London: Sherwood, Gilbert, and Piper.

Quirós, Pedro Fernández de. 1904 [1876-82]. Narrative of the Second Voyage of the Adelantado Alvaro de Mendaña, by the Chief Pilot, Pedro Fernandez de Quiros. In *The Voyages of Pedro Fernandez de Quiros, 1595-1606,* tr. and ed. Clements Markham, vol. 1, 3-146. London: Hakluyt Society.

_____. 1973 [1610]. *Relacion de un memorial que ha presentado a su Magestad el Capitan Pedro Fernandez de Quir, sobre la poblacion y descubrimiento de la quarta parte del mundo, Austrialia incognita, su gran riqueza y fertilidad: descubierta por el mismo Capitan.* Pamplona: Carlos de Labayen. In Carlos Sanz, *Australia su descubrimiento y denominación: con la reproducción facsimil del memorial número 8 de Quirós en español original, y en las diversas traducciones contemporáneas,* 37-44. Madrid: Dirección General de Relaciones Culturales, Ministerio de Asuntos Exteriores.

Quoy, Jean-René Constant. 1817-20. Corvette du roi l'Uranie. Voyage autour du monde, pendant les années 1817, 1818, 1819, & 1820. Journal. Manuscript. R-2520-11702. Rochefort, France: Service historique de la Défense, département Marine.

_____. [1820-70]. Papiers Quoy. Manuscripts. MS 2507-2510. La Rochelle, France: Médiathèque Michel-Crépeau.

_____. 1864-8. [Autobiographie]. Manuscript. MS 2507. La Rochelle, France: Médiatheque Michel-Crépeau.

_____. n.d.a. Introduction. Manuscript. MS 2507. La Rochelle, France: Médiathèque Michel-Crépeau.

_____. n.d.b. Paul Gaimard. Manuscript. MS 2508. La Rochelle, France: Médiathèque Michel-Crépeau.

[Quoy, Jean-René-Constant, and] Joseph-Paul Gaimard. 1823. Extrait d'un mémoire sur la race d'hommes connus sous le nom de *Papous*, et particulièrement sur la conformation de leur crâne; lu à l'Académie royale des sciences par M. P. Gaymard, l'un des médecins-naturalistes de l'expédition de découvertes autour du monde, commandée par le capitaine Freycinet. *Nouvelles annales des voyages, de la géographie et de l'histoire* 19:115-26.

Quoy, Jean-René Constant, and Joseph-Paul Gaimard. 1824a. *Voyage autour du monde ... exécuté sur les corvettes de S.M.* l'Uranie *et* la Physicienne, *pendant les années 1817, 1818, 1819 et 1820 ... Zoologie.* Paris: Pillet aîné.

_____. 1824b. *Voyage autour du monde fait ... sur les corvettes de S.M.* l'Uranie *et* la Physicienne *pendant les années 1817, 1818, 1819 et 1820. Histoire naturelle: zoologie. Planches.* Paris: Imprimerie en taille-douce de Langlois.

_____. 1824c. De l'homme: observations sur la constitution physique des Papous. In *Voyage autour du monde ... exécuté sur les corvettes de S.M.* l'Uranie *et* la Physicienne, *pendant les années 1817, 1818, 1819 et 1820 ... Zoologie,* 1-11. Paris: Pillet aîné.

_____. 1826. Observations sur la constitution physique des Papous qui habitent les îles Rawak et Vaigiou; lues à l'Académie des Sciences de l'Institut, le 5 mai 1823. *Annales des sciences naturelles* 7:27-38.

_____. 1830. De l'homme. In *Voyage de découvertes de l'Astrolabe ... pendant les années 1826-1827-1828-1829 ... Zoologie*, vol. 1, 15-59. Paris: J. Tastu.

_____. 1830-4. *Voyage de découvertes de l'Astrolabe ... pendant les années 1826-1827-1828-1829 ... Zoologie*, 4 vols. Paris: J. Tastu.

_____. 1833. *Voyage de la corvette l'Astrolabe exécuté pendant les années 1826-1827-1828-1829 ... Atlas zoologique.* Paris: J. Tastu.

Regnier, Edme. 1798 [an VI]. Description et usage du dynamomètre, pour connaître et comparer la force relative des hommes, celles des chevaux et de toutes les bêtes de trait ; enfin pour juger la résistance des machines et estimer les puissances motrices qu'on veut y appliquer. *Journal de l'Ecole polytechnique, ou Bulletin du travail fait à cette école, publié par le conseil d'instruction et administration de cet établissement* 2, 5me cahier: 160-78 [Paris: Imprimerie de la République].

Rensch, Karl H. 2000. *The Language of the Noble Savage: the Linguistic Fieldwork of Reinhold and George Forster in Polynesia on Cook's Second Voyage to the Pacific 1772-1775.* Canberra, ACT: Archipelago Press.

Renneville, Marc. 2000. *Le langage des crânes: histoire de la phrénologie.* Paris: Institut d'édition Sanofi-Synthélabo.

Rivers, W.H.R., ed. 1922. *Essays on the Depopulation of Melanesia.* Cambridge: Cambridge University Press.

Rudwick, Martin J.S. 1997. *Georges Cuvier, Fossil Bones, and Geological Catastrophes: New Translations & Interpretations of the Primary Texts.* Chicago: University of Chicago Press.

Ryan, Tom. 2002. 'Le Président des Terres Australes': Charles de Brosses and the French Enlightenment Beginnings of Oceanic Anthropology. *Journal of Pacific History* 37:157-86.

Sivasundaram, Sujit. 2005. *Nature and the Godly Empire: Science and Evangelical Mission in the Pacific, 1795-1850.* Cambridge: Cambridge University Press.

Smith, Bernard. 1969 [1960]. *European Vision and the South Pacific 1768-1850: a Study in the History of Art and Ideas.* Oxford: Oxford University Press.

Staum, Martin S. 2003. *Labeling People: French Scholars on Society, Race, and Empire, 1815-1848.* Montreal & Kingston: McGill-Queen's University Press.

Stepan, Nancy. 1982. *The Idea of Race in Science: Great Britain 1800-1960*. London: Macmillan.

Stocking, George W., Jr. 1968. *Race, Culture and Evolution: Essays in the History of Anthropology*. New York: Free Press.

————. 1973. From Chronology to Ethnology: James Cowles Prichard and British Anthropology 1800-1850. In James Cowles Prichard, *Researches into the Physical History of Man*, ed. George W. Stocking, Jr., ix-cx. Chicago: University of Chicago Press.

————. 1987. *Victorian Anthropology*. New York: Free Press.

Stokes, John Lort. 1846. *Discoveries in Australia; with an Account of the Coasts and Rivers Explored and Surveyed During the Voyage of H.M.S. Beagle, in the Years 1837-38-39-40-41-42-43 ...*, 2 vols. London: T. and W. Boone.

Strack, Thomas. 1996. Philosophical Anthropology on the Eve of Biological Determinism: Immanuel Kant and Georg Forster on the Moral Qualities and Biological Characteristics of the Human Race. *Central European History* 29:285-308.

Terrell, John Edward, Kevin M. Kelly, and Paul Rainbird. 2001. Foregone Conclusions? In Search of 'Papuans' and 'Austronesians'. *Current Anthropology* 42:97-124.

Urban, Manfred. 1998. The Acquisition History of the Göttingen Collection. In *James Cook: Gifts and Treasures from the South Seas: the Cook-Forster Collection, Göttingen*, ed. Brigitta Hauser-Schäublin and Gundolf Krüger, 56-85. Munich and New York: Prestel-Verlag.

Virey, Julien-Joseph. 1800. *Histoire naturelle du genre humain, ou recherches sur ses principaux fondemens physiques et moraux ...*, 2 vols. Paris: F. Dufart.

West, Hugh. 1989. The Limits of Enlightenment Anthropology: Georg Forster and the Tahitians. *History of European Ideas* 10:147-60.

White, Charles. 1799. *An Account of the Regular Gradation in Man, and in Different Animals and Vegetables; and from the Former to the Latter*. London: C. Dilly.

Williams, John. 1837. *A Narrative of Missionary Enterprises in the South Sea Islands: with Remarks upon the Natural History of the Islands, Origin, Languages, Traditions, and Usages of the Inhabitants*. London: John Snow.

Notes

[1] 'The new southern world' (Blumenbach 1781:52, original emphasis). Latin-English translations are based on Lewis and Short 1879.

[2] For a catholic sample of critical reflections on the significance of overseas field experience in the science of man in the eighteenth and nineteenth centuries, see Beer 1996; Bravo 1996; Bravo and Sörlin 2002; Gardner 2006:105-27; Liebersohn 2006; Smith 1969; Staum 2003:85-121; Stocking 1987:78-109.

[3] Blumenbach 1775:40; 1795:322; Buffon 1749a:4-7; 1749b, III:529-30; Cuvier 1817a, I:94; Cuvier et al. 1807:135, 137; Prichard 1813:3; 1836-47, I:9.

[4] The terms 'monogenist' and 'polygenist' date from the 1850s but are used here as useful labels for the extreme positions adopted by naturalists during the preceding half century in heated debates over the unity of the human species; see Chapter One (Douglas), this volume.

[5] See also Douglas 1999a, 1999b, 2003, 2006, n.d.

[6] Other partial exceptions to French predominance in the early anthropology of Oceania — though none could match the comparative span of French experience in the region — were the German Georg Heinrich von Langsdorff (1774-1852), physician-naturalist on the first Russian circumnavigation of the world in 1803-6; the French-born German naturalist and *littérateur* Adelbert von Chamisso (1781-1838), naturalist on the subsequent Russian voyage of 1815-18; the Englishman Charles Darwin (1809-1882), naturalist on HMS *Beagle's* global surveying voyage of 1831-36; and the American philologist and ethnologist Horatio Hale (1817-1896), a member of the United States Exploring Expedition to the Pacific in 1838-42 (Chamisso 1821, 1986; Darwin 1839; Hale 1846; Langsdorff 1813; see also Beer 1996; Liebersohn 2006:58-76, 273-88). William Ellis (1794-1872) and John Williams (1796-1839) of the London Missionary Society pioneered the prolific genre of missionary ethnography which dominated Pacific anthropology in the second half of the nineteenth century but few other such works were published before 1850 (Ellis 1829, 1831; Williams 1837; see also Herbert 1991:155-203; Sivasundaram 2005).

[7] See Chapter One (Douglas), this volume.

[8] Brosses's interest was avowedly inspired by a letter on the 'progress of the sciences' written in 1752 to Frederick II of Prussia by the French polymath Pierre-Louis Moreau de Maupertuis (1698-1759) who promoted the search for the *Terres australes* as the most urgent and worthy object of royal scientific patronage ([Brosses] 1756, I:i, 2-4; Maupertuis 1768:375-86). See Dunmore 1965-9, I:45-50; see also Ryan 2002 on Brosses's seminal contribution to the emergence of the anthropology of Oceania in France in the mid-eighteenth century.

[9] Blumenbach 1795:297; Darwin 1871, I:226; Duchet 1995:271, original emphasis.

[10] For parallel interpretations of Buffon, see Bernasconi 2001:x; Blanckaert 2003:135-8; 2006:458-61; Montagu 1997:69.

[11] Buffon 1749b, III:395-411.

[12] Throughout this chapter, as in the Introduction, I retain the French forms *Papou* or *Papoua* because inconsistent contemporary French usages do not always translate exactly into English 'Papuan'.

[13] Dampier 1697:297, 325-6, 456-7, 464-9; 1699:128; 181; 1703:145-9; 1709:4, 122-6, 148. Dampier (1699:176; 1709:23) used Indian in the conventional contemporary sense of an inhabitant of the East Indies, the West Indies, or the Americas generally: 'the *Indian* kind, of a swarthy Copper colour, with black lank Hair'. See Douglas 2006:7-9.

[14] Buffon 1749b, III:408-10, 433, 453-4.

[15] Buffon 1749b, III:410, 528-30.

[16] See Chapter One (Douglas), this volume; Douglas 2005:337-8.

[17] E.g., Burney 1803-17, IV:388; Cook 1955:417; Forster 1982, IV:632. See also Douglas 2006:7-8, 14, 22.

[18] Forster 1777, II:208, 226-8, 231; Forster 1778:228, 276.

[19] Forster 1778:228, 276-7, 284, 353-60; La Pérouse 1797, III:229-30.

[20] Cf. Terrell, Kelly, and Rainbird 2001.

[21] Quirós 1904:38, 143.

[22] [Brosses] 1756, II:375-80, original emphasis. Here Brosses echoed Buffon in counterposing the technical and the common meanings ('species' and 'kind') of the ambiguous term *espèce* (e.g., Buffon 1749, III:519; 1777:479); see also Chapter One (Douglas), this volume.

[23] [Brosses] 1756, I:16-17, 77-80; cf. Ryan 2002:174-84. See the Introduction (Douglas), this volume, for an outline of Brosses's threefold division of the *Terres australes*.

[24] Forster 1778:252-84, original emphasis.

[25] See Douglas 1999b:167-72.

[26] Forster 1777, II:228; Forster 1778:271-6.

[27] Kant 1785, 2001; see Chapter One (Douglas), this volume. For discussions of the Kant-Forster debate, see Agnew 2003:92-3; Bodi 1959:352-3; Gascoigne 2007:151-3; Lagier 2004:35-46; Liebersohn 2006:197-208; Strack 1996.

[28] Forster 1786:62, 77, 79-86, 156-9, 164; Bodi 1959:352-3, 356; Strack 1996:300-8.

[29] Buffon 1777:462, 478; Forster 1778:252, 258; Forster 1786:80, 159-60.

[30] E.g., Forster 1777, II:349-53, 606; 1985a:174-8; see also Eze 1995:216-21; Gascoigne 2007:157-63; Gomsu 2002; Liebersohn 2006:41-57, 200-3; Strack 1996:290-9; West 1989.

[31] Kant 2001:11-12; Kant, quoted in Strack 1996:293-4, 299; quoted in Eze 1995:237, note 70.

[32] Forster 1985a:174, 176, 178.

[33] Forster 1786:76-7, 83, 155, 157, 161-5; 1985a:174; Kant 2001:3, 12; Liebersohn 2006:203, 205.

[34] Forster 1786:78-9, 163-5; 1985b:280, my emphasis.

[35] Blumenbach 1803, I:73; 1806:55-69.

[36] See Chapter One (Douglas), this volume.

[37] Cuvier often publicly acknowledged natural history's debt to Oceanic voyagers, as in my introductory anecdote, and on one occasion credited voyage naturalists with having 'perhaps enriched' zoology more than metropolitan savants had done (1830:106).

[38] Banks [1770-1820]: 8096-8100; Blumenbach to Banks, 19 January 1799, in Banks [1770-1820]: 8098/436-7; Marx 1865:21, 31, note 2; Urban 1998. See Gascoigne 2007:164-8 on Blumenbach's global network of scholarly contacts.

[39] Blumenbach to Banks, 1 November 1793, in Banks [1770-1820]: 8098/116-17, original emphasis.

[40] Blumenbach 1795:302-22, original emphasis; 1803, I:73, 78, note.

[41] See Douglas 2001; 2003:9-11, 23, note 82.

[42] Bougainville 1771:16-17, 214, 269.

[43] In Dalrymple's translation of Quirós's 'Eighth Memorial' of 1610 (1770-1, I:164), specifically cited by Blumenbach (1795:321), 'the people of these countries are many; their colours white, negroes [*loros*, "dark brown"], mulattoes, Indians, and mixed of one and the other. The hair of some is black [*negros*], long, and lank, the others curled and woolly, and of others very red and fine'. Cf. Quirós 1973:38-9.

[44] Dalrymple 1770-1, I:164; Kelly 1966, II:309; Quirós 1973:38-9. For the link presumed between human physical diversity in the Pacific Islands and a hypothetical southern continent, see [Brosses] 1756, II:349-52; Dalrymple 1770-1, I:99-101.

[45] Blumenbach 1795:70, original emphasis.

[46] Mentelle and Malte-Brun 1804:378, 474, 577, original emphasis; see below and Introduction (Douglas), this volume.

[47] Blanckaert 2006:413-14, 429-44, 465-6.

[48] [La Pérouse] 1797, I:165-7, 253. Buffon's *Histoire naturelle* (1749-67) is cited first in the (non-alphabetical) list of works on natural history carried on the expedition and is specifically recommended to the savants by the Académie as the best source of a necessary 'common method' for zoological and anatomical description.

[49] Blumenbach to Banks, 9 October 1787, 8 May 1793, 8 January 1794, 20 December 1798, in Banks [1770-1820]: 8096/385, 8098/8-9, 213-14, 434-5.

[50] Blumenbach 1775:68; 1795:108, 211-23. However, he acknowledged the possibility that 'peculiar forms of the skull', initially forged by 'artifice', might over time become 'hereditary', 'innate', and eventually a 'second nature' (1795:221).

[51] Blumenbach 1795:xxiii-xxvi; Banks to Blumenbach, [June 1787] [draft]; Blumenbach to Banks, 20 June 1787, 12 November 1789, 9 June 1790, 9 January 1791, 8 May 1792, 6 April, 1 November 1793, 8 January, 10 March 1794, 12 June 1799, 2 January 1800, in Banks [1770-1820]: 8096/383-4, 8097/134-5, 261-2, 362-3; 8098/8-9, 114, 116-17, 213-14, 216-17; 8099/12-14, original emphasis.

[52] Cuvier 1800-5, II:13; 1817a, I:54-5; 1978:174-5.

53 Péron 1978:185; Jussieu au Ministre de la Marine, 19 thermidor an 8 [7 August 1800]; Bureau des Ports au Ministre de la Marine, 1ᵉʳ fructidor an 8 [19 August 1800], in France Marine nationale 1796-1815: BB4 997, BB4 995.

54 Bonnemains, Forsyth, and Smith 1988; Lesueur and Petit [1807], 1824; [Péron] n.d.: no. 5. The Collection Lesueur of the Muséum d'Histoire naturelle in Le Havre, France, holds nearly two hundred original sketches, drawings, watercolours, and engravings of indigenous people encountered on the voyage, the vast majority in Van Diemen's Land and New Holland.

55 Péron and Freycinet 1807-16, I:237-8, 448.

56 Péron 1978:183-4, note 10.

57 Péron and Freycinet 1807-16, I:446-84.

58 Jean Copans and Jean Jamin (1978:39) and Rhys Jones (1988:46) saw the causal nexus drawn by Péron between physical constitution and social organization as a sign of Lamarckian influence — ironically, given Péron's patronage by Cuvier, a professional enemy of Jean-Baptiste de Monet de Lamarck (1744-1829). The influence in question might equally be read as late Buffonian (1778:248).

59 Péron and Freycinet 1807-16, I:448, 458, 465-6, 471.

60 Péron and Freycinet 1807-16, II:163-4, note a, my emphasis.

61 Stocking 1968:34; Virey 1800; White 1799.

62 Péron and Freycinet 1807-16, II:164, 182.

63 'Development of Citizen Regnier's dynamometer' (Regnier 1798: plate).

64 Deleuze 1816:449; Lesson 1829:154, note 1; Péron and Freycinet 1807-16, II:164, note a.

65 An English translation of the first volume of Péron's narrative was published in 1809.

66 Copans and Jamin 1978:37-9, 47-8, 66-7; Douglas 2003:23-7; 2006:23-5, 27-9; Jones 1988:36-46; Stocking 1968:32-4, 39-41.

67 Arago et al. 1821; Cuvier 1825, 1830; Cuvier et al. 1806.

68 Dumont d'Urville 1832:19-21; Garnot 1826-30:507-9; Lesson 1826:110; Quoy and Gaimard 1824a:[ii], 9; 1830:50-3, 59; 1830-4, I:i.

69 Cuvier's official report (Cuvier et al. 1806) praised Baudin's naturalists for the unprecedented size of their zoological collection which comprised more than 2,500 new species of animals. In 1804 alone, Cuvier referred in four published articles to separate items in this collection (Bonnemains 1988). In the second edition of *Le règne animal* (1829-30, I:xxxiv; III:v), he acknowledged his debt to the 'many new objects' depicted by naturalists on the voyages of Freycinet and Duperrey and referred to Lesson's racial classification of Oceania. Cuvier (1830:104-5) also commended Dumont d'Urville's zoologists for delivering and reporting on collections of unparalleled size and value (see also Cuvier 1825).

70 Cuvier to Quoy, 11 April 1829, in Quoy [1820-70]: MS 2510, Dossier Cuvier; Quoy to Julien Desjardins, 25 December 1836, in Hamy 1906:457-8.

71 Banks 1962, I, 370-3; II:240-1; Forster 1778:276-84; Forster 1786:66; Marsden 1782; Rensch 2000:62-72.

72 Forster 1778:238, 280-1; Forster 1985a:178.

73 E.g., Blumenbach 1781:52; Chamisso 1986:248-62; Entrecasteaux 1808, I:313; Herder 1812, I:229.

74 [Greatheed] 1799:lxxxv-lxxxviii; Malte-Brun 1803:540-52; 1810b:2-4; Pinkerton 1802, II:431-519; see also Douglas 2006:25-7.

75 Malte-Brun 1803:547-8; Mentelle and Malte-Brun 1804:361-3, 377-8, 463, 474, 577, original emphasis; see also Introduction (Douglas), this volume.

76 Malte-Brun 1810a:2; 1810c:557-8; 1813:226-9, 244-54.

77 Cuvier 1825:177-82; Hamy 1906:457; Ollivier 1988:45-50; Quoy and Gaimard 1824a:[i]; Staum 2003:105-17.

78 The *Uranie* visited New Holland, Timor, Waigeo, the Marianas, the Carolines, and Hawai'i.

79 Quoy and Gaimard 1824b: plates 1, 2; 1824c. The paper was originally read to the Académie des Sciences on 5 May 1823; a long 'extract' attributed to Gaimard was published in the *Nouvelles annales des voyages* (1823); a somewhat different version appeared as the chapter 'On Man' in the *Zoologie* volume of the *Voyage* (1824c) and was republished with a few changes of wording in the *Annales des sciences naturelles* (1826).

80 See Chapter Three (Ballard), this volume.

81 Blumenbach 1806:72; Cuvier 1817a:99; Freycinet 1825-39, I:521-2, 589-90; Gelpke 1993:326-30.

[82] Quoy and Gaimard 1824c:3-6.

[83] [Quoy and] Gaimard 1823:121-6. The later versions of the paper (1824c:7; 1826:33) refer to Gall as 'this celebrated physiologist' but in 1823 he is 'this ideologue doctor' — perhaps an editorial embellishment. Cuvier was a bitter critic of Gall's 'materialist' conception of the mind-brain relationship and dismissed phrenology as a 'pseudo-science' (Gall and Spurzheim 1809; Rudwick 1997:87).

[84] Quoy and Gaimard 1824c:11; 1826:38; cf. 1823:126. See also Renneville 2000:83-96; Staum 2003:49-52.

[85] This clause appears only in the final version of the text (1826:38).

[86] 'Papuan skulls' (Quoy and Gaimard 1824b: plate 2).

[87] The *Coquille* visited Tahiti, Borabora, New Ireland, Waigeo, the Moluccas, Port Jackson, New Zealand, the Carolines, west New Guinea, and Java.

[88] Anon. 1825:215; 1830:174.

[89] Garnot 1826-30:509, 511-15, 518-20. This work was published in Lesson and Garnot's two-volume *Zoologie* of the voyage of the *Coquille* (1826-30) and subsequently expanded into an entry on 'Man' in the *Dictionnaire pittoresque d'histoire naturelle* (1836).

[90] Garnot 1836: plates 218-21.

[91] Lesson was a prolific, if repetitive publisher, prompting Quoy (1864-8:140), his senior naval medical officer and sometime patron, to lament his 'too great facility for writing'. Lesson's racial classification cobbled together several *mémoires* that had been read as scientific papers to the Société d'Histoire naturelle in Paris during 1825 and 1826 under his and Garnot's names. The composite paper was first published in Lesson and Garnot's *Zoologie* (1826-30, I:31-116) but Lesson claimed sole authorship of all but the final section and republished it as an appendix to his *Voyage médical* (1829) — the version cited here.

[92] Lesson 1829:157, 164, 168, 203-4, 214, 219. In a footnote (1829:220, note 1), Lesson insisted that his use of the term 'negro' was purely descriptive, referred only to skin colour, and implied no 'analogy' between black Africans and Oceanians (unlike Garnot's usage).

[93] Lesson 1823-4, II:275, 310, 313.

[94] 'Papou of ~~Bougainville~~ Bouca Island' (Le Jeune [1822-5]: folio 74).

[95] 'New Ireland' (Le Jeune [1822-5]: folio 20).

[96] Lesson 1823-4, II: 310, my emphasis.

[97] Dumont d'Urville borrowed the term *Mélanien* from the French soldier-biologist Jean-Baptiste-Geneviève-Marcellin Bory de Saint-Vincent (1778-1846) who applied it to the fourteenth and 'penultimate' species in his polygenist classification of the human genus (1827, I:82; II, 104-13).

[98] The *Zoologie* of the voyage of the *Astrolabe* in 1826-29 comprises four large volumes and a superb *Atlas* of 198 engraved plates (Quoy and Gaimard 1833). The expedition visited New Holland, New Zealand, Tongatapu, Fiji, New Ireland, northern New Guinea, the Moluccas, Van Diemen's Land, Vanikoro, Guam, and the Malay Archipelago.

[99] Quoy and Gaimard 1830:18. A manuscript draft of this chapter in Quoy's handwriting is held by the municipal Médiathèque in La Rochelle, France (Quoy n.d.a).

[100] Quoy and Gaimard 1830:16-17, 50-3, original emphasis; see also Cuvier 1817a, I:18-19.

[101] Quoy and Gaimard 1830:18-46.

[102] E.g., Douglas 1999a:86-7; 1999b:182-9.

[103] Quoy and Gaimard 1830:46-9.

[104] Quoy and Gaimard 1830:29, 40; see below.

[105] The published paper, 'On the Islands of the Great Ocean', is dated 'Paris, 27 December 1831' but was read to the Société de Géographie on 5 January 1832 and appeared in the 1832 volume of its *Bulletin*.

[106] Dumont d'Urville 1832:2-6, 11-15, 18-19.

[107] See Chapter One (Douglas), this volume.

[108] Kant, quoted in Strack 1996:295; Prichard 1813:iii-iv; 1826, I:80.

[109] Commerson n.d.:5v; Forster 1786:157-9, 161-2.

[110] Dumont d'Urville 1830-3, II:628, note 1; 1832:19; 1834-5, II:320.

[111] Quoy and Gaimard 1824c:2; 1830:29-30; Quoy n.d.a: passim; n.d.b:3; my emphasis; see above.

[112] See Chapter One (Douglas), this volume.

[113] Dumoutier published little about the voyage but repatriated a remarkable phrenological collection, still extant, of 51 *moulages*, plaster busts, and 51 skulls ([1838-40]) and oversaw their reproduction as lithographed photographs in the *Atlas anthropologique* of the official voyage publication ([Dumoutier] 1846). Hombron and Jacquinot, the ships' surgeons, co-authored the 5-volume *Zoologie* of the voyage (1846-54) but each independently wrote one of the first two volumes (Hombron 1846; Jacquinot 1846). The title page of the *Anthropologie* volume attributes overall responsibility to Dumoutier but the zoologist and entomologist Blanchard — not a member of the expedition — is acknowledged as the author of the text (Blanchard 1854).

[114] 'Man is the same everywhere' proclaimed Gall, the originator of phrenology (Gall and Spurzheim 1810-19, I:xxxv).

[115] Dumoutier 1837-40:441, 561; 1843:8, 15-16; n.d.:89-89v.

[116] Blanchard 1854:19, 30, 45, 49, 201.

[117] Blanchard 1854:112-36, 204, 256-7.

[118] Blanchard 1854:9, 12-13, 116-21, 128, 133, 199-218.

[119] Hombron 1846:98-9, 104-5, 131-2, 395-401.

[120] 'Ma-Pou-Ma-Hanga. Female native of the island of Manga-Réva, Gambier Archipelago' ([Dumoutier] 1846: pl. 2). I had hoped for this and the next figure to reproduce photographs of Dumoutier's original *moulages* that the Laboratoire d'anthropologie biologique at the Musée de l'Homme in Paris kindly allowed me to take in 2004. However, since my repeated requests for permission to reproduce these images have gone unanswered, I have had recourse instead to the lithographs of the *moulages* published in the *Atlas anthropologique*.

[121] 'Guenney. Native of Port-Sorelle, (Devon County), north coast of Van Diemen's Land' ([Dumoutier] 1846: pl. 22).

[122] Stocking 1973; see Chapters One (Douglas) and Six (Gardner), this volume.

[123] Blanckaert 1988:28-31; Bynum 1975:8-14; Hall 2002:67-264; Kidd 2006:121-67; Stepan 1982:1-46; Stocking 1968; 1973:xxxiii-cx; 1987:9-77; see Chapter One (Douglas), this volume.

[124] Subsequent editions are titled *Researches into the Physical History of Mankind* (1826, 1836-47).

[125] Cook and King 1784:114-17; Prichard 1813:215, 220-6, 233, 248-317.

[126] Prichard 1836-47, V:3-5, 212-16, 282-5. Prichard's neologism 'Kelænonesia' was a correlate of 'Polynesia' and was, he claimed, etymologically 'more correct' and 'more distinct' than the French alternative *Mélanésie*.

[127] Prichard 1836-47, I:vii-viii, 250-7, 298-302; V:212-57. See above and Chapter One (Douglas), this volume.

[128] Prichard 1813:2-3; 1826, I:125; 1836-47, I:vii, 9.

[129] Prichard 1836-47, V:4-5, 212-85.

[130] Forster 1778:284, 358-9, my emphasis; Dumont d'Urville 1832:19-20.

[131] E.g., [Greatheed] 1799:lxxxv-lxxxvii; Ellis 1831, I:78; Williams 1837:512-13. See Chapters Six (Gardner) and Seven (Weir), this volume.

[132] Anderson 2002:181-243; Brantlinger 2003:117-63; McGregor 1997:19-59; Rivers 1922. See also Chapters One (Douglas) and Four (Turnbull), this volume.

Chapter Three

'Oceanic Negroes': British anthropology of Papuans, 1820-1869

Chris Ballard

Captain James Cook (1728-1779) failed to see much of New Guinea or its inhabitants the Papuans. By late 1770, when the battered *Endeavour* reached the southern shores of New Guinea, Cook and his crew were on their way home and little disposed to attempt contact with the island's reportedly hostile people. But on Monday, 3 September, Cook (1955:408), 'having a mind to land once in this Country before we quit it altogether', went ashore in the pinnace in a party of twelve, accompanied by the naturalists Joseph Banks (1743-1820) and Daniel Solander (1733-1782). The first moment of encounter was pure Defoe: 'we had no sooner landed than we saw the print of Mens feet fresh upon the Sand'. Just two hundred yards further along the beach, the ship's party was attacked by three or four men throwing 'darts' and lime powder. After firing a volley, they retired, followed 'by 60 or as some thought about 100 of the natives'. From the safety of the pinnace, the Europeans:

> now took a view of them at our leisure; they made much the same appearance as the New Hollanders, being nearly of the same stature, and having their hair short cropped: like them also they were all stark naked, but we thought the colour of their skin was not quite so dark; this however might perhaps be merely the effect of their not being quite so dirty.[1]

Other than a cursory examination of their 'darts' and a short digression on the curious practice of discharging lime powder from bamboo pipes, this was about all that Cook had to say on the subject of Papuans.

The relative absence of references to New Guinea in the literature of the Cook voyages and in subsequent Cook scholarship weighed heavily on the early development of an anglophone anthropology of the Papuans, as it has also on the historiography of that anthropology. Anglophone debate about 'race' in Oceania has hinged largely on the terms established by the Cook voyage literature, most obviously through the contrast between the 'two great varieties' of South Sea Islanders identified by the naturalist Johann Reinhold Forster (1729-1798) and later re-cast as Melanesians and Polynesians.[2] Until the onset of concerted European exploration of the main island of New Guinea in the 1870s, Papuans or 'Oceanic Negroes' were the subject of much metropolitan anticipation and speculation. In his instructions for the scientists on Baudin's expedition of 1800-4 (1978:175-6), the French naturalist Georges Cuvier (1769-1832) listed a series of locations whose inhabitants were 'still insufficiently known' and first amongst them were 'the Papuans, or inhabitants of New Guinea, who have long been regarded as Negroes'. Though French voyaging scientists of the late eighteenth and early nineteenth centuries had been the first to generate systematic descriptions of Papuans,[3] their influence on European thinking about New Guinea and its inhabitants does not appear to have extended much beyond the mid-nineteenth century, perhaps because French interest in Oceania beyond its established colonial territories subsequently waned.[4]

Instead, we find repeated reference in European literature from the mid-nineteenth century to the writings and authority of a trio of British authors: the colonial administrator and philologist, John Crawfurd (1783-1868); the navigator and translator, George Windsor Earl (1813-1865); and the field naturalist and co-founder with Charles Darwin (1809-1882) of the theory of natural selection, Alfred Russel Wallace (1823-1913). Where previous observations on the inhabitants of New Guinea had derived largely from transient shipboard voyagers, each of these three authors was resident at or closely in contact with one or more of the region's early settler outposts, such as Batavia, Singapore, and Port Essington. All three published their views on the contrasting moral and physical characters of the Malay and the Papuan. Their authority as field observers was widely acknowledged and their reports furnished metropolitan debates with the means to fix these racial categories within a global schema of human difference. Most importantly, they generated their own accounts of these categories, acting as both field observers and metropolitan theorists. However, the importance they assigned to moral traits and questions of character and comportment in the distinction of racial difference sets them apart both from earlier comparative anatomists and from later anthropologists.[5] The dramatic contradictions and value reversals evident in their individual pronouncements on the Malay and Papuan 'types' neatly illustrate the struggles of an emergent nineteenth-century science of race to agree upon standards, or perhaps styles, for field observation, analysis, and comparison.

My focus here is on just three of the themes common to the writings of these authors: the increasing priority accorded to observation or presence in the field; the fundamental role of cardinality or orientation in the regional comparison of human populations; and the gathering centrality during this period of notions of racial purity and boundedness. The period of the mid-nineteenth century, immediately preceding Europe's first substantial engagements with New Guinea and with Papuans, coincided with a broad regional transition from voyager to resident or settler discourses as the principal conduits for knowledge about indigenous Oceanian people. On a global scale, this was also the era that witnessed the increasing deployment in anthropological observation of a rhetoric of precision (Bravo 1999; Ballard n.d.) and a privileging of new types of more intensive, terrestrial observation, championed by naturalist collectors such as Alexander von Humboldt (1769-1859) and Alfred Russel Wallace — developments that would prove crucial to the consolidation of a science of race.

The scientific voyages in the late eighteenth and early nineteenth centuries laid the foundations for a re-ordering of the relationships between field sites and metropolitan centres as 'ocular demonstration', or observation in the field, came to be accorded increasing privilege (Withers 2004). The first half of the nineteenth century witnessed the rise to prominence of the naturalist field observer and the Malay Archipelago and New Guinea, along with the Amazon and central Africa, were the type locations for this new genus (Driver and Martins 2005). Yet, if field observation carried new weight, this was still counter-balanced by the metropolitan or textual domination of scientific knowledge. Field observers operated very consciously with a sense of the necessity for accomplishment and the required discovery of new species and their enquiries were permeated by a keen awareness of the concerns of their metropolitan sponsors and audiences. Reports from the field on human subjects represented a complex amalgam of received and anticipated forms of expression of their differences, on one hand, and the material imprints of the encounter on the other. Despite the apparent valorization of ocular demonstration, field observers were often limited in their capacity to confront or contradict metropolitan theories of race and their reports sought systematically to exclude what Johannes Fabian (2000) has recently described as the 'ecstatic' dimension of the encounter — the excess of experience that confounds anticipation but, in descriptions of racial difference, is repeatedly elided in the translation from the relational intimacy of personal diaries to the distanced perspective of published narratives.

Presence, in this context, implies direct experience, principally through the instrument of vision; Fabian's (1983) earlier account of 'visualism' in anthropology offers a useful point of departure for an understanding of the role of observation in the representation of human difference. Visualism, in Fabian's analysis (1983:106), consists of an emphasis on visual and spatial conventions for representation. Subscription to these conventions by observers and their readers endows them with the capacity to communicate the essential character of a culture or a physical type: 'the ability to "visualize" a culture or society becomes almost synonymous for understanding it'. Fabian's visualism supplies a handy metaphor for the process of reduction of human cultural or physical complexity to a few key traits, such that information on stature for Pygmies or curly hair for Papuans becomes all that is required to convey a large body of other implied and associated knowledge about the subject under observation (Ballard 2001).

Under these terms, the physical presence of the observer assumes a heightened priority in the attribution of authority.

The cardinality of comparison is a largely overlooked element in the constitution of regional topographies of difference in Oceania. As implied by Cook's observations above on Papuans and the use of Aboriginal Australians as a comparative foil, trajectories of travel had a pronounced influence on the character of descriptions and the terms of comparison. Most of the major scientific voyages of the eighteenth and early nineteenth centuries had traversed Oceania from east to west, or south to north, approaching Melanesia by way of the central Pacific or around Australia in order to evade the political delicacies of access through the Dutch-controlled East Indies. Under these conditions, what would come to be termed Melanesia in the anglophone literature referred not so much to the island of New Guinea as it did to the extended archipelagic screen of Vanuatu, New Caledonia, and the Solomon Islands which came to serve as the primary negative poles for positive evaluations of Polynesia.[6] What emerges from a reading of the pre-twentieth-century anglophone anthropology of Papuans, however, is that the racial character of Papuans (as distinct from Melanesians) was historically defined not so much through comparison with Polynesians to the east as with Malays to the west. This is evident even in the writing of the French navigator Jules-Sébastien-César Dumont d'Urville (1790-1842) who, despite his later fame as promoter of the more limited division of the Pacific Islands into Melanesia, Polynesia, and Micronesia, nonetheless included New Guinea and Australia within his denomination 'Melanesia'. Dumont d'Urville looked both east and west in his speculations on the racial character and origins of the Papuans: 'Their name, Papuans, according to the most common explanation, indicates their black colour, *by contrast with* that of the Boughis and the copper-coloured inhabitants of the Malaysian Islands'.[7] In comparison with the more holistic vision of the French writers of the period, each of the three anglophone authors addressed here essentially approached and viewed New Guinea from the west. From this perspective, Papuans were described principally through a series of contrasts with Malays.

Finally, this chapter seeks to track the elaboration during the nineteenth century of notions of the boundedness or purity of racial types that began to emerge from the late 1820s as the central problem for a scientific knowledge of race. This development proceeded not through direct theorization of the essential character of racial purity but rather through contemplation of the problems posed by racial 'mixing' or miscegenation — a challenge that had long preoccupied slave-holding communities in the Americas and would continue to fuel racialist conceptions of difference in Oceania, as elsewhere.[8] The accounts of Papuans furnished by Crawfurd, Earl, and Wallace united what had previously been a largely disparate field of observations. The principal method in each case consisted of a willingness to distil a multitude of received and personal observations in order to produce an attractively simple opposition between fundamentally *racial* types. The significance and novelty of their contribution is best appreciated in the context of prior European representations of Papuans.

'Papuanesia'

Etymologies for the term 'Papua' are illuminating insofar as they track the semantic shifts and slippages between references to people, place, and race. Modern usage itself is scarcely fixed, with Papuans commonly identified either as the autochthonous inhabitants of the main island of New Guinea or as the residents of either of three different administrative regions: the provinces of Papua and West Papua within the Republic of Indonesia, in the western half of the island, and the former territory of colonial Papua in the southern half of what is now Papua New Guinea. Linguists, meanwhile, reserve the term 'Papuan' for a loose set of highly differentiated languages defined negatively as being 'non-Melanesian' or 'non-Austronesian', some of which extend westward to the Indonesian islands of Timor, Alor, Pantar, and Halmahera and south and east to the Torres Strait and the Bismarck Archipelago (Ross 2005). Sidney Ray (1858-1939), noting Earl's earlier work on Papuan anthropology, provided the definitive statement of 'Papuan' as a linguistic appellation in 1892:

> For these non-Melanesian languages of New Guinea I used the name Papuan. This did not imply any community of character or origin in the language so-called, but merely served as a convenient term to indicate their archaic features as the probably aboriginal languages of the great island of New Guinea (1926:24).

Solely for the purposes of this chapter, I refer to the main island as New Guinea and to the inhabitants of New Guinea and its wider fringe of associated islands as Papuans, without distinction.[9]

Since the mid-nineteenth century, conventional wisdom has derived the term Papua from a putative Malay source, *papua* or *puahpuah*, usually defined as 'frizzy-haired', with the additional implication of black or dark skin colour. Yet in his search for an origin for this association, the historian and former official of Netherlands New Guinea, Sollewijn Gelpke (1993:320-1), could find nothing earlier to substantiate this association than the series of often conflicting definitions provided by Crawfurd in 1852: "'*papuwah* (Jav. and Mal.) frizzled", "a negrito of the Indian islands; an African negro"'; "'*pâpuwah*, frizzled; the island of New-Guinea; an inhabitant of that island being of the negrito race'"; and "'Negro of the Indian Islands: Papuwah, puwah-puwah'". Crawfurd identified the 1812 dictionary of the orientalist and philologist William Marsden (1754-1836) as his key source and yet Marsden's dictionary offers only '*papūah* as "frizzled" and "crisp curled (as certain plants)"'.[10] Gelpke's careful enquiries have established that the term Papua was first documented by Portuguese explorers in the sixteenth century and referred loosely to the islands lying to the east of the northern Moluccas.[11] As Portuguese and Spanish knowledge of the region grew, the scope of the term gradually narrowed to encompass the mainland of New Guinea and the neighbouring Raja Ampat and Schouten island groups and reference was made equally to '*as Papuas*' (the Papuan islands) and '*os Papuas*' (the Papuans) (Gelpke 1993:322-6). What was initially a cardinal direction had come to identify, first, a fixed set of locations and then the inhabitants of those places, before assuming its final reference to the physical attributes of black skin and frizzly hair. By the late eighteenth century, Papua (the location) was defined in reverse as the residence of black-skinned and frizzly-haired Papuans.[12]

An additional and possibly prior sense of the term Papua is hinted at in Gelpke's research and in the writings of Iberian and other European explorers. The Portuguese Gábriel Rebelo observed in the 1560s that, '"*Papua*, em todas as linguas de Maluco diz *Cafre*" ("Papua" in all Moluccan languages, means "heathen")'.[13] *Cafre*, or *kāfir*, the Arabic term for heathen or non-believer, nicely captures this additional quality of Papuan as a negative reference to all those people of the region who remained unconverted to Islam and culturally undomesticated by the Islamic principalities of the Moluccas.[14] The *Raya Papua* or King of the Papuans, rather imaginatively described by Antonio Pigafetta in 1521, was thus the putative sovereign of the non-Moslem population of the interior of Halmahera and the islands to its east. The Spaniard Luis Váez de Torres, arriving in the Moluccas via the southern coast of New Guinea in 1606, similarly wrote that the 'Moors … carry on conquests of the people *they call* the Papuas, and preach to them the sect of Mahomet'.[15]

How then did European writers and observers come to restrict the term Papuan primarily to physical attributes and how did they set about composing an increasingly precise definition of those attributes? European voyagers apparently first heard of 'Papoia' from about 1511 and, in this moment before the actual encounter, the Portuguese Tomé Pires (1944, I:222) could still record (if not credit) accounts of Papuans couched in the medieval mode as 'men with big ears who cover themselves with them'. From 1526, when the Portuguese Jorge de Meneses landed and 'wintered' at Biak, the terms employed to describe Papuans were dominated by explicit analogy with sub-Saharan Africans. The Englishman William Dampier (1652-1715) in 1700 and the Frenchman Louis-Antoine de Bougainville (1729-1814) in 1768 were amongst the many for whom the inhabitants of New Guinea and nearby islands were 'Negroes' while others, such as the Spaniard Diego de Prado y Tovar in 1606 and the Dutchman Jan Carstensz in 1623, referred to them still more generically as 'Kaffirs' or as 'Indians'.[16] Africa's ghostly presence in the Pacific was given further substance in 1545 by the Spaniard Iñigo Ortiz de Retes when he named the main island of the Papuan archipelago 'New Guinea', reflecting both the perceived similarities between the people of New Guinea and of West Africa and the fond hope of the presence of gold through the alchemy of appellative association.

Beyond this common focus on Africa as a pole of comparison, there was little uniformity amongst the physical characteristics listed for the inhabitants of New Guinea. The variation between different Papuan communities evident to European observers was described in terms of 'types', 'peoples', 'men', 'classes', and 'nations' as well as 'races'. The word race in its modern biological sense did not obviously feature in descriptions of Papuans until the visits to New Guinea of the French Restoration scientific voyages under Louis de Freycinet (1779-1842) in 1818-19, Louis-Isidore Duperrey (1786-1865) in 1823, and Dumont d'Urville in 1827-28 and 1838-40.[17] Hair and skin colour were the two primary physical attributes upon which definitions of 'the Papuan' rested. As Douglas (Chapter Two, this volume) shows with respect to accounts of indigenous communities more generally in Oceania, the wide variation in skin colour reported both within and between different communities by observers of the sixteenth and seventeenth centuries gradually gave way to an increasingly uniform consensus on the more limited chromatic range proper to pure types or races. Where Prado and Torres could write in 1606 of adjacent communities along the south coast of New Guinea as variously 'tall and white', 'tawny', 'not very white', the 'colour of mulattos', or 'very dark' and the Dutchman Henrik Haalbos, sailing with Abel Janszoon Tasman (1603-1659) in 1643, of people along the north coast as 'tawny', 'pitch-black', or 'yellow',[18] from the time of Dampier's encounters with the inhabitants of New Guinea and the Bismarck Archipelago in 1700, Papuans were described simply and almost universally as 'black'.[19] While finer chromatic gradations continued to be discerned amongst Papuans, 'black' in an Oceanic context indicated colour within a hierarchical frame; henceforth, on any axis of comparison, Papuans could safely be presumed to be darker than most other Oceanic peoples.

A similar shift is evident in European descriptions of Papuan hair. For the earlier Iberian and Dutch voyagers, the presence or absence of facial hair was possibly more important than the form of head hair and frequent reference was made to Papuan men with 'thick beards'.[20] Again, Dampier was perhaps the first to emphasize the actual form of head hair, writing of 'Curl-pated *New Guinea Negroes*' with 'frizled' or 'short curl'd Hair'.[21] By the 1760s, Bougainville and the Englishman Philip Carteret (1733-1796) were employing the term 'woolly' along with 'frizzled' while Thomas Forrest (1729?-1802?) introduced the epithet 'mopheaded Papuas' in 1779.[22] But it was the French Restoration voyages that focused especial attention on Papuan coiffure, with lengthy descriptions and elaborate illustration of the 'mopped' or 'bushy' hairstyles sported by men in north-western New Guinea, in particular (Figure 12).[23] The coincidence of this discovery with the mid-nineteenth century re-definition of 'Papuan' as 'frizzle-haired' is surely no accident. By the 1850s, the racial metonymy was taken for granted, as in the summation of an anonymous reviewer (Anon. 1854:50): 'A black skin and a frizzly head of hair make the Papuan'.

Figure 12: Jules-Louis Le Jeune, 'Habitants du Port Dori. Nouvelle Guinée' [1823].[24]

Pen and wash drawing. SH 356. Vincennes, France: Service historique de la Défense, département Marine. Photograph B. Douglas.

A third shift over time in European accounts of Papuans has to do with the other general characteristics deemed necessary for an accurate portrayal of the differences between Papuans and other Oceanic peoples. A striking element of pre-nineteenth-century accounts is the emphasis on nudity and body decoration, whether clothing, paint, piercings, scarification, or tattoos. Without an established literature and thus a set of preconceptions about Papuans, early European observers concentrated on what was most visually arresting in their encounters. However, by the nineteenth century, clothing and decoration were increasingly of less significance to racial taxonomy than the body beneath. Nineteenth-century descriptions of encounters with Papuans moved almost immediately to questions of height, colour, hair, and bodily form, visually stripping Papuan bodies of the encumbrances of culture. Where early European explorers had imagined near-naked Oceanian people as potentially clothed and converted to Christianity (Thomas 1994:73), their later nineteenth-century counterparts, meeting clothed Oceanians, conceived them naked once again.

A history of all the other descriptive terms routinely applied to Papuans lies beyond the scope of this paper but it should be stressed that the definition of Papuan-ness for Europeans rested as much upon a host of largely negative attributions, including cannibalism, savagery, treachery, polygamy, and the poor 'usage' of women, as it did upon purely bodily characteristics. For the purposes of this chapter, however, the persistence of a specific axis of comparison for Papuans is of particular interest: for almost all those voyagers for whom encounters with Papuans were deemed worthy of extended comment, the strongest contrast lay not to the east, where apparently more subtle gradations led from what is now Fiji through Island Melanesia to New Guinea, but rather to the west, where a sharper break was commonly discerned between Papuans and Malays.

Dampier noted this contrast in 1700 in the Moluccas, where he distinguished between 'a sort of very tawny *Indians*, with long black Hair' and 'shock Curl-pated *New Guinea Negroes*'; in 1767, Carteret identified a striking break between the Admiralty Islands, peopled by 'woolly headed black, or rather copper coloured Negroes', and the Micronesian inhabitants of tiny Mapia Island, to the north of western New Guinea, whom he described as 'Indien Copper Colour'd ... [with] fine long black hair'; and Forrest differentiated 'two sorts' of inhabitants of the Molucca Islands, 'the long hair'd Moors, of a copper colour, like Malays in every respect; and the mopheaded Papuas'.[25] The Restoration French voyagers vigorously restated this distinction, with the surgeon-naturalists Jean-René Constant Quoy (1790-1869) and Joseph-Paul Gaimard (1793-1858) writing of 'a race ... similar to that of southern Africa, apparently stranded [*égarée*, literally "strayed"] in the midst of the Malay race which inhabits the archipelagos of Sunda, Borneo, and the Moluccas' (1823:117).

If 'Papua' as a location had referred initially to an area east of the Moluccas and subsequently to the inhabitants of New Guinea, during the nineteenth century it also emerged as a biologized or racialized toponym found much more widely throughout island Southeast Asia and the western Pacific. This new, racially defined region was variously named '*Mélanésie*' by Dumont d'Urville, 'Oceanic Negroland' by the English ethnologist James Cowles Prichard (1786-1848), or 'Papuanesia' by the English colonial lawyer James Richardson Logan (1819-1869) — highlighting the constantly expanding and contracting range of people identified as 'Papuans'.[26] For those authors for whom Papuan encompassed all other forms of 'Negrito', including Aboriginal Tasmanians, Andaman Islanders, and interior communities in Luzon, Mindanao, and the Moluccas, Papuanesia was both a region and a temporal layer in the racial stratigraphy of the region, representing its earliest human settlers. At its broadest extent, the boundaries of this racial zone extended from Fiji in the east, to Tasmania in the south, the Philippines in the north, and the Andaman Islands in the west (Figure 13).

Figure 13: George Windsor Earl, 'Seats of the Papuan Race in the Indian Archipelago'.[27]

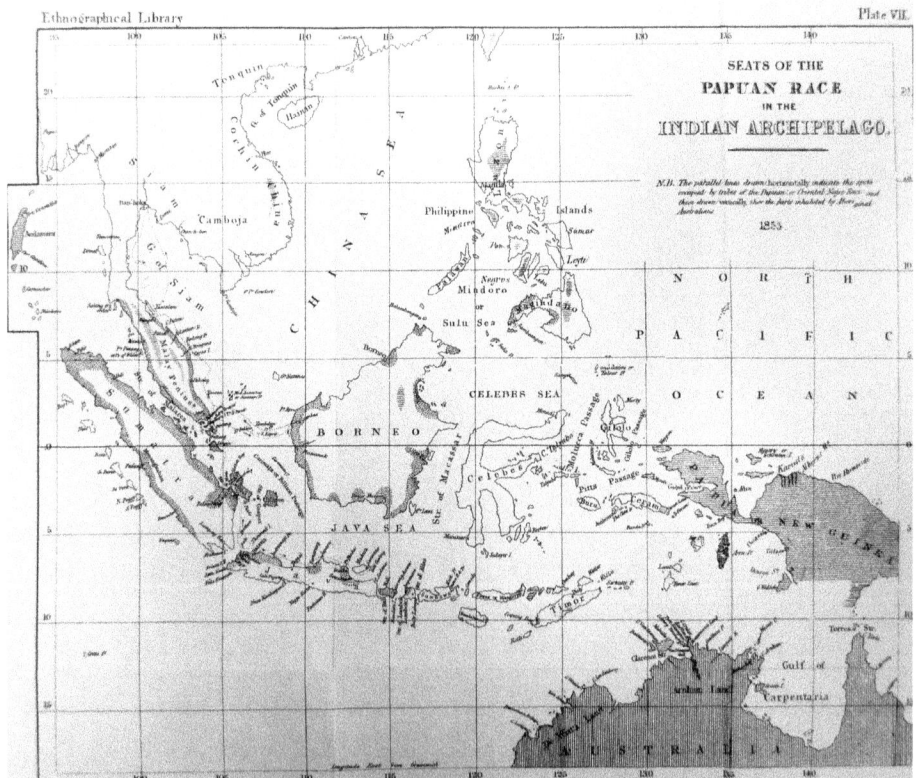

Engraving. Photograph B. Douglas.

The three anglophone authors considered here, Crawfurd, Earl, and Wallace, collectively laid the foundations for theories about Papuans during the mid-nineteenth century. The circle of acquaintance and internal reference amongst the three was almost complete: Crawfurd cited Earl approvingly (though he insisted on referring to him as 'Mr. Windsor East'), borrowed but then misplaced several of Wallace's field notebooks from the Malay Archipelago, and later clashed with Wallace;[28] Earl, in turn, cited Crawfurd's 1820 volume but might not have known much of Wallace as he died before the publication of the latter's major book on the Malay Archipelago; while Wallace had read Crawfurd's writings on the Malay or Indian Archipelago and made frequent reference to the work of Earl. All three were certainly familiar with at least some of the Dutch and French literature on New Guinea. Each of the three authors derived his authority, to a significant extent, through claims to a particular status as an observer in the field. However, the contrasts evident in their varying statements on Malays and Papuans nicely illustrate the transformation in the practice and metropolitan reception of ethnological and anthropological field observations over the passage of just forty years.

John Crawfurd — 'two separate races'

The eminent Scottish orientalist Crawfurd enjoyed a stellar career in the administration of Britain's fledgling overseas empire. Trained as a doctor, he spent five years from 1803 with the Indian Army in the Northwest Provinces. After being transferred to Penang, he took part in the British conquest of Dutch-held Java in 1811. Between 1811 and 1816, Crawfurd served as British Resident at Yogyakarta during the period of Java's British administration under Sir Thomas Stamford Raffles (1781-1826). Following a series of further diplomatic appointments — in Siam, Cochin China, Singapore, and Burma — Crawfurd returned permanently to England in 1828 where he established a reputation as a leading linguist and philologist and as an ambitious if frustrated politician.[29] Much like any writer seeking to capture the headwaters of a particular field, Crawfurd published a series of encyclopedias, general histories, and descriptive dictionaries — on the history of Java, the Indian Archipelago (1820), the Burmese court, the Malay language (1852), and the Indian Islands (1856). Combining these scholarly pursuits with a streak of ruthless ambition, he set about conquering London's academic society, a campaign recently documented in some detail by Ter Ellingson (2001).[30] In alliance with James Hunt (1833-1869), later president himself of the racialist Anthropological Society, Crawfurd engineered a coup within the largely monogenist Ethnological Society of London, of which he was elected president in 1860.

Crawfurd's views on race were decidedly individual and polygenist in all but name (Stocking 1987:100). Although strident in his opposition to slavery, (which led to his break with James Hunt and other proponents of slavery in the Anthropological Society), and contemptuous of anthropological and anatomical attempts to classify differences amongst races on the basis of physical characteristics, Crawfurd also denied any unity to mankind, insisting on immutable, hereditary, and timeless differences in racial character, principal amongst which was the 'very great' difference in 'intellectual capacity'.[31] His largely intuitive 'ethnological' approach to the question of the origins of these differences relied substantially upon the conventional skills of a gentleman philologist and ethnologist of the day (1820, I:27): 'It is by a comparison of languages,—of customs and manners,—of arbitrary institutions,—and by reference to the geographical and moral condition of the different races alone, that we can expect to form any rational hypothesis on this obscure subject'.

Crawfurd's earlier writing (1820, I:14-16) appears to acknowledge the significance of environmental elements — notably climate and staple foods — in the formation of racial differences. Championing the grains and cereals which he associated with the history of the European races, he regarded non-European staples such as sago and rice with a dislike bordering on revulsion (1856:262): 'Those tribes that live on sago, which embraces the wide region east of Celebes, including New Guinea, are either illiterate, or rude and savage, whether belonging to the Malay or Negro race'. Yet, in the same textual breath, Crawfurd (1856:264) proceeded to suggest that even where the climatic conditions existed for civilization, as on Java, there was little evidence for European-style progress and that the only possible explanation for this was the 'inferior intellectual capacity' of non-European races. The hardening racialism of Crawfurd's views was evident in a prolific series of tendentious and frequently repetitive articles on race published during the 1860s in the *Transactions of the Ethnological Society*, under his own presidency. Here (1861a:79, 85, 92), he jettisoned any residual belief in the effects of environment on fundamental human difference, denying any substantial role to either climate or diet, though he allowed for some impact of diet on 'mental development'. While he was dismissive of the Darwinians and of any attempt to align certain races more closely with the apes, Crawfurd placed considerable emphasis on the variety of human races and on the hierarchy of superiority amongst them, concluding that 'practically, the races may be considered as distinct species'.

Crawfurd's three-volume *History of the Indian Archipelago* (1820) exerted a considerable influence on early nineteenth-century thinking on race in the region.[32] Probably following the lead of Forster, who had referred his 'two great varieties' in the South Seas to 'the two different races of men' in the 'East Indian isles', Crawfurd noted the 'singular phenomenon' of an '*original* and *innate* distinction of the inhabitants into two separate races'. He defined these two 'aboriginal races' visually through the intersection of hair and skin colour attributes: the first was a 'brown' race of 'Indian islanders' with 'lank hair' and the second a 'black' or 'negro' race with 'woolly or frizzled' hair. Crawfurd sought to illustrate this contrast through an engraving that portrayed 'A Papua or Negro of the Indian Islands' alongside 'Kătut a Native of Bali one of the Brown complexioned Race' (Figure 14).[33]   Though Crawfurd explicitly denied any connection between the 'African negro' and what he variously referred to as the 'Austral', 'Asian', 'Oriental', or 'Oceanic' Negro, what was transmitted to the latter through the analogizing epithet of 'Negro' was the entire raft of negrophobic assumptions about intelligence, productivity, and so on, long associated with sub-Saharan Africans in European thinking: 'The *brown* and *negro* races of the Archipelago may be considered to present, in their physical and moral character, a complete parallel with the white and negro races of the western world'.[34]

Crawfurd then mapped this contrast across the archipelago, discerning a physical and moral gradient descending from west to east:

> Civilization originated in the west [of the archipelago], where are situated the countries capable of producing corn. Man is there most improved, and his improvement decreases, in a geographical ratio, as we go eastward, until, at New Guinea, the termination of the Archipelago, we find the whole inhabitants an undistinguished race of savages. (1820, I:15-16)

This racialized topography could be accounted for through the comfortably familiar historical scenario of the displacement of inferior by superior races:[35]

> The East Insular negro is a distinct variety of the human species, and evidently a very inferior one. Their puny stature, and feeble frames, cannot be ascribed to the poverty of their food or the hardships of their condition, for the lank-haired races living under circumstances equally precarious, have vigorous constitutions. Some islands they enjoy almost exclusively to themselves, yet they have in no instance risen above the most abject state of barbarism. Whenever they are encountered by the fairer races, they are hunted down like the wild animals of the forest, and driven to the mountains or fastnesses incapable of resistance (1820, I:24-6).

Crawfurd appears to have been largely indifferent to questions concerning the reliability of his often-uncited sources. Indeed, the extent of his personal observations on Papuans seems to have been limited to the inspection of Papuan slaves who had been brought to Java.[36] Writing in 1820, Crawfurd pronounced the Papuan to be 'a dwarf African negro', amongst whom a fully grown male measured no more than 4 feet 9 inches: 'I do not think I ever saw any that in stature exceeded five feet'. Though he recounted claims by other observers for a 'more robust' Negro in New Guinea, Crawfurd was careful to point out that he had not seen them himself — a sort of backhanded respect for the value of field observations. Having dismissed most other first-hand accounts of encounters with Papuans as 'indistinct and imperfect', he declared that of Pierre Sonnerat to be 'the best' and duly transcribed the most pejorative portions of what was perhaps the least flattering description of Papuans available at the time.[37] Sonnerat, despite the extravagant claim of the title of his book, *Voyage à la Nouvelle Guinée* (1776), never reached New Guinea.

Figure 14: W.H. Lizars, 'A Papua or Negro of the Indian Islands; Kătut a Native of Bali one of the Brown complexioned Race'.[38]

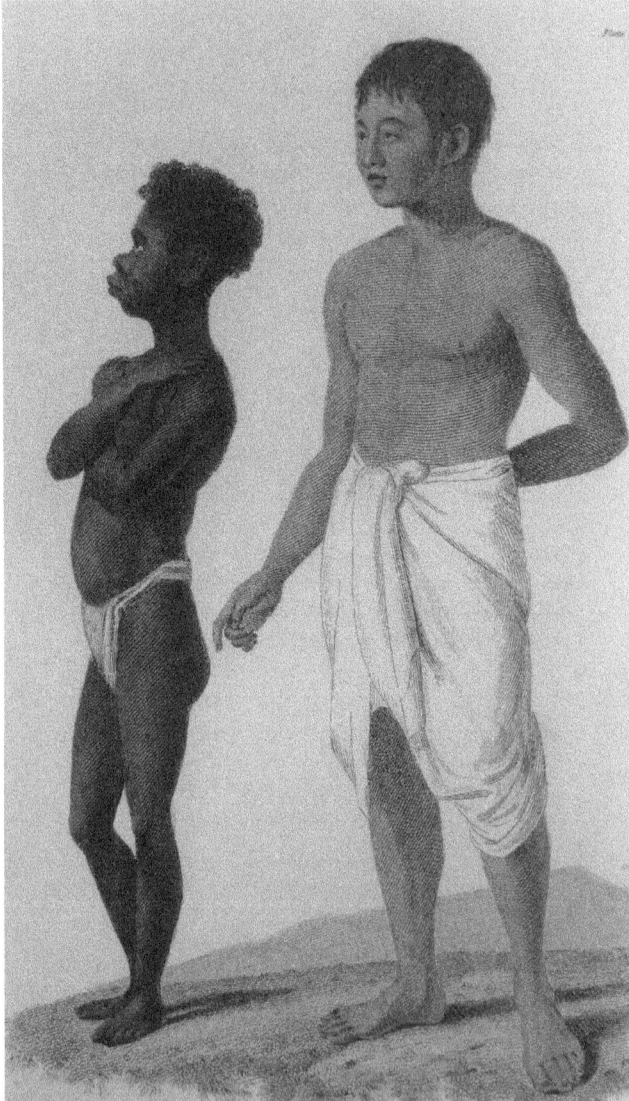

Engraving. Photograph B. Douglas.

Figure 15: William Daniell, 'A Papuan or Native of New Guinea 10 years old'.[39]

Aquatint. Photograph B. Douglas.

Yet Crawfurd was entirely aware that the 'Papuan' featured in his 1820 volume and used to illustrate the 'puny stature, and feeble frames' of Papuans generally was in fact a ten-year old slave.[40] The Papuan figure in Crawfurd's composite image was an unacknowledged reproduction of an illustration in an earlier volume by Raffles (Figure 15). Raffles (1817, II:ccxxxv) had taken the boy into his service on Bali 'under very peculiar circumstances' and later took him to

England where 'his arrival ... excited some curiosity, as being the first individual of the woolly haired race of Eastern Asia who has been brought to this country'.[41] The boy, 'whom we sometimes call Papua, and sometimes (more to his satisfaction) Dick', was duly inspected by the physician and anatomist Sir Everard Home (1756-1832), who formally described the 'particulars' in which 'the Papuan differs from the African negro'. Crawfurd's knowing employment of Raffles's image thus perpetrated a double misrepresentation: creating a general type from a known and named individual and, in support of his contrast between Malay and Papuan, wilfully ignoring the age of his subject in order to advance his claim that Papuans were 'puny'.[42]

George Windsor Earl — 'a single glance is sufficient'

Born in London, George (Samuel) Windsor Earl travelled by ship to India in 1827 as a midshipman at the age of 14 and then to Western Australia in 1830 as an indentured settler. He returned to the sea in 1832, travelling extensively between Batavia and Singapore, and rose to command his own trading brig in only two years, aged just 21. After a period back in England, he became involved in the promotion of permanent British settlement of the north coast of Australia, returning in 1838 to establish Port Essington with the North Australia Expedition. The challenges of the Port Essington settlement and several other ventures crushed Earl and he was invalided from Port Essington to London in 1845. Another attempt to launch his Australian career, this time by promoting cotton cultivation and steam transport between Sydney and Singapore, resulted again in poor health and an enforced convalescence in England. By 1855 he was once again in Australia and Singapore, shuttling from one position as a resident administrator to another until his death in 1865, en route to England from his last post at Penang.[43]

A skilled linguist, hydrographer, navigator, and draughtsman, Earl came to fame initially through the publication of a series of papers and books on the Indian Archipelago, combining his own experiences with a close knowledge of the relevant Dutch sources. He was able to secure a London publisher for his first major work, a translation of Kolff's (1840) account of his 1825 expedition to the Arafura Sea. While in London in 1845, he began to produce a series of articles on racial types for the *Journal of the Indian Archipelago and Eastern Asia*, edited by J.R. Logan, his principal sponsor, and published in Singapore. These articles were then collected and reprinted in 1853, when Earl was undergoing another period of convalescence in England, as *The Native Races of the Indian Archipelago: Papuans* — the first and, as it transpired, only volume of a planned series which was to have included separate works on Australians, 'Malayu-Polynesians', and Moluccans.

Earl's *Papuans* would remain the standard reference on the subject throughout the second half of the nineteenth century and his reputation as the first anthropologist of the Papuans endured into the twentieth. Earl's status as an authority on Papuans was widely acknowledged amongst those of his peers with regional field experience, such as the Dutchmen Jan Pijnappel (1822-1901) and Pieter Jan Baptist Carel Robidé van der Aa (1832-1887) and the Englishman John MacGillivray (1821–1867).[44] In the 1920s, reviewing the state of knowledge about the races of the Netherlands East Indies, J.P. Kleiweg de Zwaan (1925:83-8) would single out Earl as the point of departure in his canonical sequence of researchers in regional anthropology. Earl himself met or corresponded with leading ethnologists of the day such as Logan and Prichard, with the latter referring respectfully to his field experience (1847:227): 'Mr. Earle [sic] ... is better acquainted from personal observation and intercourse with the Papua race than any former voyager has been'. Even Crawfurd (1852:clxi), not known for generosity in his personal appraisals (and discounting the observations of citizens of other European nations), asserted that 'Mr. Earl saw much more of the Negroes of New Guinea than any other Englishman' and quoted him at length. Another influential metropolitan anthropologist, the Frenchman Armand de Quatrefages (1810-1872), founded his analyses of Papuans and Negritos (1895) almost entirely on Earl's writings. Earl was also cited as a local authority on more general matters by authors such as Darwin and Wallace,[45] both of whom drew on his observations on the influence of deep-sea channels on bio-geographic discontinuities in the Indian Archipelago.[46] Perhaps Earl's most enduring claim to fame, though it is poorly known, was his invention in 1850 of the term 'Indu-nesia', later adopted and modified by Logan as 'Indonesia'.[47]

Whatever his proficiencies as a navigator in the Eastern Archipelago, once amongst the shoals of metropolitan scholarly society, Earl evidently lacked either the social standing, the connections, or the cunning of Crawfurd. Though he addressed the Royal Geographical Society twice (in 1837 and 1845), he never sought to become a member, apparently because he felt snubbed by the lack of acknowledgement in a paper published by the Society of material from his 1845 address.[48] Thereafter, and possibly as a consequence of this perceived rejection, Earl (1853:23, 68) developed a deep antipathy to metropolitan scholarship, citing approvingly only what he termed the 'unbiassed testimony' of other field observers whose evidence, being 'perfectly innocent of all ethnological theories ... must be considered incontestible [sic]'.

As had Crawfurd, Earl sketched his image of the Papuan character on a canvas supplied by other inhabitants of the archipelago whom he designated the 'Malayu-Polynesians'. For Earl (1849-50:67), the distinction between the two was almost self-evident: 'The physical characteristics of the Malayu-Polynesians are so distinct from those of the Papuans, that a single glance is sufficient to detect the difference between the races'. The Malayu-Polynesians, he suggested (1849-50:3), had left their influence even in New Guinea in a 'line of improvement' that extended along the northern coast and eastwards into the Pacific.

Following established convention, Earl (1853:1, 3) opened his book on Papuans with the observation that 'their most striking peculiarity consists in their frizzled or woolly hair', deferring to Crawfurd's gloss of *pua-pua* or *papua* as 'crisped'. But in place of Crawfurd's confident 1820 account of a uniform Papuan type, Earl proposed considerable variety in features such as stature and in skin colour. Though he identified the Papuans as a single 'race', Earl (1849-50:2) found evidence for variation between at least two 'tribes': an earlier, short-statured group, limited to the interior of New Guinea, whom he actually labelled 'pygmies', two decades before Schweinfurth's more celebrated 'discovery' of African pygmies (Bahuchet 1993); and tribes of larger — or, occasionally, 'gigantic' — Papuans inhabiting the coastal zones. In his account of the Papuans, Earl (1853:6, 7) chose to challenge or directly contradict many of Crawfurd's points of contrast between the 'brown' and 'black' races. He regarded the Papuans as 'physically superior to the races of South-eastern Asia', while 'with regard to mental capacity, also, they are not inferior to the brown races'. Earl's explanation for the domination of Papuan communities by Malay traders and raiders was based not on inferiority but on the Papuan 'impatience of control' and 'want of organization'. Their 'inextinguishable hatred ... towards those who attempt to settle in their territory' he explained not in terms of an innate savagery, for Papuan slaves elsewhere in the archipelago were 'remarkable for a cheery and obedient disposition', but in terms of the history of their treatment by Malays and a desire to protect their land from foreigners. 'It is an error', he concluded, 'to suppose that these poor creatures disappear before civilization. Their chief destroyers are the wild and warlike hunting tribes of the brown race'.

Earl's lasting reputation as a field observer conceals a nice irony, however. He read voraciously and 'pumped' other travellers, such as Owen Stanley and Dumont d'Urville, for information; but, as Reece observed more generally, 'gaps in his first-hand knowledge ... did not inhibit Earl from presenting himself as an authority'.[49] Although he travelled widely between northern Australia and Singapore — evidently visiting the islands of Aru, Kai, Babar, Timor, and the neighbouring Serawatti group, for each of which he later published his own word lists (Earl 1848) — I can find no evidence that Earl ever actually laid eyes, or set foot, on New Guinea.[50]

Alfred Russel Wallace — 'Had I been blind ...'

The naturalist and zoogeographer Alfred Russel Wallace enjoys an authority that has endured beyond that of either Crawfurd or Earl, due in large part to his travels and observations in the Malay Archipelago between 1854 and 1862.[51]

Wallace's account of these travels, first published in 1869 as *The Malay Archipelago: the Land of the Orang-utan and the Bird of Paradise; a Narrative of Travel with Studies of Man and Nature* (1869a), ushered in a golden era of naturalist exploration in New Guinea and the Moluccas. Couching his developing theory of biogeography and species evolution in the form of a travelogue, *The Malay Archipelago* proved to be enormously influential not only for natural history and zoogeography in general but also more specifically for regional scholars; it is still regarded as perhaps 'the most famous of all books on the Malay Archipelago' (Bastin 1986:vii). Immediately translated into German (1869b) and Dutch (1870-71), Wallace's narrative set a standard against which much subsequent writing on the region has been measured. During the 1870s, Wallace was followed by a wave of naturalist explorers, each bearing copies of his book and consciously emulating his earlier feats: amongst them, the Russian Nikolai Miklouho-Maclay (1846-1888); Wallace's German translator Adolf Bernhard Meyer (1840-1911); and the Italians Odoardo Beccari (1843-1920) and Luigi Maria d'Albertis (1841-1901). Though Wallace's fame rests largely upon his work as a naturalist and his position as the 'moon' to Darwin's 'sun' in the development of a theory of evolution, he was equally fascinated by human as by other zoological subjects: 'The human inhabitants of these forests are not less interesting to me than the feathered tribes'.[52]

The lengthy duration of Wallace's field experience was exceptional, by any standards. As his eight years in the Malay Archipelago had been preceded almost immediately by five years of travel and collection in Brazil between 1848 and 1852, Wallace could claim to have spent twelve of these fourteen years in the field. In marked contrast to earlier observers or collectors, he operated independently, depending on the sale of his collections, and not as part of a ship's crew or a well-funded expedition — though the claim to independence conveniently ignores the colonial network of friends and acquaintances upon which Wallace leaned and the equally central contribution of his assistants, such as Charles Allen and Ali (Camerini 1996). While his predecessors had typically spent little more than a few days onshore, Wallace's visit to Dorey or Doreri Bay (Manokwari) during a period of three and a half months in 1858 marked the first sustained presence of a naturalist in New Guinea.[53]

Where Earl had insisted that 'a single glance' was sufficient to distinguish Papuans from Malays or Malayu-Polynesians, Wallace felt the contrast to be so pronounced as to almost preclude the need for visual diacritics. It was at the Kai Islands in the southeast Moluccas, on the last day of 1856, that Wallace experienced something of an epiphany in his conception of racial difference, as three or four canoes containing some fifty men approached his boat:

> I now had my first view of Papuans in their own country, and in less
> than five minutes was convinced that the opinion already arrived at by

the examination of a few Timor and New Guinea slaves was substantially correct, and that the people I now had an opportunity of comparing side by side belonged to two of the most distinctive and strongly marked races that the earth contains. Had I been blind, I could have been certain that these islanders were not Malays. The loud, rapid, eager tones, the incessant motion, the intense vital activity manifested in speech and action, are the very antipodes of the quiet, unimpulsive, unanimated Malay ... These forty black, naked, mop-headed savages seemed intoxicated with joy and excitement ... School-boys on an unexpected holiday, Irishmen at a fair, or midshipmen on shore, would give but a faint idea of the exuberant animal enjoyment of these people ... Under similar circumstances Malays *could* not behave as these Papuans did ... These moral features are more striking and more conclusive of absolute diversity than even the physical contrasts presented by the two races, though that is sufficiently remarkable (1880a:415-6, original emphasis).[54]

While Wallace advocated the comparison of moral features observed in conjunction with physical traits as a guide to racial distinction, he insisted that environmental factors exerted less influence over the moral than the physical and that moral character was thus a more durable and fundamental ground for discrimination (Brooks 1984:164).

Wallace's famous description of the Australasian and Asian faunas of the Malay Archipelago as 'two distinct faunas rigidly circumscribed, which differ as much as do those of Africa and South America',[55] was echoed in the forcefulness of his distinction between Malays and Papuans:

Between the Malay tribes, among whom I had for some years been living, and the Papuan races, whose country I had now entered, we may fairly say that there is as much difference, both moral and physical, as between the red Indians of South America, and the Negroes of Guinea on the opposite side of the Atlantic (1880a:417).

But if Wallace, like Crawfurd, had first observed Papuans as slaves, appeared to subscribe to Crawfurd's fundamental division of the Malay and Papuan, and apparently shared the latter's taste for African analogies, his description of the details of these physical and moral differences followed more closely that offered by Earl, again directly contradicting Crawfurd. In terms of stature, Wallace (1856:202-4) claimed that 'the Papuan decidedly surpasses the Malay, and is perhaps equal to the average of Europeans'.[56] For Wallace, the Papuan face possessed 'an altogether more European aspect than in the Malay' and, although he acknowledged that the 'intellect' of Papuans was 'very difficult to judge', he was 'inclined to rate it somewhat higher than that of the Malays, notwithstanding the fact that the Papuans have never yet made any advance towards civilisation'.

Equally as confident or emphatic in his pronouncements as Crawfurd, in less than half a century Wallace had produced a valuation of the differences between Malays and Papuans diametrically opposed to that of Crawfurd.

The priority of presence

Wallace's *Malay Archipelago* also marked the culmination of a progression in the significance accorded to field observation, or perhaps its very definition. Crawfurd, Earl, and Wallace all managed to combine the functions of field observer and metropolitan author and ethnologist. But where Crawfurd's contemporaries could regard his declarations on both Malays and Papuans as authoritative, Wallace's field methods, which owed as much to his formation as a surveyor as they did to established procedures amongst naturalist collectors (Moore 1997), radically raised the standard of evidence for racial discrimination.

The moral imprimatur of presence, or at least proximity, might have contributed to Crawfurd's standing; but his claim to field observation of Papuans was more the virtual presence of the well read philologist: 'I have never visited the island of New Guinea, but I have paid much attention to the subject, and ought to know something about it'.[57] For Crawfurd's critics, however, the limited scope of his observations failed to warrant his propensity to theorize. Raffles (1822:122) was not alone in his assessment that Crawfurd possessed 'a rage for generalizing on partial and insufficient data, and the substitution of bold speculation for the patient investigation of facts. With materials sufficient, perhaps, for an account of one of these islands, the author has attempted to grasp the whole'.[58]

Earl's distrust of metropolitan savants (amongst whom he would probably have numbered Crawfurd) contributed to his championing of presence in the field as the sole source of authority. The vocabulary of observation in Earl's work is considerably more precise in its identification of locations and of the position of the observer — whether that of a Dutch traveller in translation or Earl's explicit positioning of himself within the frame.[59] Earl's coyness about the exact details of his own encounters with Papuans and with the island of New Guinea is itself indicative of the significance that he attributed to personal observation in the field.

Certainly, by Wallace's time, the entire grammar of observational authority had been transformed and the distinctions between explorers, travellers, and scientific travellers more sharply drawn. Wallace proposed a commitment to field observation that went further than Earl, insisting that observers actually live amongst indigenous communities:

> It is only by a long residence among a people, by travelling through the whole district they inhabit, and by a more or less accurate knowledge of the surrounding tribes with whom they may be intermixed, that the

observer is enabled to disentangle the complexities they present, and
determine with some approach to accuracy the limits of variation of the
pure or typical race (1876:174).

The privileging of field observation through this 'residency rule' was essential
if the all-important details of moral character were to be correctly described and
made available to ethnologists: 'Ethnologists', complained Wallace, 'have too
often to trust to the information of travellers who passing rapidly from country
to country have too few opportunities of becoming acquainted with peculiarities
of national character, & scarcely even with those of physical conformation'.[60]

However, the sheer fact of presence in the field was no longer sufficient in
itself. Wallace (1880b:153) would later damn d'Albertis with faint praise in a
review of the Italian's account of his New Guinea expeditions. D'Albertis had
'all the best qualities of an explorer — enthusiasm, boldness, and resource, a
deep love of nature, great humanity, and an amount of sympathy with savages',
wrote Wallace before delivering a stinging verdict: 'To the character of a scientific
traveller he makes no claim, and those who expect to find any sound
generalizations from the results of his observations will in all probability be
disappointed'. The capacity to deliver 'sound generalizations' from their own
field observations was a trait common to Crawfurd, Earl, and Wallace, but
securing recognition for their accounts required that their senses be as keen to
the prevailing winds of scientific opinion in London and Europe as they had
been to human difference in the Malay Archipelago.

The cardinality of comparison

While field experience became increasingly valorized, the analytical aperture
of the observer's vision was becoming steadily narrowed by metropolitan theory
and the fashion of the times for a harder, more racialist conception of difference.
A critical step in this process was the development of a capacity to derive both
racial and temporal separation from location — to move from mapping difference
across space to proposing hierarchies of value that could be transposed onto
these spatialized distinctions and, ultimately, to conceive of separation in space
and in race as a fundamental difference in evolutionary time (Fabian 1983).

The function of cardinality with respect to space is similar to that of teleology
for time, imposing a moral load on locations and directions (or temporal
sequences), and linking them through gradients (or developmental trajectories).
The classic distinctions between Melanesian and Polynesian or Malay and Papuan
are also fundamentally geographic distinctions, specific valuations of particular
spatial end-points that serve to anchor racial clines. Crawfurd's physical and
moral gradient for the Indian Archipelago maps racial difference and social
evolution in space. Given his primary focus and point of departure in Southeast
Asian philology, the 'monster island' of New Guinea looms on the distant horizon

as a dark foil in Crawfurd's racial schema.[61] So, too, Earl's Malayu-Polynesian 'line of improvement' links the 'civilised' or civilizable 'brown race' of Malays and Polynesians in space, touching only lightly on the geographically intermediate but 'savage' Papuans of the north coast of New Guinea (1849-50:2-3).

Under these terms, the racial cartographer retains control only over the end points of the gradient. All else, necessarily, is shown in varying tones of grey. A concern for racial taxonomy requires rather more than gradients, however, and seeks instead to establish boundaries. If he was a keen observer, Wallace was an equally avid taxonomist and he was insistent that his human and zoological schemes matched one another (1880a:592-3): 'it is important to point out the harmony which exists, between the line of separation of the human races of the Archipelago and that of the animal productions of the same country'.[62] Though Wallace is famous for his zoogeographic boundary — dubbed the Wallace Line in 1868 by Thomas Henry Huxley (1825-1895)[63] — less well-known is his 'ethnological' line, running to the east of the Wallace Line (Figure 16):

> This line will separate the Malayan and all the Asiatic races, from the Papuans and all that inhabit the Pacific; and though along the line of junction intermigration and commixture have taken place, yet the division is on the whole almost as well defined and strongly contrasted, as is the corresponding zoological division of the Archipelago, into an Indo-Malayan and Austro-Malayan region (Wallace 1880a:590-1).

He first identified this line between human races in March 1857, locating it where it passed to the west of the island of Gilolo or Halmahera:

> Here then I had discovered the exact boundary line between the Malay and the Papuan races, and at a spot where no other writer had expected it. I was very much pleased at this determination, as it gave me a clue to one of the most difficult problems in Ethnology, and enabled me in many other places to separate the two races, and to unravel their intermixtures (1880a:316-7).

Wallace was by no means the first to propose such a line: Marsden (1834:3) had identified New Guinea as 'the common, though not the precise boundary' between his regions of Hither Polynesia (from Madagascar to the Malay Archipelago) and Further Polynesia (from Island Melanesia to Easter Island); the philologist Robert Gordon Latham (1812-1888) had written of 'lines of demarcation' separating 'the Australians, Tasmanians, and Papuans on one side, and the Malays &c. on the other' (1860:219, 222); and Dumont d'Urville (1832) had published his map of the great divisions of Oceania which showed a boundary between *Mélanésie* and *Malaisie* lying just off the west coast of New Guinea.[64]

Much as Dumont d'Urville (1832:20) had claimed his quadripartite division of Oceania and its inhabitants to be 'natural', so too Wallace (1880a:19, 591) insisted that his 'line of separation' between Malays and Papuans was 'true and natural' and 'very significant of the same causes having influenced the distribution of mankind that have determined the range of other animal forms'. A number of scholars have suggested that it was the impetus of accounting for human variation at Gilolo that led Wallace to his discovery of natural selection in animal species.[65] He was adamant that 'If mankind can be classed at all into distinct varieties, surely the Malays and Papuans must be kept for ever separate'. By this logic, if people of Malay appearance and moral composition were found to the east of this line, it was as a consequence of their 'maritime enterprise and higher civilization'.[66]

As George Gaylord Simpson (1977) has observed, Wallace's zoological line marked only the western limit of the Australasian fauna; Lydekker's Line, which approximates the submerged continental shelf of Sahul (incorporating New Guinea, the Raja Ampat and Aru islands, as well as Australia and Tasmania), eventually established the eastern limit of the Asiatic fauna but between these two lines there lay an extensive intermediate or transitional zoological zone. Much as later naturalists were vexed by questions of the significance of this intermediate zone, Wallace's ingenuity was put to the test by the problem of the process of 'admixture' or 'commixture' that, in his conception, had produced the human groups geographically intermediate between the Malay and the Papuan. His attempt to resolve this issue leads from the question of the cardinality of comparison to that of a topography of racial purity through which the geographical separation and presumed temporal sequence of Malays and Papuans became transformed into a racial hierarchy.

Topography of purity: admixture, commixture, intermixture

For all of the differences between their individual accounts of Malays and Papuans, each of the three authors considered here subscribed to the central importance of a contrast drawn between a pair of putatively pure racial types. Yet all three also moved uneasily between the security of a simple pair of types and the chaos of encounters with a visual and behavioural variability that demanded either a more complex taxonomy or a more sophisticated account of the genesis of that variation.

Crawfurd's thoroughly contrived contrast of 1820 between Papuan and Malay could hardly stand the test of time. In his later works, he sought to incorporate the reports on Papuan physical appearance by the French Restoration voyagers and others.[67] By 1848, at least, he was writing of three 'groups' (1848:330-1): one of 'brown complexion, with lank hair', which encompassed various 'divisions', including the Malays of the western and eastern portions of the archipelago and the inhabitants of what Dumont d'Urville had already labelled 'Micronesia'; a second 'division' of 'sooty complexion, with woolly hair', 'usually called Papua', but which Crawfurd here designated the 'Oriental Negro' or 'Negrito'; and a new, third group 'of brown complexion, with frizzled hair', corresponding to the earlier French descriptions of 'mop-haired Papuans' residing along the coast of New Guinea and its adjacent islands.

Crawfurd's *Descriptive Dictionary of the Indian Islands* (1856) contains three separate entries for 'Malay', 'Negro' (which included Papuans but referred only to non-African peoples), and 'Negro-Malayan Race'.[68] While he admitted that the category 'Negro' was the source of some confusion — 'there may be as many different races of negros as there are tongues, and in the present state of our knowledge, these are not countable' (1856:295) — Crawfurd claimed that his awkward 'Negro-Malayan Race' was not the result of mixture between the Malay and Negro races to its west and east, respectively. Rather, it was an intermediate race in its own right and one neatly bounded by a 'line of demarcation' on either side. Characterized by the conjunction of brown skin and frizzled hair, Crawfurd's Negro-Malay or 'quasi-negro' was to be found in the islands between New Guinea and Sulawesi — and he expressly identified Gilolo as one of the seats of this race (1848:331).

This theme resurfaced in the mid-1860s in Crawfurd's paper on the 'commixture of races' in which he sought to establish the long-term non-viability of interracial mixtures. Here (1865a:114), he drew a distinction between the 'pygmy Negro of the Malay Peninsula and Philippines' (effectively relocating his original 'puny Negro' off New Guinea's shores) and 'the stalwart Negro ... of New Guinea, New Caledonia, and the Fijis'. He insisted, however, that among these 'native races there has been little commixture, and ... none to the extent of forming a permanent cross-breed'. Crawfurd's fundamentally polygenist views could not tolerate a systematic 'admixture' of different races to account for this apparent hybridity (1856:296): 'it may be alleged to have arisen from an admixture, in the course of ages, of the Malay and Papuan races ... but we do not observe any such admixture in progress,—and from the repugnance of the races it is not likely to have proceeded to any considerable extent'.[69]

While Crawfurd could write seemingly indiscriminately of 'our [human] race', 'the Negro race', and 'two races of negroes', all within the one paper (1848), and later of 'principal' and 'minor' races and even 'hybrid' races,[70] his articulation of the notion of interracial repugnance, which was strategically subscribed to by monogenists and polygenists alike, presumed some form of racial purity and required an increasing proliferation of distinct racial types.[71] Amongst his Negroes of the Orient, Crawfurd (1852:clxv) claimed to be able to detect at least twelve 'varieties' between the Andaman Islands and the Pacific. By the 1860s (1866:238), these different 'varieties' had become 'distinct races', seven of them alone among the Oriental Negroes — of whom it could 'be safely asserted that there is nothing common to them but a black skin, a certain crispness or woolliness of hair, thick lips, and flat features'. Each separate Negro race was considered aboriginal to the island in which it was now found and no common origin for them could possibly be detected. Crawfurd (1866:232) sought to impose a strong sense of order on this seeming chaos of taxonomic elaboration in the form of a hierarchy of relative 'superiority' or 'degree of civilisation', arrived at through a process of deduction that was arbitrary even by his own standards. Thus the African Negro was 'far above all the races of Oriental Negroes' while the Andamanese in turn were superior to Pacific Negroes because the former did not practice cannibalism. Only where Oriental Negroes came into contact with Malays, as at Dorey Bay, had they 'attained a certain measure of civilisation'.

Earl, who wrote of the 'utmost purity' of the two races of the Malay Archipelago, also struggled with the racial grey zone between the heartlands of the pure Malay and Papuan. He offered an explanation in which successive waves of 'Malayu-Polynesians', each differing from the other, had distributed themselves unevenly across the archipelago, thus accounting for pockets of the 'old Polynesian race' in places such as Ceram and Timor. Unencumbered by Crawfurd's commitment to fundamental racial difference, Earl could allow for mixture, though any such mixture necessarily proceeded from an assumption about the existence of pure types from which mixtures were produced. Diametrically opposed to Crawfurd on the significance of variation amongst Oriental Negroes, for Earl 'all the Negro tribes to the eastward of the continent of Asia, belong to one and the same race'.[72]

Not surprisingly, Wallace's approach to questions of race and the origins of human difference was altogether more systematic than those of Crawfurd and Earl. Wallace appears to have selected the Malay Archipelago as a field site precisely because he regarded it as a possible point of origin for human beings; as the seat, according to the then anonymous author of *Vestiges of the Natural History of Creation* (1844), of both the 'least perfectly developed' human types, the Negro and the Malay, and 'the highest species of the quadrumana'.[73] Contrary to Crawfurd's taste for a proliferation of racial categories, Wallace's avowed preference — like Cuvier's — was for just:

> three great races or divisions of mankind … the black, the brown, and the white, or the Negro, Mongolian, and Caucasian. If we once begin to subdivide beyond these primary divisions, there is no possibility of agreement, and we pass insensibly from the five races of Pritchard [sic] to the fifty or sixty of some modern ethnologists.[74]

Somewhere in the Malay Archipelago, he reasoned, lay the faultline between two of these three 'great races'.

Wallace approached Gilolo fully anticipating that his observations on its indigenous inhabitants would equip him with the material necessary to challenge the prevailing thesis that Papuans were related to and most probably derived from Malays, as two 'classes' of a great Oceanic race; a thesis which was subscribed to by leading monogenist authors such as Wilhelm von Humboldt (1767-1835), Prichard, and his successor Latham. For these men, 'transitional' or 'intermediate' forms between adjacent races served as the guarantee for the essential unity of the human race. Latham (1850:211-2), citing Crawfurd, had even specified that a search of the 'parts about Gilolo' would yield evidence for the source of the Papuans in the form of a population 'intermediate' between the Papuan and Malay forms. As Wallace wrote later (1880a:529): 'If these two great races were direct modifications, the one of the other, we should expect to find in the intervening region some homogeneous indigenous race presenting intermediate characters'. In terms of Wallace's developing thesis of distinctly evolved zoological and anthropological domains, it was essential that the population of Gilolo mark a sharp break between Papuan and Malay. Once there, he was 'soon satisfied by the first half dozen I saw that they were of genuine papuan race' with features 'as palpably *unmalay* as those of the European or the negro'.[75]

John Langdon Brooks (1984:183-4) speculated that Wallace was seeking evidence for the dying out of intermediate forms between the Malay and Papuan in order to demonstrate the ultimate derivation of Papuan forms from an original Malay. Wallace was certainly not entirely averse to the notion of intermediate forms, invoking them to account for the great variety in his Polynesian or Great Oceanic race (1865:212). However, a more plausible explanation is that Wallace's real goal was to establish the antiquity of man more generally by linking Papuans to African Negroes as related members of the great 'Negro' race.[76] The separation of these two Negro populations by the emergence *in situ* of Malays of the great 'Mongolian' race would then demand a hitherto unsuspected temporal depth for human evolution (1880a:593): 'if these two races [Malay and Papuan] ever had a common origin, it could only have been at a period far more remote than any which has yet been assigned to the antiquity of the human race'. Even where Wallace (1880a:592) allowed for 'mongrelism', in canvassing the possibility that the Polynesians represented an 'intermingling' of Malay and Papuan, he insisted that this must have taken place 'at such a remote epoch, and ... so assisted by the continued influence of physical conditions, that it has become a fixed and stable race'. For Wallace, 'the racial differences were primitive. Malays and Papuans hailed from separate continents, like the other fauna in the archipelago. There could be no true "transitional" forms'.[77]

The problem of 'admixture' remained, however, for Wallace's Papuans at Gilolo were evidently not those of New Guinea:

> They are scarcely darker than dark Malays & even lighter than most of the coast malays who have some mixture of papuan blood. Neither is their hair frizzly or wooly, but merely crisp or waved ... which is very different from the smooth & glossy though coarse tresses, every where found in the unmixed malayan race.[78]

Here, Wallace oscillated between a verdict of relatively recent 'admixture' between Malay and Papuan, congruent with his suggestion that Malays had overrun the natural boundary between the two, and occasional acknowledgement of a possible third, intermediate race which he identified tentatively as 'Alfuru' or 'Alfuro'.[79] In his commitment to the simplicity of a single line dividing just two races, Wallace had elected to ignore the implications of the unevenness of his zoological line and the possibility that the area he assigned to this third race corresponded to the transitional zone between his line and the line to the east later identified by Richard Lydekker (1849-1915).[80]

Wallace's insistence on extending the contrast between Malay and Papuan eastwards into the Pacific would ultimately bring his ethnological scheme undone. The primacy that he accorded to the correspondence between zoological and human distributions led Wallace to identify all people east of the line, including Polynesians, as variations on a Papuan theme; indeed, his ethnological line is captioned 'Division between Malayan & Polynesian Races' (Figure 16). In this opinion, Wallace ran sharply counter to the established positions of scholars such as the naturalist and surgeon George Bennett (1804-1893) and Marsden who insisted on the closeness of linguistic, moral, and physical connections between Malays and Polynesians.[81] In order to assert 'the close affinity of the Papuan and Polynesian races, and the radical distinctness of both from the Malay', Wallace toyed initially with geological catastrophism or extensionism.[82] Rejecting the evidence of similarity between Malay and Polynesian vocabularies established and published by Marsden (which he ascribed to recent borrowings) and the oral traditions of Polynesian migration (deemed impossible against the prevailing winds), Wallace sought to bring Polynesians and Papuans together 'as varying forms of one great Oceanic or Polynesian race'.[83] This variation, Wallace argued, could be accounted for by an 'hypothesis ... which does not outrage nature, as does that of the recent derivation of the Polynesians from the Malays'; namely, that massive and ancient subsidence across the Pacific had stranded small islands of ancestral Papuans and Polynesians on isolated volcanic peaks and that, 'while man and birds were able to migrate to these, the mammalia dwindled away and finally perished, when the last mountain-top of the old Pacific sank beneath the Ocean'. So much, it would seem, for field observation.

Figure 16: Alfred Russel Wallace, 'Physical Map of the Malay Archipelago ... 1868'.[84]

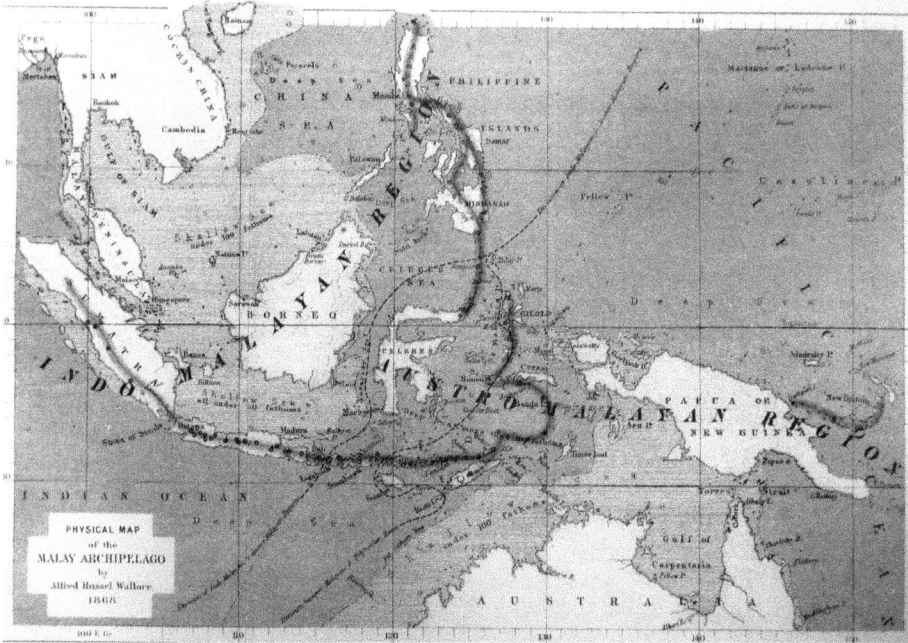

Engraving. Photograph B. Douglas.

On coming out strong

> If I live to return I shall come out strong on Malay and Papuan races, and shall astonish Latham, [Joseph Barnard] Davis, & Co.![85]

Crawfurd, Earl, and Wallace collectively laid the British foundations for the notion of a unified Papuan 'type' as an object for study and they did so principally through the device of opposition to a similarly idealized Malay type. The requirement of Papuan unity for their simple pair of racial types drastically reduced, and also effectively eclipsed, the burgeoning classificatory complexity of their French counterparts. In the cases of Crawfurd and Earl, it might be argued that the simplicity of their initial representations reflected at least in part the limits of their personal experience of Papuans. As they became acquainted with further reports, so their accounts of Papuans gradually became more elaborate and admitted increasing variability. Yet Wallace, despite his considerably more protracted engagement with people across the full breadth of the archipelago, insisted on describing Papuans and Malays in terms that were even more starkly contrasted while emphasising their internal unity to a far greater degree. What was the attraction for these writers of a simple oppositional pair of types, and why — experience apparently to the contrary

— should that attraction have proved even stronger for Wallace than it did for Crawfurd or Earl?

Raffles (1817) had contributed significantly to this opposition between Malay and Papuan in electing to publish the image of his young ward Dick Papua in a volume ostensibly devoted to Java. Eager to promote the civilized qualities of Javanese culture and history as comparable to those of Europe, Raffles was of course drawing the attention of educated London to his role in Java and thus to himself. As Forge (1994:147,150) observed, to achieve this equation Raffles needed to distinguish 'the civilised Javanese from the undifferentiated savages with which popular imagination peopled the whole archipelago'. Two of the colour plates in the first edition of his *History of Java* — the frontispiece showing a refined Javanese aristocrat looking to the left, and the final plate of the second volume, 'a misshapen and nearly naked savage looking away to the right' — served neatly to establish this contrast.[86] Hampson (2000:62) made the further point that Raffles, with Cook's fate in mind, was 'consciously setting the boundary between Cook's Pacific and his own East Indies'.

As I have suggested, Wallace had another, more theoretical agenda to service through the promotion of a profound distinction between Malay and Papuan, which was the notion of a long chronology for human evolution. As the meeting place of two of his three 'great races or divisions of mankind', the Malay Archipelago provided the perfect stage for a demonstration of the role of biogeography in asserting the depth of human antiquity. If Papuans, along with their Australasian fauna, were native to New Guinea, and Malays and their Asiatic fauna to the palaeocontinent now known as Sunda, then the essential Negroid unity of African Negroes and Papuans could only be accounted for by migrations so ancient that they predated the current form of the continents. All the narrative and rhetorical skill that Wallace could muster was thus directed at emphasizing the sharpness of the divide between Malay and Papuan.

Boon (1990:22) has argued that Wallace's emphasis on dualism in the Malay Archipelago became an all-encompassing 'totemism' in which the zoological and human distinctions that he wished to establish were condensed in the form of the bird of paradise from the Aru Islands, adjacent to New Guinea, and the orangutan of Borneo: 'each fauna pulls its human counterpart ['wild Malay' Dayaks and Papuans] towards its extreme characteristic: lyrical divinity on the one hand, bestial might (beneath apparent docility) on the other: avian grace versus animal urge'. There is something powerfully compelling about the simplicity of a dual opposition, both for the popular readership of Wallace's *Malay Archipelago* and for the intellectual peers whom Crawfurd, Earl, and Wallace each sought to impress. All three came to London to some extent as outsiders — Crawfurd from Scotland, Earl from the colonies, and Wallace from a family of reduced circumstances — and all three were concerned with advancement and keenly aware of the need, apparent to scholars then as now, to 'come out strong'.

The simple opposition of Malay and Papuan propounded by Crawfurd, Earl, and Wallace has profoundly influenced western representations of difference in the Malay Archipelago and continues to find expression in contemporary political debate. Despite the obvious flaws in detail in each of their arguments, the caricatures of Malay and Papuan created through this opposition have become entrenched in popular conception, perhaps most notably through the novels of Joseph Conrad.[87] Having failed to draw on Cook and his literature, the intertextual stream of representations of Papuans sketched in the first part of this chapter found new vigour in the writings of Crawfurd, Earl, and Wallace; which invites the hypothetical question of how Papuans and New Guinea might subsequently have been figured had Cook on each of his voyages entered the Pacific not from the east but from the west, via the Malay Archipelago and the coasts of New Guinea.

References

Allen, F. James. 1969. Archaeology, and the History of Port Essington, 2 vols. PhD thesis. Canberra: Australian National University.

Anon. 1854. Works on ethnography. *New Quarterly Review* 3:50-4.

Bahuchet, Serge. 1993. L'invention des Pygmées. *Cahiers d'études africaines*, 33 (129):153-81.

Ballard, Chris. 1993. Stimulating Minds to Fantasy? A Critical Etymology for Sahul. In *Sahul in Review: Pleistocene Archaeology in Australia, New Guinea and Island Melanesia*, ed. M.A. Smith, M. Spriggs, and B. Fankhauser, 17-23. Canberra: Department of Prehistory, Research School of Pacific Studies, Australian National University.

_____. 2001. Collecting Pygmies: the 'Tapiro' and the British Ornithologists' Union Expedition to Dutch New Guinea, 1910-1911. In *Hunting the Gatherers: Ethnographic Collectors, Agents and Agency in Melanesia, 1870s-1930s*, ed. Michael O'Hanlon and Robert L. Welsch, 127-54. New York and Oxford: Berghahn Books.

_____. n.d. The Art of Encounter: Verisimilitude in the Imaginary Exploration of Interior New Guinea, 1863-1876. In *Oceanic Encounters*, ed. Margaret Jolly, Serge Tcherkézoff, and Darrell Tryon.

Barbour, Thomas. 1944. *Naturalist at Large*. Boston: Little, Brown.

Bastin, John. 1986. Introduction. In Alfred Russel Wallace, *The Malay Archipelago: the Land of the Orang-utan and the Bird of Paradise; a Narrative of Travel with Studies of Man and Nature*. Reprint edition. Singapore: Oxford University Press.

Bennett, George. 1832. Elau, a Papuan Child. *Asiatic Journal and Monthly Register for British and Foreign India, China, and Australasia*, n.s. 7:132-6.

Blanckaert, Claude. 2003. Of Monstrous Métis? Hybridity, Fear of Miscegenation, and Patriotism from Buffon to Paul Broca. In *The Color of Liberty: Histories of Race in France*, ed. Sue Peabody and Tyler Stovall, 42-70. Durham, NC: Duke University Press.

Boon, James A. 1990. *Affinities and Extremes: Crisscrossing the Bittersweet Ethnology of East Indies History, Hindu-Balinese Culture, and Indo-European Allure*. Chicago: University of Chicago Press.

Bougainville, Louis-Antoine [Lewis] de. 1772 [1771]. *A Voyage Round the World Performed by Order of His Most Christian Majesty in the Years 1766, 1767, 1768, and 1769*, tr. John Reinhold Forster. London: J. Nourse and T. Davies.

Bravo, Michael T. 1999. Precision and Curiosity in Scientific Travel: James Rennell and the Orientalist Geography of the New Imperial Age (1760-1830). In *Voyages and Visions: Towards a Cultural History of Travel*, ed. Jás Elsner and Joan-Pau Rubiés, 162-83. London: Reaktion Books.

Brooks, John Langdon. 1984. *Just Before the Origin: Alfred Russel Wallace's Theory of Evolution*. New York: Columbia University Press.

Brown, George. 1887. Papuans and Polynesians. *Journal of the Anthropological Institute of Great Britain and Ireland* 16:311-27.

Calder, Alex, Jonathan Lamb, and Bridget Orr, ed. 1999. *Voyages and Beaches: Pacific Encounters, 1769-1840*. Honolulu: University of Hawai'i Press.

Camerini, Jane R. 1994. Evolution, Biogeography and Maps: an Early History of Wallace's Line. In *Darwin's Laboratory: Evolutionary Theory and Natural History in the Pacific*, ed. Roy MacLeod and Philip F. Rehbock, 70-109. Honolulu: University of Hawaii Press.

————. 1996. Wallace in the Field. *Osiris* 2nd series, 11:44-65.

Carteret, Philip. 1965. A Voyage Round the Globe in the Years 1766, 67, 68, & 69, by Philip Carteret Commander of His Majesty's Sloop the Swallow. In *Carteret's Voyage Round the World 1766-1769*, ed. Helen Wallis, vol. 1, 105-273. Cambridge: Hakluyt Society.

Chambers, Robert. 1994 [1844]. *Vestiges of the Natural History of Creation and Other Evolutionary Writings*, ed. James A. Secord. Chicago and London: Chicago University Press.

Clode, Danielle, and Rory O'Brien. 2001. Why Wallace Drew the Line: a Re-Analysis of Wallace's Bird Collections in the Malay Archipelago and the Origins of Biogeography. In *Faunal and Floral Migrations and*

Evolution in SE Asia-Australasia, ed. Ian Metcalfe, Jeremy M.B. Smith, Mike Morwood, and Iain Davidson, 113-21. Lisse, NL, Abingdon, OXF, Exton, PA, Tokyo: A.A. Balkema.

Cook, James. 1955. *The Journals of Captain James Cook on his Voyages of Discovery*, ed. J.C. Beaglehole, vol. 1, *The Voyage of the* Endeavour *1768-1771*. Cambridge: Hakluyt Society.

Crawfurd, John. 1820. *History of the Indian Archipelago: Containing an Account of the Manners, Arts, Languages, Religions, Institutions, and Commerce of its Inhabitants*, 3 vols. Edinburgh: Archibald Constable.

_____. 1823-25. *De Indische archipel: in het bijzonder het eiland Java beschouwd in de zeden, wetenschappen, talen, godsdienst, beschaving, koloniale belangen en koophandel van derzelver inwoners*, 3 vols. Haarlem: Loosjes.

_____. 1848. On the Malayan and Polynesian Languages and Races. *Journal of the Ethnological Society of London* 1:330-74.

_____. 1852. *Grammar and Dictionary of the Malay Language*. London: Smith & Elder.

_____. 1856. *A Descriptive Dictionary of the Indian Islands & Adjacent Countries*. London: Bradbury & Evans.

_____. 1861a. On the Effects of Commixture, Locality, Climate, and Food on the Races of Man. *Transactions of the Ethnological Society of London* 1:76-92.

_____. 1861b. On the Conditions which Favour, Retard, or Obstruct the Early Civilization of Man. *Transactions of the Ethnological Society of London* 1:154-77.

_____. 1861c. On the Classification of the Races of Man. *Transactions of the Ethnological Society of London* 1:354-78.

_____. 1865a. On the Commixture of Races of Man as Affecting the Progress of Civilisation. *Transactions of the Ethnological Society of London* 3:98-122.

_____. 1865b. On Sir Charles Lyell's 'Antiquity of Man', and on Professor Huxley's 'Evidence as to Man's Place in Nature'. *Transactions of the Ethnological Society of London* 3:58-70.

_____. 1866. On the Physical and Mental Characteristics of the Negro. *Transactions of the Ethnological Society of London* 4:212-39.

Cuvier, Georges. 1978 [1857]. Note instructive sur les recherches à faire relativement aux différences anatomiques des diverses races d'hommes. In *Aux origines de l'anthropologie française: les mémoires de la Société des observateurs de l'homme en l'an VIII*, ed. Jean Copans and Jean Jamin, 171-6. Paris: Le Sycomore.

Dampier, William. 1709. *A Continuation of a Voyage to New-Holland, &c. In the Year 1699*, vol 3, part 2. London: James Knapton.

Davis, Joseph Barnard. 1867. *Thesaurus Craniorum: Catalogue of the Skulls of the Various Races of Man, in the Collection of Joseph Barnard Davis*. London: Taylor & Francis.

Domeny de Rienzi, Grégoire Louis. 1836-8. *Océanie ou cinquième partie du monde: revue géographique et ethnographique de la Malaisie, de la Micronésie, de la Polynésie et de la Mélanésie, offrant les résultats des voyages et des découvertes de l'auteur et de ses devanciers, ainsi que ses nouvelles classifications et divisions de ces contrées*, 3 vols. Paris: Firmin Didot frères.

Douglas, Bronwen. 1999. Science and the Art of Representing 'Savages': Reading 'Race' in Text and Image in South Seas Voyage Literature. *History and Anthropology* 11:157-201.

Driver, Felix, and Luciana Martins, ed. 2005. *Tropical Visions in an Age of Empire*. Chicago: University of Chicago Press.

Dumont d'Urville, Jules-Sébastien-César. 1830-3. *Voyage de la corvette l'Astrolabe … pendant les années 1826-1827-1828-1829 … Histoire du voyage*, 5 vols. Paris: J. Tastu.

————. 1832. Sur les îles du grand océan. *Bulletin de la Société de Géographie* 17:1-21.

————. 1834-5. *Voyage pittoresque autour du monde: résumé général des voyages de découvertes …*, 2 vols. Paris: L. Tenré & Henri Dupuy.

Earl, George Windsor [W. Earle]. 1845. On the Physical Structure and Arrangement of the Islands of the Indian Archipelago. *Journal of the Royal Geographical Society* 15:358-65.

————. 1848. Specimens of the Dialects of Timor and of the Chain of Islands Extending Thence to New Guinea. *Journal of the Indian Archipelago and Eastern Asia* 2:695-704.

————. 1849-50. On the Leading Characteristics of the Papuan, Australian, and Malayo-Polynesian Nations. *Journal of the Indian Archipelago and Eastern Asia* 3:682-89; 4:1-10, 66-74, 172-81.

————. 1853. *The Native Races of the Indian Archipelago: Papuans*. London: Hippolyte Baillière.

Ellingson, Ter. 2001. *The Myth of the Noble Savage*. Berkeley: University of California Press.

Fabian, Johannes. 1983. *Time and the Other: How Anthropology Makes its Object*. New York: Columbia University Press.

_____. 2000. *Out of Our Minds: Reason and Madness in the Exploration of Central Africa*. Berkeley: University of California Press.

Fichman, Martin. 1977. Wallace: Zoogeography and the Problem of Land Bridges. *Journal of the History of Biology* 10:45-63.

_____. 2004. *An Elusive Victorian: the Evolution of Alfred Russel Wallace*. Chicago and London: University of Chicago Press.

Forge, Anthony. 1994. Raffles and Daniell: Making the Image Fit. In *Recovering the Orient: Artists, Scholars, Appropriations*, ed. Andrew Gerstle and Anthony Milner, 109-50. Chur, Switzerland: Harwood Academic Publishers.

Forrest, Thomas. 1780 [1779]. *A Voyage to New Guinea and the Moluccas, from Balambangan: Including an Account of Magindano, Sooloo, and Other Islands; and Illustrated with Thirty Copperplates. Performed in the Tartar Galley, Belonging to the Honourable East India Company, During the Years 1774, 1775, and 1776*. 2nd edition. London and Edinburgh: J. Robson, J. Donaldson, G. Robinson and J. Bell.

Forster, Johann Reinhold [John Reinold]. 1778. *Observations made during a Voyage Round the World, on Physical Geography, Natural History, and Ethic Philosophy*. London: G. Robinson.

Freycinet, Louis de. 1825-39. *Voyage autour du monde,... exécuté sur les corvettes de S.M. l'Uranie et la Physicienne, pendant les années 1817, 1818, 1819 et 1820 ... Historique,* 3 vols. Paris: Pillet aîné.

Gelpke, J.H.F. Sollewijn. 1993. On the Origin of the Name Papua. *Bijdragen tot de Taal-, Land- en Volkenkunde* 149:318-32.

Gibson-Hill, C.A. 1959. George Samuel Windsor Earl. *Journal of the Malayan Branch of the Royal Asiatic Society* 32:105-53.

Gogwilt, Christopher. 1995. *The Invention of the West: Joseph Conrad and the Double-Mapping of Europe and Empire*. Stanford, CA: Stanford University Press.

Hampson, Robert. 2000. *Cross-Cultural Encounters in Joseph Conrad's Malay Fiction*. Houndmills, Basingstoke, HAM, and New York: Palgrave.

Hamy, Ernest-Théodore. 1877. Les Alfourous de Gilolo d'après de nouveaux renseignements. *Bulletin de la Société de Géographie*, 6ᵉ série 13:480-91.

Jones, Russell. 1973. Earl, Logan and 'Indonesia'. *Archipel* 6:93-118.

Kleiweg de Zwaan, Johannes Pieter. 1925. *De Rassen van den Indischen Archipel*. Amsterdam: J.M. Meulenhoff.

Kolff, Dirk Hendrik. 1840. *Voyages of the Dutch Brig of War Dourga, Through the Southern & Little-known Parts of the Moluccan Archipelago, and along the Previously Unknown Southern Coast of New Guinea, Performed during the Years 1825 & 1826*, tr. George Windsor Earl. London: James Madden.

Labrousse, Pierre. 2000. Les races de l'Archipel ou le scientisme *in partibus* (France, XIXe siècle). *Archipel* 60:235-65.

Lamb, Jonathan, Vanessa Smith, and Nicholas Thomas, ed. 2000. *Exploration and Exchange: a South Seas Anthology, 1680-1900*. Chicago: University of Chicago Press.

Latham, Robert Gordon. 1850. *The Natural History of the Varieties of Man*. London: John van Voorst.

————. 1860 [1847]. On the General Affinities of the Languages of the Oceanic Blacks: Appendix to Jukes's Voyage of HMS Fly. In *Opuscula: Essays Chiefly Philological and Ethnographical*, 217-222. London and Leipzig: Williams & Norgate and R. Hartmann.

————. 1861. On the Pagan (non-Mahometan) Populations of the Indian Archipelago, with Special Reference to the Colour of their Skin, the Texture of their Hair, and the Import of the Term Harafura. *Transactions of the Ethnological Society of London* 1:202-11.

Le Jeune, Jules-Louis. [1822-5]. Voyage autour du monde sur la Corvette La Coquille ... Folio album of drawings. SH 356. Vincennes, France: Service historique de la Défense, département Marine.

Lesson, René-Primevère. 1829 [1826]. Mémoire sur les races humaines répandues sur les îles du Grand-Océan, et considérées sous les divers rapports physiologiques, naturels et moraux. In *Voyage médical autour du monde, exécuté sur la corvette du roi* La Coquille ... *pendant les années 1822, 1823, 1824 et 1825* ..., 153-225. Paris: Roret.

Logan, James Richardson. 1850. The Ethnology of the Indian Archipelago: Embracing Enquiries into the Continental Relations of the Indo-Pacific Islanders. *The Journal of the Indian Archipelago and Eastern Asia* 4:252-347.

MacGillivray, John. 1852. *Narrative of the Voyage of HMS Rattlesnake, Commanded by the Late Captain Owen Stanley, R.N., F.R.S. &c. During the Years 1846-1850. Including Discoveries and Surveys in New Guinea, the Louisiade Archipelago, etc....*, 2 vols. London: T. & W. Boone.

Marchant, James, ed. 1916. *Alfred Russel Wallace: Letters and Reminiscences*, 2 vols. London: Cassell.

Marsden, William. 1834. On the Polynesian, or East-Insular Languages. In *Miscellaneous Works*, 1-116. London: Parbury, Allen.

McKinney, H. Lewis. 1972. *Wallace and Natural Selection*. New Haven and London: Yale University Press.

Meinicke, Carl E. 1838. Considérations sur les races humaines de l'archipel indien. *Nouvelles annales des voyages et des sciences géographiques*, 3ᵉ série 20:44-94.

_____. 1871. Bemerkungen zu Wallace's Ansichten über die Bevölkering der indischen Inseln. *Zeitschrift für Ethnologie* 3:84-93.

Meyer, Adolf Bernhard. 1880. Sur l'ethnologie de la Nouvelle-Guinée. *Bulletins de la Société d'Anthropologie de Paris*, 3ᵉ série 3:346-62.

_____. 1882. *Über die Namen Papúa, Dajak und Alfuren*. Wien: Carl Gerold's Sohn.

Moore, James. 1997. Wallace's Malthusian Moment: the Common Context Revisited. In *Victorian Science in Context*, ed. Bernard Lightman, 290-312. Chicago: University of Chicago Press.

National Library of Australia and Australian National Maritime Museum. 1999. *Endeavour: Captain Cook's Journal 1768-71*. CD-ROM facsimile. Canberra: National Library of Australia.

Pearson, Michael B. 2005. *A.R. Wallace's Malay Archipelago Journals and Notebook*. London: Linnean Society of London.

Pires, Tomé. 1944. *The Suma Oriental of Tomé Pires; an Account of the East, from the Red Sea to Japan, Written in Malacca and India in 1512-1515 ...*, tr. and ed. Armando Cortesão. 2 vols. London: Hakluyt Society.

Pijnappel, Jan. 1853. Ethnologische studiën. *Bijdragen tot de Taal-, Land-, en Volkenkunde* 2:345-70.

Prado y Tovar, Diego de. 1930a. The Relation of Don Diego de Prado. In *New Light on the Discovery of Australia: as Revealed by the Journal of Captain Don Diego de Prado y Tovar*, tr. George F. Barwick, ed. Henry N. Stevens, 86-205. London: Hakluyt Society.

Prado y Tovar, Diego de. 1930b. The Legends on the Four Prado Maps, Translated from the Copies in the British Museum. In *New Light on the Discovery of Australia: as Revealed by the Journal of Captain Don Diego de Prado y Tovar*, tr. George F. Barwick, ed. Henry N. Stevens, 242-5. London: Hakluyt Society.

Prichard, James Cowles. 1847. *Researches into the Physical History of Mankind*, vol. 5, *Containing Researches into the History of the Oceanic and of the American Nations*. London: Sherwood, Gilbert, and Piper.

Quatrefages, Armand de. 1872. The Native Races of the Indian Archipelago. — Papuans. — By George Windsor Earl. M.R.A.S. London, 1853. *Journal des savants* October: 621-36; December: 780-93.

_____. 1895 [1887]. *The Pygmies*, tr. Frederick Starr. London: Macmillan.

[Quoy, Jean-René-Constant, and] Joseph-Paul Gaimard. 1823. Extrait d'un mémoire sur la race d'hommes connus sous le nom de *Papous*, et particulièrement sur la conformation de leur crâne; lu à l'Académie royale des sciences par M. P. Gaymard, l'un des médecins-naturalistes de l'expédition de découvertes autour du monde, commandée par le capitaine Freycinet. *Nouvelles annales des voyages, de la géographie et de l'histoire* 19:115-26.

Raby, Peter. 2001. *Alfred Russel Wallace: a Life*. London: Chatto & Windus.

Raffles, Thomas Stamford. 1817. *The History of Java*, 2 vols. London: Black, Parbury, and Allen.

[Raffles, Thomas Stamford]. 1822. Review of John Crawfurd, *History of the Indian Archipelago*. *Quarterly Review* 28 (55):111-38.

Raffles, Thomas Stamford, and John Crawfurd. 1824. *Description géographique, historique et commerciale de Java et des autres îles de l'archipel indien … contenant des détails sur les mœurs, les arts, les langues, les religions et les usages des habitants de cette partie du monde...*, tr. François Joseph Ferdinand Marchal. Brussels: H. Tarlier & Jobard.

Ray, Sidney Herbert. 1926. *A Comparative Study of the Melanesian Island Languages*. Cambridge: Cambridge University Press.

Reece, R.H.W. 1982. George Windsor Earl and the Indian Archipelago. *The Push from the Bush* 12:6-40.

_____. 2002. Introduction. In George Windsor Earl, *Enterprise in Tropical Australia*, 1-19. Darwin: NTU Press.

Ricklefs, M.C. 1971. Introduction. In John Crawfurd, *A Descriptive Dictionary of the Indian Islands & Adjacent Countries* [1856], v-vii. Facsimile edition. Kuala Lumpur: Oxford University Press.

Robidé van der Aa, Pieter Jan Baptist Carel. 1885. De verhouding der Papoes en Melanesiërs tot het Maleisch-Polynesische ras. *Tijdschrift van het Koninklijk Nederlandsch Aardrijkskundig Genootschap* 2nd series, 2:225-245.

Ross, Malcolm. 2005. Pronouns as a Preliminary Diagnostic for Grouping Papuan Languages. In *Papuan Pasts: Cultural, Linguistic and Biological Histories of Papuan-Speaking Peoples*, ed. Andrew Pawley, Robert Attenborough,

Jack Golson, and Robin Hide, 15-65. Canberra: Pacific Linguistics, Australian National University.

Sharp, Andrew. 1968. *The Voyages of Abel Janszoon Tasman*. Oxford: Clarendon Press.

Sherry, Norman. 1966. *Conrad's Eastern World*. Cambridge: University Press.

Simpson, George Gaylord. 1977. Too Many Lines: the Limits of the Oriental and Australian Zoogeographic Regions. *Proceedings of the American Philosophical Society* 121:107-20.

Smithies, Michael. 1983. A New Guinean and the Royal Society — 1816-1817. *Hemisphere* 27:365-71.

Sonnerat, Pierre. 1776. *Voyage à la Nouvelle Guinée, dans lequel on trouve la description des lieux, des observations physiques & morales, & des détails relatifs à l'histoire naturelle dans le regne animal et le regne végétal*. Paris: Ruault.

Souter, Gavin. 1963. *New Guinea: the Last Unknown*. Sydney: Angus & Robertson.

Stocking, George W., Jr. 1987. *Victorian Anthropology*. New York: Free Press.

Tcherkézoff, Serge. 2003. A Long and Unfortunate Voyage Towards the 'Invention' of the Melanesia/Polynesia Distinction 1595-1832. *Journal of Pacific History* 38:175-96.

Terrell, John Edward, Kevin M. Kelly, and Paul Rainbird. 2001. Foregone Conclusions? In Search of 'Papuans' and 'Austronesians'. *Current Anthropology* 42:97-124.

Thomas, Nicholas. 1989. The Force of Ethnology: Origins and Significance of the Melanesia/Polynesia Division. *Current Anthropology* 30:27-41, 211-13.

_____. 1994. *Colonialism's Culture: Anthropology, Travel and Government*. Cambridge: Polity Press.

Torres, Luis Váez de. 1930. The Letter of Torres, 12 July 1607. In *New Light on the Discovery of Australia: as Revealed by the Journal of Captain Don Diego de Prado y Tovar*, tr. George F. Barwick, ed. Henry N. Stevens, 214-37. London: Hakluyt Society.

Turnbull, C.M. 2004. Crawfurd, John 1783-1868. In *Oxford Dictionary of National Biography*, ed. H.C.G. Matthew and Brian Harrison, vol. 14, 90-2. Oxford: Oxford University Press.

Vetter, Jeremy. 2006. Wallace's Other Line: Human Biogeography and Field Practice in the Eastern Colonial Tropics. *Journal of the History of Biology* 39:89-123.

Wallace, Alfred Russel. [1856-61]. Malay Archipelago Journal, 4 vols. Manuscript. MS 178. London: Library of the Linnean Society of London.

_____. 1858-9. Notes on a Voyage to New Guinea. *Proceedings of the Royal Geographical Society* 3:358-61.

_____. 1864. The Origin of Human Races and the Antiquity of Man Deduced from the Theory of 'Natural Selection'. *Journal of the Anthropological Society of London* 2:clviii-clxxxvii.

_____. 1865. On the Varieties of Man in the Malay Archipelago. *Transactions of the Ethnological Society of London* 3:196-215.

_____. 1869a. *The Malay Archipelago: the Land of the Orang-utan and the Bird of Paradise; a Narrative of Travel with Studies of Man and Nature.* 2 vols. London: Macmillan.

_____. 1869b. *Der Malayische Archipel: die Heimath des Orang-Utan und de Paradiesvogels: Reiseerlebnisse und Studien über Land und Leute*, tr. Adolf Bernhard Meyer. Braunschweig: Westermann.

_____. 1870-71. *Insulinde: het Land van den Orang-Oetan en den Paradijsvogel*, tr. P.J. Veth. 2 vols. Amsterdam: P.N. van Kampen.

_____. 1876. Review of Oscar Peschel, *The Races of Man and their Geographical Distribution. Nature* 15:174-6.

_____. 1880a [1869]. *The Malay Archipelago: the Land of the Orang-utan and the Bird of Paradise; a Narrative of Travel with Studies of Man and Nature.* 7th edition. London: Macmillan.

_____. 1880b. New Guinea. *Nature* 23:152-55; 175-78.

_____. 1905. *My Life: a Record of Events and Opinions*, 2 vols. London: Chapman & Hall.

_____. 1991 [1867]. The Polynesians and their Migrations. In *Alfred Russel Wallace: an Anthology of his Shorter Writings*, ed. Charles H. Smith, 44-8. Oxford and New York: Oxford University Press.

Whitmee, S.J. 1873. Mr. Wallace on the Ethnology of Polynesia. *Contemporary Review* 21:389-407.

Williams-Ellis, Amabel 1966. *Darwin's Moon: a Biography of Alfred Russel Wallace.* London: Blackie.

Withers, Charles W.J. 2004. Mapping the Niger, 1798-1832: Trust, Testimony and 'Ocular Demonstration' in the Late Enlightenment. *Imago Mundi* 56:170-93.

Notes

1 National Library of Australia and Australian National Maritime Museum 1999:655.

2 Forster 1778:228. For more recent discussion of the history of the classification of Pacific Islanders see Douglas 1999; Terrell, Kelly, and Rainbird 2001; Thomas 1989; Tcherkézoff 2003; Chapter Two (Douglas), this volume; but hunt in vain for references to New Guinea in collections on Oceanic encounters such as those edited by Calder, Lamb, and Orr (1999) or Lamb, Smith, and Thomas (2000).

3 See Chapter Two (Douglas), this volume.

4 Labrousse (2000:258) provides a useful summary of later developments in French anthropology of the Malay Archipelago, noting the increasing influence of anglophone authors on French scholarship during the latter half of the nineteenth century.

5 E.g., with little enthusiasm, Wallace (1880a:599-602) extracted a sample of measurements for Malay, Papuan, Polynesian, Australian, and Negro crania from the *Thesaurus Craniorum* of Joseph Barnard Davis (1867), seeking to test his thesis of the distinction between Malays and Papuans, but concluded that the sample sizes were too small to be meaningful and offered no guide to the identity of individuals from any single race, amongst whom the variation was greater than that between different races.

6 As Douglas (Chapter Two), this volume, makes clear, French conceptions of the racial cartography of Oceania were considerably more elaborate and holistic in encompassing the entire region (if no less confused in their understanding of ethnic or physical differences). Between 1792 and 1840, the scientific voyages led by Entrecasteaux, Freycinet, Duperrey, and Dumont d'Urville all touched on New Guinea or its surrounding islands, arriving from a variety of directions, with each building in a relatively systematic fashion on the results of their predecessors. A sense of the proliferation of French racial types and of the sheer confusion in their distribution is conveyed in the popular work on the geography and ethnography of Oceania (1836-8) by Grégoire Louis Domeny de Rienzi (1789-1843). Largely summarizing the findings of the earlier voyages, Domeny de Rienzi identified and sought to discriminate between the *Papouas* (of island Melanesia and coastal New Guinea), the *Papou-Malais* hybrids of the Raja Ampat islands, the *Endamènes* or *Mélanesiens* of Australia and interior New Guinea, the *Pou-Andamènes* [sic] (hybrid *Papou-Endamènes*), and the *Alfouras* (see note 15). The demise in significance — for Papuan anthropology at least — of the results of these French voyages after the mid-nineteenth century may be attributed partly to the long shadow cast by the popularity of Wallace's *Malay Archipelago* but also demands a more focused examination and explanation than can be offered here.

7 Dumont d'Urville 1834-5, II:194, my emphasis.

8 Blanckaert 2003; see also Chapter Eight (Luker), this volume.

9 My use of the term 'Papuan' might seem to contribute further to the definitional confusion described in this chapter but its retention does serve to underscore the genealogical links between past and contemporary usages.

10 Marsden (1834:64) would later define *Papuah* as 'signifying crisp and curled, in the Malayan language, and applied to certain plants as well as human hair'. As Ter Ellingson (2001) has amply documented, Crawfurd was not averse to invention in the form of misplaced attribution. If *puahpuah* was a Malay term for frizzled hair, it does not appear to have been applied with reference to any other part of the Malay-speaking world, such as Timor. The more obvious Malay term for frizzled hair is *rambut keriting* (Gelpke 1993:322, 329). By 1838, the German geographer Carl Eduard Meinicke (1803-1876) (without identifying his sources) had moved one step further in confidently asserting that 'The term Papua derives from the remarkable ornament of their hairstyle' and that 'the coastal inhabitants of the Moluccas give the name Papouas solely to those natives of the great northwestern promontory of New Guinea and its neighbouring islands due ... to their peculiar hairstyle, and not in reference to their woolly hair, as has previously been believed' (1838:61, 64-5).

11 Gelpke's (1993:326-9) preferred source for the term Papua, identified in the Biak reference to the Raja Ampat islands to their west as '"Sup i papwa"', or 'the land below ... the sunset' , conveys a sense not only of place but also of the political dominance exerted over Biak by the north Moluccan sultanates to the west.

12 As early as 1779, the East India Company employee Thomas Forrest (1729?-1802?), a fluent Malay speaker, was employing 'Tanna (Land) Papua' as a synonym for 'New Guinea' (1780:v). I am indebted to Diana Carroll for this observation.

13 Gelpke 1993:325, 327-8.

[14] Forrest, travelling to the north coast of New Guinea in 1774-5 in the company of Malay ships' captains, described its inhabitants as 'Papua Coffres' to distinguish them from the 'Coffres' of other East Indies islands (1780:62, 95, 148).

[15] Torres 1930:233, my emphasis. In this respect, 'Papua' retains a category resemblance to 'Alfuro', another term for people employed widely in eastern Indonesia. Alfuro appears to be derived from the Portuguese *forrar*, 'free', compounded with the Arabic article *al*, and was a term widely used in the region to denote animist communities unconverted either to Islam or, later, to Christianity. The observation that communities designated as Alfuros were commonly found in the interior of islands in the Moluccas as well as New Guinea led European observers to conclude that they constituted an aboriginal population that preceded the subsequent arrival of both Papuans and Malays. European attempts during the nineteenth century to define the physical characteristics of Alfuros met with understandable confusion and the term had largely passed into desuetude by the early twentieth century. For a sense of the nineteenth-century debate over Alfuros, see Hamy 1877; Latham 1861; Meyer 1882.

[16] Bougainville 1772:322; Dampier 1709:100, 148; Prado 1930a:171; Souter 1963:128.

[17] See Chapter Two (Douglas), this volume.

[18] Prado y Tovar 1930a:145, 159, 171; 1930b:244; Sharp 1968:48, 49, 52; Torres 1930:229.

[19] Dampier 1709:122, 126, 128.

[20] E.g., Prado y Tovar 1930a:171; see also Sharp 1968:300.

[21] Dampier 1709:100, 126, 128, original emphasis.

[22] Bougainville 1772:342; Carteret 1965:196; Forrest 1780:68.

[23] E.g., Dumont d'Urville 1830-3, IV:604; Freycinet 1825-39, II:47.

[24] 'Inhabitants of Port Dori, New Guinea' (Le Jeune [1822-5]: folio 131).

[25] Carteret 1965:196, 201; Dampier 1709:100, original emphasis; Forrest 1780:68.

[26] Dumont d'Urville 1832:6; Logan 1850:278; Prichard 1847:213.

[27] Earl 1853: pl. 7.

[28] Crawfurd 1856:295; Wallace 1858-9; 1880a:602.

[29] For further details on Crawfurd's life, see the biographical entry by Turnbull (2004), the introduction by M.C. Ricklefs (1971) to the facsimile edition of Crawfurd's *Descriptive Dictionary* (1856), and the numerous references in Ellingson (2001).

[30] As Ellingson (2001) demonstrates, Crawfurd was also responsible for re-introducing the pre-Rousseauian notion of 'the noble savage' to modern anthropology and public discourse, crediting it wrongly (and quite deliberately) to Rousseau.

[31] Crawfurd 1861c:372ff, 368; 1865b:61.

[32] Crawfurd's *History of the Indian Archipelago* appeared fairly swiftly in both Dutch (1823-25) and French translations, with the latter combining the works of both Raffles and Crawfurd (Raffles and Crawfurd 1824).

[33] Crawfurd 1820, I:14, 17-27, my emphasis; Forster 1778:228, 281-4.

[34] Crawfurd 1820, I:18, 27-9, original emphasis. See Crawfurd 1866 for a summary of his own highly pejorative views on the 'Negro races'.

[35] See Chapter Two (Douglas), this volume, for references to the antiquity of this racialized history.

[36] 'I have myself seen in Java several of the Negroes of New Guinea as slaves, and, until better informed, believed them to be Africans — so striking, at first view, is the resemblance between the two races' (Crawfurd 1866:227). Raffles (1822:113) clearly implied that this might have been the full extent of Crawfurd's experience of Papuans.

[37] Crawfurd 1820, I:23, 24, 26-7. Sonnerat described 'the Papuans' as follows:

> Their appearance has something hideous and frightening in it. Let us imagine robust men, glistening black, but with rough, coarse skin, mostly disfigured by blotches, like those caused by elephantiasis; let us depict them with very large eyes, a squashed nose, an excessively stretched mouth, very bulging lips, especially the upper one, and frizzy hair of a shiny black or a fiery red (1776:153).

[38] Crawfurd 1820, I: pl. 2.

[39] Raffles 1817, II: ccxxxvi.

[40] Crawfurd (1820, I:24) made direct reference to this boy's connection to Raffles in the same volume and can hardly have been unaware of Raffles's own text that accompanied the original illustration. In later writings (1848:334-5), he would directly acknowledge and quote Raffles on the age of the boy, prompted perhaps by a devastating anonymous review written by none other than Raffles himself (1822:114), who declared it 'unfortunate for the author's argument, that this very individual here figured … has already attained the height of five feet two inches, the medium height, according to Mr. Crawfurd, of the brown race'.

[41] See Smithies 1983 for a review of what little else is known of the life of 'Dick Papua'. Boon (1990:37), Forge (1994), and Thomas (1994:88, 232-3) discussed his image further.

[42] Crawfurd's rendition of the Papuan boy 'Dick' continued to exert its baleful influence throughout the nineteenth century. The French anthropologist Armand de Quatrefages, for example, reproduced it as a line drawing captioned 'Negrito-Papuan (After Crawfurd)' (1895:44). Though he was aware of its origins in Raffles's *History of Java*, Quatrefages insisted on the value of this image as a representation of the type, completing Crawfurd's own argument for him (1895:61): 'To be sure, the subject is only a child of ten years, and its [sic] youthfulness may call forth criticism. But we must not forget that the physical development of these races is completed at an earlier period than among European populations. This single thought will make us understand how Earl, so good a judge in such matters, could affirm the resemblance of this portrait to adults whom he saw … He thus testifies to the accuracy of the English writers, as well as to the extension of this type in the Indian archipelagos'.

[43] For further details of Earl's life, see Gibson-Hill 1959 and Reece 2002.

[44] MacGillivray 1852, II:76; Pijnappel 1853; Robidé van der Aa 1885.

[45] Camerini 1994:85,105, note 47.

[46] Earl 1845. In private correspondence dated to 1859, Darwin, commenting on Wallace's paper 'The Zoological Geography of the Malay Archipelago' (published later in 1860), needled Wallace by drawing his attention to the priority and similarity of Earl's 1845 paper (Marchant 1916:114); Earl (1845:362) had noted the limited distribution of several marsupial species in support of his argument for delineating the 'Great Asiatic Bank' and 'Great Australian Bank' which would later be recognised as Sunda and Sahul, respectively (Ballard 1993). Wallace replied defensively, suggesting that, due to Earl's 'imperfect knowledge of the natural history of the various islands, he did not fully appreciate the important results of this observation' (quoted in Fichman 1977:51-2).

[47] Jones 1973. Like Dumont d'Urville's 'Melanesia', Earl's 'Indu-nesia' was explicitly racial in its reference (1849-50:71): 'the time has arrived when a distinctive name for the brown races of the Indian Archipelago is urgently required … By adopting the Greek word for 'islands' as a terminal, for which we have a precedent in the term "Polynesia," the inhabitants of the "Indian Archipelago" or "Malayan Archipelago" would become respectively Indu-nesians or Malayunesians'.

[48] Earl's complaint at his treatment by the Royal Geographical Society imparts something of the flavour of the competition for advancement in London's academic societies: 'it was bad enough to be snubbed by the geologists, and to have my labours for years pronounced worthless by a set of quacks who had only a smattering of the science which they professed to lead, but to find them coolly appropriating the very theory they combined to upset, is more than even my patient nature can bear' (Earl to Beaufort, 24 April 1852, quoted in Allen 1969, I:312-13).

[49] Reece 1982:20, 37; 2002:4. Sir Thomas Mitchell, the Surveyor-General of New South Wales, described him more harshly — and somewhat unfairly — as a member of the school of 'theoretical travellers' (quoted in Reece 2002:19).

[50] Quatrefages (1872:622) and other readers of Earl bemoaned the 'truly rare modesty' that had led him to reproduce the descriptions of others rather than offer his own direct observations on Papuans. The German anthropologist and ornithologist Adolf Bernhard Meyer (1880:350) asserted that Earl had travelled widely along the north coast of New Guinea; but the only published claim by Earl, who was usually quick to indicate those locations that he had personally visited, that might suggest an intimate knowledge of the island is the following rather ambiguous statement: 'My limited experience with regard to New Guinea would not authorize me to say that *no* difference exists between the coast and inland native of this great island' (1849-50:3, original emphasis).

[51] Wallace is now well served by biographers, including the recent works by Raby (2001) and Fichman (2004). See the Alfred Russel Wallace website for further details of Wallace's own publications and of writing about his work. Accessed 4 April 2005, online <www.wku.edu/~smithch/>.

[52] Wallace [1856-61]: entry 71; Williams-Ellis 1966.

[53] In the event, Wallace was ill and house-bound for much of his time in Dorey Bay, though this scarcely diminished the benefit to his reputation of his sojourn in New Guinea. Proximity to Papuans failed to translate into empathy, however. Years later, when Thomas Barbour (1944:47) sent him photographs of the Papuans of Dorey Bay, Wallace replied 'that he was sorry I had, for he disliked them so'.

[54] Vetter (2006) nicely identified the additional emphasis placed by Wallace on this contrast by comparing the account in his original journal entry with the more elaborate version published more than a decade later.

[55] Wallace to Bates, 4 January 1858, quoted in Wallace 1905, I:358-9.

[56] For emphasis, and not presumably as the result of any new data, Wallace would revise this statement in his republication of the 1865 paper as the final chapter of *The Malay Archipelago* to read 'equal, or even superior, to the average of Europeans' (1880a:586).

[57] Crawfurd, discussion, in Wallace 1858-9:359.

[58] I thank Gareth Knapman for this point. The naturalist George Bennett (1832:133) also clearly had Crawfurd in his sights when he refuted the current hypothesis of Papuans as 'a dwarfish, puny race, deficient in mental and physical powers. We are, however, too prone to form hasty general opinions from a few instances', he continued, before listing his many varied observations on Papuans throughout the region.

[59] See, for example, the manner in which Earl (1849-50:686) underwrote his authority as observer: 'The process by which these cicatrices are produced and which I have had the opportunities of watching in their progress from day to day ...'.

[60] Wallace[1856-61]: entry 63. Despite the legibility of Wallace's handwriting, there is little agreement amongst published transcripts of his journals (see, e.g., the different version of this section as rendered by McKinney 1972:88). A complete transcript of the Malay Archipelago journals and notebook is now available, held at the Linnean Society of London (Pearson 2005); while invaluable as a guide to the content of the journals, this too must be checked for accuracy against the originals.

[61] '[New Guinea] is a monster island, and, although beyond doubt God created nothing in vain, it appears to our narrow view that New Guinea was created for no earthly good purpose' (Crawfurd, discussion, in Wallace 1858-9:359).

[62] Fichman (2004:11-14, 28, 46-47) provides an excellent account of the importance of boundary-marking as an activity in Wallace's life, from his early employment as a surveyor, through his recognition of the significance of species boundaries in the Amazon, and as the impetus behind his Malay Archipelago line.

[63] Simpson 1977:108.

[64] For Dumont d'Urville's map, see Figure 2, this volume.

[65] Brooks 1984:178-80; McKinney 1972:88-9; Moore 1997.

[66] Wallace 1865:205; 1880a:19.

[67] Crawfurd's deference to the experience of the French voyagers was not entirely reciprocated, at least by the pharmacist-naturalist René-Primevère Lesson (1794-1849), who dismissed Crawfurd's denial of physical analogies between Papuans and Madagascan Negroes as 'in this case, unsupported by any positive evidence' (1829:202, note 4).

[68] Crawfurd 1856:249-53, 294-7.

[69] Crawfurd here appeared to privilege 'observation' but rather hid behind it, for nowhere did he explain how one might observe 'admixture in progress'. Only in Fiji did he allow for some 'admixture' between Oceanic Negroes and Polynesians (1865a:114).

[70] Crawfurd 1861b:169; 1865a:117.

[71] See Chapter One (Douglas), this volume, for an outline of the tangled logic and emotions of mid-nineteenth-century scientific discourses on racial mixing that formed the broader context for Crawfurd's almost neurotic aversion to the 'commixture of races'.

[72] Earl 1849-50:1, 3, 6, 9, 68, 69-70.

[73] Chambers 1994:296, 308; Moore 1997:298.

[74] Wallace 1905, II:128. See Chapters One and Two (Douglas), this volume, on Cuvier's influential general division of humanity into three major races, 'Caucasic', 'Mongolic', and 'Ethiopic'.

[75] Wallace [1856-61]: entry 127, original emphasis.

[76] Wallace (1864) had already made the case for a greater antiquity for human evolution in the form of an address to the Anthropological Society of London in which he argued that physical differences

represented a very early adaptation to different environments and modification from a single homogenous race, after which rapid moral and mental development endowed the different races with varying aptitudes and corresponding historical fates.

[77] Moore 1997:305, fn.10. Hence Wallace's oft-quoted prescription: 'no man can be a good ethnologist who does not travel, and not *travel* merely, but reside, as I do, months and years with each race, becoming well acquainted with their average physiognomy and their character, so as to be able to detect cross-breeds, which totally mislead a hasty traveller, who thinks they are transitions' (Wallace to George Silk, [1858], in Wallace 1905, I:366, original emphasis).

[78] Wallace [1856-61]: entry 127.

[79] Wallace 1865:207-8; 1880a:588.

[80] Clode and O'Brien 2001:118-19.

[81] Bennett 1832; Marsden 1834.

[82] Wallace 1865:212; 1880a:593. Fichman (1977; 2004:51-3) traces Wallace's gradual rejection of extensionism during the late 1860s and 1870s.

[83] Wallace 1991:47. Wallace was fairly swiftly and heavily criticized for his views on Polynesians by his peers, such as Meinicke (1871), as well as by missionaries who did have the requisite field experience in the region, such as George Brown (1835-1917) and Samuel James Whitmee (1838–1925) (Brown 1887; Whitmee 1873).

[84] Wallace 1880a: following 8.

[85] Wallace to George Silk, [1858], in Wallace 1905, I:366.

[86] Forge (1994:123) suggested that these two plates were the only ones in the *History of Java* which appear to have been commissioned from life for the volume, implying some particular significance of the two images for Raffles as a contrasting pair.

[87] See Sherry 1966; Gogwilt 1995; Hampson 2000.

Part Three

Consolidation: the Science of Race
and Aboriginal Australians, 1860-1885

Chapter Four

British Anthropological Thought in Colonial Practice: the appropriation of Indigenous Australian bodies, 1860-1880

Paul Turnbull

Within Australian historiography, the procurement of indigenous Australian ancestral remains by European scientists has generally been explained as resulting from the desire to produce evidence refining the core assumptions of Darwinian theory. I have argued elsewhere (1998, 1999) that the procurement of anatomical specimens through desecration of indigenous burial places in fact began shortly after the establishment of the penal settlement of New South Wales in 1788. It also seems clear that from the early 1880s indigenous burial places were plundered with a view to producing knowledge that would answer various questions about the origins and nature of racial difference that emerged as a consequence of the rapid and widespread assent given Darwinian evolutionary theory (Turnbull 1991).

In this chapter, I want to show that the motivations of British metropolitan and colonial scientists in illegally procuring body parts in the first fifteen or so years after the 1859 publication of the *Origin of Species* were intellectually more heterodox than has hitherto been appreciated. The theft of indigenous Australian bones between 1860 and the mid-1870s did not arise simply from the desire of Darwinians to verify and refine the hypothesis that humanity had developed through speciation. Rather, the plunder of ancestral burial sites occurred because Aboriginal bones took on disparate meanings within the context of rivalry between prominent early Darwinians and the leadership of the Anthropology Society of London. As is well known to historians of racial thought, in early 1863 a split occurred in the Ethnological Society.[1] A faction of about a dozen members led by James Hunt (1833-1869) and C. Carter Blake (c. 1840-1887) broke away to form a new organization, the Anthropological Society of London. For several years this group had sought to reform the Ethnological Society from within, arguing that race was the true foundational principle of anthropological research. By this reasoning, differences in lifeways, social institutions, and forms of cultural expression were all manifestations of racial difference and only truly explicable when interpreted in the light of comparative anatomical delineation of presumed physiological and psychological differences amongst the races of man. Moreover, they believed racial differences to be biologically immutable and highly suggestive of the plurality of human origins — the doctrine that by the mid-nineteenth century was known as polygeny.

For Hunt and his supporters, race was all. They had grown increasingly frustrated by the polite reception the Ethnological Society gave admirers of the writings of Johann Friedrich Blumenbach (1752-1840) and James Cowles Prichard (1786-1848) who had explained human racial differences as having arisen through environmental modifications of a single ancestral type.[2] However, what provoked them to form a new organization was the growing epistemological credence given within the Ethnological Society to the Darwinian theory of organic evolution through speciation (Van Keuren 1982:29-30). The acrimonious relations between leading Darwinians and the leadership of the Anthropological Society have been appraised by several historians of Victorian anthropological thought.[3] This chapter explores one of the key consequences of these metropolitan debates — their stimulation of scientific trafficking in indigenous remains from Australia and elsewhere.

It was largely in the context of seeking to establish Darwinian evolutionary theory as scientific orthodoxy against the claims of members of the Anthropological Society that scientists such as Thomas Henry Huxley (1825-1895), George Busk (1807-1886), and George Rolleston (1829-1881) sought out the bones of indigenous Australians. Because they saw skeletons and skulls as reflecting the evolutionary history of specific human populations from one ancestral form, they eagerly encouraged the desecration of burial places by colonial agents. However, members of the Anthropological Society were equally energetic in seeking to procure indigenous Australian remains. Indeed, the most successful collector of indigenous Australian skeletal material of the Victorian era, Joseph Barnard Davis (1801-1881), was no Darwinian but one of the most prominent among the early 'Anthropological' critics of the idea of human speciation. Davis confidently believed that comparative anatomical examination of mainland Australian and especially Tasmanian indigenous bones would yield compelling proof of the historical immutability of racial difference. By proving the unchanging racial characters of these native races, such theorists would not only overturn the Darwinian account of organic development but also strengthen their own case for reforming anthropological practice to focus on investigating how race determined the varying lifeways and social institutions of the different people of the earth.

The chapter also touches on how the appropriation of Aboriginal remains within rival branches of metropolitan science between 1860 and the mid-1870s had profound and pernicious consequences for indigenous Australians. I suggest that such remains were instrumental in transforming widespread European perceptions of indigenous population decline into proof of the inevitability of Aboriginal extinction. For both Darwinians and members of the Anthropological Society — for different reasons — were led by their examination of what we now know to be superficial anatomical peculiarities to conclude that indigenous Australians were racially incapable of adapting to the changes to their way of life wrought by European colonization. This shared intellectual position resonated fatally with decades of colonial assumptions on the settlement frontiers of Australia.

The ubiquity of race

I begin by examining how race was fundamental to the conceptual vocabulary of both Darwinians and their Anthropological Society critics, but understood in very different ways. One economical yet informative way of doing this is to consider the controversial reception of one of the most infamous of mid-Victorian racial texts, James Hunt's *The Negro's Place in Nature* (1864). In this widely circulated pamphlet, Hunt outlined a prima facie case for classifying African people as a species distinct from and inferior to Europeans. Having already gained notoriety in intellectual circles in London because of his sympathy for the Confederate States and their defence of slavery, Hunt provocatively read the first part of *The Negro's Place in Nature* as a paper before the 1863 meeting of the British Association for the Advancement of Science. Not unexpectedly, advance publicity ensured that his audience included abolitionists who loudly hissed as he spoke; but what proved unsettling for Hunt was finding himself entangled in debate with William Craft (1824-1900), an ex-slave.[4]

In the question time following Hunt's paper, Craft introduced himself, ironically, as one 'not of pure African descent' but nonetheless 'black enough to say a few words' about Hunt's taking the skull as a reliable indicator of racial origin and intellectual prowess. Craft rejected the notion that measuring the characteristic differences in cranial shape between European and African peoples produced clear evidence of the latter's racial inferiority. He did not dispute that there were morphological differences, notably in the relatively greater thickness of the bones of Negro skulls. Where he differed was in seeing this variation as 'wisely arranged by Providence'. For had God not provided Africans with thick skulls, he declared, the tropical climate they inhabited would have ensured that their brains would 'probably have become very much like those of many scientific gentlemen of the present day'. Craft did not dispute the existence of racial peculiarities but found it sorrowful 'that scientific and learned men should waste their time in discussing a subject that could prove of no benefit to mankind', instead of accepting the wealth of evidence exemplifying the 'independence of character and intellectual power on the part of the Negro' (Hunt 1863:389).

To Hunt's annoyance, Craft's critique triggered additional testimony from members of the audience with first-hand experience of social conditions in the West Indies and Africa, to the effect that slavery and colonial oppression were the true causes of what Hunt claimed was an innate African incapacity for civilization. Hunt's supporters moved to close discussion, praising his determination to argue purely from the basis of facts and regretting that 'philanthropy' had clouded what had been a purely scientific discussion. Smarting from Craft's moral dissection, Hunt could not forgo securing the final word. In doing so, however, he stepped outside the limits of scientific discourse. In a manner reminiscent of the celebrated 1860 debate on evolution between Bishop Samuel Wilberforce and Thomas Henry Huxley, Hunt (1863:391) resorted to ridicule and in doing so severely damaged his scientific credibility by social impoliteness. Like Craft he too was sorry, he exclaimed — sorry that scientific discourse should be opposed 'by poetical clap-trap, or by gratuitous and worthless assumptions'.

Craft's defence of the African illustrates the widespread salience that monogenetic environmentalist accounts of racial difference still enjoyed in Britain during the 1860s. He was able to reaffirm the fundamental truth claims of this tradition by demonstrating its continuing capacity to explain historical events and providing eyewitness testimony as to the intellectual power of men and women of African descent. He did so particularly by exposing the thin evidence on which Hunt's correlation of African bodily peculiarities with recorded or observable behaviour rested. In the absence of robust evidence to the contrary, Craft had argued, the fact that anatomical studies had shown Africans to have thicker skulls did nothing to unsettle the case for providential design as the most plausible account and, indeed, a more scientific explanation than any Hunt had produced, by virtue of its commensurability with the wealth of testimony to the intellectual abilities of Africans who had secured their freedom.

Craft's critique of Hunt further serves to illuminate the fact that Darwinians and Anthropological Society members were consciously engaged in a contest to reinterpret the monogenetic environmentalist tradition. It was, moreover, a contest in which Darwinians enjoyed a distinct intellectual advantage. For by the early 1860s, subscribers to monogenetic environmentalism could draw upon two powerful explanatory resources. One was the encyclopaedic research of James Cowles Prichard. The other was the widely admired philosophical comparative anatomy of Richard Owen (1804-1892). Prichard and Owen equally regarded the diversity of life as the expression of the divine mind. By virtue of its perfection, the divine will obviated the need for the subsequent emergence of new organic forms though, as the fossil record showed, it allowed for the extinction of certain species. Species might come to exhibit diversity but only to the extent that they reflected the divine intention that each be perfectly suited to inhabit a preordained place in the order of creation. Hence, this tradition was able to envisage human history as evolutionary insofar as it accepted that organisms were subject to biological processes designed to ensure that they became most perfectly suited to the environment which they were providentially destined to inhabit (Rupke 1994:224-30). Darwinians consequently found themselves sharing substantial common ground with monogenetic environmentalists. Where they disagreed was on how far humanity could undergo organic change (Stocking 1973:lv-lvi). By way of contrast, the static physical anthropology espoused by Hunt and his circle had little if any commensurability with monogenetic environmentalism.

Though they stressed that Hunt had merely sought to present the 'simple facts' of race, the leaders of the Anthropological Society were aware that the empirical evidence for classifying Europeans and Africans as separate species was far less substantial than it needed to be. In fact, we should do well to read *The Negro's Place in Nature* as a manifesto for the new Anthropological Society. As the pamphlet makes clear, its founders envisaged the new society as providing an institutional basis and direction for a new science of race, anchored in the study of racial anatomy. In doing so, they looked enviously towards France. Indeed, they chose the name Anthropological Society because of the widespread use of the term 'anthropology' by French anatomists since the early years of the nineteenth century to describe the comparative study of human anatomy, morphology, and physiology. French state sponsorship of the biomedical and natural sciences from the revolutionary era had provided a stronger institutional context for the study of humanity than the network of national and provincial scientific societies and clubs that characterized British intellectual life during the first two-thirds of the nineteenth century. By virtue of its location within Parisian biomedical institutions, the study of human difference had developed a more coherent program of research that was informed by, and in turn gave additional intellectual weight to, the body of theory relating to the nature and origins of organic life-forms propounded by Georges Cuvier (1769-1832), Etienne Geoffroy Saint-Hilaire (1772-1844), and their successors. This research had also become more focused on employing instrumentation to determine statistical regularities in the typical form of organic structures.

Several figures closely associated with the Anthropological Society had either studied medicine in Paris or with Parisian-trained researchers. The most influential was Robert Knox (1791-1862), the charismatic Edinburgh anatomist. Knox (1823-4) had first become interested in the anatomical differences between African peoples and Europeans while serving as an army medical surgeon in southern Africa between 1817 and 1820. During the course of subsequent continental studies, he embraced and idiosyncratically sought to synthesize and refine the transmutationist views of Jean-Baptiste de Monet de Lamarck (1744-1829) and Geoffroy Saint-Hilaire (Goodsir 1868:26-7). After establishing himself as an anatomy teacher in Edinburgh, Knox began to offer special lectures on comparative human anatomy in which he reflected a growing conviction that differences in the typical form of bones within indigenous African, American, and Australian populations were so pronounced as to suggest that they were separate species which had developed from different ancestral forms. For the remainder of his life, Knox sought to refine his racial taxonomy through anatomical inquiries. As recalled by Carter Blake (1870:335), an ex-pupil of Knox and member of the first executive of the Anthropological Society, the anatomist 'could not glance at a cranium for the common descriptive anatomy without speaking of its ethnological bearings.... [E]ven when walking along the streets thronged with men and women, he was always on the *qui vive* for race features'. Disgraced by his involvement in the Burke and Hare body-snatching scandal of 1828-9 and then near-bankrupted by the inclusion of anatomy in the Edinburgh University medical curriculum in the mid-1830s, Knox was severely constrained in his own ability to procure and examine comparative anatomical specimens. Nonetheless, he vigorously encouraged those of his past students who had found employment as naval surgeons or colonial medical officers to gather as much information as they could about non-European peoples they might encounter and, most importantly and wherever possible, to procure skeletal material and soft tissue structures for metropolitan anatomical collections.

During the 1840s, Knox turned to popular lecturing on race. His lectures (1850) were a heady mix of anatomical demonstration and racial reinterpretation of history peppered with scathing criticisms of contemporary religious leaders, intellectuals, and politicians for downplaying the crucial significance of race as the principal determinant of human affairs. Knox died just before the foundation of the Anthropological Society but he was a powerful source of inspiration to its leadership which envisaged the new society as a source of institutional support and intellectual direction to the anatomical study of racial difference. However, the society's claim to be the first and sole body truly devoted to disclosing the meanings of race through empirical study was vigorously disputed by leading Darwinians who regarded themselves as more rigorously committed to elucidating the meanings of racial difference through inductive reasoning.

Francis Galton (1822-1911), for example, heard and was unimpressed by Hunt's discourse on African inferiority at the 1863 meeting of the British Association for the Advancement of Science. By this time, Galton (1908:288) had been led by the *Origin of Species* 'to pursue many new inquiries ... clustered round the central topics of Heredity and the possible improvement of the Human Race'. While it was not until the mid-1880s that Galton felt confident he could adequately describe how hereditary characteristics were transmitted, by 1863 he was convinced that Darwin's concept of natural selection was far more powerful an explanation than the static racialism propounded by Knox and his admirers in the Anthropological Society. For if, as Hunt now claimed, members of primitive races inherited identical qualities of intellect, how could they explain the wealth of empirical evidence for the production by even the most primitive races of at least some 'able men capable of taking an equal position with Europeans'? Indeed, Galton asked Hunt after his paper, if no racially pure African had the psychological capacity to embrace civilization, as Hunt had claimed, how could 'so degraded a people … furnish men capable of constructing nations out of the loosest materials?' (Hunt 1863:387-8).

Galton's treatment of Hunt was gentle in comparison to that of other influential Darwinians. In the course of delivering the 1864 Hunterian Lectures at the Royal College of Surgeons, Huxley (1872:20) gleefully catalogued Hunt's 'aberrations from scientific fact or fair speculation' when reviewing what leading continental anatomists had actually discovered by post-mortem dissection of black corpses over the previous thirty years. Rolleston, a fellow Darwinian and Oxford's Linacre Professor of Anatomy and Physiology, openly belittled Hunt's scientific pretensions and privately queried whether he was in the pay of Confederate agents (Desmond 1994:326). Hunt and several other prominent members of the Anthropological Society responded by accusing Huxley in particular of having wilfully misrepresented Hunt's intentions. *The Negro's Place in Nature* was never intended as a definitive account of African inferiority but as a call for focused research into the racial distinctiveness of the African and other primitive races. The fact that Huxley and his colleagues seemed uninterested in undertaking such research underscored the rationale for establishing the Anthropological Society (Anon. 1863:107). Society members also charged Huxley with having attacked Hunt because of his pro-slavery views and queried whether his antagonism was unconnected with the fact that key elements of Darwin's theory — such as the existence of intermediate forms between species — lacked empirical verification.[5]

While the leadership of the Anthropological Society steadfastly believed that its program of anatomical research would produce evidence proving beyond doubt the plural origins of humanity and the immutability of racial difference, they were conscious of only having begun to place the study of race on a truly scientific basis. There is no reason to doubt that Hunt was sincere in protesting that his views on African inferiority were in many respects tentative and open to revision. While claiming that anatomical examinations strongly suggested the typical African brain to be smaller in size than the European, Hunt (1864) nonetheless readily conceded that cranial capacity alone was insufficient proof of intellectual capacity. What was needed was extensive research aimed at identifying and correlating what might possibly be complex and racially unique matrices of interrelated traits. The few published accounts of individual post-mortem dissections of adult men and women of African descent, for example, suggested to him that the African brain was more akin structurally to that of a European child. The African brain also supposedly differed markedly in terms of colour and exhibited less numerous and more massive convolutions. What had so far been found through close anatomical scrutiny of the African body suggested interesting correlations between the physical structure of the brain and what were allegedly typical African behavioural traits. But only comprehensive anatomical inquiry, he concluded, would disclose the full scientific significance of these and many other racial peculiarities likely to be found distinguishing the peoples of the earth.

Where Hunt could justly be accused of being disingenuous was in depicting his Darwinian critics as uninterested in anatomical investigation of racial characteristics. From as early as 1861, Rolleston, for example, had sought to obtain brains of the different varieties of mankind so as to illuminate whether psychological differences might be explained by racially typical aspects of cerebral structure.[6] He also studied homologies in shoulder musculature and teeth enamel in some detail with a view to disclosing evidence of evolutionary processes (F[lower] 1881). Huxley (1900:205-9) documented cranial variations between the fossil crania and modern 'primitives' to show how they formed a series highly suggestive of evolutionary refinement. In short, for all the differences between Darwinians and their polygenist opponents, both regarded the human body as an ensemble of markers of racial affiliation. Irrespective of their selection of bones or soft tissues or their methods of measurement, both camps implicitly assumed that the true course of human natural history would only be disclosed through regimented, statistically significant measurement and racial differentiation of bodily structures.

The lure of Aboriginal bodies — the Darwinians

The centrality of bodily measurement within anatomical and anthropological circles meant that much of the interaction between metropolitan racial scientists and their Australian colonial correspondents during the 1860s centred on the procurement of indigenous bodies and the interpretation of their supposed racial characteristics. Darwinians sought indigenous Australian bodily remains in the belief that they would yield important evidence of ancestral relations between races that over time had come to exhibit morphologically distinct physical and psychological characteristics. Those who subscribed to static racialist explanations of human origins were equally, if not more, anxious to amass evidence of racial peculiarities, believing that accurate determination of the contours of race would show the immutability of certain key racial characteristics, thus proving that humanity could not have evolved from a common ancestral type.

However, in seeking to map racial characteristics, researchers faced a serious difficulty. As Berthold Seeman (1825-1871) warned fellow members of the Anthropology Society in June 1863, skulls alone were insufficient to determine racial identity. In many instances, it was also necessary to examine soft tissue. Indeed, he told the society, 'I myself should like to see in London an anthropological garden, something on the same principle as the Zoological

Gardens, where living specimens of the principal varieties of the human race might be seen and compared'.[7] Yet, as the Darwinian palaeontologist George Busk lamented in 1861:

> while in the case of animals and plants, copious collections can be made and stored up in museums for accurate and leisurely examination and comparison ... at best but few perfect specimens of pure or unmixed races (to use an indefinite term) can be obtained, and the Anthropologist at home is compelled to rely for the materials of his studies upon such fragmentary portions of the body as can be easily obtained and transported.... A Gorilla or a Chimpanzee can be caught and sent alive to the Zoological Gardens, or killed and forwarded in a cask of rum to the British Museum, but loud would be the outcry were similar attempts made to promote the study of Anthropology (1861:348-9).

Busk knew first-hand from over twenty years as visiting surgeon to the Dreadnought hospital ship at Greenwich how few opportunities for studying racially interesting soft tissue occurred.[8] Accepting that the study of human racial difference should necessarily be restricted to bones, Busk (1861) believed it essential that they be made to reveal as much as possible and to this end he personally invested much time developing new cranial measuring techniques and instruments. However, by the early 1860s, he and many fellow anatomists feared that they were working against time. Opportunities for procuring even skeletal material were threatened by what seemed the impending extinction of the world's more primitive and scientifically interesting races.

The concept of racial extinction was hardly novel. At least since the 1830s, many British intellectuals and colonial administrators had thought it possible that some races would disappear as a consequence of the expropriation of their homelands by European settlers. By this time, it was common knowledge that in South Africa and the Australian colonies resistance to settler ambition had frequently led to the indiscriminate killing of indigenous peoples. However, few if any ethnographers believed that settler violence alone explained the collapse of native populations. Rather, a wealth of eyewitness testimony to the impact of diseases and the prevalence of infertility and supposed social anomie was interpreted as highly suggestive that the demise of peoples such as the 'aborigines of New Holland' was providentially ordained.

What was new in the early 1860s was the conviction amongst racial scientists that the pace of extinction had accelerated to the point that several races were on the verge of disappearing. Indeed, the fact that only several 'full-blooded' native Tasmanians remained alive convinced such theorists that the race had effectively become extinct. This conviction, moreover, gained cognitive strength from the additional empirical weight that the apparent decline of indigenous populations gave to the core theoretical assumptions of both Darwinians and static racialists. Darwinians saw the drama of racial extinction supposedly being played out in the Australian colonies as further proof that, like all other forms of organic life, humanity had evolved through natural selection. With the spread of settler society, the native Australian race was naturally being subsumed by the more advanced European. Critics of Darwinian explanations who believed in the plurality of human origin interpreted the supposed extinction of races such as the Tasmanians as one further historical episode in which two races of unequal physiology and intellect had sought to occupy the same territory. For polygenists, the scientific significance of studying the typical bodily characteristics of these vanquished races lay in producing evidence that racial conflict did not result in hybrid beings who over time would become the ancestors of a new race.

The new intellectual salience assumed by the premise of racial extinction during the 1860s heightened the desire of both Darwinians and polygenists to secure anatomical evidence likely to prove the truth of their respective accounts of human natural history. It made authorities in both camps even more concerned to secure the bones of races believed to be close to extinction. To this end, they sought to enlist the help of colonial scientists, museum personnel, medical practitioners, and amateur naturalists, representing the collection of remains as a means for them to make an invaluable contribution to the progress of British anthropological science.

Amongst Darwinians, Rolleston was particularly active in cultivating Australian collectors. Until his death in 1881, Rolleston was successful in promoting a slow but steady flow of indigenous skeletal material to Oxford by two avenues. One was through his brother Christopher Rolleston (1817-1888) who had been nearly thirty years in New South Wales when he was appointed auditor-general of the colony in 1864. Among the specimens yielded through this family connection were four skulls stolen from a burial place on a cattle station owned by Christopher in western central Queensland.[9] The other means by which George Rolleston secured remains was through former students practicing medicine in the Australian colonies. In 1869, for example, he received the skull of a Wiradjuri woman from H.M. Rowland, by this time a physician in the Bathurst district. The skull had been removed from a burial place unearthed during the clearing of scrub.[10] In the same year, Rolleston received a case containing five skulls obtained from another former pupil residing in Adelaide who had employed a local natural history collector to secure him skulls from a traditional burial site near the Murray River entrance. Two of the skulls, belonging to a man and his wife only buried in 1862, were the last remaining at the site. However, as the collector informed Rolleston's former student:

> If you should wish to have any more skulls I may have opportunities of obtaining some, but at present I do not know for certain of any place

where I could get some. Those from freshly dead natives would of course be most valuable, & those I do not know how to get. I think I would undertake to clean them myself if I had them, as I have often prepared the skulls of lower animals.[11]

The question of how Aboriginal people reacted to these desecrations is beyond the scope of this paper. However, there is a wealth of archival evidence and oral testimony illustrative of Aboriginal determination to protect the dead (Turnbull 2002).

Around 1870, Rolleston received the complete skeleton of a man from the Port Augusta region of South Australia from another former pupil, J. Marshall Stokes, who informed Rolleston that the man, who had died in 1869, was in his opinion 'considerably below the average stature of his tribe and I always fancy weakly so as not to be taken as a type of his race physically'. While he was a willing participant in the production of racial knowledge, Stokes's encounters with living indigenous Australians had left him convinced that the common perception of the Australian race as limited in intellectual capacity was 'very mistaken'.[12] Also in Rolleston's hands by 1872 was a skull procured from a burial place on a sheep station (ironically named Oxford Downs) 130 kilometres west of Mackay in central Queensland. The skull had been obtained for him by George Marten who had been an undergraduate at Pembroke College in the early 1860s. Marten, now growing sugar in the Mackay district, had acquired the skull on learning of Rolleston's desire for aboriginal remains from a neighbour, W.R. Davidson, another ex-student of the anatomist. In sending the skull, Marten wrote that he would be 'glad to know if there is any special objects of interest that I might be in the way of procuring in Queensland' and 'glad to do anything we could in the cause of science'.[13]

Lacking a network comparable to that enjoyed by Rolleston, other Darwinians proved less successful in securing donations of Australian skeletal material. Busk, for example, managed to obtain no more than two or three crania. Huxley had better but still relatively limited success. Among the colonists he approached was the mining engineer and colonial ethnographer Robert Brough Smyth (?-1899), author of the compendious *Aborigines of Victoria* (1878). Interestingly, Smyth — unlike Darwin himself — had no difficulty in reconciling the latter's theory of organic development through speciation with the essential truths of Christianity as they were understood within liberal Anglican circles. In a lecture to the Bendigo Working Men's Club in 1886 (1856-89:4 [c]), he declared that providence had bestowed on man two books of supreme wisdom: the Bible and *The Origin of Species*. As secretary and later chair of Victoria's Board for the Protection of Aborigines during the 1860s, Smyth accordingly saw no tension between administering a regime in which conversion to Christianity was regarded as an essential precondition for civilizing the colony's indigenous inhabitants and subjecting them to scientific examination of their presumed racial peculiarities on behalf of leading metropolitan Darwinians. Nor indeed did Smyth (1856-89:4 [d]) have any qualms about approaching Victoria's colonial secretary to procure the skeleton of an Aboriginal elder given Christian burial in the Melbourne general cemetery. Through Smyth, Huxley came in contact with Christopher D'Oyly H. Aplin (1819-1875), a surveyor with the Victorian Geological Survey Office. Aplin in turn willingly approached landowners on Huxley's behalf, eventually securing him three skulls. One, Aplin wrote, was 'found by some friends of mine in an excavation made by them for the purpose of examining the nature of the large mounds or "myrnong heaps" rather numerous in the Western Districts of the colony'. The other two were obtained after being exposed by erosion in sand dunes at Port Fairy.[14]

Amongst those whose aid Huxley sought to enlist was Johann Ludwig Gerard Krefft (1830-1881), curator of Sydney's Australian Museum from 1864 to 1872. By the time of his appointment, Gerard Krefft had established a modest reputation as a taxonomist with leading metropolitan British anatomists. Since the late 1850s, he had supplied numerous rare vertebrate fossils to Richard Owen at the British Museum and published descriptions of new Australian reptiles and fish species in several London scientific journals. Krefft had closely followed the debates between Darwinians and followers of Owen and could not have been unaware that the question of human origins was now a tripartite contest in which both Owenites and Darwinians alike were targets of the static physical anthropologists of the Anthropology Society. Indeed, Krefft realized that by virtue of his ability to procure and examine native Australian bodies, he was uniquely situated to gain fame in metropolitan scientific circles by producing knowledge to help resolve the question of the significance of human racial differences. One of his first moves on being appointed curator was to instruct the Museum's assistant George Masters (1837–1912) to remove remains from indigenous burial places encountered on collecting expeditions. In May 1865, Masters wrote to Krefft on returning from the countryside west of Ipswich, in southern Queensland, informing him that he had shipped to the Museum a variety of skins and skeletons, including the bones of an Aboriginal woman.[15] Krefft also alerted the many amateur naturalists who regularly donated zoological specimens that the Museum particularly desired Aboriginal skeletons. One of the first naturalists to oblige in this respect was a pastoralist in central Queensland who wrote to Krefft in September 1865 that he had not only 'got the bones of an alligator for you as soon as they are fit to send away' but 'also two blackfellows buried in a paddock of mine on purpose to get the skeletons to send you'. The pastoralist gave no indication of how he had procured the bodies.[16] In the same year, the Museum also received another two skeletons of central Queensland Aboriginal people donated by George Rolleston's old student W.R. Davidson.[17]

On being approached by Huxley in 1866, Krefft provided him with basic cranial measurements of the Museum's collection and promised to help him secure skulls through James Wilcox (1823–1881), a farmer in the Grafton district of New South Wales who for some years had supplemented his income by selling bird and marsupial specimens to the Australian Museum and the Museum of Victoria. Wilcox was also known to be willing to plunder Aboriginal graves.[18] However, this was as far as Krefft was prepared to help Huxley, being concerned to ensure that he did not enhance his relationship with metropolitan authorities at the expense of failing to enrich the holdings of his own Museum. Krefft was now unwilling to pass over any opportunity to acquire Aboriginal or other racially interesting human remains. By the early 1870s, the Museum had acquired four complete skeletons and some eighty skulls, mostly of Aboriginal and Oceanic origin (Maddock 1874:78). When Huxley again approached Krefft in 1872 wanting additional remains and in particular female Aboriginal pelvic bones, Krefft deflected the request by sending Huxley photographs of Aboriginal skulls in the Museum's collection while stressing that it was becoming increasing rare to discover burial places. 'I wish I could', he told Huxley, 'but it is very difficult — we have 2 female skeletons in the Museum but I cannot send them'. He had again told a collector 'a few days ago to look out for same', but added, 'I suppose the greater portion of the native graves are obliterated'.[19]

By the early 1870s, Krefft had two further interrelated reasons for not wanting to see remains shipped to Britain. Although he had come to believe that humanity had evolved through speciation, he was sceptical of Darwin's claim that new species emerged by a purely random process. In common with influential metropolitan figures such as George Campbell, Duke of Argyll (1823–1900), and the geologist William Dawkins (1837–1929), Krefft was inclined to think that, while variation occurred through natural selection, some underlying law determined that the flow of variations moved in a purposeful direction.[20] However, unlike these British authorities who had sought to reconcile speciation with Christian belief in the subordination of nature to providential design, Krefft appears to have been influenced less by Darwin's writings than by the radical pantheistic account of evolutionary processes championed by Ernst Haeckel (1834-1919), the Prussian zoologist.[21] The second reason why Krefft was unwilling to part with Aboriginal bones was that he had himself become greatly interested in the question of Aboriginal origins, largely as a result of having discovered in 1869 what he took to be a fossilized human tooth during the excavation of a cave in the Wellington Valley of central-western New South Wales.

Metropolitan ideas and the colonial 'field'

By 1872, Krefft was convinced that the Aboriginal remains collected by the Australian Museum bore striking anatomical similarities to the ancient 'stone age' remains recently discovered in the limestone cliffs of the Vézère river valley in the Dordogne region in France. As Krefft had learned from reading the 1869 address by Paul Broca (1824-1880) to the Académie des Sciences, the most important of these discoveries had been the fossilized remains of four adults and an infant in a rock shelter uncovered during the construction of a railway line at Cro-Magnon (Broca 1873:305-9).

Broca (1873:426-8) was fascinated by what he and other French researchers presumed, on the basis of animal bones and various items of material culture found with the Cro-Magnon skeletons, to have been the development of an ancient race through three distinct societal stages before sudden extinction. They took the Cro-Magnons to have been a morphologically distinct race whose bodily characteristics bore no relation to less ancient remains found in barrow mounds or to modern Europeans. The thigh bones, for example, were much thicker than in any modern human race though seemingly closer in shape to modern men than were those of the higher apes. The skulls were much longer than those of modern European races with cranial sutures sufficiently similar to those of modern 'savage nations' to encourage the conclusion that they were probably on the same level in terms of social sophistication. Even so, Broca believed that their skulls showed 'signs of a powerful cerebral organisation' which he took as suggesting that they might have been constrained in achieving their full evolutionary potential by unknown environmental or social factors. Indeed, Broca was drawn to speculate that their extinction was due to their having been a peaceable people who were intellectually and technologically incapable of resisting the intrusion into the Vézère of a more aggressive and better-armed race.

Krefft was inspired by Broca to see remarkable affinities between the apparent course of human evolution in prehistoric Europe and the drama of racial supersession seemingly being played out in the Australian colonies, although the question remains open as to whether Krefft, in embracing Broca's reasoning as to the fate of the Cro-Magnons, also accepted Broca's polygenist explanation of human origins. Broca's fascination with the Cro-Magnon remains was in large measure due to his seeing them as providing clear morphological evidence that humanity had not evolved as Darwinians suggested through the evolutionary transformation of one ancestral type.

Whatever he thought of Broca's polygenist transformism, Krefft, over several newspaper articles published in Sydney during early 1873, argued that Australia's indigenous race exemplified the same three stages of societal development posited by Broca for the race whose remains had been discovered at Cro-Magnon. 'Comparing the weapons of our savages with these descriptions of the learned Frenchman', he wrote (1873b), 'we must acknowledge that he has hit the proper distinction to a point'. In Western Australia, he added, there lived 'savages with scarcely any covering except a cape of wallaby skin, without possum rugs and with the roughest lump of granite embedded in grass-tree gum for a hatchet'. These people clearly corresponded to the earliest era of Cro-Magnon society whereas the people living along the Murray and inhabiting coastal New South Wales were in Krefft's estimation obviously 'more advanced'. Like the socially more advanced Cro-Magnons, they fashioned stone hatchets with ground edges and carved or drew hunting scenes. Finally, in Krefft's eyes, the inhabitants of New Guinea were modern counterparts to the Cro-Magnon race in the third phase of social development preceding their extinction. By contrast, the Maori of New Zealand were a distinct, more advanced, 'intelligent' race who might in different circumstances have colonized Australia where they 'would have made short work with our gentle savages' and 'given future invaders more trouble than they gave them in their limited islands, though even there they proved hard to conquer'.

Krefft's conjectural racial history appears to have attracted no public comment in either Sydney or London media. Possibly, as he later claimed in a letter to Darwin, his evolutionary beliefs were a factor in his dismissal from the post of curator of the Australian Museum in 1874 (Butcher 1994:52-4). However, regardless of its reception, Krefft's comparative prehistory vividly illustrates how, by the mid-1870s, competing racial discourses licensed the imaginative reconstruction of human history as a universal narrative of racial struggle and supersession.[22] Yet Krefft did not simply bring the Darwinian conception of speciation together with Broca's speculative human history. Certainly, his collecting of Aboriginal bodily remains is a striking instance of convergence between seemingly disparate discourses on the issue of examining those remains. Moreover, the implications of that discursive convergence were doubly pernicious for Indigenous Australian people, given shared polygenist and Darwinian expectations of racial supersession and extinction. However, Krefft's position at the hub of colonial collecting practice also shows that Australia increasingly served as a critical zone of intellectual feedback to the metropole, with practical ramifications for diverse strands of the European science of race.

The lure of Aboriginal bodies — the polygenists

Darwinians were not alone in hunting indigenous bones. Leading members of the Anthropology Society proved equally keen to encourage the flow of indigenous Australian remains into scientific hands. Indeed, one of them, Joseph Barnard Davis, proved by far the most successful collector of racial crania and skeletons of the nineteenth century, amassing just over 1700 specimens by the late 1870s.[23] What is particularly remarkable about Davis's achievement is that, unlike Huxley or Rolleston but like most of his 'anthropological' colleagues, he was an amateur student of comparative human anatomy. Shortly after completing his medical studies in the late 1820s, Davis settled in the Staffordshire village of Shelton where he worked as a private physician and medical officer until his death in the 1880s. He was a confirmed believer in the immutability of racial characteristics who was especially critical of Huxley's argument (1862) that affinities between the shape of the Neanderthal skull discovered in 1856 and that typical of modern Australian crania suggested strongly that humanity had evolved through monogenetic speciation. The Neanderthal find, Davis argued (1864), was clearly pathological and of relatively modern origin. He wrote of Huxley to John Beddoe (1826-1911), a medical colleague and fellow member of the Anthropological Society: 'He is maddened that I have demolished the first and only foundation stone of human Darwinianism and can't help showing it'.[24] Even so, Davis was cautious in what he claimed could safely be inferred about human origins from cranial research and never positively affirmed publicly that humanity had arisen from plural origins.

Davis's racial thinking was greatly shaped by an intimate acquaintance with indigenous Australian bodily remains. By his own account, he began collecting and systematically mapping the racial peculiarities of crania in the late 1840s and it seems clear that his intellectual stimulus was the research into racial difference pursued since the early 1830s by the American anatomist Samuel Morton (1799-1851). In *Crania Americana* (1839), Morton had presented comparative measurements of the shape and internal capacity of some eighty indigenous north and south American skulls, believing that the sum of these cranial measurements 'of more than forty Indian nations' proved beyond dispute that they were a distinct race exhibiting no signs of having originated in Asia. In fact, Morton claimed, the typical form of the indigenous American skull justified the conclusion that racial distinctions were purely the product of physiological processes and that humanity was adapted 'from the beginning' to particular geographical regions (Morton and Combe 1839:3). By the mid-1840s, further research, based in part on 137 skulls procured from ancient Egyptian burial sites, had convinced Morton (1844:66) that humanity was comprised of separately-originating races and that the 'physical or organic characters which distinguish the several races of men, [were] as old as the oldest records of our species'.

At the time of his death in May 1851, Morton had only published detailed comparative measurements of American and Egyptian crania but it was well known in anthropological circles that he envisaged these works as preliminary instalments of a comprehensive base map of human racial diversity. The supposition that Davis saw himself as completing the polygenist Morton's research is strengthened by the fact that from the early 1850s he began energetically seeking the help of colonial administrators and medical practitioners to procure crania of European, Asian, Oceanic, and particularly mainland Australian and Tasmanian origin. As John Beddoe recalled (1910:205), 'Davis's enthusiasm for his subject was wonderful, but sometimes it verged on the ghoulish.... [He] looked on heads simply as potential skulls'.[25] Davis had no qualms about encouraging the theft of Tasmanian skulls during post-mortems or from graves at the settlements on Flinders Island and Oyster Cove where the survivors of the infamous campaigns of the 1820s were exiled. He informed one correspondent in 1856 (Rae-Ellis 1981:133): 'Were I myself in the colony, I could with very little trouble abstract skulls from dead bodies without defacing them at all, and could instruct any medical gentleman to do this'.

By the late 1860s, Davis had acquired the remarkable number of sixteen Tasmanian crania and the complete skeleton of a thirty year-old Tasmanian man. He bought several skulls at sales but acquired others through contacts with colonial administrators and medical colleagues. They included Joseph Milligan (1807-1884), the superintendent and medical officer of the Flinders Island and Oyster Cove settlements between 1843 and 1855 who had kept Tasmanian remains he came across in the course of his duties. Having retired to England by the early 1860s on a meagre colonial pension, Milligan was well aware of the value placed on bones in metropolitan anatomical circles but was loath to be seen to be trafficking in human remains (Davis 1867a:1). Davis regarded one of the skulls he had bought from Milligan as 'perhaps the finest and most perfect specimen in any Museum. Of great rarity and value'. It was from a Tasmanian man aged about twenty-four who had been killed in 1831 during an attack on a shepherd's hut in the Surrey Hills. Several other specimens Milligan sold Davis bore testimony to the viciousness of frontier conflict in Tasmania, notably the skull of a woman shown to Milligan by a boy of her clan. The boy 'told Milligan that his party some years before had been fired into by a white man when a woman was injured … she had been shot through the eye'.[26]

Davis's quest for Tasmanian specimens also led him to cultivate the friendship of George Augustus Robinson (1791-1866), Tasmania's first protector of Aborigines, who by the early 1860s had retired to the English spa town of Bath. Over the years, Robinson had acquired a skeleton and at least six crania, two of which were most likely procured during post-mortems at the Aboriginal settlement on Flinders Island.[27] Not content with the gift of one skull from Robinson, Davis sought to acquire the entire collection after the protector's death in 1866, together with his copious journals — though his plans in this regard were foiled by Robinson's family.[28]

From 1869, Davis found Tasmanian remains harder to obtain as a result of the infamous affair of the post-mortem mutilation of William Lanne, allegedly the last man of the Tasmanian race. As is well known, Lanne's corpse became the focus of scientific rivalry between the Hobart surgeon William Crowther (1817-1885), who sought to procure the skeleton for the Royal College of Surgeons in London, and leading members of the Royal Society of Tasmania. The mutilation of Lanne's corpse by the competing camps caused widespread public outrage over the willingness of medical authorities to transgress morality and the law in order to secure anatomical specimens, regardless of race (Petrow 1988:20). The scandal meant that few amongst the colony's elite were henceforth prepared to risk public association with the procurement of body parts through dissection or, particularly, the exhumation of graves.

While the Lanne affair greatly restricted both inclination and opportunities to procure Tasmanian remains, Davis was fortunate that one of his Tasmanian correspondents was prepared to risk moral censure for grave-robbing. This was Morton Allport (1830-1878), a Hobart lawyer and prominent member of the Royal Society of Tasmania. Davis appears to have begun corresponding with Allport after the latter sought in 1871 to become a corresponding member of the Anthropological Society and ensured his election by presenting the society with a complete skeleton exhumed in great secrecy from the Aboriginal cemetery on Flinders Island. At about the same time, Davis doubtless also learnt that Allport (1850-78:9-10) had presented the Royal College of Surgeons with two complete Aboriginal skeletons and had professed his readiness to send a third if the College would give Lanne's skull and vertebrae to the Royal Society of Tasmania. Davis's cultivation of Allport eventually led to his receiving a skull and bones in May 1872 that Allport had taken 'no small trouble to see ... were disinterred from a spot where none but other Aborigines were buried'. The following January, Allport (1850-78:107) sent news that he had secured 'a treasure for you in the shape of an adult male Skeleton of Tasmanian native all but absolutely perfect except as to the styloid processes which always seem very fragile'. However, this was to be one of the last skeletons that Allport removed from Flinders Island. As he explained in a letter of May 1874 to Charles Gould, son of the famous ornithologist, he had been approached for skeletal material by Professor Wyville Thompson, then visiting the Australian colonies as naturalist on the *Challenger* expedition. 'He also wants a *specimen* from Flinders', Allport confided to Gould, but remains had been discovered when a packing crate of 'geological specimens' was opened and he now feared that the Tasmanian government would move to protect indigenous Tasmanian burial places.[29]

Davis was to play an influential part in the contest between the 'anthropologicals' and their Darwinian opponents during the 1860s as a consequence of his ruthless pursuit of racially significant non-European skulls and skeletons. His unrivalled collection of Australian and indigenous remains from many other parts of the world proved a valuable resource for generating craniometric evidence that Davis (1864) and other leading 'anthropologicals' deployed against the evolutionary claims of Huxley and other leading Darwinians. The Darwinians responded by dismissing or ignoring the worth of Davis's findings. Even so, they were respectful if not jealous of his success in procuring racially significant remains. And while dismissive of the conclusions that Davis drew from measuring crania, they were equally convinced of the fundamental importance of comparative examination of the bones of ancient and modern 'primitive' peoples in reconstructing the true course of human evolutionary development. In the cause of racial science, Darwinians and 'anthropologicals' were equally willing to disregard the religious and moral sensitivities of their contemporaries and those of the people whose dead they defiled.

Conclusion

By the early 1880s, Darwinian evolutionary theory had become scientific orthodoxy in British anthropological circles. On his death in 1881, Davis received faint praise from evolutionist critics for his tenacity as a collector and for donating his wealth of specimens to the Royal College of Surgeons. In contrast, his Darwinian rival George Rolleston, who died less than a month later and had also examined large numbers of crania using much the same metrical techniques as Davis, was feted as Britain's leading craniologist. The failure of the static, polygenist ideas of the 'anthropologicals' owed much to the lack of explanatory power their interpretation of the meanings of race were deemed to have in comparison to those of the Darwinians. Moreover, while at its height in the mid-1860s the Anthropological Society boasted over 700 members, it was only a small inner circle within the society that actively propagated static racialism. These men were largely amateur researchers like Davis who worked outside the professional scientific establishment of mid-Victorian Britain. In contrast, many leading Darwinians enjoyed positions and rising influence within universities and the medical establishment. They had many more opportunities to convince professional colleagues and students of the validity of their ideas. Furthermore, the Darwinian conceptualization of the demise of indigenous people as a natural process rather than the outcome of human agency in the form of inter-racial conflict was culturally and morally a far more attractive vision of human natural history.

I have shown in this chapter that the contest between the Darwinians and their 'anthropological' opponents put indigenous Australian bones at the heart of a disturbing practical juncture between long-standing colonial assumptions about the inevitable extinction of 'inferior' races and the divergent logic of opposed branches of the science of race. The apparent correspondence of theory and experience had sinister consequences. It not only stimulated the plunder of Aboriginal burial places and scientific trafficking in bodily remains but strengthened white perceptions that the Aboriginal body itself proved the reality of profound and insurmountable biological differences between indigenous Australians and colonial settlers. This entanglement of metropolitan intellectual controversies with colonial experience, phobias, and actions firmly established race as the dominant cognitive foundation for envisaging and managing the destiny of Aboriginal Australians.

References

Allport, Morton. 1850-78. Morton Allport — Records. Letter Book 1871-1874. Manuscripts. Hobart: Allport Library and Museum of Fine Arts.

Anon. 1863. On the Relations of Man to the Inferior Animals. Review of T.H. Huxley, *Man's Place in Nature*. *Anthropological Review* 1:107-17.

Anthropological Society of London. 1863. Ordinary Meeting, 22nd June, 1863. *Transactions of the Anthropological Society of London* 1:xviii-xxvi.

Australian Museum. 1853-83a. Australian Museum Letters Received pre-1883. Correspondence Series 14. Manuscripts. Sydney: Australian Museum Archives.

————. 1853-83b. Letters Received 1853-1883. Correspondence Series 7/5. Manuscripts. Sydney: Australian Museum Archives.

Beddoe, John. 1854-73. Correspondence. General, Anthropological Society, Lectures, Published Papers, Etc. Manuscripts. Bristol: Bristol University Library.

————. 1910. *Memories of Eighty Years*. Bristol: J.W. Arrowsmith.

Blake, C. Carter. 1871. The Life of Dr Knox. Review of Henry Lonsdale, *The Life of Robert Knox, the Anatomist. Journal of Anthropology* 1:332-8.

Blumenbach, Johann Friedrich. 1781. *De Generis Humani Varietate Nativa*. 2nd edition. Goettingae: Abr. Vandenhoek.

————. 1795. *De Generis Humani Varietate Nativa*. 3rd edition. Gottingae: Vandenhoek et Ruprecht.

Broca, Paul. 1873. The Troglodytes of the Vezere. *Nature* 7:305-8, 326-9, 366-9, 426-8.

Busk, George. 1861. Observations on a Systematic Mode of Craniometry. *Transactions of the Ethnological Society of London*, new series 1:341-8.

Butcher, Barry W. 1994. Darwinism, Social Darwinism, and the Australian Aborigines: a Reevaluation. In *Darwin's Laboratory: Evolutionary Theory and Natural History in the Pacific*, ed. Roy MacLeod and Philip F. Rehbock, 371-94. Honolulu: University of Hawaii Press.

Clark, William, ed. 1862. *Catalogue of the Osteological Portion of the Specimens Contained in the Anatomical Museum of the University of Cambridge*. Cambridge: Cambridge University Press.

Craft, William, and Ellen Craft. 1860. *Running a Thousand Miles for Freedom: or, The Escape of William and Ellen Craft from Slavery*. London: William Tweedie.

Davis, Joseph Barnard. 1864. *The Neanderthal Skull: its Peculiar Conformation Explained Anatomically*. London: Taylor and Francis.

_____. 1867a. *Thesaurus Craniorum: Catalogue of the Skulls of the Various Races of Man, in the Collection of Joseph Barnard Davis*. London: Taylor and Francis.

_____. 1867b. Davis Catalogue of Crania. Manuscript. MS 42/c/37. London: Royal College of Surgeons Library.

Desmond, Adrian J. 1982. *Archetypes and Ancestors: Palaeontology in Victorian London, 1850-1875*. London: Blond and Briggs.

_____. 1994. *Huxley: the Devil's Disciple*. London: Michael Joseph.

Ellingson, Ter. 2001. *The Myth of the Noble Savage*. Berkeley: University of California Press.

F[lower], W[illiam] H[enry]. 1881. George Rolleston, M.D., F.R.S. *Nature* 24:192-3.

Galton, Francis. 1908. *Memories of my Life*. London: Methuen.

Goodsir, John. 1868. *The Anatomical Memoirs of John Goodsir*, ed. William Turner. Edinburgh: A. and C. Black.

Haeckel, Ernst. 1866. *Generelle Morphologie der Organismen: allgemeine Grundzüge der organischen Formen-Wissenschaft, mechanisch begründet durch die von Charles Darwin reformirte Descendenz-Theorie*, 2 vols. Berlin: G. Reimer.

Hunt, James. 1863. On the Physical and Mental Characters of the Negro. *Anthropological Review* 1:386-91.

_____. 1864. *The Negro's Place in Nature: a Paper Read Before the London Anthropological Society*. New York: Van Evrie, Horton.

Huxley, Thomas Henry. 1825-95a. Huxley Papers. Manuscripts. MF4/216. Sydney: Mitchell Library.

_____. 1825-95b. Notes and Correspondence. Anthropology. Scientific Notebooks, Drawings and other Papers. Manuscripts. London: Archives of Imperial College of Science and Technology.

_____. 1862. A Lecture on the Fossil Remains of Man. *Lancet* 79:165-7.

_____. 1872 [1870]. *Lay Sermons, Addresses, and Reviews*. New York: D. Appleton.

_____. 1900 [1894]. *Man's Place in Nature and Other Anthropological Essays*. New York: D. Appleton.

Knox, Robert. 1823-4. Inquiry into the Origin and Characteristic Differences of the Native Races Inhabiting the Extra-Tropical Part of Southern Africa. *Memoirs of the Wernerian Natural History Society* 5:206-19.

_____. 1850. *The Races of Men: a Fragment*. Philadelphia: Lea and Blanchard.

Krefft, Gerard. 1873a. Remarks on New Hypotheses. *Sydney Mail* 12 July 1873.

_____. 1873b. Savages, Fossil and Recent. *Sydney Mail* 19 July 1873.

Maddock, William. 1874. *Visitors' Guide to Sydney: Comprising a Description of the City and its Institutions with which is Incorporated the Tourists' Handbook and the Resources of New South Wales*. 2nd edition. Sydney: W. Maddock.

Morton, Samuel George. 1844. *Crania Ægyptiaca: or, Observations on Egyptian Ethnography, Derived from Anatomy, History and the Monuments*. Philadelphia: John Penington.

Morton, Samuel George, and George Combe. 1839. *Crania Americana: or, a Comparative View of the Skulls of Various Aboriginal Nations of North and South America to Which is Prefixed an Essay on the Varieties of the Human Species*. Philadelphia: J. Dobson.

Museum of Victoria. 1854-99. Correspondence Boxes A - Z 1854-1899. Manuscripts. Melbourne: Museum of Victoria.

New South Wales, Parliament. 1866. *Votes and Proceedings of the Legislative Assembly*. Sydney: Government Printer.

Petrow, Stefan. 1997-8. The Last Man: the Mutilation of William Lanne in 1869 and its Aftermath. *Australian Cultural History* 16:18-44.

Prichard, James Cowles. 1813. *Researches into the Physical History of Man*. London: John and Arthur Arch.

_____. 1836-47. *Researches into the Physical History of Mankind*, 5 vols. 3rd edition. London: Sherwood, Gilbert, and Piper.

Rae-Ellis, Vivienne 1981 [1976]. *Trucanini: Queen or Traitor?* 2nd edition. Canberra: Australian Institute of Aboriginal Studies.

Reddie, James. 1864. On Anthropological Desiderata, Considered with Reference to the Various Theories of Man's Origin and Existing Condition, Savage and Civilised. *Journal of the Anthropological Society of London* 2:cxv-cxxxv.

Robinson, George Augustus. 1788-1866. Journals, Papers and Letters. Manuscripts. MS A7089. Sydney: Mitchell Library.

Rolleston, George. c. 1850-81. Rolleston Papers: Miscellaneous Archaeological and Anthropological Letters and Papers. Manuscripts. Oxford: Ashmolean Museum.

Rupke, Nicolaas A. 1994. *Richard Owen: Victorian Naturalist*. New Haven, CT: Yale University Press.

Smyth, Robert Brough. 1856-89. Papers. Manuscripts. Box 1176. Melbourne: La Trobe Library.

_____. 1878. *The Aborigines of Victoria: with Notes Relating to the Habits of the Natives of Other Parts of Australia and Tasmania*, 2 vols. Melbourne: Government Printer.

Stocking, George W., Jr. 1973. From Chronology to Ethnology: James Cowles Prichard and British Anthropology 1800-1850. In James Cowles Prichard, *Researches into the Physical History of Man*, ed. George W. Stocking, Jr., ix-cx. Chicago: University of Chicago Press.

_____. 1987. *Victorian Anthropology*. New York: Free Press.

Turnbull, Paul. 1991. 'Ramsay's Regime': the Australian Museum and the Procurement of Aboriginal Bodies, c. 1874-1900. *Aboriginal History* 15:108-21.

_____. 1998. 'Outlawed Subjects': the Procurement and Scientific Uses of Australian Aboriginal Heads, ca. 1803-1835. *Eighteenth-Century Life* 22:156-71.

_____. 1999. Enlightenment Anthropology and the Ancestral Remains of Australian Aboriginal People. In *Voyages and Beaches: Pacific Encounters, 1769-1840*, ed. Alex Calder, Jonathan Lamb and Bridget Orr, 202-25. Honolulu: University of Hawai'i Press.

_____. 2002. Indigenous Australian Peoples, their Defence of the Dead, and Native Title. In *The Dead and their Possessions: Repatriation in Principle, Policy and Practice*, ed. Cressida Fforde, Jane Hubert, and Paul Turnbull, 63-86. London: Routledge.

Van Keuren, David Keith. 1982. Human Science in Victorian Britain: Anthropology in Institutional and Disciplinary Formation, 1863-1908. PhD thesis. Philadelphia: University of Pennsylvania.

Young, Robert J.C. 1995. *Colonial Desire: Hybridity in Theory, Culture and Race*. London and New York: Routledge.

Notes

[1] The Ethnological Society of London was founded in late 1843 through the agency of Richard King, a physician and secretary of the Aborigines Protection Society. King and several other members of the Aborigines Protection Society believed that the world's 'savage' nations were destined to extinction in the wake of colonialism and that it was of crucial scientific and philosophical importance that their physical and moral characteristics be studied before they became no more than a history memory. See especially Stocking 1987:240-5.

[2] Blumenbach 1781, 1795; Prichard 1813, 1836-47. See Chapter One (Douglas), this volume.

[3] See especially Ellingson 2001; Stocking 1987; Van Keuren 1982; Young 1995.

[4] Hunt 1863; Craft and Craft 1860.

[5] E.g., Anon. 1863:114-17; Reddie 1864:cxv-cxix.

[6] This is clearly evident from items of correspondence in the Rolleston Papers detailing his efforts to secure non-European brains from British port cities (Rolleston c. 1850-81: Box 2).

[7] Anthropological Society of London 1863:xxiii.

[8] See, e.g., Clark 1862:106.

[9] Rolleston c. 1850-81: Box 4.

[10] Rolleston c. 1850-81: Box 2.

[11] Rolleston c. 1850-81: Box 4.

[12] Rolleston c. 1850-81: Box 2.

[13] Rolleston c. 1850-81: Box 4.

[14] Huxley 1825-95b: XVI, 2: 143.

[15] Australian Museum 1853-83a: C: 40.65.5.

[16] Australian Museum 1853-83b: C: 30.65.24.

[17] New South Wales Parliament 1866:4, 909.

[18] Museum of Victoria 1854-99: Box W.

[19] Huxley 1825-95a: ff. 291-v.

[20] Desmond 1982:175-86; Krefft 1873a.

[21] In his *Generelle Morphologie der Organismen* (1866), Haeckel sought to transform Darwin's theory into a monistic *naturphilosophie* grounded in the idea that through the agency of fundamental causal laws, all living organisms and inorganic matter were more or less complex expressions of the same substance.

[22] See Chapter Two (Douglas), this volume, for earlier conjectural histories of racial displacement.

[23] Davis's collection was acquired by the Royal College of Surgeons of England shortly before his death in May 1881. The size of his collection can be gauged from Davis 1867a.

[24] Davis to Beddoe, 18 Feb. 1866, in Beddoe 1854-73.

[25] Beddoe recounted further: 'Once when [Davis] visited us I took him to the infirmary, and showed him a Morlachian sailor from near Ragusa, whom I was trying to cure of gangrene of the lung, resulting from having been half-drowned — a fine, handsome fellow, but desperately ill. "Now", said my friend, "you know that man can't recover; do take care to secure his head for me when he dies, for I have no cranium from that neighbourhood". After all, the poor Morlach made a wonderful recovery, and carried his head on his own shoulders back to the Herzegovia' (1910:205).

[26] Davis 1867b:1, 1128, 1120.

[27] Robinson 1788-1866: Vol. 68[a], f. 517; Davis 1867a:270-1.

[28] Robinson 1788-1866: Vol. 68[a], ff. 583, 591, 595, 603, 607.

[29] Allport 1850-78:56-7, orig. emphasis.

Chapter Five

'Three Living Australians' and the Société d'Anthropologie de Paris, 1885

Stephanie Anderson

To search through nineteenth-century French anthropological writings about Indigenous Australians means ingesting a great deal of material that is highly offensive and injurious to Aboriginal people. In this discourse, Australian Aborigines were almost invariably assigned to the *dernier échelon*, the bottom rung, of the human racial ladder. This was their epistemological 'slot'.[1] The prevailing view about Aborigines that had become established in travel accounts and periodicals such as the *Journal des Voyages* was of a people barely human who at worst showed many simian characteristics and at best were living fossils, contemporary manifestations of Stone Age people. The scientific view as reflected in the anthropological literature, in particular the journals produced by the Société d'Anthropologie de Paris, founded in 1859, scarcely departed from these gross representations.

Aboriginal Australians in 19th-century French anthropology

Early French studies devoted in part or in whole to Australian Aborigines form part of the body of texts which constituted the French (and wider European) discourse of the science of race, *raciologie* in French terminology. The history of French anthropology in the nineteenth century is a growing field and a number of excellent studies has been produced but the focus of research is primarily on metropolitan thinkers rather than their indigenous subjects.[2] This chapter takes a different approach in looking at what happened when a particular group of Australian Aborigines fell under the lens of French anthropologists who for raciological purposes generally took them as representative. How did Aborigines fit the raciological theories of the day? How exactly were they represented in French anthropological discourse? And what do such representations reveal about the construction and practice of raciology? With these questions in mind, I tackle French anthropological discourse relating to Indigenous Australians through a specific episode: the presentation of three Aborigines from North Queensland to a small group of French anthropologists at the Société d'Anthropologie in Paris in 1885. The record of the meeting was published in the dense and voluminous *Bulletins de la Société d'Anthropologie de Paris*, the official publication of the Société along with the *Mémoires*. The story of the world tour of the Aboriginal troupe presented by the American impresario Robert Cunningham has itself been the subject of a touring exhibition in Australia and a recent book by Roslyn Poignant (2004).[3] The report of the Paris meeting was merely a sideline to that tour but it condenses many aspects of French anthropological interest in Australian Aborigines in particular and the study of non-European people as racial specimens more generally. It is an unwitting *mise en abyme*, a representation in miniature, of the ideology and practices of late nineteenth-century racial anthropology in France.

Influential figures in this anthropological milieu were Paul Broca (1824-1880), Paul Topinard (1830-1911), and Ernest-Théodore Hamy (1842-1908),[4] all of whom feature in this chapter. Broca presided over the French anthropological scene for twenty years after playing a key part in founding the Société d'Anthropologie de Paris and serving as its first secretary-general. Broca proselytized an anthropometrical approach characterized by a dogmatic empiricism which, for a time, was the dominant paradigm for the study of human others among members of the Société and beyond. Topinard and Hamy are important here not only because of their views and writings on the subject of Aborigines but because they were directly involved with the three Aboriginal Australians while they were in Paris and brought them to the attention of the Société. Topinard was a particular protegé of Broca's whose influence showed in Topinard's anthropological focus on the observable and the measurable. The difficulties this approach entailed when he came to synthesize the mass of information he had collected about Aborigines are discussed below.

If, in representational terms, the 1885 meeting of Aborigines and scholars typified raciological discourse and method, in practice it was atypical because it brought together elements in nineteenth-century French anthropology that were usually quite separate: namely the objects of study and those undertaking the analysis, the 'armchair' anthropologists. As Nélia Dias (1994:38) pointed out, the functions of collecting data (skeletal material, observations, photographs) and its analysis were not normally undertaken by the same person. In this case, when the analysts actually came face to face with those they were studying, the preconceptions about non-Europeans underpinning raciology stood out all the more clearly. Because I use the meeting to highlight aspects of raciological discourse and methods, my discussion moves back and forth between this exceptional Aboriginal-French encounter in Paris and the broader anthropological setting in which it occurred. In presenting the three Aborigines to the Société d'Anthropologie, the secretary-general Topinard drew on information provided in a memoir by two Belgian anthropologists, Emile Houzé (1848-1921) and Victor Jacques (1853-?), who had examined seven members of Cunningham's troupe when they were on exhibition at the Musée du Nord in Brussels. The Belgian memoir provides some illuminating comparisons and contrasts to the French report as does one by Rudolf Virchow (1821-1902) who had examined the Queenslanders in Berlin, but to whom Topinard made scant reference.[5]

Cunningham's troupe and Topinard's 'presentation'

Cunningham's troupe was composed of nine Aborigines from the Palm Islands and Hinchinbrook Island off the coast of North Queensland. We do not know whether they went with him willingly and knowingly but their job was to play the role of wild savages as they toured North America in Barnum's Circus, appearing at fairs and dime museums.[6] They went on to England and Europe where they performed and were displayed at popular venues and were made available to anthropologists for examination and study. When the group arrived in Paris, only four of the nine were still alive — Toby and Jenny who were married, their child little Toby, and another man, Billy. The other five had succumbed to illness and died along the way. While in Paris, the four survivors stayed at the Jardin d'Acclimatation, gardens established to introduce and acclimatize exotic plants and animals. In the latter part of the nineteenth century, a number of such groups from exotic places was temporarily put on display there for the entertainment of the Parisian crowds but the Queensland group actually performed at the Folies-Bergère.[7]

The core of Topinard's 'Présentation de trois Australiens vivants' (1885) is a short report to the audience attending this 'live' demonstration on what he distinguished as the salient anthropological features of the three individuals. It should be noted that Jenny, Billy, and perhaps little Toby were actually present as Topinard spoke to his colleagues.[8] We do not, however, know how the room was set up or what the three subjects did while they were being discussed. Despite their reported linguistic skills, it is unlikely that they had picked up sufficient French during their short stay to enable them to follow the scientific discussion. They were probably addressed in English,[9] a second language for both the Aborigines and the French. Topinard (1885:683-6) began by describing how the presentation came about. The eminent anthropologist Hamy had learned of the troupe's stay in Paris from a colleague. He and Topinard visited them twice at the Jardin d'Acclimatation and also arranged for them to be examined at the laboratory of the Ecole d'Anthropologie. When Topinard and Hamy made their first visit, the fourth surviving member of the group, Jenny's husband Toby, was in hospital suffering from tuberculosis. He died the following day. Topinard said: 'I did all that I could, but to no avail, to have his body sent to the Broca laboratory, to be dissected'. During the anthropologists' second visit, Billy gave a display of his skills with the boomerang, an object of wonder to European scientists.[10]

After a brief account of the Aborigines' world tour, Topinard (1885:686-7) noted that its members had been measured by other anthropologists. He then described the physical appearance of the man, the woman, and the child. Physical appearance — what could be observed from the outside and measured — was seen as crucial. Their skin colour was a 'deep yellowish chocolate'. The description and classification of their hair proved more problematic. Topinard dismissed previous reports of Aboriginal hair as straight and went into comparative detail about the diameter of the whorls of hair of the 'most favoured negroes' and 'the most inferior', the Bushmen. He maintained that the Australians' hair was closer to the 'woolly' hair of negroes than to the straight hair of the 'yellow races' and concluded that it was 'modified negro hair' formed of 'numerous but rather broad whorls'. He described their faces as follows:

> With a full, rounded forehead, bulging and protuberant brow ridges, a deep root of the nose, very pronounced prognathism, particularly in the woman. The nose short vertically, wide at the base, triangular when it is seen face on, massive, with coarse and dilated wings; in brief what is called the *Australoid nose* (1885:688, original emphasis).

He generalized 'the Australoid nose' as 'Melanesian', by which he collectively meant 'Papuan, New Caledonian, Australian and Tasmanian', and deemed it 'so characteristic that by this feature alone an expert anthropologist can recognise a subject's Melanesian origin at first glance'. For Topinard (1885:688), the nasal index of the living subject — the ratio of maximum width to length of the nose — was of primary importance in classifying human races into the three basic divisions of white, yellow, and black. He found this feature at 'its maximum development' in the Australians.

Topinard (1885:689-90) used the figures obtained by his Belgian colleagues Houzé and Jacques for body measurements despite disagreeing with their figures and methods for the nasal index. He included a table comparing measurements of body height and the length of the head, trunk, leg, arm, hand, and foot for Billy, Jenny, and 'average European men'. He found that the Aboriginal man was shorter and had a smaller head, a longer trunk, a shorter leg, a longer arm, and a smaller hand (although the measurement in the table shows a larger hand) than 'the European', now singularized, but had much the same sized foot. The differences between the Aboriginal man and woman were not exactly 'average' but he cautioned against drawing firm conclusions from individual cases: 'What is typically true of a race is only to be found in its averages'. And yet Topinard's juxtaposition of individual physical measurements for Billy and Jenny with the European male average epitomized the metonymic use of individuals as specimens to stand for a whole race, a practice particularly marked in the raciological photography of this era.

The concluding paragraphs of Topinard's presentation (1885:690-1) focused on the question of Australian Aboriginal racial types, because, as he reminded his colleagues, he had already explored this subject at length in his article 'Sur les races indigènes de l'Australie' (1872), a review of mainly English-language literature about Aboriginal physical anthropology drafted as instructions to travellers to Australia concerning the collection of appropriate material. Topinard had argued there that the indigenous population was composed of two quite different racial types, one tall and handsome, the other small and ill-favoured, which could still be distinguished even though they had now interbred. Now, he provided his audience with a visual demonstration of this thesis in a photograph showing 'King Billy and his three wives' and a fifth individual, of a notably different 'type', who was 'relatively handsome' and 'very reminiscent of the true Ainu type'. He concluded: 'The three Australians here before us would represent the ugly type, the inferior race'.

Topinard's presentation was followed by discussion with contributions from about a dozen members, amongst whom the most prominent were Eugène Dally (1833-1887), Abel Hovelacque (1843-1896), a linguist and founder of the *Revue de Linguistique*, Hamy, Joseph Deniker (1852-1918), author of *Les races et les peuples de la terre* (1900), and the embryologist Mathias Duval (1844-1907). The record of the discussion is longer than the text of the presentation. It is immediately striking that all but one of the questions and comments relate not to the anthropometrical data gathered by Topinard and the Belgian anthropologists but to culture — that is, to ethnographic issues. The discussion ranged over the intelligence and dispositions of the Australians, their language, their numeracy, the systems of numeration of Aboriginal languages, scarification, cannibalism, and the Aboriginal sense of time. It concluded with a request from one member that 'the two Australians be made to speak aloud in their own language and also to sing'. It was recorded that 'The man performs with good grace and sings, accompanying himself by beating time with one stick against another' (Topinard 1885:697-8).

The published report includes two full-page engravings of Jenny after photographs taken by Prince Roland Bonaparte (1858-1924)[11] — a full-face portrait and a profile (Figure 17). In both, the top of Jenny's show dress is folded down to her waist revealing her breasts and her shoulders which are marked by cicatrices. She is wearing a number of bracelets and bead necklaces. She does not look directly at the lens of the camera but slightly off to the side and into the distance. The portraits are arresting because there is so little by way of illustration in the pages of the *Bulletins* — these are the only visual representations of a person in the seven hundred or so pages of this volume. They are also disturbing because we cannot now simply read her state of mind off the engravings and yet we know that this woman has experienced the deaths of most of her group during the tour and, depending on exactly when these photographs were taken, that her husband is either very ill in hospital or has just died.

Figure 17: Anon. after Prince Roland Bonaparte, 'Jenny'.[12]

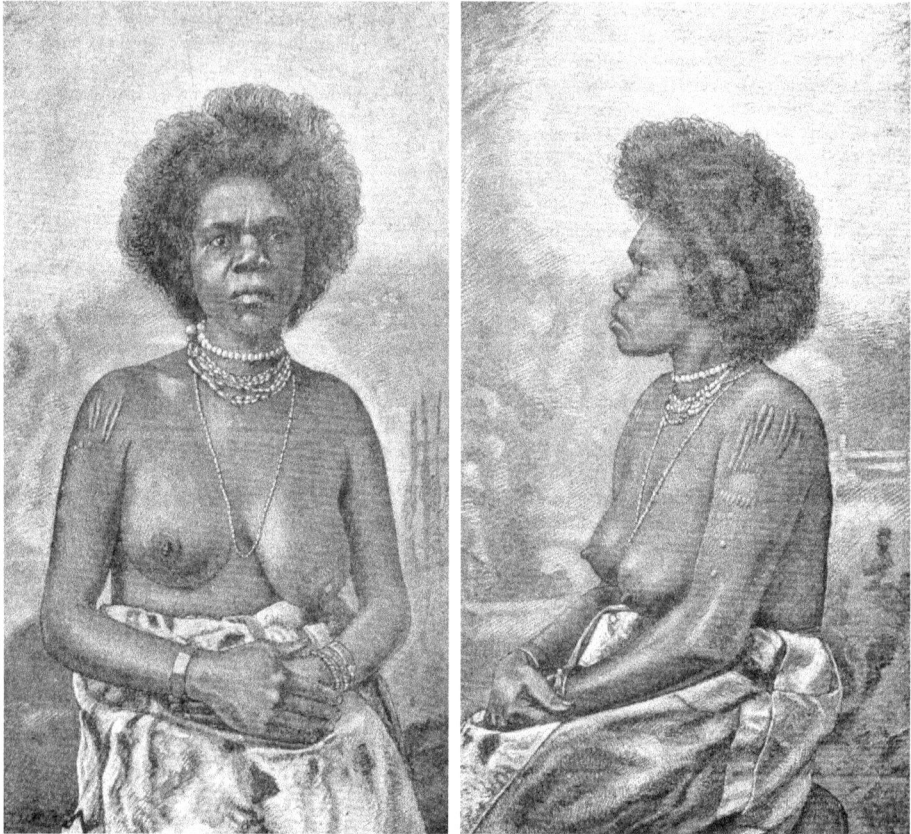

Engraved photographs. Photograph: ANU Photography Services.

Curiosity about Indigenous Australians had been awakened in France in the late eighteenth century during the great era of European voyaging in Oceania. In 1793, idyllic encounters were recorded between Tasmanians and members of Joseph Antoine Bruni d'Entrecasteaux's expedition. Nicolas Baudin's expedition of 1800-04 was the first to undertake 'anthropological' fieldwork and reporting and collected significant material about mainland and Tasmanian Aborigines.[13] But following the cessation of French voyaging on a grand scale after 1840, face-to-face interactions between French and Aboriginal people were rare. Henceforth, French scientists and the interested French public alike had to rely mainly on information about Aborigines written in English by British explorers, missionaries, settlers, and officials in the Australian colonies and on sensationalized popular accounts. Very few French anthropological reports about Aborigines, or indeed about non-European people generally, had been based on first-hand familiarity with living indigenous subjects.[14] Anthropologists either discussed the information they had obtained in their laboratories from measuring skulls and skeletons or borrowed ethnographic descriptions from accounts by observers on the spot. Their scientific texts were thus representations of representations. In this context, the visit to Paris of Cunningham's depleted troupe provided a rare opportunity to study Aboriginal people but even my brief synopsis suggests that it was an opportunity *manqué* because the scientists involved refused to engage with the Aborigines as fellow human beings but objectified them as racial specimens. By returning long after the heyday of raciology to this singular episode, it is possible to read off it some key elements in the intersections of French anthropology and Australian Aborigines, highlighting the ways in which Aborigines figured in the vigorous anthropological debates of the day.

'Arguments about Aborigines'[15]

Les Australiens featured regularly in the discussions of the Société d'Anthropologie. Its members were interested in where the Aborigines had come from or whether they were autochthonous, in their 'civilization' (what would now be called 'culture'), and, given its perceived paucity, their presumed closeness to nature. More precisely, information about Aborigines was seized upon as ammunition in two debates. The first hinged on the question of whether or not there was a distinct *règne humaine*, 'human kingdom', set apart from the animal world. In the nineteenth century, advances in various branches of scientific knowledge that impinged on human origins — archaeology, geology, biology, linguistics — and the burgeoning information about indigenous people around the world gave particular urgency to the age-old question of what it is to be human. Debates recorded in the *Bulletins* and *Mémoires* reveal the passionate interest in this question. A variety of non-European groups which were judged to be inferior, frequently Australians and Tasmanians, was routinely invoked as a test case of either humanity or bestiality.

The second and related issue which drew on Aboriginal evidence was that of monogeny versus polygeny, the common or multiple origins of the 'races of man'. Monogenists saw humankind as ultimately one, the descendants of a single pair of human ancestors; polygenists posited that different racial groups had separate and different origins. The monogenist position was conservative, its adherents likely to be Christian believers who rejected as heretical the proposition that there had been human beings other than the first divinely created pair. Polygenists were able to conceive a non-Biblical view of human origins and were prepared to countenance the unsettling of scriptural teaching and hence religious institutional authority. The intellectual and political radicalism of the racialist polygenists is disconcerting to liberal-minded modern scholars but for these scientists of the Third Republic, political progressiveness was consonant with the intellectual assumption of significant hereditary differences between human groups.[16] The racial rhetoric of both monogenists and polygenists is abhorrent to present sensibilities but that used by polygenists to discuss human difference and supposedly inferior forms of humanity is especially noxious.

It is beyond the scope of this chapter to examine the ways in which doctrines such as polygeny and the supposed likely extinction of inferior races, much discussed by members of the Société,[17] related to accelerated French colonial expansion in the second half of the nineteenth century. Material about Aborigines was only indirectly relevant to French colonialism per se but was nonetheless pertinent comparatively to the process of imposition of French colonial rule over indigenous populations.

Broca and human hybridity

Paul Broca was the foremost French polygenist and the leading physical anthropologist of his time. He located humankind squarely in the animal kingdom in close relationship to the anthropoid apes. The title of his *Recherches sur l'hybridité animale en général et sur l'hybridité humaine en particulier considérées dans leurs rapports avec la question de la pluralité des espèces humaines* (1860) expressly denotes polygenism, as does the use of the term 'genus' in the title of the English translation, *On the phenomena of hybridity in the Genus Homo* (1864). This work — which reads today like a racialist tract — advanced Broca's thinking about the relationship of racial interbreeding to the issue of polygeny. The question of whether interbreeding between different human groups produced fertile unions that continued over time was of much interest to anthropologists. Broca first investigated the products of interbreeding between closely related species such as rabbits and hares. When he turned to human groups, he proposed a range of types in terms of fertility of the offspring that he suggested were the result of different kinds of interracial union.[18] Quite a large proportion of this work is devoted to Australian Aborigines.

Broca sought to reveal what happened when the two most divergent human types — the purportedly most superior and most inferior — interbred. He designated the Germanic (Anglo-Saxon) as the most superior race and the Aboriginal Australians and Tasmanians as the most inferior, in line with the received hierarchical ranking of human groups by the scientists of the day. His only other contenders for the position of most inferior were the so-called Hottentots (Khoikhoi),[19] but he considered that they at least showed signs of 'improvability' while the Aborigines 'seem absolutely incorrigible savages'. While he expressed disgust at the 'execrable atrocities' visited upon them by the British, he wrote (1864:45-6) that 'the Tasmanians are, or rather were, with the Australians, nearest to the brutal condition'. Indeed, at the beginning of this work, he singled out the Australians, among all groups, as satisfying the conditions of a separate human species:

> The term species, has, in classical language, an absolute sense, implying both the idea of a special conformation and special origin, and if some races — the Australians, for instance — unite these conditions in a sufficient degree, to constitute a clearly marked species, many other pure or mixed races escape, in this respect, a rigorous appreciation (1864:11).

Broca (1864:49) maintained that the 'ugliness and dirty habits of the native women' were not enough to deter men's sexual interest and went on to explain what he believed to be the scarcity of mixed-race children in the Australian colonies not in terms of the absence of sexual encounters between Europeans and Aborigines but as the consequence of a dysgenic match, of too great a separation between two racially quite distinct human types. His final conclusion (1864:60) about human hybridity as it related to Aborigines was 'that the lowest degree of human hybridity in which the homœogenesis is so feeble as to render the fecundity of the first crossing uncertain, is exhibited in the most disparate crossings between one of the most elevated [Anglo-Saxons] and the two lowest [Aborigines and Tasmanians] races of humanity'.

Broca's premise that unions between different combinations of races would produce differing degrees of fertility in future generations rested on a spurious hierarchical ranking of human groups. And his conclusions about the infertility of Aboriginal-European unions were later shown to be absurd. Here, then, is an egregious example of what Elkins (1999:169) termed 'ugly' racism, racism involving sexual revulsion or attraction. Broca's comments about 'native women' certainly suggest a sexual element. What it was that made him and many of his colleagues so ready to jump from anatomical researches to quite unsubstantiated and abusive rhetorical pronouncements about relative racial worth is a complex question that writers such as Gilman (1985) and Jahoda (1999) have tackled on a wide cultural, historical, and psychological canvas and Fausto-Sterling (1995) on a smaller scale relevant to this discussion. Whatever the particular combination of reasons in Broca's case, he was enormously influential. He died in 1880 but the imprint of his thinking about Aboriginal Australians can be discerned in the discussion that followed Topinard's 1885 presentation and particularly in Topinard's own contributions, Topinard habitually referring to Broca as his 'master'.

Topinard and Aboriginal Australians

Eugène Dally, one of the progressives, started the discussion by adding some details about Billy and Jenny. Intelligence was the issue but first he noted that the man and the woman, not of the same tribe, could not stand each other. He went on: 'Their intelligence is very minimal. The mode of counting is of the most rudimentary. They count on their hands up to ten, then they begin again to go any further' (Topinard 1885:691). This pronouncement accords exactly with the stereotype of low Aboriginal intelligence and the scientific dictum promoted by Broca of small Aboriginal cranial capacity. Topinard responded with further information, piqued at the inference that after hours spent in the company of the three Australians he and Hamy had learnt nothing of their intelligence.[20] Then follows the most telling comment of the whole record:

> The man appears reserved: he is cold, self-obsessed, but well behaved. He showed little surprise at the Jardin d'Acclimatation, and had no trouble recognising the animals of his country. The woman, on the other hand, appears dazed [abrutie], quite removed from what is going on around her. One can get something out of the first, nothing out of the second (1885:691).

Here, Topinard not only told us something about the mental state of Billy and Jenny but revealed his own frustration and disquiet that he could get no response from Jenny. He then (1885:691-2) described Billy's recitation of the names of the cities he had visited while on tour (but demeaned this feat of memory as 'entirely automatic'), his lack of animation except when examining or throwing a boomerang or thinking about his lunch, and his vanity about the ivory stick in his nose, before returning to Jenny and her state:

> With the woman I could awaken no idea of coquettishness or otherwise. The death of her husband, here in Paris, has not affected her, Mr Cunningham assures me. I am not so sure; you would say that there is some kind of sadness about her which could be related to that. Once, though, I did see her laugh freely, opening a disproportionately large mouth, when one of us at the Jardin d'Acclimatation tried to throw the boomerang. According to Mr Cunningham, the intelligence of these indigenes has not improved at all since they have been exhibited far and wide; in this regard he has the lowest opinion of them: 'downright brutes', he says; and he gives me evidence of this that I think it best not to repeat (1885:692).

Topinard did not condemn other races like Broca. His comments about Jenny reveal both his inability to transcend thinking about Aborigines in stereotypical terms and confusion provoked by the barriers to communication with another human subject whose emotions he sensed but could not grasp. If he could not reach her, then, as a dedicated empiricist, he would have to doubt his judgements about her.

No member of the Société had greater knowledge of the literature on Aboriginal people than Topinard and he kept up correspondence on the subject with French visitors to Australia. His first study of Aboriginal Australians was

'Etude sur les Tasmaniens' (1868), a study of the eight skulls from Tasmania then held in the Muséum de Paris. The Tasmanians were of interest to French anthropologists on a number of counts: the common belief that they had been exterminated by the British colonists; their epistemological status as one of the most remote human groups, both geographically and culturally, along with such people as the Fuegians and Eskimos; and their racial origins as connected or unconnected with mainland Aborigines. French anthropologists of this period, like other non-British European travellers and reporters (McKenna 2002:75), could be highly critical of the British colonial enterprise in terms of its treatment of indigenous people.

Topinard's 'Etude' starts on an elegiac note (1868:307): 'The newspapers have advised us that the last of the Tasmanians died five or six months ago and that, of these islanders, who numbered seven thousand when Van Diemen's Land was discovered, just one woman is now left; and I think that she may have just succumbed'. The scientist then stepped in quickly: 'It therefore seemed to me that the time had come to study the several skulls of this race that were held in the Museum of Paris, without concerning myself about what could have been written on this subject'. The 'Etude' is an assemblage of measurements of aspects of the skull, brain cavity, and facial structure, comparing the Tasmanian set of skulls with others, including those of Parisians and especially mainland Aborigines. It would be fatuous to dismiss the intellectual labour involved in such anthropometrical studies and Topinard's scientific integrity and ability strike me as impressive. In its osteological detail, the 'Etude' holds little meaning for non-experts and so my reading looks not so much to the information provided but rather to the manner of its presentation. Topinard emphasised its empirical base in a footnote:

> I could not, in fact, put too much emphasis on the fact that in this work I have deliberately avoided bringing in elements foreign to the anatomical pieces that are its object, I have looked for what they were saying to me, I have analysed them and compared them with others, nothing more (1868:326, note 1).

But it was not a case of 'nothing more'. In a slide from fact to value, Topinard took the physical features of the skulls, which provided his data, as an index of the degree of racial superiority or inferiority. When he boasted (1868:319) about a plaster cast of an Aborigine as 'the superb trophy owned by the Society', we might ask him what that cast was 'saying' to him. Why was it 'superb', why was it a 'trophy'?

Topinard (1868:322, 325-6) concluded that the more pronounced prognathism of the Australian mainlanders, a putatively primitive feature, indicated that they were 'greatly inferior' to the Tasmanians and of lesser intellect and that the two groups constituted 'two distinct races'. The Tasmanians, he suggested, were midway between 'the black autochthonous race', 'highly dolichocephalic and prognathous', spread over different areas of the Pacific region, and another grouping who are 'sub-dolichocephalic and only slight prognathous', including the New Zealanders, northern Polynesians, and Tahitians. He remained undecided as to whether they represented the vestiges of an isolated autochthonous group or were the result of 'a crossing between the black autochthonous race and one of the invading groups of the great Polynesian family'. But he judged that the Tasmanians did not deserve to be classed with those like the Australians and the Hottentots who were 'truly inferior'.

Topinard and the two races theory

Topinard (1872:211) subsequently turned his attention to these mainland Australians when Eugène Simon, the French consul in Sydney, and a Dr Jules Goyard requested instructions regarding the anthropological observations of Australian Aborigines that travellers might make where the opportunity arose. These 'instructions' were published in the *Bulletins* (Topinard 1872). They show that when Topinard applied himself to a detailed study of the available literature, the racial judgments he had earlier made of the mainland groups were tempered by reflection on the information before him. He formed the view that the Aboriginal population of mainland Australia comprised 'three orders of tribes': inferior and superior, with an intermediate type that showed a blend of features arising from their intermixing. Topinard had taken up the first-hand observations of a number of explorers, officials, and missionaries,[21] combined these with his own studies of the Australian skulls in Paris, and reworked this material to propose a theory of an inferior negroid type occupying mainly the coastal regions and a superior type, the 'bush Australian', inhabiting the remoter parts of the continent. He described the superior type as handsome, tall, and well proportioned, stately in bearing, proud, brave, intelligent, and with long, wavy hair; the inferior type he portrayed as ugly, small, and stupid with frizzy hair, using such demeaning terms as 'ill-favoured' (*disgracié*), 'repulsive' (*hideux*), 'wretched' (*misérable*), and 'puny' (*chétif*). According to Topinard, his two types were the descendants, no longer existing in their pure form, of two original 'races', the superior 'Dravidian' race having displaced the 'negroid' type.[22] He maintained that the favoured race took over the best land leaving the less fertile littoral regions to the 'pariah race'. The pariahs, he supposed, were autochthonous and belonged to the 'true Melanesian race'. They were identical to the 'black New Caledonians' who represented his pure Melanesian type.[23]

When Topinard met Billy, Jenny, and little Toby, he saw physical confirmation of his two races theory, immediately assigning them to his second category. His difficulty in seeing beyond physical appearance is evident here and contrasts with Virchow's report on Cunningham's troupe who had spent several weeks performing in Berlin in 1884. Virchow (1884:414-16), like Topinard, had been most concerned to conduct an anthropometrical appraisal of the Queenslanders. But, unlike Topinard, he had no difficulty in making a distinction between inner states and capacities and outer appearance. He found the Queenslanders physically unattractive but, as if addressing a racially hostile interlocutor, he took pains to make a number of relatively positive observations about the mental and psychological qualities of different members and of the group as a whole when compared to Europeans. He responded to each of the Aborigines as separate individuals with distinct personalities. He praised the grace, composure, and prowess of their physical performances. And, as a committed monogenist, he had no hesitation in seeing them as 'true men' in every respect.

Much of Topinard's 1872 paper 'Sur les races indigènes de l'Australie' rehearses descriptions of the way Aboriginal men and women looked to the voyagers and explorers who wrote about them. When it came to aesthetic evaluations of different ethnic or indigenous groups, most commentators unquestioningly applied European standards of beauty. The narratives and scientific treatises issuing from voyages of exploration were especially detrimental to Aboriginal Australians in their physical descriptions, as Topinard (1872:229, 231) acknowledged in relation to the writings of Dumont d'Urville. Topinard explained the reported differences in Aboriginal appearance in terms of his theory of two distinct racial types and an intermediate form:

> So can be explained the diversity of portraits that have been made of the Australians, why navigators have depicted them in different ways, why travellers in the centre have found them to be better built, more handsome than those on the coast, why for such a long time they have been considered as the most hideous beings in creation, while today, through over-reaction one is inclined to take them as models for statuary (1872:240).

In particular, Topinard's review of reports about the appearance of Aboriginal women shows how easily the science of race could descend into fantasizing and voyeuristic attraction or repulsion. In keeping with his two types thesis, he found two extreme versions of Aboriginal womanliness (1872:261): 'one of them, everything that is most hideous, bestial and repulsive in the world; the other composed of women who are well formed, with broad backs, slim waists, ample and well developed busts, and with very pleasant features and overall appearance'. In such an intellectual climate, gender and race stereotyping easily became conflated and intensified. Topinard (1872:252) imagined continual 'crossings' between the two main racial types over the centuries and maintained that 'It is the female sex which preserves the most pronounced characteristics of the most primitive type for the longest time and it is there that we will find its purest traces'. His unease about Jenny and the harshness of his descriptions of her suggest this kind of conflation and intensification of stereotyping in relation to an anthropological subject who is disturbingly and doubly different.[24] Yet, this is easy to say and to condemn, as if sexual, gender, and identity anxieties were purely nineteenth-century phenomena, ignoring our own era's investment in such critiques.[25]

Topinard was always primarily concerned with anatomical and morphological data as shown in his presentation of the members of Cunningham's troupe. This blinkered perspective limited his capacity to comprehend human differences. The ethnographic information paraphrased in his 1872 study (1872:278, 285) gave him no insights into Aboriginal social and cultural life. With respect to religious sentiment, for example, he pronounced negatively: 'They have neither cult, nor ceremony, nor idol, nor any object of worship that might take their place'. The chastity of Aboriginal women was a 'thing unknown'. But writing several years later in another register, Topinard was much more alert to positive aspects of Aboriginal adaptation to the Australian environment and reproved the British colonizers:

> The intelligence of the Australians was perfectly adapted to the resources they had at their disposal, their hunting territories were huge, there was a place for everyone … But today space is becoming limited and is no longer adequate for this type of existence, the game flees, their weapons can no longer reach them: there is sadness, anaemia, infertility, their nakedness is no longer offset by an iron-clad constitution, they are dying: 'You whites', said an Australian, 'should give us blacks your cows and sheep now that you have wiped out our possums and our kangaroos; we have nothing to live on and we are hungry' (1879:644).

In fact, Topinard's two races theory of Aboriginal origins can be read as an expression of his ambivalence about the contemporary anthropological zeal for ranking human groups on a scale from higher to lower, superior to inferior, forms of humanity. He had reviewed a large volume of literature about Aboriginal Australians and found the evidence contradictory. But his binary theory enabled him both to praise and condemn Aborigines. The human ladder was a major blindspot of raciology which scarcely questioned the scientific, let alone the humanitarian validity of ranking. Once the human 'varieties' of the eighteenth century became reified as 'races',[26] measurable and observable features such as skin colour, head shape, hair type, nasal index, prognathism, ratio of upper leg to lower leg — features overwhelmingly associated with stereotyped sub-Saharan Africans — were assigned values indicating higher or lower. With the accumulation of comparative data, unexpected mixtures of putatively inferior and superior features in the one race, such as the dark skin of Indigenous Australians combined with non-'negroid' hair, led either to confusion or to implausible qualifications by scientists who had to explain the presence of superior features in what was held to be an inferior race, or vice versa.[27]

In a detailed and historically useful discussion of the notion of race, Topinard (1879:660) referred only once to the concept of a racial hierarchy when he concluded his paper with Broca's definition of the term 'ethnology' as the description and determination of human races, including 'their respective position in the human series'. This is an anodine formulation for ranking by race which ultimately Topinard accepted as a basic tenet of anthropology.[28] He did not, however, follow Broca's pronouncements about unproductive unions between Europeans and Aborigines. Indeed, he cited the historian James Bonwick (1817-1906) to the effect that the children of Tasmanian Aborigines and English 'are as fertile as the Europeans and are prospering' and he anticipated a future racial melting pot, where in effect the multiplicity of human origins had given way to increasing human uniformity — but the 'inferior' races had died out.[29]

Topinard was wholly committed to the natural science approach to the study of human difference in which humans beings had to be subject to the same objective methods applied to animals. In his famous manual *L'Anthropologie* he proclaimed:

> As for the method to be followed, there can be no possible doubt, it is identical for man and the animals: intuition, a priori reasoning, and other methods relying on feelings and impressions will be mercilessly banished. Whatever man's brilliant role on our planet and his place at the pinnacle of natural organization, whether he represents his own separate branch, the *human kingdom*, or is only the first of the primates, the same procedures of observation apply to him (1876:4).

Hamy and the push for ethnography

Topinard's (1879:660) vision of anthropology left little place for ethnography which he defined rather dismissively as 'the description of peoples' and the source of raw material for ethnology. However, by the time of his presentation of the three Australians to the Société, ethnography was receiving more consideration from some of his colleagues. Hamy, who had first learned of the group's presence in Paris and had visited them with Topinard at the Jardin d'Acclimatation, was at the forefront of this shifting emphasis. Three years earlier he had founded the *Revue d'Ethnographie* and in his introduction (1882:ii) had lamented the neglect of ethnography at a time when 'The white races, in their movement of expansion across the earth, saw the indigenous races of the newly occupied countries disappear in their wake almost everywhere'.

Hamy's career began in 1864 as an intern for Jean-Martin Charcot (1825-1893) (whose demonstrations of his psychiatric patients Sigmund Freud famously attended) at the Salpêtrière psychiatric hospital in Paris. There he met Broca and went to work in his anthropological laboratory as his student and assistant. Hamy held various positions in the Muséum national d'Histoire naturelle, succeeding the prominent defender of monogenism in France, Armand de Quatrefages (1810-1892), in the Chair of Anthropology in 1892. His greatest achievement was the ultimate success of his efforts to establish France's first ethnographic museum, the Musée du Trocadéro (the modern Musée de l'Homme), which opened in Paris in 1880.[30]

Hamy (1891) made an invaluable contribution to the history and ethnography of Aboriginal Australians, especially Tasmanians, through his pursuit of lost artwork from Baudin's voyage, a portfolio of drawings by Nicolas-Martin Petit.[31] However, Hamy's historical and ethnographic sense, which might have led him out of the racialist assumptions of his training, did not translate into cultural sensitivity, at least in his writings. In this, he differed from his mentor Quatrefages (1988) who later in his career had drawn on Bonwick's works to write in humanistic terms about the moral worth and vanquished rights of the Tasmanians. Hamy's commitment to a social evolutionary schema that classified human groups into higher and lower races meant that his sociocultural focus rested no less on hierarchical assumptions than did the craniometry of Broca or Topinard. For example, in an early article in the *Bulletins de la Société d'Anthropologie de Paris* (1872:622), he wrote that the 'negritos', while occupying 'a very low position in the scale of human races', were not yet 'the last of men' — the Australians had that distinction by virtue of their level of material progress.

Hamy made only a very limited contribution to the discussion following Topinard's presentation. He confined himself to some remarks about practices of scarification and a brief appraisal of the memoir by Houzé and Jacques: 'if the anthropological conclusions of the first of these colleagues leave something to be desired, at least the ethnographic and linguistic part is treated with the greatest precision' (Topinard 1885:693). Indeed, the memoir in question shows a marked lack of fit between Houzé's extreme polygenism and, for the time, Jacques's relatively detailed, sensitive ethnographic and linguistic reporting and analysis (Houzé and Jacques 1884-5). This disjunction no doubt resulted from the separation of physical anthropology from ethnography, the first tackled by Houzé and the second by Jacques.

Houzé and polygeny

Houzé's polygenism was of the order of Broca's. He used the word 'pithecoid', ape-like, to describe a whole range of Aboriginal physical characteristics from the head to the foot,[32] concluding, with specific reference to Cunningham's troupe of Queenslanders, that:

we are justified in retaining the epithet of inferior for any human race that presents, in the way it is organized, in the proportions of its limbs, a large number of features that are found in monkeys; these features, attenuated by crossings and by evolution, appear as atavistic reminders (Houzé and Jacques 1884-5:92).

Houzé made much of Darwin's pronouncement in *The Descent of Man* concerning the relative atavism of male and female forms (Houzé and Jacques 1884-5:92). In this respect, the final conclusion to his report is reminiscent of Topinard's stereotyping conflation of sexual and racial prejudices to malign not only Aboriginal Australians but women generally:

we shall emphasise again the fact that woman presents many more atavistic features than man, just as much in the white [race] as in the Australian. Woman has remained true to the primitive type; she is the guardian of hereditary features, she is basically conservative; in her skeleton as in her moral aspects, she belongs to the past, while man is progressive; in his [physical] organization he is more distant from the base-type; in his mental faculties he belongs to the future.[33]

Jacques's contribution to the memoir takes us into quite different territory from his colleague's. It also contrasts favourably with the feeble ethnographic efforts of the members of the Société d'Anthropologie de Paris and the scant information they obtained from the remnants of Cunningham's troupe. The circumstances whereby most members of the group successively succumbed to fatal illnesses meant that the Belgians had some advantage over the French since seven of the original nine were still alive when they reached Brussels. However, in retrospect, Jacques's comments about Toby's lack of animation spoke to the state of health that ended with his death in a Paris hospital. The Belgians had decided to vaccinate the seven Aborigines against smallpox owing to an outbreak of the disease in Brussels but most suffered a severe reaction (Houzé and Jacques 1884-5:63). The doctors no doubt acted with the best intentions but it is likely that, uprooted, debilitated, and suffering from the Northern cold, the Australians were further weakened by the reaction.

The contrast between Jacques's study and Topinard's presentation and the subsequent discussion highlights the inherent conflict between the perspectives of the physical anthropologists and those more interested in the cultural dimensions of human groups. Anthropology's brief was to bring within its purview everything relating to the study of man, in nature and in the world. Its domain was both the natural history of man and the study of past and present human groups in their geographical distribution and all the diversity of their languages, 'manners and customs', and material cultures. However, Broca, Topinard, Houzé, and their like, whose first interest was man in nature, had no sense of their discipline as humanistic. Indeed, their conception of the anthropological enterprise expressly precluded humanism, as Houzé made clear in relation to Australia:

> The authors who have described the different Australian tribes are often in disagreement, even for identical localities; we are not at all surprised by these differing opinions, because we know how difficult it is to describe and especially to observe, and how it is necessary to resist the deceptive impulses of our illusions. Art and feeling have not to intervene in anatomical research, and we almost always take the wrong direction when they guide us in our observations, what is necessary in this research is the arid and brutal truth (Houzé and Jacques 1884-5:53-4).

By contrast, a humanistic anthropology is one in which the subject becomes 'the object of observation for himself', as Franz Pruner-Bey (1808-1882), a former president of the Société d'Anthropologie de Paris, put it in his inaugural address, appealing to the Socratic dictum 'Know thyself'.[34] Such an anthropology would accept that other human beings were fully human which was precisely what polygenism called into question.

Jacques and the cultural perspective

Jacques certainly did not see the Aborigines as equal but simply different. However, unlike the French anthropologists, he did convey the sense that he had established some rapport with them and at least viewed them as people with their own concerns, culture, language, identities, history, and present suffering while in thrall to Cunningham. He began his section of the paper by giving his transcription of the Aborigines' names, as did Virchow (1884), an acknowledgement of their autonomy as individuals and foreign visitors not accorded them by Topinard.[35] Jacques then described the dubious circumstances in which they had joined Cunningham's troupe and queried what they might have made of the study to which he and his colleague subjected them. In this and other respects, he recorded their exercise of a measure of personal agency:

> We came before these unfortunate people armed with strange instruments, whose use their understanding certainly did not allow them to divine. Immediately after our arrival we took one by the head and we palpated it all over, then another, and another, without explanation. They suffered all of this with the resigned air of victims, no doubt intimidated by the presence of their master. But when it came to approaching them with a compass in hand, there was a revolt and we were greeted by a quite categorical refusal to be touched (Houzé and Jacques 1884-5:98).

Jacques compiled a comparative vocabulary of 198 words for Palm Islands and Hinchinbrook Island, together with notes relating to other Aboriginal languages, but was regretful about the quality of his linguistic observations for 'these languages that were so interesting'. He described his difficulties in trying to learn their pronunciation and included a vignette showing Aboriginal methods as teachers: 'When we had not properly understood after two, three or four tries, they leaned towards us and repeated the word several times very softly in our ear. I mention this as a proof of their intelligence and way of reasoning'. However, Jacques's conclusions about Aboriginal intelligence were mixed. He found the members of the troupe to be childlike, 'like all primitive people', their memories prodigious, their senses acute, their sense of numeracy limited, their sense of time absent — on both the latter counts he was Eurocentrically blind to other systems of quantification than Roman numerals or to other ways of reckoning time than in named days of the week, weeks, and months. He provided some details about marriage rules but concluded this discussion by remarking, with no sense of irony: 'There are still some other details in the rules which besides are rather complicated; but these we shall spare you' (Houzé and Jacques 1884-5:101, 104, 130).

A frequent point of debate among anthropologists at this time was whether different indigenous groups did or did not hold religious beliefs, seen as a mark of full humanity.[36] The monogenists,[37] as believers themselves and proponents of the idea of the 'human realm', sought and found religious belief in indigenous communities denied it by their opponents who engaged in sometimes facetious commentary on the moral and religious capacities of animals.[38] Jacques maintained that the Queenslanders had no religion, in the sense of believing in a deity, but proceeded to describe their supernatural beliefs in some detail, having also retold a myth about the origin of different languages and presented it as a rival to the Biblical story of Babel. He did not, however, hesitate to question other prominent stereotypes in contemporary anthropological literature on the basis of his own observations of the Aboriginal group. Thus, he described Toby and Jenny's marital relationship as harmonious in opposition to the general view of the lowly status and ill-treatment of Aboriginal women by their husbands as pronounced by Charles Letourneau (1831-1902). In contrast to Topinard's difficulty in attributing Jenny's stunned state to grief, Jacques related another proof of marital affection by describing Sussy's grief-stricken reaction to Tambo's death (Houzé and Jacques 1884-5:102-3, 131).

One of the most persistent and titillating tropes in nineteenth-century imaginings was the cannibal savage.[39] Here again, there is an interesting contrast between the several reports. Jacques claimed that he 'was never able to obtain a definite answer' to his inquiry whether the Queenslanders sometimes ate human flesh: 'one might have said that they were trying to avoid an embarrassing question'.[40] Cunningham had 'assured' him that one circumstance in which it was practised was after a battle but that he thought it was not otherwise prevalent. Jacques then stated seriously that, unlike 'the Western tribes', the Queenslanders did not eat their old people but took very good care of them (Houzé and Jacques 1884-5:133). During Topinard's presentation (1885:695), Dally asked Billy about anthropophagy but reported a different answer from that given by Jacques: Billy 'admitted that he had eaten the flesh of his fellows several times'. The judgement was then pronounced that cannibalism indicated nothing about the relationship of carnivorous instincts to physical organization since Billy's and Jenny's teeth were small, neat, and worn in a circular pattern. Both reports reinvoked the spectre of cannibalism but while Jacques sought to explain it in cultural terms, Topinard and Dally invoked bestiality.

A final word is needed about the photographs which illustrate each of the two reports: those taken by Prince Roland Bonaparte and included in Topinard's presentation and those taken by the president of the Association belge de Photographie, Pierre-Alexandre de Blochouse (1821-1901), for Houzé and Jacques's memoir. In France, the evidential promise of photography meant that this new technology was welcomed by anthropologists such as Broca and a genre of racial photography quickly developed as a tool of anthropology (Dias 1994; Jehel 2000). The genre rested on a metonymical logic: one type specimen of a racial group visually stood for all, just as Jenny's and Billy's measurements in Topinard's table stood tacitly for all Aborigines when placed against figures for average European males. The subjects of such photographs were typically posed against a neutral background, preferably without clothes, and taken full face and in profile. Blochouse's photographs of Sussy, Bob, Jenny, and Toby conform to the genre except that the Queenslanders are wearing their show clothes. They might have refused to disrobe for the photographer as Jacques reported that they would not undress for him, though he declined to attribute their refusal to modesty — another human emotion denied to indigenous people by physical anthropology — but instead invoked vanity and the climate (Houzé and Jacques 1884-5:124). Although these particular photographs by Bonaparte appear to be raciological in design, they do not conform simply to the dehumanizing, objectifying genre of racial photography. They are also individual portraits with a story to them which makes them all the more disconcerting.[41]

Conclusion

Topinard's presentation of the three living Australians and the discussion which followed is a demonstration of how raciology used comparative anatomical measurements as well as judgments about reported manners and customs to assign particular groups of human beings to different rungs on the human racial ladder. Yet when scientists tried to collate all the information available about an indigenous group, in this case Aboriginal Australians, the results did not match their preconceptions. Not only did ethnographic information and physical evidence frequently conflict but evidence from physical features alone could not deliver a clear verdict of racial inferiority. Topinard's response to such tensions was to invoke his two races theory as an umbrella explanation to reconcile the wide range of diverging evidence about what Aborigines were really like.

The comparison between Topinard's presentation and Houzé's report, on the one hand, and Jacques's and Virchow's reports, on the other, exemplifies two opposed perspectives on human difference: physical anthropology and an ethnographic or cultural approach. A particularly harsh variety of physical anthropology was dominant in France for much of the nineteenth century though it was by no means uncontested, as shown in the ambivalent humanist caveats offered by other scientists such as Pruner-Bey and Quatrefages. The encounter between the surviving members of Cunningham's troupe and the scientists of the Société d'Anthropologie de Paris demonstrates clearly that at this period French raciologists denied common humanity to the people they studied, even when they came face to face with them. By treating the Queenslanders anthropometrically as bodies and behaviourally as typical savages, these French anthropologists failed to establish any rapport or any human connection with their subjects — and saw no need to do so. The methodological strictures of an observation-based science excluded feeling, imagination, and intuition. Furthermore, this human failure entailed an epistemological failure. The episode is emblematic of the way in which the brand of anthropology promoted by Broca and Topinard in the early years of the Société was stunted by its raciological premises which foreclosed any prospect of achieving the comprehensive human science to which they aspired.

References

Anderson, Stephanie. 2000. French Anthropology in Australia, a Prelude: the Encounters between Aboriginal Tasmanians and the Expedition of Bruny d'Entrecasteaux, 1793. *Aboriginal History* 24:212-23.

_____. 2001. French Anthropology in Australia, the First Fieldwork Report: François Péron's 'Maria Island: Anthropological Observations'. *Aboriginal History* 25:228-42.

_____. 2006. Clichés of Australian Aborigines: Photograhy and Raciology, Paris 1885. In *Reading Images, Viewing Texts/Lire les images, voir les textes*, ed. Louise Maurer and Roger Hillman, 13-30. Berne: Peter Lang.

Arens, William. 1979. *The Man-eating Myth: Anthropology & Anthropophagy.* New York: Oxford University Press.

Barker, Francis, Peter Hulme, and Margaret Iversen, ed. 1998. *Cannibalism and the Colonial World.* Cambridge: Cambridge University Press.

Blanckaert, Claude. 1988. On the Origins of French Ethnology: William Edwards and the Doctrine of Race. In *Bones, Bodies, Behavior: Essays on Biological Anthropology*, ed. George W. Stocking, Jr., 18-55. Madison: University of Wisconsin Press.

Blanckaert, Claude, ed. 1996. *Le terrain des sciences humaines (XVIIIe — XXe siecle)*. Paris: L'Harmattan.

Broca, Paul. 1860. *Recherches sur l'hybridité animale en général et sur l'hybridité humaine en particulier considérées dans leurs rapports avec la question de la pluralité des espèces humaines*. Paris: J. Claye.

————. 1864 [1860]. *On the Phenomena of Hybridity in the Genus Homo*, tr. and ed. C. Carter Blake. London: Longman, Green, Longman & Roberts for the Anthropological Society.

————. 1866. Discours sur l'homme et les animaux. *Bulletins de la Société d'Anthropologie de Paris* 2e série, 1:53-79.

Cauvin, Charles-Jean-François. 1882. *Mémoire sur les races de l'Océanie*. Paris: Imprimerie nationale.

————. 1883. Sur les races de l'Océanie (analyse). *Bulletins de la Société d'Anthropologie de Paris* 3e série, 6:245-56.

Deniker, Joseph. 1900. *Les races et les peuples de la terre: éléments d'anthropologie et d'ethnographie*. Paris: Schleicher frères.

Dias, Nélia. 1994. Photographier et mesurer: les portraits anthropologiques. *Romantisme* 84:37-49.

Douglas, Bronwen. 2003. Seaborne Ethnography and the Natural History of Man. *Journal of Pacific History* 38:3-27.

Elkins, James. 1999. *Pictures of the Body: Pain and Metamorphosis*. Stanford, CA: Stanford University Press.

Fausto-Sterling, Anne. 1995. Gender, Race, and Nation: the Comparative Anatomy of 'Hottentot' Women in Europe, 1815-1817. In *Deviant Bodies: Critical Perspectives on Difference in Science and Popular Culture*, ed. Jennifer Terry and Jacqueline Urla, 19-48. Bloomington and Indianapolis: Indiana University Press.

Gilman, Sander, L. 1985. *Difference and Pathology: Stereotypes of Sexuality, Race, and Madness*. Ithaca: Cornell University Press.

Goldman, Laurence, ed. 1999. *The Anthropology of Cannibalism*. Westport, CT: Bergin & Garvey.

Hammond, Michael. 1980. Anthropology as a Weapon of Social Combat in Late Nineteenth-Century France. *Journal of the History of the Behavioral Sciences* 16:118-32.

Hamy, Ernest-Théodore. 1872. Sur un négrito des forêts de l'Inde centrale. *Bulletins de la Société d'Anthropologie de Paris* 2ᵉ série, 7:619-22.

_____. 1882. Introduction. *Revue d'Ethnographie* 1: i-iv.

_____. 1889. Les origines du Musée d'Ethnographie. *Revue d'Ethnographie* 8:305-417.

_____. 1891. *L'œuvre ethnographique de Nicolas-Martin Petit, dessinateur à bord du 'Géographe' 1801-1804*. Paris: G. Masson.

Harvey, Joy. 1983. Evolutionism Transformed: Positivists and Materialists in the Société d'Anthropologie de Paris from Second Empire to Third Republic. In *The Wider Domain of Revolutionary Thought*, ed. David Oldroyd and Ian Langham, 289-310. Dordrecht, Boston, London: D. Reidel Publishing.

Hiatt, L.R. 1996. *Arguments about Aborigines: Australia and the Evolution of Social Anthropology*. Cambridge: Cambridge University Press.

Houzé, Emile, and Victor Jacques. 1884-5. Communication de MM. Houzé et Jacques sur les Australiens du Nord. *Bulletin de la Société d'Anthropologie de Bruxelles* 3:53-155.

Jahoda, Gustav. 1999. *Images of Savages: Ancient Roots of Modern Prejudice in Western Culture*. London: Routledge.

Jehel, Pierre-Jérôme. 2000. Une illusion photographique: esquisse des relations entre la photographie et l'anthropologie en France au XIXe siècle. *Journal des anthropologues* 80-81:47-70.

McKenna, Mark. 2002. *Looking for Blackfellas' Point: an Australian History of Place*. Sydney: UNSW Press.

Martin de Moussy, Jean-Antoine-Victor. 1866. La religiosité est-elle un des caractères spéciaux du genre humain? *Bulletins de la Société d'Anthropologie de Paris* 2ᵉ série, 1:105-20.

Maxwell, Anne. 2000. *Colonial Photography and Exhibitions: Representations of the 'Native' and the Making of European Identities*. London: Leicester University Press.

Mondière, A.-T. 1886. Les Australiens exhibés à Paris. *Revue d'Anthropologie* 3ᵉ série, 15:313-17.

Obeyesekere, Gananath. 2005. *Cannibal Talk: the Man-Eating Myth and Human Sacrifice in the South Seas*. Berkeley and Los Angeles: University of California Press.

Péron, François. 1983. Maria Island: Anthropological Observations: Interview with the Natives of this Island and Description of a Tomb Found on the Northern Shore of East Bay, Ventose an. 10 [February 1802], tr. N.J.B. Plomley. In N.J.B. Plomley, *The Baudin Expedition and the Tasmanian Aborigines 1802*, 82-95. Hobart: Blubber Head Press.

Pickering, Michael. 1999. Consuming Doubts: What Some People Ate? Or What Some People Swallowed? In *The Anthropology of Cannibalism*, ed. Laurence R. Goldman, 51-74. Westport, CT: Bergin & Garvey.

Poignant, Roslyn. 1992. Surveying the Field of View: the Making of the RAI Photographic Collection. In *Anthropology and Photography 1860-1920*, ed. Elizabeth Edwards, 42-73. New Haven, CT, and London: Yale University Press in Association with the Royal Anthropological Institute.

_____. 1993. Captive Aboriginal Lives: Billy, Jenny, Little Toby and their Companions. In *Captive Lives: Australian Captivity Narratives*, ed. Kate Darian-Smith, 35-57. London: Sir Robert Menzies Centre for Australian Studies, Institute of Commonwealth Studies, University of London.

_____. 2002. Les Aborigènes: 'sauvages professionnels' et vies captives. In *Zoos humains: de la vénus hottentote aux reality shows*, ed. Nicolas Bancel, Pascal Blanchard, Gilles Boetsch, Éric Deroo, and Sandrine Lemaire, 103-10. Paris: Éditions de la Découverte.

_____. 2004. *Professional Savages: Captive Lives and Western Spectacle*. Sydney: University of New South Wales Press.

Poirier, Jean. 1968. Histoire de la pensée ethnologique. In *Ethnologie générale*, ed. Jean Poirier, 3-179. Paris: Encyclopédie de la Pléiade.

Pruner-Bey, Franz. 1860. Reprise de la discussion sur la perfectibilité des races. *Bulletins de la Société d'Anthropologie de Paris* 1ère série, 1:479-94.

_____. 1865a. Discours d'ouverture. *Bulletins de la Société d'Anthropologie de Paris* 1ère série, 6:1-9.

_____. 1865b. L'homme et l'animal. *Bulletins de la Société d'Anthropologie de Paris* 1ère série, 6:522-62.

Quatrefages, Armand de. 1890. *The Human Species*, tr. unknown. 5th edition. London: Kegan Paul, Trench, Trübner, & Co. Ltd.

_____. 1988 [1884]. *Hommes fossiles et hommes sauvages: études d'anthropologie*. Paris: Jean Michel Place.

Renneville, Marc 2000. *Le langage des crânes: une histoire de la phrénologie*. Paris: Sanofi-Synthélabo.

Staum, Martin S. 2005. Nature and Nurture in French Ethnography and Anthropology, 1859-1914. *Journal of the History of Ideas* 65:475-95.

Stocking, George W., Jr. 1968. French Anthropology in 1800. In George W. Stocking, Jr., *Race, Culture and Evolution: Essays in the History of Anthropology*, 13-41. New York: Free Press.

Topinard, Paul. 1868. Etude sur les Tasmaniens. *Mémoires de la Société d'Anthropologie de Paris* 1ère série, 3:307-29.

_____. 1872. Sur les races indigènes de l'Australie. *Bulletins de la Société d'Anthropologie de Paris* 2e série, 7:211-327.

_____. 1875. Sur les métis australiens. *Bulletins de la Société d'Anthropologie de Paris* 2e série, 10:227-40.

_____. 1876. *L'anthropologie*. Paris: C. Reinwald et Cie.

_____. 1879. De la notion de race en anthropologie. *Revue d'Anthropologie* 2e série, 2:589-660.

_____. 1885. Présentation de trois Australiens vivants (Séance du 19 novembre 1885). *Bulletins de la Société d'Anthropologie de Paris* 3e série, 8:683-98.

_____. 1888. Les dernières étapes de la généalogie de l'homme. *Revue d'Anthropologie* 3e série, 3:298-332.

Trouillot, Michel-Rolph. 1991. Anthropology and the Savage Slot: the Poetics and Politics of Otherness. In *Recapturing Anthropology: Working in the Present*, ed. Richard G. Fox, 17-44. Santa Fe, NM: School of American Research Press.

Virchow, Rudolf. 1884. Australier von Queensland. *Zeitschrift für Ethnologie* 16:407-18.

Williams, Elizabeth. A. 1985. Anthropological Institutions in Nineteenth-Century France. *Isis* 76:331-48.

_____. 1987. The Science of Man: Anthropological Thought and Institutions in Nineteenth-Century France. Ann Arbor, MI: University Microfilms International [PhD thesis, Indiana University, 1983].

Notes

[1] I use in a different context the concept contained in the term 'savage slot' as coined by Michel-Rolph Trouillot (1991) for the epistemological domain of anthropology itself.

[2] Elizabeth Williams's study (1987) is the first comprehensive history of French anthropology in the nineteenth century and a basic reference point. See also Blanckaert 1988, 1996; Hammond 1980; Harvey 1983; Poirier 1968; Renneville 2000; Staum 2005; Stocking 1968; Williams 1985.

[3] The exhibition 'Captive Lives: Looking for Tambo and his Companions', curated by Roslyn Poignant, assisted by Irene Turpie, was held at the National Library of Australia from November 1997 to March 1998. It toured Australia extensively until mid-2000 and is now permanently housed at the Museum of Tropical Queensland in Townsville. Poignant's book (2004) presents her meticulous research into the story of Tambo and the other members of the group: how the unscrupulous Cunningham formed his troupe; their tour through North America and Europe in 1883-7 with its tragic outcome for most of them; and their objectification by both popular and scientific curiosity, even as they themselves adapted as performers to the roles they were expected to play as 'professional savages'.

[4] Like many of their colleagues in the Société d'Anthropologie de Paris, all three had trained in medicine.

[5] Houzé and Jacques 1884-5; Virchow 1884; see also Poignant 2004:125-36.

[6] Poignant 2004:16-25, 59-104. There was a public outcry in Australia and questions were raised in parliament about the departure of the group (Poignant 1993:46; Houzé and Jacques 1884-5:97-8).

[7] See Topinard's editorial note in Mondière 1886:313; see also Poignant 2004:115-16, 164.

[8] Despite the title of the report, it is unclear whether little Toby was actually present. He is not mentioned in the presentation or the discussion and reference is made at the end to 'the two Australians'.

[9] Houzé and Jacques had used English in their meetings with the troupe in Belgium.

[10] E.g., Houzé and Jacques (1884-5:134-8) devoted some pages to a description of the dimensions and manipulation of the boomerang. Virchow (1884:417) was equally fascinated, marvelling at the complicated aerodynamics of its movement combined with the simplicity of the tool itself.

[11] Prince Roland Bonaparte was a great traveller, polymath, and generous sponsor of scientific research. He made early use of photography as a means of anthropological recording. Among his anthropological portraits, the photographs he took of the three surviving members of Cunningham's troupe have aroused considerable interest and were the starting point for Poignant's important work in bringing this episode to light (see Poignant 1993:37). These photographs are also discussed in Poignant 1992; 2004:4-7; Maxwell 2000; Anderson 2006.

[12] Topinard 1885:684-5.

[13] See Anderson 2000 and 2001 for the embryonic ethnographic dimension of the two expeditions and Douglas 2003 for a discussion of the links between voyage ethnography and anthropological thought in the late eighteenth and early nineteenth centuries.

[14] Exceptions include François Péron's (1983) account of the Aborigines of Maria Island, Van Diemen's Land, based on field observations made in 1802 during Baudin's expedition, and much later memoirs by the naval doctor Charles Cauvin (1882, 1883) who saw several Aborigines when his ship called at Melbourne and Sydney in 1879 but nonetheless concentrated on Australian skulls and skeletons held in French institutions.

[15] I borrow the title of L.R. Hiatt's book (1996) in which he examines the controversial issues in British and Australian social anthropology that so often centred on Aboriginal Australians.

[16] E.g., Broca (1864:69-71) was himself emphatic that polygenism had been wrongly equated with support for slavery. See also Hammond 1980; Harvey 1983.

[17] See Chapters One (Douglas) and Four (Turnbull), this volume.

[18] See Chapter One (Douglas), this volume.

[19] See Fausto-Sterling 1995:22-3 on the inappropriate use of the term Hottentot.

[20] A subtext of the discussion is the hostility between Topinard and political radicals such as Hovelacque who would be part of a successful push to oust him from his chair at the Ecole d'Anthropologie in 1889 (see Harvey 1983:301-3).

[21] His sources of information were extensive, including the explorers Ludwig Leichhardt and Edward John Eyre, the explorer and colonial governor Sir George Grey, the American expedition leader Charles Wilkes, the botanist and explorer Allan Cunningham, the palaeontologist and museum curator Gerard Krefft, the missionary and Congregationalist minister George Taplin, who had a deep interest in Ngarrindjeri culture, and the Spanish Benedictine missionary, later bishop, Rosendo Salvado.

[22] In the second half of the nineteenth century, there was much speculation about the nature of the relationship between Aboriginal Australians and Indian groups among linguists and anthropologists who addressed the question of Aboriginal settlement of the Australian continent.

[23] Topinard 1872:232, 236-7, 239-40, 259, 278, 316-17, 325-6.

[24] Cf. Gilman 1985: ch.3; Fausto-Sterling 1995.

[25] See Elkins 1999:169-92.

[26] See Chapter One (Douglas), this volume.

[27] Topinard 1879:660. Armand de Quatrefages (1810-1892) was one anthropologist who came to doubt the validity of using external features to judge relative racial worth. In *The Human Species* he wrote:

> Influenced by certain habits of thought, and by a self-love of race which is easily explained, many anthropologists have thought that they could interpret the physical differences which distinguish men from one another, and consider simple characteristic features as marks of inferiority or superiority. Because the European has a short heel, and some Negroes have a long one, they have wished to consider the latter as a mark of degradation. Is the fundamental superiority of one race really betrayed outwardly by some material sign? We are still in ignorance upon this point. But when we examine it more closely, we are led to think it is not so (1890:350).

[28] An advertisement for a course given by Topinard at the École d'Anthropologie in 1886-7 is more pointed, perhaps in order to attract an audience: 'GENERAL ANTHROPOLOGY: Paul Topinard, professor, Tuesday, 4 o'clock. *Programme*: the professor will stress the superior and inferior characteristics of the human races' (*Revue d'Anthropologie* 1886:745).

[29] Topinard 1875:236; 1879:646; 1888.

[30] Williams 1987:166-9. Hamy's sense of the history of the discipline shows in his paper 'Les origines du Musée d'Ethnographie' (1889) which traces the history of the Musée du Trocadéro from the first royal collections in the reign of François Premier until its opening in 1880. The essay was published together with more than 200 pages of documents.

[31] Hamy (1891:3) had become obsessed with finding Petit's portfolio when assembling anthropological and ethnographic material collected or produced by French expeditions. He wanted to see Petit's drawings of Tasmanians and Australians for comparative raciological purposes.

[32] For Houzé's summary of supposedly atavistic or simian characteristics in his subjects, see Houzé and Jacques 1884-5:92-4.

[33] Houzé and Jacques 1884-5:94; see also Topinard 1872:252.

[34] Pruner-Bey 1865a:4. Pruner-Bey was one member of the Société who defended non-European groups, particularly Aboriginal Australians (see especially 1860:481-9). He deserves a prominent place in the story of such defenders because of his sensitivity to culture and language and his awareness of the problems involved in knowing and speaking about another culture, having himself spent many years in Egypt.

[35] I have not reproduced these names because there is some discordance between the two lists which, as Poignant (1993:40) noted, may suggest that some of the names proffered by the Queenslanders were group rather than personal ones. Poignant also noted the reluctance of some Aboriginal groups to tell their names. Furthermore, it is appropriate to be circumspect in the use of such names in recognition of Aboriginal practices and sensitivities about deceased relatives.

[36] See Chapter Six (Gardner), this volume.

[37] E.g., Pruner-Bey 1865b:548-55.

[38] E.g., Broca 1866. See also the exchange between Jean-Antoine-Victor Martin de Moussy (1810–1869) and Eugène Dally (Martin de Moussy 1866).

[39] Cannibalism remains a contentious issue in anthropology (e.g., Arens 1979; Barker, Hulme, and Iversen 1998; Goldman 1999; Obeyesekere 2005). With respect to Aboriginal Australians, Pickering (1999:67) concluded, on the basis of an extensive study of historical and ethnographic records, that 'the evidence, or rather lack of evidence, is more than sufficient to refute arguments that cannibalism was a traditional institution in Aboriginal societies'.

[40] Virchow (1884:413) reported a different response again from Toby who, he claimed, boasted of having killed men but said that he had never personally eaten them, though he had seen 'others' eating people.

[41] See Figure 17. Cf. Poignant 1993, Anderson 2006.

Part Four

Complicity and Challenge: the Science of Race
and Evangelical Humanism, 1800-1930

Chapter Six

The 'Faculty of Faith': Evangelical missionaries, social anthropologists, and the claim for human unity in the 19th century[1]

Helen Gardner

In his influential *Account of the English Colony in New South Wales* (1804:354), the deputy judge-advocate David Collins (1756-1810) dismissed claims by an 'eminent divine, that no country has yet been discovered where some trace of religion was not to be found' and pronounced the Aborigines of Port Jackson free of any trace of a religious state or knowledge: 'It is certain, that they do not worship either sun, moon, or star; … neither have they respect for any particular beast, bird, or fish'. The question of Aboriginal belief engaged the minds of those eighteenth-century Britons who were eager for details on the new colony. Captain Watkin Tench (c. 1759-1833), whose lively *Account of the Settlement at Port Jackson* was published in 1793, was frequently asked on his return: "'Have these people any religion: any knowledge of, or believe [sic] in a deity?—any conception of the immortality of the soul?"' (1793:183-4). In complete opposition to Collins, Tench (1793:186) responded with a close description of Aboriginal belief in supernatural forces and closed by 'expressing my firm belief, that the Indians of New South Wales acknowledge the existence of a superintending deity'.

Heathens and the capacity for religious thought

In the century that followed, descriptions of religious activity from around the world became evidence in debates on whether the capacity for religious belief was a universal human attribute and whether the supposed presence or absence of religion could help define the nature or extent of human difference. This chapter traces these discussions in Britain and the Australian colonies, focussing on the personal, theological, and political tensions that shaped the observations and the theoretical texts from which they were formulated. The evidence and the findings tacked between two related questions. First, whether indigenous people had a priori religious beliefs — a question that went to the heart of the relationship between faith and humanness in the debate over single or multiple human origins. Second, whether such people had the intellectual or spiritual capacity to respond to Christian doctrine. Those who believed that all people did have such a capacity tended to presume that all non-Christians held some form of spiritual belief, however erroneous. Yet the questions were distinct and the evidence relating to them was used to service different arguments.

Prior to the nineteenth century, across different eras and religious denominations, Europeans concerned with European exploration and expansion had debated the relationship between indigenous rights and the capacity for religious thought. The sixteenth-century Spanish jurist and theologian Francisco de Vitoria (1486?-1546) argued for the political and legal status of Native Americans (1991:233-92), contending that, while they were barbarians and unbelievers, they undoubtedly carried the capacity for Christian knowledge and that it was the duty of the Spanish representative to present the means for their salvation. In his theological musings on the question (1992:75), the Dominican friar and contemporary of Francisco, Bartolomé de las Casas (1474-1566), argued for the natural faculty by which men are led to 'the worship of God, or of what they believe to be God'. Therefore regardless of the barbarity or state of the nation, human society could not exist 'without the worship of the true or false deity'. The Moravian Count Nicolaus Ludwig von Zinzendorf (1700-1760) insisted that the nature of heathen deities was less significant than their existence. Any spiritual response to the natural world was proof of God's immanence. He sent his missionaries to the field in 1734 with the comforting text from Paul's letter to Roman Christians on the heathen experience of God: 'for what can be known about God is plain to them, because God has shown it to them. Ever since the creation of the world his eternal power and divine nature, invisible though they are, have been understood and seen through the things he has made. So they are without excuse ...' (Romans 1:19-20).[2] Therefore, Zinzendorf insisted, the heathen 'know already that there is a God' and are ignorant 'only of the Son' (Hutton 1923:21).

The 'eminent divine' referred to by Collins was Hugh Blair (1718-1800), Professor of Rhetoric at the University of Edinburgh and a significant figure in what came to be known as the Scottish Enlightenment, whose *Sermons* were among the best-selling works of the English language in the eighteenth century.[3] Blair (1777-1801, I:4-5) preached on natural religion, arguing that if there is any sense 'which man is formed by nature to receive, it is a sense of religion.... Cast your eyes over the whole earth.... You may discover tribes of men without policy, or laws, or cities, or any of the arts of life: But no where will you find them without some form of religion'. The theological argument that humanity possessed a natural capacity for faith was central to debates amongst Calvinist Evangelicals in the eighteenth century over whether civilization should precede Christianity. The historian Brian Stanley (2001:180) described it as the belief in an 'innate moral sense or conscience' by which the Holy Spirit, in conjunction with the human will and the essential knowledge provided by the missionary, could bring about salvation.[4]

In the nineteenth century, the question of the presence or absence of natural religion was contested on scientific as well as legal and theological grounds. The battle line was drawn initially and most sharply between Christians who supported missionary work, a task predicated on the universal capacity for religious thought, and certain 'natural historians' or 'philosophers'. Some men of science sought to prove either that multiple human species had developed from separate origins that could be tracked through evidence of physical, intellectual, or religious distinctions or that long isolation had created physical differences which reflected the intellectual or moral divergence of different races. The former position, which was professed by relatively few philosophers or naturalists, was completely beyond the pale for all Evangelical Christians. The latter — that differences in intellectual or spiritual abilities had developed as a result of the early separation of human populations — was more common but was equally threatening to the missionary project. As the discipline of anthropology was being established in British universities in the late nineteenth century, the argument over the significance of religion in the role of human unity changed. Now, the absence or presence of a religious sensibility became a sign of the evolution of the psyche and implicit evidence for the maturation of human beings from apes. Here, theorists such as Edward Burnett Tylor (1832-1917) and Friedrich Max Müller (1823-1900) lined up against Charles Darwin (1809-1882) and John Lubbock (1834-1913) on the evidence, or otherwise, for a 'primitive' religious sensibility, particularly amongst Aboriginal people in the Australian colonies.

The development of the British missionary movement in the late eighteenth and early nineteenth centuries coincided with Evangelical alarm about increasingly strident philosophical assertions against original human unity emanating in particular from France (Stanley 2001:11). In a sermon preached in 1824, Reverend Richard Watson (1781-1833), a Methodist intellectual and secretary of the Wesleyan Methodist Missionary Society that had been founded eight years earlier, advocated the religious instruction of the slaves in the West Indies. Taken from the text 'Honour all men' (1 Peter 2:17), Watson's sermon was a direct attack on literature which claimed that black people were either immutably distinct or a different species altogether from Europeans. Watson dismissed as self-serving the observations of slave owners on the essential inferiority of their charges and castigated those who used Biblical texts to claim Negro inferiority. Noah's curse on Ham, he argued, was not on Africans but on the Canaanites who were made the slaves of the Israelites. Therefore the curse, if it could be said to exist in any general sense, was on a tiny portion of Asia rather than any of the African tribes. Watson also turned his scorn on 'minute *philosophers*', one of whom, he said, had claimed in the previous twelve months that the degeneracy of Africans denied 'all cultivation of mind, and all correction of morals'. He dismissed as 'affected philosophy' attempts to 'measure mind by the rule and compasses; and estimate capacity for knowledge and salvation by a scale of inches and the acuteness of angles!' While acknowledging the supposedly low state of African civilization, Watson insisted that it was the result of political oppression by the 'civilized' nations, which had systematically enslaved millions of Africans over centuries, and not of the base nature of the African people.[5]

Against those who 'by the dreams of a theory' challenged the concept of a single human species and in so doing banished millions 'out of the *family* of God', Watson put forward one criterion for essential and original human unity. In a test that simultaneously denied human difference, claimed Christian jurisdiction, and was a call for missionaries to the cause, he insisted that unity between humankind could be proved where congregations showed themselves to be 'capable of loving God'. The findings from this test were already to hand: missionaries to the slave plantations of the Caribbean and in the missions to Africa described their converts as 'flashing with the light of intellect, and glowing with the hues of Christian graces'.[6] Watson's sermon was a clever subversion of the philosophical discussion on the 'natural' state of man and the claims that black people were intellectually and morally inferior. He urged mission supporters and philosophers alike to look to the outcomes of Christian preaching for the proof of human similarity. Addressed to a large and respectable congregation, Watson's sermon was a triumph: it was immediately published and went rapidly to a fourth edition. The readership included Members of Parliament and non-Methodists who found it an eloquent statement on human difference and the role of Christian mission during the turbulent years when church-goers backed the Anti-Slavery League and became increasingly involved in questions of Christianity and civilization amongst the native populations in the colonies of Tasmania, New South Wales, and New Zealand.[7]

There were at least two possible candidates for Watson's unnamed philosopher who disputed African equality. In the previous twelve months, the French naturalist Julien-Joseph Virey (1775-1846) had published the second edition of his *Histoire naturelle du genre humain*, 'Natural History of the Human Genus' (1824), in which he claimed that black Africans were biologically, mentally, and morally inferior to whites as a result of separate origins (Augstein 1996:xxvi). Less heterodox but still unacceptable to Evangelical missionaries was a popular edition of *Lectures on Physiology, Zoology and the Natural History of Man* (1822) by the anatomist William Lawrence (1783-1867). Lawrence (1822:473) upheld the important doctrine of the unity of the human species but insisted that differences of 'physical organisation and of moral and intellectual qualities' between the 'several races of our species' were the result of 'native or congenital varieties' which were then transmitted to offspring in 'hereditary succession'. This analysis was an insidious challenge to Evangelical Christians for it implied that human difference, while classified as 'varieties' rather than as original, was nonetheless immutable or biological. Lawrence (1822:423) even claimed to provide proof that members of the 'black variety' were aware of their inferiority with the poignant tale of an African found weeping and moaning that 'black men are nothing'. His volume amounted to an attack on the primary theology of imago dei, that man is made in God's image with universal abilities. It was also a threat to important new political initiatives such as the establishment of Liberia in 1821 as a haven for former slaves, an experiment that was followed keenly by naturalists and Evangelical missionaries alike.[8]

Data for Lawrence's lectures came from around the world and included a large footnote transcribed from Collins's account of the Aborigines of Port Jackson. Based on Collins's relatively benign descriptions, Lawrence (1822:413, 433) wrote a damning analysis: these were a people of 'remorseless cruelty, … insensible to distinctions of right and wrong, destitute of religion, without any idea of a Supreme Being, and with the feeblest notion … of a future state'. He acknowledged tensions with the Evangelical movement with a nod to their motivations of 'philanthropy and benevolence' but insisted that his analysis was based on unsentimental reason and that political decisions relating to slaves and colonized people 'must be limited by the natural capabilities of the subjects'.

Indigenous Gentiles: human unity and missions

Missionaries to the Australian colonies faced frequent charges that their efforts were beyond the mental capabilities of their flocks. Such threats could even come from the clergy. After early failures to persuade Aboriginal children to remain in his household, Samuel Marsden (1764-1838), the colonial chaplain to New South Wales who was instrumental in bringing the gospel to Maori in Aotearoa New Zealand, doubted that Aborigines were capable of civilized or Christian responses and was increasingly reluctant to extend limited funds to missionary efforts in New South Wales.[9] Responding to a request from his archdeacon for information on the state of New South Wales Aborigines in 1826, Marsden (1974:349) admitted their essential humanity but questioned their capacity for religious thought: 'the want of reflection upon their past, present and future, which is so strikingly apparent in the whole of the conduct of the Aborigines, opposes in my mind the strongest barrier to the work of a Missionary'.

This passage must be considered in the context of the debate then running between Marsden and his enthusiastic subordinate, Lancelot Threlkeld (1788-1859) of the London Missionary Society, who was dependent on Marsden for maintaining funds to his mission to the Awabakal people of Lake Macquarie. Threlkeld's description of his intermittent congregation was written in the same year as Marsden's comments, amid considerable settler hostility towards Aborigines and with the fear that the mission was at risk of losing its funding. While acknowledging that the religious ideas of his flock were false, Threlkeld (1974, I:52) found them no more 'contemptible than the pretended finding of the golden-plates and the magic spectacles, through which alone the book of Mormon could be read by the impostor Joe Smith'. Threlkeld held that the beliefs of his congregation indicated their religious sensibility and he made close analogies between Jewish, Christian, and Awabakal rituals that can be read both as a plea for universal ability and an implicit claim for continued support of the mission. The point also had legal implications: on the basis that Aborigines did not believe in a 'Supreme Being' and therefore could not swear an oath, Aboriginal testimony was inadmissible in the law courts of New South Wales until 1876 (Wright 2001:140). Against numerous detractors, Threlkeld insisted:

> It matters not how simple soever the act may be which is done as a testimony of acknowledgment of the power of a superior being, whether that Being be the Almighty true and only God, or the mere imaginary Demon of the Gentiles; whether the child be sacrificed as a burnt offering to Devils, or a tooth knocked out as a security against the anger of *Puttikán* an imaginary supernatural Being of whom the aborigines in these parts of the colony stand in dread; or whether the evidence of belonging to the ancient people of God under the Old Testament dispensation be the circumcision of the fore-skin, or in the dispensation of the New Covenant, the holy people use water as the witness of the external purification of the flesh, symbolical of the internal baptism by the holy spirit of God, or ever we can enter into the kingdom of heaven (1974, I:61).

Ultimately, Threlkeld's arguments for the mission failed and it was closed in 1828. He believed that the principal reason the funding was stopped was because he disputed the common belief that 'Aborigines are incapable of civilization and instruction' and he acknowledged that on this point he was in opposition to Marsden. Against many settlers, significant sectors of the colonial administration, and even his own superior, Threlkeld (1828:65) argued that 'Aborigines are not "Baboons", that they have no "innate deficiency of intellect"', and that they might be brought eventually to 'sit at the feet of Jesus, clothed in their right mind'. He was aware that evidence of the religious sensibility of Aborigines strengthened their claims for political, legal, and economic rights. For this reason, he was strategic in his choice of terms. Along with many other missionaries, Threlkeld used 'Gentile' rather than 'heathen' to describe his congregations. 'Gentile' sidestepped the Christian/heathen, civilized/savage oppositions and drew Aboriginal people closer to Biblical history where belief in the Jewish God was an ongoing matter of theological debate and discussion rather than a scientific, moral, or intellectual sign of human difference and ability.

During the first half of the nineteenth century, the most important British theorist to draw on reported observations of newly-encountered people was James Cowles Prichard (1786-1848), described by his counterpart in the second half of the century, Edward Burnett Tylor, as the 'founder of modern anthropology' (Stocking 1973:x). Prichard's use of physical evidence might have left him vulnerable to Watson's invective against those who 'measure mind by the rule and compasses' but he remained true to his devout Quaker upbringing and later membership of the Evangelical wing of the established church and maintained his belief in the orthodox view that humankind was born of a single origin.[10] Prichard's major ethnological publication, *Researches into the Physical History of Man(kind),* was revised three times between 1813 and 1847. The first volume of the third edition includes a new chapter that marks a significant shift from the physical focus of his earlier work. Titled 'the psychological comparison of human races', the chapter is based almost entirely on Moravian missionary accounts of Bushmen, Eskimos, and sub-Saharan Africans.[11] Prichard readily accepted Moravian conversion accounts as psychological evidence that all people share the 'same mental endowments, similar natural prejudices and impressions, the same consciousness, sentiments, sympathies, propensities, in short, a common psychical nature or a common mind'. The evidence for religious and by extension moral and intellectual parity could be found in the common 'tendencies to superstitious belief, as well as the same moral impressions as the rest of the human family'. Prichard believed he had defined a 'new subject of enquiry'.[12] His modern editor George Stocking, Jr. (1973:lxxxiv) argued that Prichard had extended the human unity discussion from the physical to the psychological realm, a position developed in the second part of the nineteenth century as the 'psychic unity of man'. Evangelical Christians of the period who were familiar with the text, however, almost certainly viewed Prichard's use of missionary texts as an important scientific confirmation of the general unity of the human species, viewed in Christian terms and confirmed by missionary observations.

Debates on the unity or otherwise of the human species were influenced by political events and often coalesced around societies and institutions.[13] The year after Prichard published the first volume of his third edition, the Aborigines Protection Society was established in Britain to agitate for indigenous rights. While the fight for legislation against slavery in the colonies had been won in 1833, Evangelical Christians were increasingly concerned by the more insidious dangers of colonization. In 1838, the Anglican Church Missionary Society petitioned the British Parliament against the granting of a major charter to colonize New Zealand, arguing that European colonization had 'disastrous consequences to the Aborigines of uncivilised countries in their rights, their persons, their property and moral condition' (Stenhouse 1994:399). However, there was no single missionary stance on colonialism in the Pacific throughout the nineteenth century. Denominational differences, political circumstances, both internal and international, as well as changing ideas of the relationship between subject and state meant that missionaries occupied the spectrum of political responses to colonization and often advocated European intervention, particularly in the face of settler encroachment on indigenous land.[14]

During the early nineteenth century, many missionaries proceeded to the field on the assumption that humanity could be defined by the capacity to form a relationship with the Christian God. Once in the field, and particularly when they began to translate the Scriptures into local languages, missionaries became profoundly entangled in indigenous beliefs as they searched for concepts that could bridge the differences between Christian doctrine and cosmology on the one hand and local ideas on the other.[15] Evidence for human unity and God's immanence could be found in a variety of sources. The Protestant call to translate the Bible into all tongues was based on the belief that every language had been created by God and therefore contained the means to describe the revelation of Jesus (Sanneh 1989:201). In 1850, John Geddie (1815-1872), a Presbyterian missionary on the island of Aneityum in what is now Vanuatu, wrote of translating the New Testament (1975:63): 'The study, however, is one of intense interest and delight; and those are privileged indeed, whom God permits to prepare the key which will unlock the hidden treasure of divine truth, which makes the soul rich for all eternity'. While the presence of heathen spirits or gods was generally taken by missionaries as evidence of degeneration, it could also serve the more significant purpose of proving the essentially spiritual nature of the unconverted. Geddie's colleague John Inglis (1808-1891) insisted that the Aneityumese idea of spirit possession indicated a spiritual — as opposed to secular — nature that corresponded closely to the Christian idea of the spirit and revelation. As with Threlkeld, Inglis made ready analogies between local and Jewish beliefs. He believed that Aneityumese messages from the spirits were:

> not the inspiration of genius, as accepted by a sceptical or a secular philosophy, but a personal inspiration … distinct from the man's soul, speaking through the lips of the poet; the Scriptural idea of inspiration as expressed by David in his last words, when he said, 'The Spirit of the Lord *spake* by *me,* and *His word* was in *my tongue*' (1882:xxxvi, original emphasis).

Such analogies served the dual purpose of bringing the heathen into the Christian world and indicating to sceptics that they shared their history and humanity with the frequently despised native. For many missionaries, conversion was not merely proof of the indwelling God but was a significant marker of their own faith for it proved the universal appeal of Christ and, by extension, the unity of humankind.

'The faculty of faith': evidence and theories

As Geddie and Inglis were establishing the Aneityum mission, the German scholar and linguist Friedrich Max Müller, who remained a committed Lutheran despite the theological and scientific debates that raged around him, was settling into Oxford as professor of modern languages and later comparative philology (Chaudhuri 1974:69). Over the next thirty years, Müller was to prove an important advocate for human congruity, particularly on the issues of faith and intellect. Profoundly influenced by the German philosopher Friedrich Schelling (1775-1854), Müller developed an essentially evolutionist theory that 'myth' was the product of an 'indwelling law' through which religious belief was expressed. Thus, Christianity was inherent in all faiths as it found expression in different phases along the path to the godhead (Trompf 1969:202). While believed by many to be profoundly Darwinian, Müller refused to admit the mechanism of natural selection in relation to the development of language and held that the capacity for speech constituted the demarcation point between human beings and animals. In 1873, he delivered a series of lectures on this point against Darwin's theory (Müller 1873). Darwin, acknowledging Müller's intellect and standing, pronounced him a 'dangerous man' and wrote that being criticized by him made him feel 'like the man in the story who boasted he had been soundly horsewhipped by a Duke' (Chaudhuri 1974:258). Müller was a friend and correspondent of a number of missionaries in the field, including the Bishop to the Melanesian Mission John Coleridge Patteson (1827-1871), his colleague Robert Codrington (1830-1922), and the Methodist Lorimer Fison (1832-1907).[16]

For some clergy and missionaries, the debate about religious sensibility was formulated on the idea of degeneration: the belief that, after the deluge and the dispersal of the tribes, some had wandered so far across the world and been separated from God for so long that they had lost the ability to think in religious terms. For others, less concerned with Biblical literalism, 'degeneration' was merely the loss of the conscious knowledge of God: indigenous beliefs, while misguided, were proof of an inherent spiritual capacity which indicated their place in the family of God. Still others professed, along with Müller, a form of evolutionism in which races gradually passed through stages of religious belief led by the indwelling Spirit towards the pinnacle of Christian knowledge.

The text from the Australian colonies that was to prove most influential in British debates in the 1860s and 1870s on the religious sensibility of Aborigines was *Queensland, Australia* (1861) by Reverend John Dunmore Lang (1799-1878). The book was primarily intended as an invitation to immigrants but also includes a long essay on Queensland Aborigines based on Lang's attempt in 1837 to establish a mission at Nundah, Queensland, which was abandoned in 1843. As a result of this failure, Lang was dubious about the intellectual or religious ability of Aborigines (Bridges 1993:12). While Lang's numerous publications ensured his reputation in Britain, in the Australian colonies his relationships were so rancorous that he defended a number of libel charges over the course of his career, including one from Threlkeld whom he sought to have dismissed.[17] In *Queensland, Australia*, Lang focused his well-honed scorn on a successful publication by Paul Edmund de Strzelecki (1797-1873), *Physical Description of New South Wales and Van Diemen's Land* (1845). In this account, Strzelecki (1845:339) claimed that indigenous Australian 'recognise a God, though they never name him in their vernacular language, but call him, in English, "Great Master," and consider themselves his slaves.... They believe in an immortality, or after-existence, of everlasting enjoyment, and place its locality in the stars, or other constellations'.[18] Lang's response to Strzelecki showed the minister's theological opposition to the notion of a universal religious sensibility and probably harked back to his opposition to Threlkeld. 'I have always been very sceptical in regard to the ideas alleged by certain travellers to be entertained by barbarous tribes on the subject of God', wrote Lang (1861:375-6). He acknowledged that it was against the 'preconceived ideas, or the philosophical system, of certain writers, to admit that there is any portion of the human race living entirely without a religion' and yet missionaries reported such evidence not only amongst the 'Papuan aborigines of Australia' but also in the fledgling congregations of Greenland and Southern Africa.

In the second half of the nineteenth century, religious belief, or the lack thereof, became fertile ground for the discussion of the relationship between human beings and animals. Lang's testimony became evidence for both sides of an unexpected alliance between, on the one hand, clergy or religious people who believed in degeneration and were horrified by the suggestion that heathen beliefs shared anything with the Christian promise of salvation; and, on the other hand, scientists who were keen to minimize the distinction between some human beings and animals in order to strengthen evolutionary arguments about the ultimate origin of mankind within the animal kingdom or to prove that human races were the outcome of multiple origins. In a short address to the Anthropological Society of London in 1864 on the 'Universality of Belief in God, and in a Future State', the Archdeacon of Westminister, the Very Reverend Frederic W. Farrar (1831-1903), who was later chaplain to Queen Victoria, quoted Lang, amongst others from around the world, to claim (1864a:ccxvii): 'there are not only isolated tribes, but whole nations who are so degraded as to live with no knowledge of their Creator'. For Farrar (1864a:ccxviii), the revelation of Christ and the Judeao-Christian God had no parallel with the spirits of 'savages' whose religious beliefs could be compared to the involuntary reactions of animals: 'a vague fear of the Unknown is found even among animals, and is widely different from a belief in God'. The assembled members then debated the paper and revealed a range of possible positions on the issue. Alfred Russel Wallace (1823-1913) described the absence of belief amongst the 'wild tribes of Molucca and of New Guinea' with whom he was familiar. A Reverend Kerr commented that in his parish work in Liverpool he had found many who had 'but little notion of a God'. Another insisted that he had never met an African Negro who did not believe in the existence of a good or bad spirit. The president of the Anthropological Society, James Hunt (1833-1869), a professed polygenist, believed that Farrar's evidence against the general assumption of universal belief was of particular importance to anthropology. For his part, Farrar held that he was merely confirming the Biblical claim that 'there were people who knew not God' (1864a:ccxix-ccxxi). However, his second paper, 'On Hybridity' (1864b), which was then read to the members, was based on a scientific argument about interracial infertility that revealed he had a close knowledge of polygenist theories on the failings of the human 'hybrid' and his analysis implied separate human origins.

In the early 1870s, several anthropological texts addressed the question of a universal religious sensibility in relation to the distinction between human beings and animals. In their respective publications *The Descent of Man* (1871) and *The Origin of Civilisation* (1870), Darwin and Lubbock implied that the absence of religious belief amongst some human groups could be likened to a psychic missing link that was evidence for the maturation of human beings from apes.[19] Opposing them, from a different intellectual tradition, were Tylor, who published *Primitive Culture* in 1871, and Müller, whose *Introduction to the Science of Religion* (1873) argued for a universal and innate religious sensibility in all human groups.[20]

In *The Origin of Civilisation*, Lubbock (1870:212) stated that the 'evidence of numerous trustworthy observers' opposed the belief that 'religion is general and universal'. Lang was held to be a particularly trustworthy observer as his findings were believed to be in opposition to his Christian beliefs. Yet here Lubbock was either ignorant of Lang's degenerationism or misrepresented him. Degenerationism as professed by Lang meant the loss of the knowledge of God to the point where a religious sensibility was completely absent. Lang (1861:377) held that 'Papuan' ignorance of the 'knowledge of God' was to be expected for 'almost every trace of divine knowledge ... [had] disappeared at a comparatively early period in the history of the postdiluvian world, among all the other Gentile nations'. This position was distinct from evolutionist theories such as Lubbock's which claimed that the gradual development of man from ape could be mapped on to existing populations using evidence such as religious sensibility. Without acknowledging Lang's degenerationism, Lubbock (1870:212) simply used his work as evidence for his own implicit claim of the essential similarity between the 'lowest races' and animals: 'we must admit that the feeling of a dog or a horse towards its master is of the same character; and the baying of a dog to the moon is as much an act of worship as some ceremonies which have been so described by travellers'.[21]

Lubbock's friend and mentor Darwin published *The Descent of Man* the following year. In a chapter comparing the 'Mental Powers of Man and the Lower Animals', Darwin (1871, I:53-62) responded to those who insisted that the gulf between human beings and animals could not be bridged by his theory. 'Instincts' shared with animals, such as maternal affection, curiosity, imitation, attention, were the primary foci of the chapter but he also included discussion on language with an oblique attack on Müller. The chapter finishes with a sub-section on 'Belief in God — Religion' (1871, I:65-9). In an attack on Tylor's explicit claim for a universal religious sensibility and his implicit argument that this was a primary division between human beings and animals (Tylor 1866:71-81; 1870:370), Darwin insisted:

> There is no evidence that man was aboriginally endowed with the ennobling belief in the existence of an Omnipotent God. On the contrary there is ample evidence, derived not from hasty travellers, but from men who have long resided with savages, that numerous races have existed, and still exist, who have no idea of one or more gods, and who have no words in their languages to express such an idea (1871, I:65).

Darwin (1871, I:65-7) did allow that amongst 'the less civilised races' there was a universal belief in 'spiritual agencies' but held that this did not mark the divide between human beings and animals because a similar belief could be found in his dog, a 'very sensible animal' who growled at the movement of a parasol in the wind, attributing it to some 'strange living agent'.

In his conclusions, Darwin (1871, II:394-5) acknowledged the importance of the debate over an innate religious sensibility to his theory of the development of human beings from animals: 'The belief in God has often been advanced as not only the greatest, but the most complete of all the distinctions between man and the lower animals'. He even provided a salve to religious sensitivities concerned about the point of human development where man developed an immortal soul and he stopped short of the explicit suggestion that 'primitive man' was not part of the family of God. Ultimately, however, Darwin insisted that it is 'impossible to maintain that this belief [in God] is innate or instinctive in man'.

E.B. Tylor's *Primitive Culture*, also published in 1871, is primarily a work on religion. The anthropologist Adam Kuper (1988:77) argued that during this early period of anthropology there was a shift from questions of political development to the relationship between belief and rationality. Thirteen of Tylor's twenty chapters in the two-volume work are concerned with rites, rituals, mythology, and animism. The chapters on animism begin with the question posed in his two earlier articles on religion: 'Are there, or have there been human tribes so low in culture as to have no religious conceptions whatever?'[22] While Tylor insisted that the question had been asked over centuries, in this instance it was clearly formulated against Lubbock and Darwin. The observations of J.D. Lang were immediately in Tylor's firing line. Recognizing the degenerationism in Lang's analysis that Aborigines were without belief in a god, Tylor applied some of Lang's other findings of evil or benign spiritual agents to his own definition of what constituted religious thought, based on his theory of animism. By this criterion, Tylor (1871, I:379) found that Lang's observations were proof that 'the natives of Australia were at their discovery, and have since remained, a race with minds saturated with the most vivid belief in souls, demons, and deities'.

Tylor supported this argument with page after page of careful depositions against similar claims for the absence of religious thought amongst indigenous people. He held that the primary error committed by those who failed to acknowledge a religious sensibility in their observations was the definition of religion as 'the organised and established theology of the higher races' (1871, I:380). The words that follow dramatize the divide between earlier anthropologists such as Prichard, who had been sympathetic to missionaries and uncritically accepted the quality of their accounts, and their more sceptical successors who held that missionary observations were invariably tainted by an overt Christian agenda. Tylor believed that missionaries who acknowledged the pre-Christian beliefs of their congregations were rare and enlightened souls. He claimed, however, that for the most part the '"religious world"' despised heathen beliefs and that missionaries had neither the time nor the capacity to understand them. Kuper convincingly argued that the implication to be drawn from Tylor's theories on religious evolution was that nineteenth-century man was developing beyond belief and theology to the superior knowledge of science. The most progressive vantage point from which to view 'primitive religion', therefore, was that of the scientific observer. According to Tylor, missionary observations were intrinsically tainted, owing to the beliefs of the observer, and belonged to an earlier system of data collection (Kuper 1988:80).

The strongest definition of the role of faith in the unity of humankind came from Müller's series of lectures published in 1873 as *Introduction to the Science of Religion*. In a thesis that sustained his attack against Darwin's attempt to minimize the human/animal divide, Müller described the religious sensibility as one of the two faculties that defined man as utterly distinct from animal:

> As there is a faculty of speech, independent of all the historical forms of language, so there is a faculty of faith in man, independent of all historical religions. If we say that it is religion which distinguishes man from the

animal, we do not mean the Christian or Jewish religion; we do not mean any special religion; but we mean a mental faculty, that faculty which, independent of, nay in spite of sense and reason, enables man to apprehend the Infinite under different names and under varying disguises. Without that faculty, no religion, not even the lowest worship of idols and fetishes, would be possible; and if we will but listen attentively, we can hear in all religions a groaning of the spirit, a struggle to conceive the inconceivable, to utter the unutterable, a longing after the Infinite, a love of God (1873:17-18).

As with Prichard, Müller believed that the correlation between faith and human unity was proved by a capacity for religious thought rather than an adherence to a specific religion. His final sentence in the above passage shows the usefulness of developmental theory as a means both to describe and prescribe differences between human groups. As Stocking (1968:73) has shown in relation to Tylor's use of the singular for 'culture' in his famous definition of the term, Müller's reference to the 'lowest worship of idols and fetishes', followed by the use of upper case and singular for 'God', suggests similarly that religious evolutionism described difference as stages along a single defined path toward a Christian end.

George Brown, Frazer, and the origins of totemism

As these debates were being conducted in London in the 1870s, missionaries were establishing new fields throughout the western Pacific and were forming links with metropolitan theorists, particularly Tylor and Müller.[23] In 1875, George Brown (1835-1917), who had begun his mission career for Methodism in Samoa in 1860, was founding a new mission on the Duke of York Islands in the Bismarck Archipelago of what is now Papua New Guinea. Shortly afterwards, he began to publish articles on anthropological matters and made contact with Tylor just prior to the theorist's appointment to Oxford University as the first lecturer in Anthropology. Brown and Tylor communicated intermittently over the next twenty years (Gardner 2006a:111-27).

Brown was one of a number of missionary anthropologists familiar with metropolitan literature. He read Müller while in Samoa and was enthusiastic about Lubbock's *Origin of Civilisation* which he read in his final years in the Bismarck Archipelago, despite the scorn of many of his colleagues who were generally scathing about Lubbock's ethnological pastiches.[24] Many of Brown's published articles were concerned with the debates on an ethnological division of the Pacific which he addressed most comprehensively in his book *Melanesians and Polynesians* (1910). Brown's response to Tylor's edited publication *Notes and Queries on Anthropology* (1874) reflected the symbiotic but ambivalent relationship between missionaries and contemporary anthropology. Indeed, the text itself points to the great split between the Ethnological and Anthropological Societies of London that had been resolved three years prior to its publication.[25] Part One, entitled 'Constitution of Man', was compiled by John Beddoe (1826-1911), a former president of the racialist Anthropological Society who was then engaged in the comprehensive measuring of the British population (Stocking 1987:66). The section was exclusively concerned with physical anthropology and included questions on the 'form and size' of 'living subjects' and instructions on how to measure the human body (Tylor 1874:1-6). While these questions might not have been abhorrent to the ornithologist in Brown, they were clearly incompatible with his Evangelical ideals of human unity. He largely ignored the section on physical anthropology except for a few terse responses that show little more than his desire to subvert the spirit of the inquiry. He was clearly more comfortable with Part Two of *Notes and Queries* and the questions on 'Culture' that were compiled by E.B. Tylor, long affiliated with the humanitarian Ethnological Society. Brown answered most of the questions from these sections, often with long and detailed explanations that readily agreed with the mode of investigation. He similarly refused to use physical evidence as a means of classifying difference across the putative Melanesia-Polynesia division (1887:312), arguing that the difficulties were such that the evidence was inherently unsound.

In 1889, Brown received a letter and a copy of 'Questions on the Customs and Superstitions of Savages' from James Frazer (1854-1941), then a fellow at Trinity College, Cambridge.[26] By this link, Brown was drawn into the great late-nineteenth century question regarding religious sensibility, the relationship between magic and science. Central to the debate was the anthropological term 'totemism' which was defined as the origin of erroneous magical thinking and the mechanism by which the 'lowest races' sought spiritual answers for material phenomena. From the base line of totemism, human evolution led to increasingly sophisticated religious thought and then finally to science. The implication was that, by this route, humanity was progressively freed from religious falsehood.[27] Melanesia was proving to be a rich field in the study of the relationship between totemism and marriage classes and Frazer actively courted Brown as one who was 'intimately acquainted with the local people'.[28] The two men corresponded over the next twenty-five years and in *Totemism and Exogamy* (1910), in a chapter on 'Totemism in Northern Melanesia', Frazer (1910, II:119,122-3) quoted extensively from Brown's 1877 paper on the Bismarck Archipelago as well as from *Melanesians and Polynesians*. To Frazer (1910, II:151), the Bismarck Archipelago offered 'pure' forms of totemism that rested easily within prescribed definitions. It also fitted the expected correlation between race and development — Melanesians had totems while Polynesian forms had purportedly 'developed' into religion. In this scheme, the Palau Islands, which were reported as having both totems and religion, provided the link between the two regions.

Frazer closed *Totemism and Exogamy* with his final theory that totemism originated from the failure to identify the role of the male in human conception.[29] He based his theory on the fieldwork of the biologist Baldwin Spencer (1860-1929) and the Alice Springs postmaster Frank Gillen (1856-1912) who spent some months amongst the Aranda (now Arrernte) people of central Australia in the last years of the nineteenth century. In reply to their question, asked ad nauseum, the people told the researchers time and time again 'the child was not the direct result of intercourse' (Wolfe 1994:180). Frazer (1910, IV:61) believed that the apparent failure to attribute conception to intercourse was the source of totemism and, according to evolutionist theory, the origin of all religion:

> Ignorant of the true causes of childbirth, they imagine that a child only enters into a woman at the moment when she first feels it stirring in her womb, and accordingly they have to explain to themselves why it should enter her body at that particular moment ... The theory of the Central Australians is that a spirit child has made its way into her from the nearest of those trees, rocks, water-pools, or other natural features (1910, IV:57).

While Brown was a keen informant for anthropological theorists, he clearly believed that Frazer's theory came too close to defining the Arrernte as a proto-religious group. His problems were twofold. First, there were political dangers for the Arrernte people implicit in such a definition. It could be argued that this period marked the high tide of European claims for Aboriginal inferiority and their anticipated extinction. Second, Brown was alert to the threat to Christianity in Frazer's suggestion that religion was little more than a long progression from an original erroneous explanatory system to the eventual triumph of science. In his response to Frazer's 'conceptional' theory in a paper to the Australasian Association for the Advancement of Science (1911), Brown made pointed arguments against Frazer's findings. He held that Frazer did not properly account for a number of beliefs that would have to have been present before the 'conceptional' belief could occur: for example, there must have been a prior belief in 'totem spirits' as well as a prior belief in both a 'spirit child' who entered the mother's womb and the ability of the mother to receive the 'totem'. Brown concluded, against Frazer: 'there must, in fact, have been totems before the totemic spirit could enter the womb of the woman'. The aging missionary then made a bold statement on the unity of humankind through the faculty of faith:

> For the origin of totemism, we must, I think, go back to a period far earlier than that which is indicated by the conceptional idea ... when man first became conscious of the existence of a power, or powers, outside of himself.... How that consciousness was created or evolved is a matter with which I am not at present concerned. I myself, while accepting all the facts, and believing some of the theories, of evolution and quite

prepared to find some day that, so far as the body of man is concerned, every proof has been given of our ascent from the most primitive forms of life, also believe, with Mr A.R. Wallace and many others, that in everything which differentiates man from all other creatures he is a special creation of God. I believe this ... because he alone has the religious instinct, and that is found amongst men everywhere, even in the lowest states of culture (1911:403-4).

Frazer's analysis troubled Brown's uneasy adherence to cultural evolutionism. He described the data as 'so abnormal and contrary to experience' that some other explanation had to be available and he concluded that Gillen and Spencer were probably missing vital information. Brown's alternative theory was that 'knowing herself to be pregnant (as all women do)' the Arrernte woman simply takes the 'necessary steps to fix the totem of her child' (1911:407-8). Therefore the two beliefs, biological conception and the entering of the 'totemic spirit' into the womb, could be held simultaneously. Brown's outburst on the religious instinct showed his unease that evolutionist speculations on the gradual development of all aspects of human ability undermined the theology of human unity. Brown maintained the place of an innate and universal capacity for belief, human reasoning, and intelligence and questioned the implication that Arrernte (and by extension other Aboriginal groups) marked the very origin and therefore the lowest level of intellectual and religious states.

Conclusion

Throughout the nineteenth century, evidence and debates about the role of faith in the unity and/or original diversity of humankind shaped metropolitan theories as well as observations from the periphery. Most observers were aware of the debates on the issue and structured their reports according to their positions which could encompass a range of theological, political, and scientific theories. The question of 'The Faculty of Faith' was loaded with implications for the conceptualization of relationships between human groups and eventually between human beings and animals. Along with other Evangelical missionaries such as Threlkeld and Inglis, Brown constantly and anxiously patrolled contemporary debates about human difference and was alert to the political, religious, and moral implications of philosophical and scientific theories. Brown's anthropological interests and the terms on which he agreed to debate human difference were directed by his Christian insistence on human similitude. While he joined many of his fellow missionaries in accepting the logic of social evolutionist theory, he simultaneously sought to temper the implications of its findings. Theorists such as Tylor and Müller consistently argued for the psychic unity of man and the universal intellectual and religious capabilities of all human beings. Müller, secure in his own faith, was never concerned with suggestions that human beings were progressing beyond religion. Tylor, however, mapped out a particularly modernist position where faith became the preserve of the primitive and the less advanced and could only be successfully investigated by the post-Christian scientific anthropologist. Lubbock and Darwin sought to downplay the sophistication of native faith in order to minimize the division between people and animals and advance the theory that human ability, whether religious, moral, or intellectual, was neither innate nor universal but developed through time and could be mapped on to contemporary human populations.

By the end of the nineteenth century, the issue of the 'faculty of faith' appeared to have lost its relevance to the discipline of anthropology. Anthropologists generally seemed to have accepted the Tylorian position that all belief in spirits was evidence of religion. However, the evolutionist theory on the gradual development of religious belief from animism to monotheism to science was a popular idea that maintained the opposition between 'civilized' and 'primitive'. While it is beyond the scope of this chapter to move into the twentieth century, it would seem that secular modernism created new implications for the question of primitive belief. In the popular imagination, the question suggested two possible answers: either indigenous peoples had maintained 'traditional' beliefs which were clearly outdated by rational thought; or they had been 'coerced' into Christianity, a level of religious belief which many believed to be beyond their cultural and moral capacity.

References

Augstein, Hannah Franziska, ed. 1996. *Race: the Origins of an Idea 1760-1850*. Bristol: Thoemmes Press.

Blair, Hugh. 1777-1801. *Sermons*, 5 vols. Edinburgh and London: W. Creech, W. Strahan, and T. Cadell.

Bridges, Barry. 1993. John Dunmore Lang. In *Presbyterian Leaders in Nineteenth Century Australia*, ed. Rowland Ward, 1-22. Melbourne: Rowland S. Ward.

Brown, George. 1876-80. Letterbooks, 1876-1880. Manuscripts. ML A1686-3. Sydney: Mitchell Library.

————. 1877. Notes on the Duke of York Group, New Britain and New Ireland. *Journal of the Royal Geographical Society* 3:137-50.

————. 1877-1914. Scientific and Ethnological Papers, 1877-1914. Manuscripts. ML A1686-22. Sydney: Mitchell Library.

————. 1879-1917. Papers, 1879-1917. Manuscripts. MSS 952. Sydney: Mitchell Library.

————. 1887. Papuans and Polynesians. *Journal of the Anthropological Institute of Great Britain and Ireland* 16:311-27.

_____. 1910. *Melanesians and Polynesians: their Life-Histories Described and Compared*. London: Macmillan.

_____. 1911. The Conceptional Theory of the Origin of Totemism. In *Report of the Twelfth Meeting of the Australasian Association for the Advancement of Science, Held at Brisbane, 1909*, ed. John Shirley, 402-11. Brisbane: Government Printer.

Casas, Bartolomé de las. 1992. *A Short Account of the Destruction of the Indies*, tr. and ed. Nigel Griffin. London: Penguin Books.

Chaudhuri, Nirad. 1974. *Scholar Extraordinary: the Life of Professor the Rt. Hon. Friedrich Max Müller P.C*. London: Chatto and Windus.

Collins, David. 1804 [1798-1802]. *An Account of the English Colony in New South Wales, from its First Settlement, in January 1788, to August 1801: with Remarks on the Dispositions, Customs, Manners, &c. of the Native Inhabitants of that Country ...*, ed. Maria Collins. Abridged 2nd edition. London: T. Cadell and W. Davies.

Darwin, Charles. 1871. *The Descent of Man and Selection in Relation to Sex*, 2 vols. London: J. Murray.

Dwyer, John. 1987. *Virtuous Discourse: Sensibility and Community in Late Eighteenth Century Scotland*. Edinburgh: John Donald Publishers.

Farrar, Frederic William. 1864a. Universality of a Belief in God and in a Future State. *Anthropological Review* 2:ccxvii-ccxxii.

_____. 1864b. On Hybridity. *Anthropological Review* 2:ccxxii-ccxxix.

Frazer, James George. 1910. *Totemism and Exogamy: a Treatise on Certain Early Forms of Superstition and Society*, 4 vols. London: Macmillan.

Gardner, Helen Bethea. 2006a. *Gathering for God: George Brown in Oceania*. Dunedin, NZ: Otago University Press.

_____. 2006b. 'New Heaven and New Earth': Translation and Conversion on Aneityum. *Journal of Pacific History* 41:293-311.

Geddie, John. 1975. *Misi Gete: John Geddie, Pioneer Missionary to the New Hebrides*, ed. R.S. Miller. Launceston: Presbyterian Church of Tasmania.

Goldhawk, Norman. 1978. The Methodist People in the Early Victorian Age: Spirituality and Worship. In *A History of the Methodist Church in Great Britain*, ed. Rupert Davies, A. Raymond George, and Gordon Rupp, vol. 2, 113-43. London: Epworth Press.

Gunson, Niel. 1965. Missionary Interest in British Expansion in the South Pacific in the Nineteenth Century. *Journal of Religious History* 3:296-313.

_____. 1974. Introduction. In *Australian Reminiscences & Papers of L.E. Threlkeld, Missionary to the Aborigines, 1824-1859*, ed. Niel Gunson, vol. 1, 1-37. Canberra: Australian Institute of Aboriginal Studies.

_____. 1978. *Messengers of Grace: Evangelical Missionaries in the South Seas 1797-1860*. Melbourne: Oxford University Press.

Hutton, Joseph Edmund. 1923. *A History of Moravian Missions*. London: Moravian Publication Office.

Inglis, John. 1882. *A Dictionary of the Aneityumese Language*. London: Williams and Norgate.

Kuper, Adam. 1988. *The Invention of Primitive Society: Transformations of an Illusion*. London and New York: Routledge.

Lang, John Dunmore. 1861. *Queensland, Australia: a Highly Eligible Field for Emigration, and the Future Cotton-Field of Great Britain: With a Disquisition on the Origins Manners, and Customs of the Aborigines*. London: Edward Stanford.

Lawrence, William. 1822 [1819]. *Lectures on Physiology, Zoology and the Natural History of Man delivered at the Royal College of Surgeons*. London: Benbow.

Lubbock, John. 1865. *Pre-historic Times as Illustrated by Ancient Remains, and the Manners and Customs of Modern Savages*. London: Williams and Norgate.

_____. 1870. *The Origin of Civilisation and the Primitive Condition of Man: Mental and Social Condition of Savages*. London: Longmans, Green, and Co.

Mallet, Shelley. 1995. Bearing the inconceivable. In *Work in Flux,* ed. Emma Greenwood, Klaus Neumann, and Andrew Satori, 41-58. Melbourne: History Department, University of Melbourne.

Marsden, Samuel. 1974. Reverend Samuel Marsden's Report to Archdeacon Scott on the Aborigines of N.S.W. (2 December 1826). In *Australian Reminiscences & Papers of L.E. Threlkeld, Missionary to the Aborigines, 1824-1859*, ed. Niel Gunson, vol. 2, 347-9, Appendix 8. Canberra: Australian Institute of Aboriginal Studies.

Maxwell, Ian. 2001. Civilization or Christianity? The Scottish Debate on Mission Methods. In *Christian Missions and the Enlightenment,* ed. Brian Stanley, 123-41. Grand Rapids, MI: William B. Eerdmans.

Metzger, Bruce M., and Roland E. Murphy, ed. 1991. *The New Revised Standard Bible, Oxford Annotated*. New York: Oxford University Press.

Müller, Friedrich Max. 1873. *Introduction to the Science of Religion: Four Lectures Delivered at the Royal Institution, with Two Essays on False Analogies, and the Philosophy of Mythology*. London: Longmans, Green and Co.

_____. 1976 [1902]. *The Life and Letters of the Right Honourable Friedrich Max Müller*, ed. Georgina Adelaide Müller, 2 vols. New York: AMS Press.

Mulvaney, John. 1981. Gum Leaves on the Golden Bough. In *Antiquity and Man: Essays in Honour of Glyn Daniel*, ed. John D. Evans, Barry Cunliffe, and Colin Renfrew, 52-64. London: Thames and Hudson.

Owens, John. 1970. Religious Disputation at Whangaroa 1823-7. *Journal of the Polynesian Society* 79:289-303.

Prichard, James Cowles. 1836-47. *Researches into the Physical History of Mankind*, 5 vols. 3rd edition. London: Sherwood, Gilbert, and Piper.

Rivière, Peter. 1978. Introduction. In John Lubbock, *The Origin of Civilisation and the Primitive Condition of Man,* ed. Peter Rivière, i-lxviii. Chicago: University of Chicago Press.

Samson, Jane. 2001. Ethnology and Theology: Nineteenth Century Missionary Dilemmas. In *Christian Missions and the Enlightenment*, ed. Brian Stanley, 99-123. Grand Rapids, MI: William B. Eerdmans.

Sanneh, Lamin. 1989. *Translating the Message: the Missionary Impact on Culture*. Maryknoll, NY: Orbis Books.

_____. 1996. *Religion and the Variety of Culture: a Study in Origin and Practice*. Valley Forge, PA: Trinity Press International.

Sher, Richard B. 1985. *Church and University in the Scottish Enlightenment: the Moderate Literati of Edinburgh*. Edinburgh: Edinburgh University Press.

Stanley, Brian. 1990. *The Bible and the Flag: Protestant Missions and British Imperialism in the Nineteenth and Twentieth Centuries*. Leicester: Apollos.

_____. 2001. The Enlightenment in English Evangelical Mission Thought. In *Christian Missions and the Enlightenment*, ed. Brian Stanley, 169-97 Grand Rapids, MI: William B. Eerdmans.

Stenhouse, John. 1994. The Darwinian Enlightenment and New Zealand Politics. In *Darwin's Laboratory: Evolutionary Theory and Natural History in the Pacific,* ed. Roy MacLeod and Philip F. Rehbock, 395-425. Honolulu: University of Hawai'i Press.

Stocking, George, W., Jr. 1968. *Race Culture and Evolution: Essays in the History of Anthropology*. New York: Free Press.

_____. 1973. From Chronology to Ethnology: James Cowles Prichard and British Anthropology 1800-1850. In James Cowles Prichard, *Researches into the Physical History of Man*, ed. George W. Stocking, Jr., ix-cx. Chicago: University of Chicago Press.

_____. 1987. *Victorian Anthropology*. New York: Free Press.

_____. 1996. *After Tylor: British Social Anthropology, 1888-1951*. London: Athlone.

Strzelecki, Paul Edmund de. 1845. *Physical Description of New South Wales and Van Diemen's Land: Accompanied by a Geological Map, Sections and Diagrams, and Figures of the Organic Remains*. London: Longman, Brown, Green and Longmans.

Tench, Watkin. 1793. *A Complete Account of the Settlement at Port Jackson, in New South Wales, Including an Accurate Description of the Situation of the Colony; of the Natives; and of its Natural Productions*. London: G. Nicol and J. Sewell.

Threlkeld, Lancelot Edward. 1828. *A Statement Chiefly Relating to the Formation and Abandonment of a Mission to the Aborigines of New South Wales; Addressed to the Serious Consideration of the Directors of the London Missionary Society*. Sydney: Government Printer.

_____. 1974. *Australian Reminiscences & Papers of L.E. Threlkeld, Missionary to the Aborigines, 1824-1859*, ed. Niel Gunson, 2 vols. Canberra: Australian Institute of Aboriginal Studies.

Trompf, Garry W. 1969. Friedrich Max Müller: Some Preliminary Chips from his German Workshop. *Journal of Religious History* 5:200-17.

Tylor, Edward Burnett. 1866. The Religion of Savages. *Fortnightly Review* 6:71-86.

_____. 1870. The Philosophy of Religion among the Lower Races of Mankind. *Journal of the Ethnological Society* 2:370-81.

_____. 1871. *Primitive Culture: Researches into the Development of Mythology, Philosophy, Religion, Language, Art and Custom*, 2 vols. London: John Murray.

Tylor, Edward Burnett, ed. 1874. *Notes and Queries on Anthropology, For the Use of Travellers and Residents in Uncivilised Lands*. London, British Association for the Advancement of Science.

Tyrrell, Alex. 1993. *A Sphere of Benevolence: the Life of Joseph Orton, Wesleyan Methodist Missionary (1795-1842)*. Melbourne: State Library of Victoria.

Virey, Julien-Joseph. 1824 [1800]. *Histoire naturelle du genre humain*, 3 vols. 2nd edition. Paris: Crochard.

Vitoria, Francisco de. 1991. *Francisco De Vitoria: Political Writings*, ed. Anthony Pagden and Jeremy Lawrance. Cambridge: Cambridge University Press.

Walls, Andrew. 2001. The Eighteenth Century Protestant Missionary Awakening. In *Christian Missions and the Enlightenment,* ed. Brian Stanley, 22-44. Grand Rapids, MI: William B. Eerdmans.

Watson, Richard. 1824. *The Religious Instruction of the Slaves in the West India Colonies, Advocated and Defended: a Sermon Preached before the Wesleyan Methodist Missionary Society, in the New Chapel, City-Road, London, April 28, 1824.* 4th edition. London: Butterworth and Son and Kershaw.

Wolfe, Patrick. 1994. 'White Man's Flour': Doctrines of Virgin Birth in Evolutionist Ethnogenetics and Australian State Formation. *History and Anthropology* 8:165-205.

Wright, N.E. 2001. The Problem of Aboriginal Evidence in Early Colonial New South Wales. In *Law, History and Colonialism: the Reach of Empire,* ed. Diane Kirkby and Catharine Coleborne, 140-56. Manchester: Manchester University Press.

Yarwood, A.T. 1977. *Samuel Marsden, the Great Survivor.* Carlton, VIC: Melbourne University Press.

Notes

[1] I acknowledge the fruitful discussions with Robert Kenny in which much of this paper was conceptualized.

[2] Biblical citations are from the *The New Revised Standard Bible, Oxford Annotated* (Metzger and Murphy 1991).

[3] Dwyer 1987:19; Sher 1985:13.

[4] The ontological debate on the relationship between people and God meant that the response to preaching was deeply entwined with ideas on the natural or God-given state of all people. These debates were marked by denominational distinctions: for example, in the mid-eighteenth century, the Presbyterian theologian Robert Wallace was convinced that the success achieved amongst Native Americans by the Baptist missionary David Brainerd and the conversions brought about in England and Scotland by the Evangelical Anglican George Whitefield resulted from the unfortunate excitation of natural passions that were present in all religions rather than from an appeal to natural reason or superior powers that could be found only in Christianity (Maxwell 2001:125).

[5] Watson 1824:4, 7, 8-9, original emphasis. Watson was an active supporter of the Anti-slavery Society and in 1830 he persuaded the Methodist Conference to depart from Wesley's argument against political involvement and urge Methodists to vote against slavery (Goldhawk 1978:119).

[6] Watson 1824:4, 7, original emphasis.

[7] Maxwell 2001:127; Tyrrell 1993:49.

[8] See Chapter One (Douglas), this volume, for detailed consideration of the scientific positions on man taken by Virey and Lawrence.

[9] Stanley 2001:187; Gunson 1974:10-11; Yarwood 1977:241.

[10] Samson 2001:109; Stocking 1987:48-53.

[11] Prichard 1836-47, I:165-216. The Moravians were the first of the modern Protestant missionary societies. In an outburst of missionary zeal between 1734-37, this church sent missionaries to slaves in the West Indies, to Greenland, South Africa, the Dutch East Indies, and to Amerindians under the instructions and patronage of Count von Zinzendorf. Andrew Walls (2001:30-2) claims that the British Evangelical and missionary movement owed much to Continental Pietism and the Moravian example. John Wesley was converted at a Moravian meeting in London.

[12] Prichard 1836-47, I:170, 212; Prichard, quoted in Stocking 1973:lxxxiv.

[13] E.g., in London, the tensions and differences between the Ethnological and Anthropological Societies can be read in their responses to the Jamaica uprising in 1866 that was brutally suppressed by Governor Edward John Eyre (1815-1901). The Ethnological Society joined humanitarians in condemning Eyre's response while the Anthropological Society, believing that Negroes were a different species, held that the suppression of the uprising was proper given the immutable distinctions between black and white people (Stocking 1987:251).

[14] Gardner 2006a:89; Gunson 1965:310; Stanley 1990:68-78.

[15] Gardner 2006b; Owens 1970:289-303; Sanneh 1989:193-7.

[16] Müller 1976, I:302-3; Stocking 1996:18, 34, 44.

[17] Bridges 1993:34; Gunson 1974:24-5.

[18] It is evidence of the significance of the debate that the Aborigines who gave this account to Strzelecki were almost certainly making some syncretic analysis of the Christian God and Aboriginal belief. Strezlecki was dealing with Aboriginal groups who had been in direct or indirect contact with Europeans for up to fifty years. Therefore, they would almost certainly have heard something about the European religion prior to their meeting with the explorer. Yet the point was politically significant and Strzelecki made it within the context of the debate about Aboriginal humanity.

[19] As a young boy, Lubbock was befriended by his near neighbour Darwin who oversaw his first scientific publication. The geologist Charles Lyell (1797-1875) sponsored Lubbock's election to the Geological Society and he was acquainted through his membership of royal societies with most of the well known scientific figures of the period, including Huxley, Wallace, Spencer, Tylor, and Galton (Rivière 1978:xix).

[20] I concur with Stocking that it is important not to overdraw the connections between Darwinian evolution and theories of cultural development. While theorists such as Tylor and Müller were clearly in discussion with Darwinian notions of natural selection, the primary influences on their ideas of cultural change were pre-Darwinian, in particular the work of Prichard (Stocking 1968:91-109).

[21] The point was particularly pertinent to Archbishop Richard Whately's case against evolutionism which Lubbock addressed in an appendix to *The Origin of Civilisation* (1870:337-62). The appendix includes a counter-attack on the Duke of Argyll's degenerationist arguments against Lubbock's earlier work *Pre-historic Times* (1865) (Stocking 1987:160).

[22] Tylor 1866:71; 1870:370; 1871, I:378.

[23] Gunson 1978:21; Müller 1976, I:302; Stocking 1996:34.

[24] Brown to Fison, 6 January 1872; Brown to Pratt, 4 April 1879, in Brown 1876-80. Many of Brown's contemporaries had also read Lubbock. His colleagues Lorimer Fison and Robert Codrington were both disdainful of the text (Stocking 1996:17, 40). However, Fison's partner in his anthropological work, the Victorian police magistrate and anthropologist A.W. Howitt, was inspired by Lubbock's earlier book *Pre-historic Times* (Mulvaney 1981:57).

[25] Stocking 1987:248-62; see Chapter Four (Turnbull), this volume.

[26] Frazer to Brown, 9 February 1889, in Brown 1877-1914.

[27] Kuper 1988:76-91; Sanneh 1996:43.

[28] Frazer to Brown, 9 February 1889, in Brown 1877-1914.

[29] This discussion resurfaced in the late twentieth century. Wolfe (1994:165-205) proposed a problematic reading of the correlation between the conclusions formulated on Arrernte theories of conception and subsequent colonial policies to contain miscegenation whereas Mallet (1995:41-58) discussed the issue reflectively.

Chapter Seven

'White Man's Burden', 'White Man's Privilege': Christian humanism and racial determinism in Oceania, 1890-1930

Christine Weir

The contribution of Protestant Pacific missionary correspondents, including Robert Henry Codrington (1830-1922) and George Brown (1835-1917), to the development of anglophone social evolutionary theories during the latter half of the nineteenth century is well documented by scholars.[1] The theorists Henry Maine (1822-1888), John Lubbock (1834-1913), John McLennan (1827-1881), Lewis Henry Morgan (1818-1881), and Edward Burnett Tylor (1832-1917) were writing in the metropoles and were thus reliant for their data on firsthand accounts of exotic people produced by others. These theorists attempted in various ways to systematize the assumption — longstanding and sometimes explicit as in the writings of the eighteenth-century Scottish stadial theorists — that human beings progress through a universal sequence of stages from primitive to civilized. To comprehend the origins of modern civilized society, one had to look to the 'primitive' societies of the contemporary present. The presupposition, variously identified as 'classical evolutionism' or 'social evolutionism', that the non-European world provided theorists with a living museum of the history of present-day Western society was well entrenched by the middle of the nineteenth century. As Stocking neatly put it:

> Contemporaneity in space was therefore converted into succession in time by re-arranging the cultural forms coexisting in the Victorian present along an axis of assumed structural or ideational archaism — from the simple to the complex, or from that which human reason showed was manifestly primitive to that which habitual association established as obviously civilized (1987:173).

The equation of the European past with the primitive present and the consequent establishment of developmental rules appealed to the legal minds of Maine and McLennan. But it was also a profoundly progressivist notion containing the implicit assumption that Europeans had climbed furthest up the universal ladder of social progress.

The growing attractiveness of a social evolutionist understanding of human difference was influenced but not determined by Darwinism. Maine's 1861 treatise on the development of legal structures, *Ancient Law*, used Old Testament and Roman history to surmise that law had originated with status-based patriarchal authority and moved towards a contractual state only in recent times.[2] This was not a universal approach amongst evolutionary theorists: McLennan, in his work on the development of marriage, attempted to explain the institution of marriage 'in naturalistic developmental terms' rather than using Biblical evidence (Stocking 1987:167). But all saw contemporary Western Christian (male) society as the zenith of human achievement and saw the increasing complexity of religious concepts and practice as fundamentally linked to changes in other elements of society. In working out their theoretical models, the early anglophone anthropologists drew heavily for ethnographic evidence on the writings of missionaries, especially those stationed in Oceania. Oceanic missionaries contributed to learned anthropological journals and their expertise was acknowledged by Tylor, Sir James Frazer (1854-1941), Maine, and Morgan.

Armchair anthropology and missionary ethnography

Missionary collaboration with metropolitan theorists was welcomed at least in part because of the increased interest in religious belief and practice emanating from the studies in language and religion of Friedrich Max Müller (1823-1900), as well as in marriage patterns or forms of legal authority, as indicators of evolutionary status.[3] Tylor, continuing such investigations, corresponded with missionaries in Oceania and assisted in publishing their ethnographic descriptions of indigenous religions in such periodicals as the *Journal of the Royal Anthropological Institute* (later *Man*). He did so despite the tendency of missionaries to dispute theoretical generalizations in order to assert the uniqueness and value of the communities they knew and lived amongst. At least in principle, missionary arguments and ethnography were always underpinned by the assumption that all human beings were capable of progress towards a 'higher state' since all were valuable in God's sight.[4] They took seriously St. Paul's dictum that 'there is neither Greek nor Jew, circumcision nor uncircumcision, Barbarian, Scythian, bond nor free: but Christ is all, and in all' (Colossians 3:11).[5] Those working in Melanesia also had a particular desire to prevent 'their' people from being placed near the bottom ranks of any theoretical model. Helen Gardner (2006:114-20, 127) has documented the unease of the Methodist George Brown, writing from experience in Samoa and New Britain, with the widely held distinction drawn between Polynesians and Melanesians. Brown's disagreement with Frazer over totemism demonstrated the 'tension' between Brown's acknowledgement of 'the logic of social evolutionist theory' and his simultaneous resolve 'to temper the implications of its findings'. This subversive impulse came from his 'Christian insistence on human similitude' but also from a deep and close familiarity with the people amongst whom he had long lived. Broad generalizations satisfied few of the missionary ethnographers who had personal knowledge of counter-examples. In his academic writings, the Anglican missionary Codrington (1881:313) disputed Tylor's contention that the belief in souls originated in speculation about the meaning of dreams, for his personal experience amongst the Banks Islanders (of what is now north Vanuatu) was that no such link was made. Codrington (1889:310) complicated any easy relationship between forbidden foods and totems, suggesting that many taboos were of a recent origin and somewhat ad hoc in nature. Although direct and prolonged contact with Islanders led to writing which emphasized local specificity, potentially subverting universalist developmental models, such empirically-based ethnographic work by missionaries remained acceptable in metropolitan scientific circles.

John Barker (1996:111) has suggested that the collaboration with metropolitan theorists also changed missionary attitudes with their scientific work 'mark[ing] a notable instance of the "capture" of missionary ethnography by a professionalizing anthropology, based on the discourse of the natural sciences'. Yet he also noted that this scientific turn was complemented by a 'gradually liberalizing mood in the missionary movement as a whole', with a complex interaction between different perspectives. The collaboration with metropolitan theorists strengthened a tendency, which had been apparent in some considerably earlier missionary writings such as those of the Methodist Thomas Williams (1815-1891) on Fiji, to see traditional religion in systematic terms rather than just as a collection of abhorrent practices. In his representation of a Fijian religious system (1858), Williams began to valorize it in powerful, positive terms (Herbert 1991; Weir 1998), thus anticipating the social evolutionary view that all people had some form of religion which marked a definable stage in human religious and social development. By around 1890, the view was widely held both by theorists and by many of their missionary collaborators that early religions should be 'respected for their place in preparing humankind for higher religions' (Gunson 1994:303). This opinion was especially strong amongst Anglicans but John Henry Holmes (1866-1943) of the London Missionary Society (LMS), who worked with members of the 1898 Cambridge anthropological expedition to Torres Straits and with other anthropologists, expressed similar attitudes. In his own writings, partly under the influence of the leader of the Torres Straits expedition, Alfred Haddon (1855-1940), Holmes moved from a position of revulsion at the religious practices of the Elema of the Papuan Gulf to a sensitivity to the importance of their traditional beliefs, in particular in the lives of older people (Reid 1978).

The naturalness of race and the challenge of experience

However, between 1900 and the 1920s, in the context of the institutionalization of a fieldwork-based professional ethnography, this publicly acknowledged symbiosis between missionary informant in the field and metropolitan theorist gradually broke down. While the Anglican priests Charles Elliot Fox (1878-1974) and Walter George Ivens (1871-1940), as well as the LMS missionaries William James Viritahitemauvai Saville (1873-1948) and Holmes, continued to publish in anthropological journals until the 1930s, scientific contributions from anglophone missionaries declined though they remained acknowledged experts in the linguistic field. Before and during this period, missionary activity in Oceania was in transition from the exuberance of the era of early conversions to the routine work of educating and guiding converts — less glamorous and more frustrating than pioneer work. Some of the perceived faults in converts, seen originally as manifestations of heathenism, persisted. Missionaries began to question whether such faults were also the result of 'inferiority' or 'backwardness'. In times of frustration, they tended to endorse what had long been a widespread popular sentiment — that supposed 'backwardness' and 'inferiority' were inherently *physical* qualities, deemed either immutable or capable of change only in the very long term, rather than attributes of the presence or absence of heathenism. Such distinctions were often couched in terms of the varying levels of progress achieved by different 'races'.

A belief in the existence of separate, physically discrete races was held by many writers, secular and religious, over most of the period under discussion. Indeed, the term race was embedded in contemporary discourses, its meaning ranging from a generally benign descriptor of physical human appearance to a highly value-laden and proscriptive demarcator of unbridgeable human difference. Missionaries tended to use race in something approaching the former sense. This paper investigates some of the nuances in their understanding of human difference. Such beliefs were rooted in their Christianity and yet partook of widely-held ideas originating in contemporary scientific or legal circles.

Racialist assumptions informed the gloomy evolutionism which saw the Methodist John Burton (1875-1970) equate long-Christian Fijians with 'adolescents' who are 'proverbially difficult to manage' and 'make unreasonable demands on patience and resource' (1926:3). His colleague William Bennett (1914:475-6) found teaching Fijians 'a slow and tedious process' and complained of a 'half-knowledge ... ready to beget a loud-mouthed boasting'. Yet Bennett held such views in tension with his confidence that 'a native Church indigenous to the soil, withal so strong and stable in Christian character that it can stand of itself', was being developed. Another Methodist, John Francis Goldie (1870-1954), referred to the people of Roviana in the western Solomon Islands as having recently been 'Stone Age savages' (1927:4). But earlier he also described his weekly class, listing each man by name (1914:574-6): one was 'a living epistle, a monument of God's power to save'; another was Goldie's constant and valued assistant. Goldie and Bennett knew and respected individual Islanders. Evolutionist language, normalized in popular discourse, slipped into their writing and yet was tempered by personal experience of individual Islanders which moderated any racial generalizations and confirmed their underlying Christian belief in human similitude. Just as missionary anthropologists tended to subvert the developmentalist paradigm by insisting on the discrete nature of their subjects and resisted their placement within a rigid theoretical framework, so many of the writers in the Methodist centenary volume (1914), edited by James Colwell (1860-1930), emphasized the skills, the positive attributes, and the great progress achieved by the people with whom they worked. The celebratory nature of the volume accentuated this tendency: these 'darkness-to-light' stories, rooted within the great narrative tradition of Christian progress, generally eschewed evolutionary language. Any overt or tacit acceptance of social evolutionism based on biological or racial presuppositions remained interwoven with descriptions of particular societies and individuals with unique value and potentiality in the sight of God. The trajectory envisaged for them was a rather different developmental path, from 'heathen darkness' to the 'light' of Christianity, through which they could realize their human potential in this life and have salvation in the next.

The concurrent acceptance within missionary and church circles of varying, even antithetical, discourses about human beings can be seen in two 'Study Circle books' on the Pacific Islands: John Burton's *The Call of the Pacific* (1912) and Frank Paton's *The Kingdom of the Pacific* (1913).[6] Both were designed to instruct Protestant congregations in Britain and Australia about missionary endeavours in the Pacific Islands and to foster their financial and moral support or, as Burton (1912:1) put it, 'to set forth … the great needs which still clamour from the Isles of the Seas'. Yet there are some distinct differences between the two books, unremarked at the time in reviews or advertisements — which may show how common it was for apparently divergent discourses and vocabulary to be used in tandem. Burton's work incorporated more strident social evolutionist language and concepts than was usual in missionary texts. He ranked Islanders according to well-established stereotypes. Of Fijians, he commented:

> The people are of a lower grade than the Tongans, Samoans, Tahitians, and Maoris. They have not nearly the same intellectual development, and their civilization is of a coarser order. They are, in turn, superior to the Western peoples of New Hebrides, New Britain, and New Guinea. The race gives evidences of greater capability than has had opportunity to realise itself. There seems a sort of 'arrested development' (1912:92-3).

Burton's relative lack of confidence in the abilities of Islanders and his readiness to use normalized evolutionist judgements about them must be seen against his personal experience. He had served as a missionary in the Pacific region for ten years but worked mostly with indentured Indians in the Rewa area of Viti Levu in Fiji, though he was involved in industrial training schemes for Fijian boys. What he lacked was any personal knowledge of Fijian village communities and his limited familiarity with the Fijian chiefly system left him unimpressed.[7] In writing *The Call of the Pacific*, Burton relied on the accounts of secular writers and other missionaries; this lent a degree of detachment and a somewhat theoretical air to his writing. The personal did not complicate his theoretical hierarchies.

By contrast, Frank Paton (1870-1938) had lifelong experience of Islanders. Born and brought up on his father's mission station in the New Hebrides (now Vanuatu), he returned there after education in Australia and Europe as a missionary in his own right for several years. His personal appreciation of certain Islanders was such that he ended his earlier book about his years on Tanna with the words (1903:311): 'We may travel far afield in the providence of God, but we shall never meet with nobler or more Christlike men than Lomai and his brave fellow teachers. They are heroes, every one of them, God's Heroes'. Any ranking of Islanders, such as Burton's which put New Hebrideans near the bottom of an evolutionary hierarchy, offended Paton's childhood experiences and most that had come after it.

Accordingly, *The Kingdom in the Pacific*, though published only a year after Burton's book, used different language and arguments. Paton (1913:2-3) did not hesitate to expound on the 'evils' of the pre-Christian Pacific Islands, cannibalism, war, and widow-strangling, and like most other missionary commentators saw this 'depravity' as induced by the thraldom of pagan religion. But the relatively unsophisticated lifeways of Pacific Islanders were attributed to geographic isolation rather than an inherent lack of ability. He employed a discourse of Christian humanism which was universalist in its assumption of human value, emphasized economic and geographic explanations for differing levels of human development, and stressed European responsibility for aiding human progress in the Pacific region. Burton (1912:299), while regarding independent indigenous churches as the ultimate aim of missionary endeavour, believed that 'these newly-won people require the greatest care in treatment ... we must not force their growth'. Paton (1913:76) envisaged the development of indigenous churches with a 'strong native ministry, composed of men and women who are filled with faith' as a closer reality.

Internationalism and its enemies

Paton's resistance to theoretical racial hierarchy, based on personal experience particularly in Melanesia, was not new — Codrington and many other humanitarians had written in a similar vein. Where Paton marked new ground was in the degree of his conviction about metropolitan responsibility for the welfare of Pacific Islanders, not just in converting them to Christianity but in ensuring justice, education, and a place for them in a rapidly changing world. Paton (1913:142-3) consciously introduced a new international discourse of Christian humanism into the Pacific missionary world: he cited the discussions of the World Missionary Conference held in Edinburgh in 1910, a worldwide ecumenical gathering incorporating most of the mainline English-speaking Protestant missions, as the authority for his opinions.[8] This gathering, attended by metropolitan mission administrators, serving (white) missionaries, and also by some indigenous African and Asian church leaders, was seen by many missionaries as their first opportunity to consider their own work in an international context. As Charles Fry Rich (1872-1949), an LMS missionary from Papua, put it (Anon. 1910:148): 'We climbed high enough to behold the need of a whole world for a whole gospel of redemption, carried to it by a whole Church'. The conference discussed, amongst other things, the role of the churches in education, the growth of the indigenous priesthood and independent churches, and 'the growing desire of Eastern peoples to realize themselves, to work out their particular national life, and not to be cast into Western moulds', an aspiration which was regarded with 'strong sympathy' (Anon. 1910:146).

Influenced by such internationalist rhetoric, Paton's appeal to European obligation was couched in wide terms. To an unusual degree, the prime villain was European influence in general. While his father John G. Paton, a veteran missionary in the New Hebrides, had denounced labour traders and beachcombers at length and with vigour (Weir 2003:95-142), Frank Paton cast doubt on the whole colonial enterprise. After enumerating the evils of alcohol, guns, and labour-recruitment, he concluded that they were not outweighed by the benefits of settled government or new opportunities. He asked:

> Can we look back upon the record of our impact upon the black man without a blush of shame? We have done them much good, but more evil … If it is true that we who are strong ought to bear the burden of the weak, then we have a terrible past to atone for, and a great work before us which we have hardly begun to touch as yet. Surely this is a national duty, the white man's burden and the white man's privilege (1913:35).

This passage includes allusions to two texts which became particularly popular in internationalist missionary discourse through the 1920s: 'we who are strong ought to bear the burden of the weak' comes from Paul's letter to the Romans 15:1; 'the white man's burden' derives, of course, from Rudyard Kipling's poem of the same title (1899).[9] Thus the secular and religious responsibilities of strong and powerful nations were linked, as educators and protectors of native peoples, as beneficent colonial administrators, and also as evangelists.

Ideas such as Paton's gained new urgency in response to the stridently determinist racist rhetoric emanating immediately after World War I from American secular writers such as Madison Grant (1865-1937) and Lothrop Stoddard (1883-1950). Grant (1921, 1920) and Stoddard (1920, 1922) began writing during the War but their works had greatest impact in the 1920s when they were reprinted, translated, and widely disseminated. They warned of an impending global race war as the 'natural' superiority of the European races was challenged by recent internal civil war (which was how they represented World War I) and by resistance from other races. Colonized people would fight to be free of domination, claimed Stoddard. Africa, important as 'the natural source of Europe's tropical raw materials and foodstuffs', and Latin America could not possibly 'stand alone'; strong European rule was essential (Stoddard 1920:89, 103).

The basis of their arguments lay in biological determinism. Grant (1920:xix) claimed that the 'great lesson of race is the immutability of somatological or bodily characteristics, with which is closely associated the immutability of psychic disposition and impulses'. He invoked Weismann's work on cellular structure and his theory of 'germ plasm' to decry the 'fatuous belief in the power of environment' which he saw as an idea stemming from 'loose thinkers and sentimentalists' (Grant 1921:15-16). Several other scientific tendencies around the turn of the century also reinvigorated a popular view of heredity based on biological determinism. Galton's statistical modelling and the rediscovery of Mendelian genetics provided a mechanism for Darwinian natural selection (Shipman 1994:113-16).[10] These developments, along with the 1904 foundation of the Eugenics Record Office in the US and Charles Davenport's studies of eugenics conducted at Cold Spring Harbor Laboratory, gave a certain credibility to the demands of Grant and Stoddard for 'world-eugenics' to avoid the mixing of races and to encourage the 'highest' to reproduce.[11] Since the laws of nature determined that biology and heredity were everything, Grant and Stoddard claimed, then direct rule by those of 'worth and merit' should be the norm, thus undermining democracy. Only amongst the most advanced of the Europeans, the 'Nordics',[12] should it even be considered. Biological determinists could attack democracy and socialism on racial grounds and discount them as sentimental.

In Australia, Christian writers concerned with inter-racial issues believed that such doctrines had to be confronted. John Burton's acceptance of something approaching a biologically-determined evolutionism and his use of evolutionist language in describing Fijians, evident in *The Call of the Pacific,* must be seen alongside the campaign he waged from around 1909 against the indenture of Indians in the Fiji sugar-fields (Weir 2003:163-83). Burton (1909:15-16) raised the ire of colonial officials by describing plantation accommodation where 'coolies are herded together like so many penned cattle amid the most insanitary conditions and indescribable filth' and in concluding that 'the difference between this state and slavery is merely in the name and the term of years'. This humanitarian concern was coupled with respect for the Hindu religious and philosophic system, especially as expressed by the more learned members of the community. Accounts of his dialogues with Hindu leader Totaram Sanadhya present two intelligent men, each determined not to be converted by the other, enjoying a stimulating debate about life, death and everything in between.[13] Burton (1903:8) also described encounters with other Hindu religious leaders. He was prepared to pray and worship with Hindus, even if he found the music 'weird'. But this respect for Indian culture and religion was contrasted with his ambivalence about Fijian customs which he essentialized and framed with evolutionist assumptions. Fijians had practical skills, Indians intellectual ones.

John Burton's position moved closer to that of Paton after the First World War — during which he served as a YMCA chaplain in London — and the peace settlement. His writing developed greater emphasis on obligation and showed less use of evolutionist language. Influencing this shift was Burton's increased involvement in the International Missionary Council, growing friendship with Frank Paton, and further academic studies in philosophy at the University of Melbourne.[14] His increasing personal knowledge and appreciation of individual Fijian missionaries and other Islanders through his visits to Papua and New Britain as General Secretary of the Australian Methodist Missionary Society in the 1920s appear to have changed his thinking further. On these visits he saw Fijian teachers and ministers working effectively: the earlier disdain bred mostly of ignorance was replaced by respect for individuals (Burton 1926).

The degree to which the discourse of humanitarian obligation complemented Burton's earlier evolutionist assumptions becomes clear in his reactions to the vociferous biological evolutionism emanating from the United States. In his review of Stoddard's pro-eugenics tract *The Revolt against Civilization*, Burton (1922:11) advanced ethical and spiritual claims to counter the determinism of biology, notwithstanding his own earlier recourse to biological images: 'Biology deals only with a fraction of life; its fingers are too clumsy and its methods too coarse to deal with the soul of man'. The individual could be changed purposefully by wise men under the guidance of God. Christian commentators saw the violence and appeal to force implicit in the writings of Stoddard and Grant as dangerous and immoral. The very stridency of the new recourse to biological determinism forced critics to modify, if not entirely reject, their own much milder use of such arguments. In another review, Burton (1924:1) described Stoddard's later book *The Rising Tide of Color* as 'striking but shallow'; it tried 'to foment feeling against other races' and in doing so was 'unchristian'.

The 'sacred trust of civilization' in New Guinea

This shifting emphasis and its accompanying discourse were exemplified in the debates within Australia on the League of Nations mandate over New Guinea. Many Christians accepted the ideals inherent in the League of Nations as a mechanism that would maintain peace and ensure the past war could never be repeated. This vision, most notably connected with the United States President Woodrow Wilson (1856-1924), aimed to 'vindicate the principles of peace and justice in the life of the world as against selfish and autocratic power' through councils of collective security which would intervene to prevent quarrels escalating.[15] Wilson, the son of a Presbyterian minister, was profoundly motivated by Christian belief and ethics which underpinned his public life. He believed in a covenant between God and human beings within which human beings had the responsibility to strive to give the world structure and order (Mulder 1978:269-77). The Covenant of the League of Nations, with its provision for regular conferences, marked the culmination of that vision — but the failure of the United States to ratify the covenant or take part in conference deliberations undermined the whole system. Grant's (1920:xxx) demand that the 'Nordic' race 'discard altruism' and the 'vain phantom of internationalism', which he believed to be both unscientific and potentially dangerous, resonated with the views of more conservative American politicians. Subsequent judgement on the League of Nations has been harsh but the major powers systematically deprived it of any ability to be effective, mostly by absenting themselves. Yet in Australia and the Pacific Islands, the League of Nations Covenant did have a particular importance, perhaps validating the comment by Norman Davies (1996:950) that the League 'played a major role in the management of minor issues, and a negligible role in the management of major ones'. For under the terms of Article 22 of the Covenant, Australia gained a mandate over the former German New Guinea. While Wilsonian principles generally disapproved of colonialism and supported self-government for smaller states, it was recognized that some peoples were 'not yet able to stand by themselves under the strenuous conditions of the modern world'. In such cases their 'well-being and development ... form[ed] a sacred trust of civilization', a duty which, in the case of New Guinea, devolved to Australia.[16]

But if Christians accepted the responsibility inherent in such a mandate, much popular and government opinion disagreed with them. In May 1921, the military government of the former German New Guinea was replaced by a civilian administration under the terms of the League of Nations mandate. Exactly what this mandate meant was the source of considerable tension within Australia. Prime Minister William Morris Hughes (1862-1952) saw control of New Guinea as a strategic matter, ensuring that 'the great rampart of islands stretching around the north-east of Australia' would, as he had demanded at Versailles, be 'held by us or by some Power in whom we have absolute confidence'. For Hughes, possession of New Guinea formed a sizeable part of the reparations due to Australia (Hudson 1980:27-30).[17] He rejected Wilsonian idealism and regarded the adoption of the Fourteen Points as 'an error — of judgement if you like'.[18] That was in public. His language in private was much less temperate and his hostility to Wilson unrelenting.[19] Others agreed with him in seeing New Guinea's importance in terms of what it might offer to Australia and not vice versa. The majority (Attlee Hunt and Walter H. Lucas) of the commissioners considering the form of administration for the mandated territory stated that 'the best and most humane principles' should govern the treatment only if this was 'consistent with the promotion of industrial enterprises tending to the benefit of the whole community', which included a large number of returned soldiers to be settled on the ex-German plantations. The 'evolution of the native' would consist in his moving 'from being a mere chattel of an employer to becoming an asset of the State'. The 'sacred trust of civilization' demanded by the mandate could be fulfilled by abolishing flogging.[20]

An alternative view was put by Hubert Murray (1861-1940), the chair but also the minority voice on the Commission. Murray had been Administrator of the Australian colony of Papua since 1906; his mode of government, though subject to both contemporary and modern criticism, was widely seen as taking into serious account the interests and concerns of the indigenous people and he regarded his administration as the obvious model for the newly mandated territory of New Guinea. The demands of Article 22 could not be satisfied if the development of the country was 'solely in the interests of the European settler' and if the 'natural duty of the native' was perceived to be 'to assist the European with his labour'.[21] Hence he advocated maintaining expropriated German plantations as a Government-owned business 'in the public interest'.[22] But Murray's vision did not prevail, and the majority report was accepted.

However, there were also strands of public opinion which supported Murray's view that the mandate was a 'sacred trust', expressed by people who, as far as they could, monitored the administration of the mandated territory. In May 1921, the month that the Australians assumed the mandate administration of New Guinea, the Methodist *Missionary Review* carried a remarkable image, apparently designed as a poster (Figure 18). The creator of the image is not named but it was probably Burton who was actively involved with the *Missionary Review* in 1921 and formally took over as editor in May 1922. Entitled 'Our Two Mandates', the poster juxtaposes state and Christian responsibilities. The left side carries two texts: the quotation from Article 22 of the League Charter concerning the 'sacred trust' and the first stanza of Kipling's poem 'The White Man's Burden' invoke the responsibilities of the Commonwealth. Balancing these on the right are the same citation from Paul's letter to the Romans earlier used by Paton and part of the missionary hymn by Bishop Heber of Calcutta, 'From Greenland's icy mountains', marking the responsibilities of the Australian churches. The dominant stress is on obligation, both secular and religious, with the implicit assumption that they were complementary. There is no distinction on the map between the mandated territory and Papua; the obligations are assumed to apply to both. Interestingly, the Melanesian figure is not, as in many appeals, that of a child or young woman but an adult male with traditional facial markings and body ornamentation. This could be read as conveying the depth of the need and the difficulty of the endeavour; certainly it is no mere sentimental appeal.

Yet alongside the language of duty and obligation and the reference to modern secular political realities, indeed, immediately below the words of the Covenant of the League of Nations, recourse is had to the ongoing language of social evolution: 'the Brown Pacific' needs the 'help and guidance of a higher race'. The word 'paternalism', with its inherent tensions, sums up this attitude — in both its more usual negative sense and in its appeal to fatherly care. This is made explicit in a lecture Burton gave in 1921 in which he compared humanity to a family with older, stronger members and also young, weak, 'less-equipped and undeveloped members'.

> The true objective, if the family is to be perfect in all its relations, is to bring [the weak] into such a position where they might rightfully claim, without danger to themselves or others, the fullest privileges and the highest powers. 'Self-determination' is only latently theirs; and processes of education and training must be devised in order that they may come to full stature, and thus be able to discharge their responsibilities.
>
> This is only possible when the stronger members are prepared to aid, to the utmost of their powers, the weaker and less advantaged members (1921:3).[23]

To perform this task was the reason, and the only reason, why Australia had been granted the mandate over New Guinea. In a striking conjunction of social evolutionism and humanist insight, Burton represented New Guineans as simultaneously 'inferior races' but with 'undeveloped' potential:

> The Mandate is over undeveloped races. They have some measure of skill and capacity; but it is the skill of the stone age; the capacity of an untutored savage. We are asking them to perform a stupendous feat. We are proposing to them that in one gigantic leap they spring from the Stone Age, where we found them yesterday, to the Steel Age, where we are today. Consider what mental and social adjustment is required in such a movement! We have only to think back over a modern period in our own history, to provide ourselves with an illustration of the

difficulties connected with such a change ... What patient help and gracious chivalry then ought we not to extend to these inferior races who are asked to make adjustments far more profound that those we have attempted in our superior life (1921:5).

Figure 18: Anon., 'Our Two Mandates'.[24]

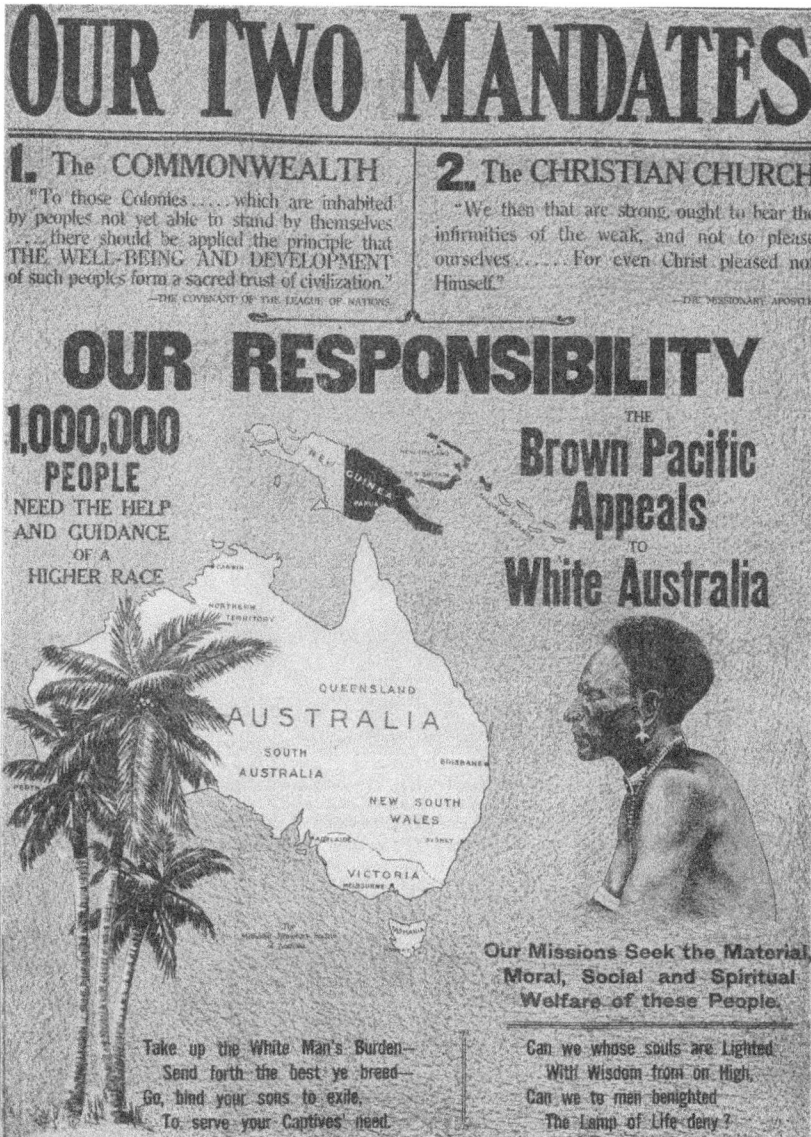

OUR TWO MANDATES

1. The COMMONWEALTH

"To those Colonies ..... which are inhabited by peoples not yet able to stand by themselves ... there should be applied the principle that THE WELL-BEING AND DEVELOPMENT of such peoples form a sacred trust of civilization."

—THE COVENANT OF THE LEAGUE OF NATIONS

2. The CHRISTIAN CHURCH

"We then that are strong, ought to bear the infirmities of the weak, and not to please ourselves ...... For even Christ pleased not Himself."

—THE MISSIONARY APOSTLE

OUR RESPONSIBILITY

1,000,000 PEOPLE NEED THE HELP AND GUIDANCE OF A HIGHER RACE

THE **Brown Pacific Appeals** TO **White Australia**

AUSTRALIA

NORTHERN TERRITORY
QUEENSLAND
SOUTH AUSTRALIA
NEW SOUTH WALES
VICTORIA

Our Missions Seek the Material, Moral, Social and Spiritual Welfare of these People.

Take up the White Man's Burden—
Send forth the best ye breed—
Go, bind your sons to exile,
To serve your Captives' need.

Can we whose souls are Lighted
With Wisdom from on High,
Can we to men benighted
The Lamp of Life deny?

Poster. JAF 266.7MIS. Canberra: National Library of Australia.

The poster and the lecture, with their blend of evolutionism and the discourse of philanthropic/humanitarian obligation, epitomize the support for a vision of the League of Nations which existed both within the churches and outside. An active League of Nations Union in Melbourne aimed to educate citizens 'to equip themselves to discharge their responsibilities for a National undertaking' (Eggleston 1928: frontispiece). In seminars and 'round tables' about the mandate for New Guinea addressed by both church and secular figures, the desire was expressed to administer New Guinea with greater humanity than had been achieved with Aboriginal people. The League of Nations was seen as the model. Within church circles, enthusiasm was not confined to the Methodists and the claims made for the League of Nations could be effusive. The editor of the Anglican *A.B.M. Review* saw the Covenant's 'great principles of international brotherhood, co-operation and responsibility' as 'fundamentally Christian principles' and their adoption as 'due to Christian missionary work'.[25] W.N. Lawrence, an LMS missionary writing from Papua, believed that the formation of the League was 'a step towards the realization of the brotherhood of man and the Kingdom of God on the earth' (*Chronicle*, March 1919:41). The Australian Student Christian Movement backed the League of Nations as 'an institution whose principles were entirely in harmony with Christian ethics', welcomed the New Guinea Mandate, and urged members to use their influence 'to encourage the Federal Government in carrying out the high ideals of Article xxii of the Covenant'. International topics, including the White Australia Policy and policy towards the mandated territories, should be studied by student groups.[26]

In New Guinea, any interference by 'do-gooder anthropologists, missionaries, or presumed agents of the League of Nations' was resented by the new Administration and by European settlers (Nelson 1998). This did not stop continued surveillance by interested Christian and secular parties over the administration of the mandate. In 1928, Burton castigated the military ethos of the administration for 'hasty and dogmatic' decision-making, over-use of the indenture system which took men away from their villages, inadequate attention to preventative health measures, and an unsuitable (that is, too literary) education system; his essay (1928) was published in an academic political science study. Concern about the mandate and issues surrounding its administration meant that Australian Christian voices were now taking part in international debates. The issues of justice, social concern, and international relations which had been discussed within a limited milieu at the 1910 World Missionary Conference were now at the international centre stage and Australians, as citizens of a mandated power, had become major players.

Christianity and the race problem

People like Burton who were trying to promote an alternative to biological determinism welcomed the publication in 1924 of J.H. Oldham's *Christianity and the Race Problem.* In December of that year, Burton (1824), as editor of the Methodist *Missionary Review*, devoted his editorial to an extended review of this work, noting that it was only one of many on the subject, for 'books on the problems of race are pouring forth from the press at an astonishing rate, and the popular magazines are printing numbers of articles dealing with the "menace" of the coloured peoples'. Joseph Houldsworth Oldham (1874-1969) had been a missionary in India in the 1890s who became organizing secretary for the Edinburgh World Missionary Conference and then the editor of the *International Review of Missions*, a journal instigated at the Edinburgh Conference. He was never ordained but brought a more secular internationalist outlook to missionary affairs. His book, rather than talking of 'menace' or of 'fan[ning] the flames of race hatred and jealousy', advocated that Europeans 'cultivate the friendly spirit, help the backward peoples and build up the City of God on this fair earth', an aim of which Burton approved (1924:1-2). The book was widely recommended in missionary circles in Australia and Europe.[27]

Here was a cogently argued rebuttal of the 'scientific' racism of Stoddard and Grant. While he did not entirely eschew evolutionary language, Oldham's treatise is a sophisticated attempt to develop an alternative Christian analysis of racial relations by attacking the determinism of Stoddard and Grant, both of whom are cited, on scientific, economic, and ethical grounds. Where Stoddard saw biological race as the determining factor, Oldham's explanation for what he took as differential development incorporated history, culture, and geographic circumstance. This essentially environmentalist argument, which saw race (though he preferred the word 'peoples') as a sociological rather than a biological concept, recognized a potential for progressivist change and development and reasserted the principle of the psychic unity of mankind.[28] Oldham (1924:52-3) even questioned the dominance of the idea of natural selection, suggesting that the Lamarckian theory of transmission of acquired characteristics had not been disproved. With this assumption, he emphasized education and argued that social and economic gaps could thus be bridged (1924:76, 164).[29] But communities of blood or culture should not override the importance of the individual, each of whom was important with a 'uniqueness and value' in the sight of God. With this emphasis on the individual, Oldham (1924:82) undercut statistics which purport to show differential racial intelligence and mental characteristics. Using material from Franz Boas (1858-1942) — and thus tapping into the developing anthropological critique of social evolutionism (Stocking 1968:202-33) — he observed that racial 'averages' say nothing about individual capability.

The other counter to Stoddard was to accentuate another non-genetic factor, the economic causes behind racial tension. Oldham (1924:136-7, 172, 229) pointed out that the objection to Asian immigration to the United States and Australia was really a fear of undercutting wages. He noted that unequal access to economic opportunity based on race militated against the growth of real friendship which he saw as the answer to racial tension. For 'the fundamental issues in racial relations are not ethnological or biological but ethical'. Such analysis rested on the older assumption of psychic unity (1924:80): 'The differences between men … are differences within a unity. Underlying all differences of race there exists a common humanity'. When exploitation and injustice were ended, the hostility would be taken out of the issue. Oldham saw difference as a good thing, part of God's great variety. But only the growth of true respect and economic equity would counter the growth of hostility. In a synthesis of Oldham's views as they applied to the Pacific regional situation, the Australian lawyer Kenneth Bailey (1924:18, 8) questioned the morality of the White Australia policy if the land of northern Australia was not developed economically and he acknowledged widespread exploitation of non-European labourers throughout the British Empire.[30]

Conclusion

Buoyed by Christian idealism, Oldham and his admirers in Australia and the Pacific region saw no reason why difference should lead to hostility. Rather than countering scientific determinism on its own terms, Oldham, Paton, and Burton opposed it on ethical grounds, based in the Christian belief in the essential unity of humankind. Although their writing did not move away entirely from notions of racial hierarchy, it reframed them in the language of obligation. While arguments based on moral and humanitarian grounds were explicitly denounced by biological determinists, missionary writers drawing on them were able to appeal to a new authority — that of the League of Nations and a new internationalism. This had considerable resonance in Australia as the new mandate over New Guinea triggered reflection within and beyond missionary circles. Attempting to engage a secular as well as a religiously committed audience, missionaries and other humanitarians employed the discourse of international relations and the associated new science of economics to further their constant message of Christian humanism as the principle which should guide relations with the Pacific Islands and with Pacific Islanders.

References

A.B.M Review. 1920-25. Sydney: Australian Board of Missions, Anglican Church of Australia.

Anon. 1910. What the Conference Means to me: Impressions of Workers from the Field. *Chronicle,* August 1910:146-50.

Australia, Commonwealth of. 1919. *Parliamentary Debates*, vol. 89. Melbourne: Government Printer.

Australian Student Christian Movement. 1895-1997. Records. Manuscripts. NLA MS 980. Canberra: National Library of Australia.

Bailey, Kenneth H. 1924. *Racialism and Christian Missions*. Melbourne: Methodist Layman's Missionary Movement.

Barker, John. 1996. 'Way Back in Papua': Representing Society and Change in the Publications of the London Missionary Society in New Guinea, 1871-1932. *Pacific Studies* 19:107-42.

Bennett, William E. 1914. Fiji. In *A Century in the Pacific*, ed. James Colwell, 439-76. Sydney: William H. Beale.

Bowler, Peter J. 1984. *Evolution: the History of an Idea*. Berkeley: University of California Press.

Burton, John W. 1903 An Indian Service in Fiji. *Missionary Review,* January 1903:7-8.

————. 1909. *Our Indian Work in Fiji*. Suva: Methodist Mission Press.

————. 1910. *The Fiji of Today*. London: Charles H. Kelly.

————. 1912. *The Call of the Pacific*. London: Charles H. Kelly.

————. 1921. *The Australian Mandate in Relation to our Duty to Native Races*. Melbourne: Australian Student Christian Movement Corporation.

————. 1922. 'The Revolt Against Civilization' (book review). *Missionary Review*, December 1922:10-11.

————. 1924. 'Christianity and the Race Problem' (book review). *Missionary Review*, December 1924:1-5.

————. 1926. The Old Tasks and the New. *Missionary Review*, January 1926:1-5.

————. 1928. The Australian Mandate in New Guinea. In *Studies in Australian Affairs: Issued by the Institute of Pacific Relations, New South Wales Branch*, ed. Persia Campbell, R.C. Mills, and G.V. Portus, 218-240. Melbourne: Macmillan & Co. Ltd. in association with Melbourne University Press.

————. n.d. The Weaver's Shuttle: Memories and Reflections of an Octogenarian. Manuscript. ML MSS 2899. Sydney: Mitchell Library.

Chronicle. 1910-1924. London: London Missionary Society.

Codrington, R.H. 1881. Religious Beliefs and Practices in Melanesia. *Journal of the Royal Anthropological Institute* 10:261-316.

————. 1889. On Social Regulations in Melanesia. *Journal of the Royal Anthropological Institute* 18:306-13.

Colwell, James, ed. 1914. *A Century in the Pacific*. Sydney: William H. Beale.

Davies, Norman. 1996. *Europe: a History*. Oxford: Oxford University Press.

Douglas, Bronwen. 2001. From Invisible Christians to Gothic Theatre: the Romance of the Millennial in Melanesian Anthropology. *Current Anthropology* 42:615-50.

Eggleston, F.W., ed. 1928. *The Australian Mandate for New Guinea: Record of Round Table Discussion: Issued for the Victorian Branch of the League of Nations Union*. Melbourne: Macmillan & Co. Ltd. in association with Melbourne University Press.

Gardner, Helen Bethea. 2006. *Gathering for God: George Brown in Oceania*. Dunedin, NZ: Otago University Press.

Goldie, John F. 1914. The Solomon Islands. In *A Century in the Pacific*, ed. James Colwell, 559-85. Sydney: William H. Beale.

_____. 1927. The Frontiers of the Kingdom. *Missionary Review*, July 1927:1-6.

Grant, Madison. 1920. Introduction. In Lothrop Stoddard, *The Rising Tide of Color Against White World-Supremacy*, i-xxxi. New York: Charles Scribner and Sons.

_____. 1921 [1916]. *The Passing of the Great Race: or, The Racial Basis of European History*. 4th edition. London: G. Bell and Sons.

Greenslade, William. 1994. *Degeneration, Culture and the Novel 1880-1940*. Cambridge: Cambridge University Press.

Gunson, Niel. 1994. British Missionaries and their Contribution to Science in the Pacific Islands. In *Darwin's Laboratory: Evolutionary Theory and Natural History in the Pacific*, ed. Roy MacLeod and Philip F. Rehbock, 283-316. Honolulu: University of Hawaii Press.

Herbert, Christopher. 1991. *Culture and Anomie: Ethnographic Imagination in the Nineteenth Century*. Chicago: University of Chicago Press.

Higham, John. 1955. *Strangers in the Land: Patterns of American Nativism 1860-1925*. New Brunswick, NJ: Rutgers University Press.

Hudson, W.J. 1980. *Australia and the League of Nations*. Sydney: Sydney University Press and Australian Institute of International Affairs.

Kipling, Rudyard. 1899. The White Man's Burden. *McClure's Magazine* 12.

Knock, Thomas. 1992. *To End All Wars: Woodrow Wilson and the Quest for a New World Order*. New York: Oxford University Press.

Kuper, Adam. 1988. *The Invention of Primitive Society: Transformations of an Illusion*. London: Routledge.

Lal, Brij V., and Yogendra Yadav. 1995. Hinduism under Indenture: Totaram Sanadhya's Account of Fiji. *Journal of Pacific History* 30:99-111.

Maine, Henry James Sumner. 1861. *Ancient Law: its Connection with the Early History of Society, and its Relation to Modern Ideas.* London: John Murray.

Missionary Review. 1903-27. Sydney: Board of Missions, Australian Methodist Missionary Society.

Mulder, John M. 1978. *Woodrow Wilson: the Years of Preparation.* Princeton, NJ: Princeton University Press.

Nelson, Hank. 1998. Frontiers, Territories and States of Mind. Paper to States and Territories workshop, 10-12 December 1998. Manuscript. Canberra: Division of Pacific and Asian History, Australian National University.

Offer, Avner. 1989. *The First World War: an Agrarian Interpretation.* Oxford: Clarendon Press.

Oldham, J.H. 1924. *Christianity and the Race Problem.* London: Student Christian Movement.

Paton, Frank H.L. 1903. *Lomai of Lenakel, a Hero of the New Hebrides: a Fresh Chapter in the Triumph of the Gospel.* London: Hodder and Stoughton.

_____. 1913. *The Kingdom in the Pacific.* London: London Missionary Society.

Prichard, James Cowles. 1836-47. *Researches into the Physical History of Mankind,* 5 vols. 3rd edition. London: Sherwood, Gilbert, and Piper.

Reid, R.E. 1978. John Henry Holmes in Papua: Changing Missionary Perspectives on Indigenous Cultures 1890-1914. *Journal of Pacific History* 13:173-87.

Royal Commission on Late German New Guinea. 1920. Final Report. *Papers of the Parliament of the Commonwealth of Australia, session 1920-21,* vol. 3, 1539-1621. Melbourne: Government Printer.

Sanadhya, Totaram. 1991. *My Twenty-One Years in the Fiji Islands.* trans. John D. Kelly and Uttra Kumari Singh. Suva: Fiji Museum.

Shipman, Pat. 1994. *The Evolution of Racism: Human Differences and the Use and Abuse of Science.* New York: Simon and Schuster.

Stocking, George W., Jr. 1968. *Race, Culture and Evolution: Essays in the History of Anthropology.* New York: Free Press.

_____. 1987. *Victorian Anthropology.* New York: Free Press.

_____. 1996. *After Tylor: British Social Anthropology 1888-1951.* London: Athlone Press.

Stoddard, Lothrop. 1920. *The Rising Tide of Color Against White World-Supremacy.* New York: Charles Scribner and Sons.

_____. 1922. *The Revolt against Civilization: the Menace of the Under Man*. London: Chapman and Hall.

Weir, Christine. 1998. Fiji and the Fijians: Two Modes of Missionary Discourse. *Journal of Religious History* 22:152-67.

_____. 2003. The Work of Missions: Race, Labour and Christian Humanitarianism in the South-West Pacific, 1870-1930. PhD thesis. Canberra: Australian National University.

Williams, Thomas. 1858. *Fiji and the Fijians*, ed. George Stringer Rowe, vol. 1, *The Islands and their Inhabitants*. London: Alexander Heylin.

Notes

[1] Barker 1996; Douglas 2001; Gardner 2006 and Chapter Six, this volume; Gunson 1994; Stocking 1996.

[2] Kuper 1988:17-34; Stocking 1987:121-8.

[3] See Chapter Six (Gardner), this volume.

[4] But see Chapter Six (Gardner), this volume, for instances of senior clergymen in the Australian colonies who, frustrated in their efforts to evangelize Aboriginal people, had henceforth denied their capacity for religion.

[5] Biblical citations are from the King James Version of 1611, the version most commonly used by anglophone Protestants in the period under discussion.

[6] The Study Circle movement, important in the 1910s and 1920s in Protestant churches in Britain and Australia, was part of increased lay involvement. Small groups studied books about missionary activity, aiming to 'understand the wholeness of Christ's mission and claim, and the wholeness of man's need and duty' (*Chronicle*, January 1912:21).

[7] See Burton 1910:190, 229-36 for his detailed opinions on the chiefly system.

[8] Burton (1912:298, 302) also briefly referred to the Edinburgh conference but it was much less of a focus for his book. Edinburgh was the first of several international missionary conferences attended by both the leaders of metropolitan missionary societies and indigenous church leaders. These conferences were the forerunners of the World Council of Churches.

[9] An identical juxtaposition of these two texts is found in Burton, *Fiji of Today* (1910:173), a book steeped in evolutionist judgments — which may again indicate how common it was for missionaries (and others) simultaneously to hold varying discourses in tension.

[10] Mendelian theory was not fully developed until the work of R.A. Fisher (1890-1962) and J.B.S. Haldane (1892-1964) on population genetics in the late 1920s but by around 1920 the basic outlines were clear. Haldane himself had grave reservations about the way such science was used by policy makers, describing eugenics as 'largely the product of a class struggle based on the desire of the governing class to prove their innate superiority' (Greenslade 1994:254-5).

[11] Bowler 1984:286-96; Higham 1955:152-3; Shipman 1994:111-28.

[12] The division of Europeans into three 'races' — 'Nordics', 'Alpines', and 'Mediterraneans' — originated with William Z. Ripley (1867-1941) in 1899 in an attempt to maintain a distinction between old and new immigrants to the United States. Both Grant and Stoddard then adopted it (Higham 1955:154).

[13] Accounts of these discussions exist written by both Burton and Totaram Sanadhya: see Burton 1910:323; Sanadhya 1991:73-79; Lal and Yadav 1995:99-111.

[14] These factors comprise Burton's own explanation for his changing understandings over these years (n.d.:89-102). The International Missionary Conferences were the successors to the 1910 World Missionary Conference in Edinburgh; Burton attended the 1921 meeting in the USA.

[15] Woodrow Wilson, Speech to the United States Senate, 2 April 1917, cited by Knock (1992:121). In this speech Wilson promulgated his Fourteen Points which became the basis of the League of Nations Covenant.

[16] The text of the League of Nations Covenant is reprinted by Hudson (1980:208-14).

[17] For further discussion of Australian policy and official attitudes towards the mandated territory, see Nelson 1998.

[18] W.M. Hughes, Speech to the House of Representatives, 10 September 1919, Commonwealth of Australia 1919:12173, 12167. On Hughes's attitude to the Peace Conference, see also Offer 1989:371-6.

[19] See, e.g., Hudson 1980:21-4.

[20] Report by Majority of Commissioners, 29, in Royal Commission on Late German New Guinea 1920.

[21] Report by Chairman, 55, in Royal Commission on Late German New Guinea 1920.

[22] Report by Chairman, 68-9, in Royal Commission on Late German New Guinea 1920.

[23] This lecture was delivered in the Melbourne Town Hall on 21 July 1921 under the auspices of the Victoria Branch of the League of Nations Union but was published by the Australian Student Christian Movement — another example of secular and religious linkage.

[24] *Missionary Review*, May 1821:7. The population figure of one million given in the image was the estimated population of both territories in 1921; Australians did not know of the existence of the large populations of the highlands region until the 1930s.

[25] *A.B.M. Review*, September 1920:104. The editor added that the Covenant had only twice been surpassed — by the Ten Commandments and the Sermon on the Mount — and twice equalled — by the Magna Carta and the Constitution of the United States of America.

[26] Report of the Commission to Consider the World Student Christian Federation International Findings, 14 May 1923, in Australian Student Christian Movement 1895-1997: Box 65, Item 3/5. The same report noted the view of the commission that the White Australia Policy could only be justified if 'Australia were to be used to the full by citizens of British stock and traditions'. If such a population did not completely occupy the continent, then other groups should be admitted; anything else was a 'dog-in-the-manger attitude'.

[27] Reviews and recommendations appeared in *Missionary Review*, September 1924:18-19; December 1924:1; *A.B.M. Review*, August 1925:9; *Chronicle*, August 1924:190.

[28] Belief in the psychic unity of mankind derives from the Pauline assumptions already discussed of the equality of all human beings before God, particularly as developed by Evangelicals such as James Cowles Prichard in *Researches into the Physical History of Mankind* (1836-47). See Weir 2003:28-33 and Chapter Six (Gardner), this volume.

[29] Oldham had a life-long interest in education, both in India and Africa. A member of the British Government's Advisory Committee on Native Education in Tropical Africa, he wrote definitive policy statements on African education together with Lord Lugard.

[30] Bailey did not acknowledge that he was developing Oldham's ideas in spite of virtually verbatim citation from his book.

Part Five

Zenith: Colonial Contradictions and
the Chimera of Racial Purity, 1920-1940

Chapter Eight

The Half-Caste in Australia, New Zealand, and Western Samoa between the Wars: different problem, different places?[1]

Vicki Luker

Something called the 'half-caste problem' was noted in many colonial situations during the interwar period. Numerous books and chapters addressed it.[2] At least one global survey was attempted (Dover 1937). Half-castes also figured in fiction, images, and song. Noel Coward, better known for 'Mad Dogs and Englishmen', sang a ballad 'Half-caste Woman' which I listened to from an old record as a child.[3] Later, during the course of research that was not particularly concerned with miscegenation, I was struck by contrasting attitudes towards half-castes in several locations in the southwest Pacific during these decades. Two questions puzzled me. First, why, in New Zealand, was indigenous and European miscegenation actually celebrated by some proponents while advocates of a parallel process in Australia were less than jubilant? Second, why did New Zealand administrators revile and vituperate half-castes in Western Samoa when politicians and officials back home rejoiced in their nation's outstanding men of mixed race? While these views on half-castes were not universally held in their time and place, they were nevertheless prominent and I wondered how their differences could be explained. The following discussion is my attempt to do so.

I begin by reviewing the ancestry of the term 'half-caste', comment on the 'half-caste problem' between the wars, and outline some very general variants — in time, space, and racial reasoning — that can help explain the contrasting evaluations of miscegenation to which my opening questions refer. I then turn to the three main sites of this inquiry — Australia, New Zealand, and Western Samoa — while also drawing some illustrations from Australia's mandated territory of New Guinea and the British Crown Colony of Fiji. Although writing for a volume devoted to the science of race, I remain uncertain as to how the science of race can be defined in these locations and how its influence on policy and action can be tracked and measured.[4] Instead, I suggest some differences in broad patterns of racial thinking relating to half-castes and correlate them with the differences between the imperatives of 'settler' and 'managerial' colonialisms, at least in this quarter of the world — imperatives which were in turn determined to a considerable degree by environment. Though I have no qualms about alluding to environmental influences upon colonial formations, in conclusion I mention some of the difficulties in proposing the 'imperatives' that I outline as historical explanations, despite the fact that my own efforts have led me to them. These difficulties raise questions that remain unanswered as I finally reflect on the postcolonial fortunes of the term half-caste.

The half-caste

The word half-caste has an imperial genealogy going back to the Roman Empire, which exported the Latin adjective *castus*, 'pure', 'unpolluted', to its subjects. From these origins, modern English derives 'chaste' but half-caste was a later child of linguistic miscegenation between the empires of Portugal and Britain. In Portuguese, the adjective *casta* in the phrase *casta raça*, 'pure race', was nominalized and from the mid-sixteenth century came to denote the large endogamous groupings of India.[5] The English adapted this Portuguese term and from the late-eighteenth century, in order perhaps to differentiate this specialized sense from all the meanings associated with the homonym 'cast' (the verb of non-Latinate derivation meaning 'to throw'), began spelling 'caste' with a final 'e'. Simultaneously, the term half-caste appeared. Referring to persons of combined European and Indian parentage, it coincided with the introduction of employment policies in the British East India Company that discriminated against men of mixed race. From the start, half-caste had pejorative connotations. It also appealed to what the British understood as 'Indian notions of birth', with the concept of caste, more so than race, entailing injunctions of physical, sexual, and marital exclusiveness (Ballhatchet 1980:4, 97-8). With the expansion of Britain's empire, half-caste was applied loosely to any person of mixed race.

The 'half-caste problem' between the wars

Several factors appear to have contributed to the interwar prominence of the 'half-caste problem'. First, ideologies of race were perhaps most widely popularized and implemented by governments during these years — even though the intellectual bases of racial science were already under assault in Britain and the United States (Barkan 1992). Half-castes were significant because they affronted ideals of racial purity and challenged the real or imagined structures, including colonial structures, founded thereon.

Second, many colonial rulers were now keenly feeling the vulnerability of empire to moral objection and coloured revolt. As one former British Under-Secretary of State for the Colonies remarked, a wave of restlessness had swept the world since the Great War (Shiels 1933:321). In tropical possessions, wherever Europeans constituted managerial minorities, the question of where to place and how to treat the mixed-blood descendants of the ruling race was, in theory and practice, often problematic. Where the male half-caste was spurned by his father's people, they sometimes feared him as, metaphorically, a potential parricide. This spurning was painfully true of the British imperial tradition — though, as will be seen, there were exceptions, and the stereotypes which characterize French, Spanish, Portuguese, and Dutch colonialisms as more accepting of racial mixing do not entirely survive scrutiny.[6] The half-caste woman was depicted as dangerous in a different way: she was tragically alluring, for in tempting a white man to marry she could bring him, it was often said, to social and racial ruin.[7]

Third, half-castes were in effect metonyms for interracial sex. Male or female, they were its proof and product. If female, from a white man's viewpoint they were often seen to invite it. The accentuated sensitivity to racial divisions in these years therefore only served further to eroticize in the European imagination those who appeared to embody the sexual transgression of these divides. In societies of mass European settlement with indigenous minorities, such as Australia and New Zealand, the half-caste was perhaps not feared as such a potentially violent threat and was perhaps less eroticized. But here, too, 'the half-caste problem' was symbolically charged and complicated the process envisaged for shaping a national identity.[8]

Differing evaluations of miscegenation

I suggest three general axes of variation to help explain the different evaluations of miscegenation that this chapter will address. The first is chronological. The conditions of frontier, as distinct from later colonialism often conduced to the acceptance of interracial liaisons and their offspring. This initially relaxed attitude to interracial sexual relations was partly a matter of sexual pragmatics since white women were usually scarce on the frontier. It could be partly strategic, since liaisons with local women could help white men gain useful knowledge and relationships. The children born of these unions, especially if their fathers or paternal associates cared for them, often became entrepreneurs in the frontier economies.

The photographs in Figures 19 and 20 — the first of a white father and the second of an indigenous mother and their son — illustrate certain significant features of frontier miscegenation. The son, Clem Leahy, was one of three mixed-race half-brothers by the same father, Michael Leahy, who led the first European expeditions into the New Guinea highlands during the 1930s and met Clem's mother, Yamka Amp Wenta, in the Mt Hagen area when she was sent to him by her husband. Though Michael Leahy did not acknowledge his children by local women, missionaries targeted his sons. All three were schooled by Christian missions and became successful businessmen.[9]

Figure 19: Anon., 'Michael Leahy in the Wahgi Valley, 1934'.[10]

Photograph. nla.pic-vn4198892. Canberra: National Library of Australia.

Figure 20: Robin Anderson, 'Clem Leahy and his Mother, Yamka Amp Wenta, 1983'.[11]

Photograph. © Robert Connolly and Penguin Group. Photograph B. Douglas.

More fundamentally, the parents in these photographs display the archetypically gendered ancestry of the European half-caste: father white, mother coloured.[12] There were of course cases — usually later — in which the mother was white and the father coloured but this occurrence was relatively rare and such sexual relations aroused hostility in European, especially male European, observers. Fernando Henriques (1974:78-92), in his classic survey of miscegenation beautifully entitled *Children of Caliban*, explored this antagonism. It was the subject of Amirah Inglis's (1975) examination of the White Women's Protection Ordinance in Papua. Claudia Knapman (1986:113-35) analyzed it in her study of white women in Fiji. Ann McGrath (1987:73) discussed it too in the 'cattle country' of Australia's Northern Territory. The most vivid cameos from my archival research relate to the nineteenth century. In Fiji in 1892, the white widow of a Colonial Sugar Refinery employee was living as wife with a Fijian chief. The administration denied him chiefly honours and the disgust of white officials is almost palpable on the page: 'The case is bad as it is'.[13] Still earlier, an elderly white woman who granted intercourse to Fijians for a small fee caused intense official indignation. She was deported.[14]

The photographs make a further chronological point. In many parts of Melanesia, such as the New Guinea highlands, empire was just beginning at or near the close of the imperial era. A map of Australia by the entomologist turned anthropologist Norman B. Tindale (1900-1993) traces further such examples.[15] During the decades following World War I, Australian frontiers were still advancing in the continent's north and centre and these areas were also the zone of first generation half-castes. But time cannot always be so neatly mapped. Different times may coexist. Elements of the culture of frontier can survive into later periods. As John Owens (1992:53) commented, 'Old New Zealand' — romanticized by some as the 'good old days' of the Pakeha-Maori, a term referring to Pakeha, 'Europeans', who 'went native' — continued in remoter areas. These social survivals combined with persisting values and memories derived from an earlier era to nourish, even to the present, an alternative tradition of race relations in New Zealand. A similar statement could be made for all the countries discussed here.

My second axis of variation is latitudinal. Throughout the colonial era and into the twentieth century, Europeans tried to explain the apparent toxicity, to them, of the tropics where they tended to sicken and die (Curtin 1990:136-8). One theory, not so very far from Alfred Crosby's (1986) classic explanation of the ecological determinants of European expansion, was that Europeans were constitutionally ill-suited to tropical climates. If the tropics were bad for white men, they were believed to be worse for white women. Aside from the usual scarcity of white women in such locations, these beliefs supported arguments in favour of interracial liaisons and also strengthened the case for hybrid progeny.

For European enterprise in the tropics, half-castes could inherit from their fathers a loyalty, training, and taste for the activities of empire and from their mother — aside from contacts and local knowledge — acclimatization to their surroundings. These considerations probably influenced the vision splendid of one Wesleyan missionary in the 1840s, Walter Lawry (1739-1859), who looked forward to the day when a proud race of industrious Christians, descended from native mothers and white fathers, would populate the isles of the Pacific (1850:135).[16]

Beliefs in the toxicity of the tropics continued, however, into the interwar era. In Australia, though doctors like Raphael Cilento (1893-1985) — who liked to walk in the tropical sun without a hat — proclaimed that medical conquests, if combined with stringent racial segregation and sanitary discipline, now enabled white settlement of the nation's north, some expert and much popular opinion was less certain.[17] These doubts still supported certain arguments in favour of miscegenation. Thus Cecil Cook (1897-?), from 1927 Chief Medical Officer and Chief Protector of Aborigines in the Northern Territory, buttressed his case for marriage between mixed-race women and white men by saying that their children would derive, through their mothers, biological protection against skin cancer (a condition, incidentally, that plagued Cilento!).[18]

Associated with the idea of the toxicity of the tropics was the common contrast between temperate and tropical forms of colonization. Temperate regions were usually environmentally benign to Europeans and what Crosby (1986) calls their 'portmanteau biota' which included their associated plants and animals. Tropical colonies, however, were ecologically less hospitable to this European package. Broadly, different demographic histories and patterns of race relations correlate with these environmental differences. In the first, precipitous indigenous population decline, due to sickness, dispossession, and violence, was often accompanied by heavy European immigration, conflict over land, and troubled political relations between the indigenous minority and European majority in the subsequent evolution of a new, shared nation. In the second, whether or not the indigenous people were susceptible to introduced diseases, white populations rarely took deep root or abundantly flourished. Typically they amounted to no more than a minority who held managerial positions in administration, business, and the Christian missions. There was no comparable 'demographic takeover' (Crosby 1994:29-31).[19]

My third axis of variation is along a particular line of racial logic that sometimes favoured half-castes and sometimes not. The characterization of half-castes as infertile, prone to illness, lacking vitality, and combining the worst elements of both parental lines was commonplace. But derogatory assessments often coexisted with enthusiastic appraisals.[20] For example, in a lengthy official report into the reasons for the decrease of the indigenous Fijian population, published in 1896 and revived and feted between the wars, negative statements about half-castes can be read alongside arguments strongly in favour of racial mixing. The authors — all civil servants — were for instance keen to import Barbadians to interbreed with Fijians in order to produce a robust new racial hybrid (Stewart et al. 1896:184-7). One of these authors, Basil Thomson (1861-1939), like innumerable English writers since Defoe, also gloried in the mongrel vigour of the British.[21] How can these apparently divergent assessments of miscegenation be reconciled?

Here the concept of racial distance is pivotal and can be illustrated by reference to animal breeding. The examples of the mule and the racehorse were often invoked. The mule was an age-old symbol of hybridization (and hence the term 'mulatto' for persons of mixed European and Negro ancestry).[22] It supposedly demonstrated the law that strains too far removed from one another mated unnaturally and produced defective offspring. The main defect of the mule was infertility. The racehorse, however, showed that by crossing distinctive but related strains and carefully mating their offspring in ensuing generations, a magnificent new breed could be produced (Pitt-Rivers 1927:6, 97). Of course, we could argue with such evaluations (what about, for instance, the virtues of a mule or the deficiencies of a racehorse?), but the influence of models drawn from animal breeding and horticulture was profound in both lay and specialist thinking about half-castes.[23]

For human miscegenation, the lesson usually drawn was therefore that crosses between races regarded as sufficiently close to one another were likely to prove beneficial while those between races considered too distant would not (e.g., Broca 1864:16-66). The historian Stephen Henry Roberts (1901-1971) clearly applied this principle in a chapter on race mixing in the Pacific (1927:352-86). He acknowledged the old prejudice that all hybrids invariably combined the worst features of both parents. He acknowledged some experts who condemned even crossing closely related races. He also admitted the great diversity of opinion on all matters relating to race — including the repudiation of race as an entity. But Roberts did nevertheless confidently confirm this rule of racial distance. Thus, on the basis that Polynesians and Micronesians were deemed to be relatively close to Europeans and 'Asiatics', their mixture with European or Asian strains could be approved. Melanesians, however, were too distant from either Europeans or 'Asiatics' in Roberts' racial schema to be profitably combined with either. Roberts made no mention of Aborigines. Since a consensus of both expert and popular opinion had characterized the indigenous people of Australia as among the most primitive on earth,[24] the rule of racial distance did not favour the results of Aboriginal miscegenation with so-called higher races. But, as we shall see, racial distance was elastic.

The 'half-caste problem' in Australia

Australia and New Zealand were colonies of mass-European settlement. In both, the status and future of their indigenous minorities complicated the ideal and attainment of nationhood. As McGregor (1993:57) observed in relation to Australia, the belief that national cohesion depended upon 'a large degree of racial homogeneity' — displayed and symbolized in 'whiteness' — was standard. During the interwar period, among white New Zealanders particularly, similar values and metaphors resonated and scholars have explored the significance of 'whiteness' for both nations.[25] Though Belich has argued that a more appropriate descriptor of New Zealand's racial template was 'Aryan' rather than 'white', the quest for racial consistency provides a common ground for considering approaches to miscegenation on both sides of the Tasman in the era examined here.

In Australia between the wars, the half-caste problem was most vividly perceived on the frontier where the children of Aboriginal mothers and European fathers were often described as destitute. Paul Hasluck (1905-1993), later Minister for Territories, said that most had 'no chance to be anything but hangers-on' (1938:3-4). The historian Gordon Briscoe (2001), who was born at a native institution in Alice Springs in the late 1930s, has described how Aboriginal mothers living near the transport and communication links of central Australia survived under great stress, without support from the white fathers of their children but also reluctant to live a tribal life and fearing tribal men. Unusually severe droughts in Central Australia during the 1920s also compelled many people of Aboriginal descent to depend more heavily on support than before. The Great Depression then denied incomes to many who had been earning money.[26] Demographic trends were also apparently dramatic. Population data were unreliable but seemed to show that half-caste numbers had steeply increased.[27] To some observers, half-castes promised either to form an ever-growing, impoverished, illiterate, coloured population or, alternatively, to merge back with 'full-blood' Aborigines and swell their numbers (Briscoe 2001; Hasluck 1938:6).

At a conference held in Canberra from 21-23 April 1937, Commonwealth and State Aboriginal authorities addressed the half-caste problem. It resolved that 'the destiny of the natives of aboriginal origins, *but not the full-blood*, lies in their ultimate absorption by the people of the Commonwealth, and it therefore recommends that all efforts be directed to that end'.[28] Tindale (1941), following a survey of Australia's half-caste populations conducted in 1938 and 1939, ultimately agreed. He rhetorically posed four options. The sterilization of half-castes he immediately dismissed. He also rejected the desirability of cultivating a new but distinct half-caste race — though in a few circumscribed communities he saw the process under way and some missionary opinion supported the idea (e.g., Webb n.d.). Tindale considered current policies, characterized by inconsistency and drift, as undesirable too.[29] Assimilation through miscegenation, which required the removal of mixed-race children, was the remaining option. Within government circles, Cook in the Northern Territory and A.O. Neville (1874-1954), the Commissioner of Native Affairs for Western Australia, were the most energetic proponents of this policy which gained increasing favour in the late 1930s (Wilson 1997:32-5).

More than one motive or justification can be discerned in the policy of child removal. Certainly, the image of half-castes as destitute and outcast often misrepresented their situation. Even among those in difficult circumstances, there is piercing testimony to the strength of caring ties that connected persons of mixed ancestry with parents and kin — whether white, 'full-blood', or within evolving half-caste communities.[30] The vital contribution of Aboriginal and mixed-race men and women to the rural economy was also widely admitted. J.W. Bleakley (1879-1957), the Chief Protector of Aborigines in Queensland, remarked in an official report that the pastoral industry in the Northern Territory was 'absolutely dependent' upon them (1929:7; McGrath 1987). Others referred to half-caste families 'owning their own property, paying rates, educating their children, managing their affairs', and functioning within white society, if at a modest grade (Hasluck 1938:23). Some alluded too to half-castes of high social status within white society, such as the landowning '5/8 Aboriginal of wealth, married to a white woman' whose class was inferior to her husband's (Tindale 1941:113, 119). Nevertheless, the removal of mixed-race children harmonized with the established practice of institutionalizing children deemed neglected or deprived.

Measures to remove mixed-race children were not confined to Australia. Indigenous writers of New Zealand and Canada have discovered similar histories of child removal.[31] In managerial colonies, too, Europeans were often averse to the sight of light-skinned children growing up 'native'. In the Australian mandate of New Guinea, indigenous parents hid their 'white' children from missionaries and others in authority and some coercion was used to remove Clem Leahy and his half-brothers from their families for missionary schooling.[32] Occasional files in the colonial archives of Fiji also concern the removal of 'white' children from indigenous communities. The Methodist missionary Joseph Waterhouse (1828-1881), for instance, appealed for the removal of two white boys from Fijian households, insisting that these children should have 'the education and advantages common to those of their colour'. Even before colonial rule in these islands, he remarked, half-caste families never allowed their children to live with Fijians.[33]

Clearly, then, some white onlookers within and beyond Australia objected to the exclusion of such children from their paternal heritage and believed that church or state should assume a responsibility for them, as an uncle might acknowledge the offspring of an errant brother by adopting the role of father. These are complicated feelings in which arguably emotions and ideas about kinship, paternal responsibility, and rights of inheritance were translated into a discourse on race. But at a certain level of interpretation, the teleological force of the vision of a 'white Australia' seems difficult to deny. 'Full-blooded' Aborigines were not such an issue. Whether they totally died out, as many commentators still believed they would, or whether small populations could survive inviolate under secluded conditions, made little difference to this vision.[34] Half-castes, however, had to be a transitional category for the goal of white Australia to be reached.

Yet two basic difficulties bedevilled this long-range process. First, it relied on the intermarriage of half-caste women with European men but left unanswered the question of what to do with half-caste men (McGregor 1997:167-8). The second difficulty related to the supposed racial distance between Aborigines and Europeans. A policy favouring marriage between half-caste women and white men had, in effect, to shorten that distance. Advocates of such a policy tried to do precisely this. They insisted that no harmful effects of Aboriginal ancestry could be discerned in the children resulting from intermarriage with whites: unlike 'Negro blood' which allegedly produced occasional 'throwbacks' to the Negro-type among white descendants, 'Aboriginal blood' disappeared after a few generations. Indeed, Neville (1947:63) averred that among whites and Aborigines, the opposite kind of 'throwback' occurred, with a child of an Aboriginal mother sometimes reverting to the colour of a white grandfather. Moreover, increasing stress appears to have been laid on racially classifying Aborigines as 'Caucasian'.[35] The geographer Griffith Taylor (1880-1963) joined a chorus repeating that 'blood-tests of Australian aborigines agree more closely with those of west Europeans than with similar tests of most intervening races'.[36] Thus, with assurances rather than celebration, the racial distance between Europeans and Aborigines was narrowed.

Half-castes in New Zealand: not a problem?

In New Zealand, however, the biological amalgamation of Maori and European sent some commentators into transports of eugenic delight. Of the various theories of Maori origins propounded during the nineteenth and early twentieth centuries, that proposing their Aryan origin informed much thinking in the interwar era and, like the Caucasian Aborigine, brought indigenes and whites racially closer in the settler imagination.[37] To combine and paraphrase a few texts from that time: the Maori, our distant relatives, are manly and the bravest and most intelligent of the Polynesians; after the long voyage to New Zealand, which only fine human specimens would undertake or survive, subsequent generations were invigorated, intellectually and physically, by the bracing climate; just as

Maori represent the best of their race, so white New Zealanders are the best of the British (better than those left behind — and infinitely superior to Australians). Thus, in New Zealand the superb blood of two fine peoples mixed.[38]

Proponents of these views were not all European. At least one eulogist was of mixed Maori and Pakeha ancestry. Peter Buck (c. 1877-1951) was a doctor, politician, and ethnologist, later knighted and also known as Te Rangi Hiroa. He recalled his horror, as a student, reading a sign in the Otago Medical School advertising Maori skulls, pelves, and skeletons for sale, and yet subsequently devoted much of his professional energy to Maori somatology.[39] In later life, he directed the Bernice P. Bishop Museum in Honolulu and when he died, Sorrenson (1973:193) recalled, New Zealand's 'politicians vied with one another to bring back his ashes'. As one of a group of outstanding men of Maori parentage — including Sir James Carroll (1857-1926), Sir Maui Pomare (1876-1930), and Sir Apirana Ngata (1874-1950) — Te Rangi Hiroa was a national trophy, displaying the unique triumph of race relations in New Zealand. One patriot remarked that these men 'would grace any gathering of any race or any nation' (Nash 1927:36). Several could have been called 'half-castes' but that appellation appears to have been rarely, if ever, applied. Notwithstanding their mixed race, Pakeha often celebrated them as Maori.[40]

Following the 'Aryan' tradition, Te Rangi Hiroa supposed an original homeland for the Polynesians in northern India. During their subsequent travels, he believed (1938:8, 25), they were infused with the blood of other races but remained fundamentally Europoid (or Caucasian). In an earlier essay (1924:365, 369), he described how New Zealand had changed those Polynesians who had landed there. For five centuries, 'the temperate climate had toughened ... [the] constitution of the Maori, sharpened his mentality, and altered his material culture'. This evolutionary process set Maori apart from tropical Polynesians. And, after weathering 'the storm of extinction' that followed European settlement, Maori numbers had recovered. From their nadir in 1871, when there were an estimated 37,520 Maori, by 1921 they had increased to 52,751.

But Te Rangi Hiroa did not believe that Maori would survive as a distinct race. Their future was intermixture and absorption. The fate of Maori in New Zealand's South Island seemed already to endorse this prediction. By the end of the nineteenth century, so rapid and far-reaching had been the effects of miscegenation and cultural assimilation that — according to the prehistorian Atholl Anderson (1991:31), himself a product of this history — very few descendants of South Island Maori culturally identified with Maoridom (though this is not the case today). Te Rangi Hiroa (1924:371) argued that neither white New Zealanders nor Maori could object to 'another intermixture' since each side 'was long ago deprived of any pretensions to purity of race'. 'Miscegenation', he continued (1924:374), 'has stepped in, as it has all down the ages'. He challenged the earlier, much cited pontifications of Alfred Kingcome Newman (1849-1924), a medical doctor and businessman, who had predicted (1881:50, 475-6): 'In the course of a few generations the Maoris will die out and leave no trace of their union with the whites'. Instead, Te Rangi Hiroa (1924:371) argued that Maori would shape 'the evolution of a future type of New Zealander in which the best features of the Maori race will be perpetuated for ever'.[41]

Favourable evaluations of Maori and Pakeha miscegenation, the way in which national figures like Te Rangi Hiroa seemed to demonstrate its attractiveness, and the distinctive features of race relations in New Zealand deserve more consideration than can be given here. Until the 1970s, white New Zealanders continued to take pride in what they saw as their unique success with Maori. As late as 1971, the historian Keith Sinclair (1971:125-7) wrote a short piece entitled 'Why are race relations in New Zealand better than in South Africa, South Australia or South Dakota?', particularly stressing the special influence of Christian and humanitarian ideals. A few years later, the historian Kerry Howe's (1977) study of race relations in New Zealand and Australia acknowledged ideological factors but qualified their importance, referring to environmental determinants in an argument to which my discussion will return. For most New Zealand historians of the last three decades, however, Sinclair's question might seem to validate a self-congratulatory assumption that they have energetically repudiated. No longer is New Zealand projected as an exception to the sorry history of settler colonialism but, as historian Claudia Orange (1987:5) remarked, a variation on the general pattern.[42]

The menace of the half-caste in Western Samoa and Fiji

I now shift from settler to tropical empire in order to reflect upon the contrast between New Zealand's domestic eulogizing of miscegenation and the tirades directed against half-castes in New Zealand's territory of Western Samoa. In 1914, New Zealand troops seized these islands from Germany and the League of Nations granted New Zealand the mandate after the War. New Zealanders were qualified for this administrative role, according to some spokesmen, because their record with Maori had demonstrated a gift for administering Polynesians (Cocker 1927:37). Yet some New Zealanders' attitudes to and treatment of half-castes in Western Samoa indicate a very different set of racial logics and imperatives.[43]

Though my ultimate destination is Western Samoa, I stop en route in Fiji, as was normal for passengers travelling by sea from Auckland to Apia. As sites of broadly similar tropical or managerial colonialism, Fiji and Western Samoa shared certain characteristics. The largest component of their populations was indigenous (though in Fiji, the Indian population, descended mostly from indentured labourers, was growing rapidly and would outnumber indigenous Fijians by the census of 1946). Europeans were a minority. Those Europeans born and raised in Fiji and Samoa included men and women of mixed race who were classed as Europeans, usually through a legally recognized European patriline.[44] The colonial administrations of Fiji and Western Samoa adhered similarly to the principle of the primacy of native interests. This was the proclaimed moral basis of the British administration in Fiji. The German administration of Western Samoa, which New Zealand inherited, had also subscribed to this ideal. After World War I, an ethic of modern, imperial responsibility, explicitly promoted by the League of Nations, endorsed it too. This principle needed, of course, a prior definition of the 'native' which tended to rely heavily on racial terminology. Between the wars, the principle of native primacy coexisted with a process whereby the categories race and class appear, in the anglophone managerial tradition of empire manifested in these colonies, to have been congealing into functional colonial castes.

This process was very marked in Fiji and contributed to the indignation some British officials felt towards European tourists disembarking from visiting ships during the twenties and thirties.[45] The relaxed behaviour of these white tourists and their friendliness with Fijians in the streets flouted the rules of social distance that expressed the division of the races. In Fiji's hierarchy of colour, Europeans were on top, with indigenous Fijians beneath them, and Indians at the bottom. The role of Europeans was to rule. The role of Fijians was simply to exist and reflect well on the administration by thriving and in some ways modernizing.[46] The role of Indians was to underpin the sugar industry through their labour. Race, for this colony, was an organizing principle, an identifier, and a value.[47] But as the discomfort caused by white tourists to some officials shows, this racial schema had difficulty accommodating people whose behaviour or colour did not fit the prescribed categories. While the political and economic aspirations of Indians posed the greatest challenge to Fiji's racial hierarchy, half-castes were threatening too. Those (of white, Chinese, Indian, or any other ancestry) reared as Fijians were controversial and offensive to the ideal of racial purity (Lukere 1997:211-34). But half-castes who were classed for legal purposes as Europeans were a problem felt even more keenly by the administration.

Much class differentiation could be found within this mixed-race category. The course of Fiji's colonial development had reduced opportunities for such people and most half-castes classed as Europeans were poor. White, expatriate managerial elites in the 1920s and 1930s increasingly rejected them.[48] The dominant ethnic Fijian in administrative circles, Ratu Sir Lala Sukuna (1888-1958), described the problem thus: half-castes wanted greater political involvement but their educational level was little higher than that of Fijians. Socially rejected by Europeans and Fijians, 'they are easily carried away by appeals based on notions of equality'. Their numbers were rapidly increasing and they would soon swamp the vote of true whites: 'At no distant day the European electorate', said Sukuna (1983:176), 'will be white only in name, enlightened only in memory'. With its founding creed of native welfare, the administration had real difficulty with the political aspirations of those subjects who were racially excluded from the core relationship between indigene and ruler.

New Zealand interpreted the League of Nations mandate as placing Samoans in its sacred trust.[49] For the New Zealand administration, the category 'Samoan' did not include half-castes of Samoan ancestry who were classed as Europeans. In 1930, out of Western Samoa's total population of 40,722, persons of mixed descent classified as Europeans numbered roughly 2,320 (Keesing 1934:32).[50] As in Fiji, they were increasing rapidly and even greater class differentiation obtained among them. The majority were poor, landless, culturally closer to Samoans than Europeans, but proud of their European status. A minority were affluent. Unlike Fiji and also unlike American Samoa, Western Samoa had supported a comparatively large, nationally diverse European community numbering some 600 individuals in 1914.[51] Intermarriage was common between Samoan women and white men with longstanding business interests in the islands. Germany's relatively late imposition of effective colonial government in 1899 had prolonged the experience of a frontier ethic that was more accepting of interracial liaisons and no doubt helped to promote the exuberance of the mixed-race commercial community.[52] In the 1920s, Keesing (1934:461) observed that many of the older white men were dying off and nearly 200 Germans had left the territory. Consequently, children of mixed descent were inheriting family property and business. Many had been educated as Europeans but also participated in networks of Samoan kin. Indeed, there was sometimes economic advantage in their doing so. Such men, Keesing noted, lived 'in both mental worlds and know both moralities'. They occupied positions of considerable commercial and political influence.

New Zealand officials found both poor and well-off half-castes classed as 'Europeans' difficult. Regarding the former, one high official explained: 'It would not be fair to the Samoan in whose interests the islands are governed and the preservation of whose race is considered to be our duty, to give the half-caste the same status as the native with regard to the land ... the half-caste must be left to sink to his level in the scale of humanity' (quoted in Keesing 1934:463). 'Europeans' who enjoyed traditional Samoan titles and use of Samoan land through their maternal kin were blocked from converting that land to freehold and were discouraged from exercising the political power associated with their titles. To represent Samoans in the Legislative Council, these 'Europeans' were required to abandon their European legal status and surrender associated rights, which none was keen to do (Meleisea 1987:171). Men of mixed race were also excluded from employment in government service.

Despite and perhaps partly because of New Zealand's zeal to run a model mandate primarily for the benefit of 'pure' Samoans, local Europeans, including prominent half-castes classed as Europeans, ganged up with other leading Samoans against the administration. The resulting mass Samoan movement of non-cooperation, the Mau, disabled New Zealand rule for several years in the late 1920s and early 1930s. The death of high chief Tupua Tamasese Leolofi after he was shot by New Zealand police at a peaceful demonstration of the Mau on 'Black Saturday', 28 December 1929, became a sombre symbol for Samoan nationalists of their people's resistance to colonial domination and their quest for political independence.

However, many contemporary European observers instead viewed the Mau in terms of the menace of the half-caste. The Mau was often described, especially in the early days, as a half-caste movement that lacked real Samoan support — for Samoans, so officials believed at the outset, did not like half-castes.[53] Demonstrations by the women's Mau were wont to be dismissed by officials as the actions of a rag-bag of half-caste women accompanied by well-known damsels of loose morals.[54] Many saw O.F. Nelson (1883-1944), a mixed-race businessman of girth, wealth, and intellect who also commanded high traditional status among Samoans, as the root cause of the trouble (see Figure 21).[55] When he and others were exiled to New Zealand, supporters of the Mau demanded to know why, if mixed-race men of Maori mothers were accepted as Maori leaders, the government rejected mixed-race men of Samoan mothers as leaders of Samoans (Anon. 1929). The official language vilifying Samoan half-castes — alleging their perfidy and cunning, their desire to oust European officials, their exploitation of naïve indigenous Samoans, the deplorable fact that so little British blood flowed in their veins (Nelson had none while German blood was said to vitiate most Samoan 'Europeans') — and the proposal, before the Mau came to a head, to solve the half-caste problem in the territory by exporting them all to New Zealand, demonstrate a striking difference between New Zealand's domestic and external racial lexicon and manners.[56]

Figure 21: Anon., 'Samoan Patriots'.[57]

‖Samoan Patriots

(From reader's left to right): High Chief Tuimaleaiifano, Mr. A. G. Smythe, Hon. O. F. Nelson, Mr. E. W. Gurr, and High Chief Faumuina.

Photograph. JAF Newspaper 079.9614NZS, Canberra: National Library of Australia.

The significance of place

The administration's handling of the Mau caused outcry and controversy in New Zealand. Many commentators found it difficult to explain why half-castes in this island territory had proven so problematic. The psychologist and ethnologist Ernest Beaglehole (1906-1965) later reflected that perhaps the legacy of earlier German attitudes towards Samoan half-castes was somehow to blame (1949:56-7).[58]

But the attractiveness and assimilability of the Maori half-caste, in the lines of thought described in this chapter, and the contrasting indigestibility of the Samoan half-caste perhaps derived in part from differences in broad colonial requirements. During this era in the settler societies of Australia and New Zealand, to achieve the goal of a racially coherent nation that was some shade of white, indigenous elements had logically to be absorbed into the majority population. Despite New Zealand's founding Treaty of Waitangi — which authorized the coexistence of two distinct peoples and two ways of life, one indigenous and one European — Te Rangi Hiroa and like-minded thinkers in New Zealand shared with the advocates of intermarriage between half-castes and whites in Australia a similar national vision and ideal of racial homogenization — even if in New Zealand they saw it as a more distant goal. By contrast, managerial colonialism in Samoa and Fiji required service to the ideal of native preservation. Fiji was in principle for Fijians, Samoa in principle for Samoans. The performance of social roles as conceived in these colonies relied on the language of race for the definition of their agents. This was a political vision — and ideal — of racial differentiation.

These statements of contrasting racial ideals and imperatives, though big, loose, and abstracted, nevertheless remind us that place is more than an historical site: it can be an historical actor too. At least one Maori observer of New Zealand's troubles in its territory of Western Samoa sensed this. The barrister and parliamentarian Sir Apirana Ngata stressed the radically different nature of the race relations necessitated by mass white settlement in his ancestral lands, gently challenging the conceit that white New Zealanders' colonial record with Maori fitted them to administer Samoans and also underscoring the more profound upheaval that his own people had had to survive. If Western Samoa, he wryly remarked, had been a temperate country suitable for European settlement, then the motto 'Samoa for Samoans' — first coined by the New Zealand administration though the Mau appropriated it — would have justified the taking of land from Samoans as in the Samoans' best interest.[59] In terms of my initial three axes of variation, Ngata seemed to see the latitudinal as ultimately the most important determinant of colonial racial ideology. And while I argue that the particular attitudes towards miscegenation in Australia and New Zealand that have been addressed here share fundamental similarities, their contrast — measured in differing degrees of enthusiasm for the biological absorption of indigenous elements within the white majority — can also be explored, as Howe has argued (1977), in terms of comparative colonial histories ultimately and crucially shaped by place.

Yet while this chapter has tried to give an answer to the opening questions, even within these terms of reference I am uneasy with my conclusions. In Australia's case, for instance, just how important was a teleology of a white Australia? I feel its undertow and some of the writers cited here stress its power. Patrick Wolfe (2001; 1999:32) talked in language stronger than mine of a 'logic of elimination' that corresponded with settler colonialism and he dubbed Australia's policy of biological assimilation a 'eugenic *realpolitik*'. But even if we concede this teleology, the removal of mixed-race children could occur without it; some individuals who aspired to a white Australia did not support a policy of 'breeding out the colour'; while a few in favour of racial mixing rejected this national ideal as unattainable. I have previously alluded to examples of the removal — or attempted removal — of mixed-race children in the mandated territory of New Guinea and colonial Fiji where no logic of absorption towards the telos of white nationhood pertained. Leading promoters in Australia of 'breeding out the colour' also admitted that one of the greatest obstacles to this policy was 'colour prejudice' and that during the interwar years prejudice against half-castes was increasing.[60] Such views, though they typically accompanied support for a white Australia, could obstruct this particular process as a means for achieving it. On the other hand, some proponents of racial mixing, like Griffith Taylor, remained unconvinced that a white Australia was possible (Anderson 2002:165-68).

Other key questions remain outside my terms of reference: about the diversity of views and practices relating to miscegenation; the existence of and potential for multiple explanations; and the ways in which actors themselves saw the world and understood their own motivations. Given that the removal of half-caste children is, along with the killing of Aborigines on the frontier, central to a broad and polarized debate over whether white Australians carry the guilt or not of attempted genocide, these are volatile questions (Manne 2001). It is difficult, for example, to reconcile the interpretation of assimilation in Australia advanced by Wolfe (1999:32; 2001), who conflated biological and cultural assimilation, with that offered by Paul Hasluck who as Minister for Territories helped formulate and direct the post-World War II policy of cultural assimilation. Hasluck (1988:67-68; 1995:50) argued that even those attending the 1937 Canberra conference were not proposing a 'solution' to a 'single problem' or following one particular abstract doctrine; and he insisted that, far from implementing a racial policy, most of the supporters of assimilation, including himself, were implementing their opposition to race. Arguments such as that developed by Suzanne Parry (1995) can mediate these opposed positions by proposing that well-meaning people could support or engage in actions that were facilitated by ideologies of nationalism, patriarchy, and racism without explicitly invoking them — and, I suppose, perhaps even though they might explicitly reject them. Nevertheless, such mediations do not help us to understand the different worlds in which people subjectively lived and acted.

Postcolonial fortunes

I conclude by considering the postcolonial fortunes of the word half-caste. The end of World War II entailed a retreat from racial language and the concept of race in most of the European world and a process of decolonization for the managerial colonies. In 1962, Western Samoa became the first Pacific island colony to decolonize and one of O.F. Nelson's grandsons served twice as the new nation's prime minister. In Australia, although the removal of half-caste children continued into the 1970s, the emphasis on biological assimilation had passed. Arguments for cultural assimilation, which had sometimes been separate but were also combined with the case for physical miscegenation between the wars, now prevailed. In New Zealand, the deaths of Sir Apirana Ngata and Sir Te Rangi Hiroa were mourned in 1950 and 1951 respectively, marking the departure of men who in their prime had embodied what some called the first Maori renaissance. And on both sides of the Tasman, the term half-caste continued to be used.

Then the politics of indigeneity shifted. From the 1970s, many persons who had been labelled half-castes, together with those who acknowledged lines of indigenous ancestry, asserted a primary indigenous identification. Simultaneously, new sites proliferated — in schools, universities, political organizations, and welfare groups — to which people identifying as indigenous, whether or not they had received from their own family a great deal of explicit lore or custom, could come for cultural enrichment.[61] This shift, and in Australia the related, painful issue of the past policy of child removal, charged the word half-caste with new political significance. By calling someone 'half-caste', the speaker could be understood as denying that person's indigeneity or more generally as discounting the survival of an indigenous identity and tradition. The word has since come to be used less often than at any stage in the last two hundred years.

In Fiji and Samoa, however, local renditions of 'half-caste' remain current and can involve ambivalence.[62] With independence, many people of mixed ancestry who had formerly stressed their European connection began to stress the indigenous.[63] In 1987, the historian Malama Meleisea (1987:56) noted that, over the previous decade, almost half the parliamentarians in Western Samoa 'were once classified as "Europeans" or are the sons of men so classified'. More recently, in Fiji, George Speight, the coup leader of mixed European and Fijian descent, stood as an indigenous champion. But in Samoa and Fiji, too, claims to indigenous status by persons of mixed ancestry can also be disparaged by calling them half-caste. Speight was thus discredited by his critics. The leader of Fiji's earlier coups, Sitiveni Rabuka, was also reported to have said: 'I am still waiting for him [Speight] to make his announcement in Fijian'.[64]

The geography of time, however, is complex. Riccardo Orizio's survey of what he called *The Lost White Tribes* (2001) documented a tenacious pride in being 'European' among many distant descendants of white forebears in former colonies. In places where racial mixture can derive from multiple sources, a European bloodline is also sometimes vaunted above others — a point made in Teresia Teaiwa's poem (2000) describing the bitter coldness of part-European snobbery in today's Suva. There is also an echo in some more recent Maori writing of the celebration of miscegenation and the old language of race — praising, for instance, 'half-caste children for their beauty, a product of hybrid vigour' (Walker 1996:28). Thus, ironically, do elements of earlier discourses about the half-caste persist.

References

Allen, John S. 1994. Te Rangi Hiroa's Physical Anthropology. *Journal of the Polynesian Society* 103:11-27.

Anderson, Atholl. 1991. *Race against Time: the Early Maori-Pakeha Families and the Development of the Mixed Race Population in Southern New Zealand.* Dunedin, NZ: Hocken Library.

Anderson, Warwick. 2002. *The Cultivation of Whiteness: Science, Health and Racial Destiny in Australia.* Carlton South, VIC: Melbourne University Press.

Andrews, C.F. 1937. *India and the Pacific.* London: George Allen & Unwin.

Anon. 1929. *When a Samoan is not a Samoan.* New Zealand Samoa Guardian, 30 May 1929.

Austin, Tony. 1990. Cecil Cook, Scientific Thought and 'Half-castes'. *Aboriginal History* 14:104-22.

Australian Broadcasting Commission. 2003. Awaye! Presents Red Hot Hip Hop Writing from the Honouring Words Indigenous Writers Festival Held in Canada Late Last Year. *Awaye!* 28 March 2003. Sydney: ABC Radio National. Accessed 31 March 2003, online <http://www.abc.net.au/message/radio/awaye/stories/s815475.htm>.

Ballantyne, Tony. 2002. *Orientalism and Race: Aryanism in the British Empire.* Houndmills, Basingstoke, HAM: Palgrave.

Ballara, Angela. 1986. *Proud to be White? A Survey of Pakeha Prejudice in New Zealand.* Auckland: Heinemann.

Ballhatchet, Kenneth. 1980. *Race, Sex and Class under the Raj: Imperial Attitudes and Policies and their Critics 1793-1905.* London: Weidenfeld & Nicolson.

Barkan, Elazar. 1992. *The Retreat of Scientific Racism: Changing Concepts of Race in Britain and the United States between the World Wars.* Cambridge: Cambridge University Press.

Beaglehole, Ernest. 1949. The Mixed-Blood in Polynesia. *Journal of the Polynesian Society* 58:51-7.

Belich, James. 1986. *The New Zealand Wars and the Victorian Interpretation of Racial Conflict.* Auckland: Penguin Books (NZ).

_____. 1996. *Making Peoples: a History of the New Zealanders from Polynesian Settlement to the End of the Nineteenth Century.* Auckland: Penguin Books (NZ).

_____. 2001. *Paradise Reforged: a History of New Zealanders from the 1880s to the year 2000.* Honolulu: University of Hawai'i Press.

Bleakley, J.W. 1929. *The Aborigines and Half-Castes of Central Australia and North Australia*. Melbourne: Parliament of the Commonwealth of Australia.

Boxer, C.R. 1963. *Race Relations in the Portuguese Colonial Empire 1415-1825*. Oxford: Clarendon Press.

Briscoe, Gordon. 2001. The Half-Caste Problem: Revisiting the Stolen Generation Metaphor 1900-1944. Paper to the Australian Institute of Aboriginal and Torres Strait Islander Studies, 15 November 2001. Manuscript. Canberra: Australian Institute of Aboriginal and Torres Strait Islander Studies.

_____. 2003. *Counting, Health and Identity: a History of Aboriginal Health and Demography in Western Australia and Queensland 1900-1940*. Canberra: Aboriginal Studies Press.

Broca, Paul. 1864 [1860]. *On the Phenomena of Hybridity in the Genus Homo*, tr. and ed. C. Carter Blake. London: Longman, Green, Longman, & Roberts for the Anthropological Society.

Brown, Malcolm. 2000. *Waste of Speight*. Sydney Morning Herald, 3 June 2000.

Campbell, Ian. 1999. New Zealand and the Mau in Samoa: Reassessing the Causes of a Colonial Protest Movement. *New Zealand Journal of History* 33:92-110.

Cilento, Raphael. 1933. The Conquest of Climate. *Medical Journal of Australia*. 1:421-32.

_____. 1959. *Triumph in the Tropics: an Historical Sketch of Queensland*. Brisbane: Smith and Paterson Pty Ltd.

Cocker, W.H. 1927. The Aims and Aspirations of New Zealand. *News Bulletin, Institute of Pacific Relations*, Honolulu, Hawaii, September 1927:34-7.

Colony of Fiji. 1874-1941a. Colonial Secretary's Office. Suva: National Archives of Fiji.

_____. 1874-1941b. Confidential Files. Suva: National Archives of Fiji.

_____. 1874-1941c. Provincial Council Minutes. Suva: National Archives of Fiji.

Condliffe, J.B. [1971]. *Te Rangi Hiroa: the Life of Sir Peter Buck*. [Christchurch]: Whitcombe & Tombs.

Connell, John. 1987. *New Caledonia or Kanaky? The Political History of a French Colony*. Canberra: National Centre for Development Studies, Australian National University.

Connolly, Bob, and Robin Anderson. 1987. *First Contact*. New York: Viking.

Coward, Noel. 1982. *The Noel Coward Diaries*. London: Weidenfeld & Nicolson.

Crosby, Alfred W. 1986. *Ecological Imperialism: the Biological Expansion of Europe, 900-1900*. Cambridge: Cambridge University Press.

_____. 1994. Germs, *Seeds and Animals: Studies in Ecological History*. Armonk, NY: M.E. Sharpe.

Curtin, Philip D. 1990. The Environment Beyond Europe and the European Theory of Empire. *Journal of World History* 1:131-50.

Davidson, J.W. 1967. *Samoa Mo Samoa: the Emergence of the Independent State of Western Samoa*. Melbourne: Oxford University Press.

Dover, Cedric. 1937. *Half-Caste*. London: Martin Secker & Warburg.

Gilson, Richard. 1970. *Samoa 1830 to 1963: the Politics of a Multi-Cultural Community*. Melbourne: Oxford University Press.

Hage, Ghassan. 2003. *Against Paranoid Nationalism: Searching for Hope in a Shrinking Society*. Annandale, NSW: Pluto Press.

Hasluck, Paul. 1938 [1836]. *Our Southern Half-Caste Natives and their Conditions*. Perth: Native Welfare Council.

_____. 1988. *Shades of Darkness: Aboriginal Affairs 1925-1965*. Carlton, VIC: Melbourne University Press.

_____. 1995. *Light that Time has Made*. Canberra: National Library of Australia.

Hegarty, Ruth. 1999. *Is that you Ruthie?* St Lucia, QLD: University of Queensland Press.

Henriques, Fernando. 1974. *Children of Caliban: Miscegenation*. London: Secker & Warburg.

Howe, K.R. 1977. *Race Relations, Australia and New Zealand: a Comparative Survey 1770s-1970s*. Wellington: Methuen.

Inglis, Amirah. 1975. *The White Women's Protection Ordinance: Sexual Anxiety and Politics in Papua*. New York: St Martins Press.

Jones, Frederic Wood. 1934. *Australia's Vanishing Race*. Sydney: Angus & Robertson.

Keesing, Felix M. 1928. The Maoris of New Zealand: an Experiment in Racial Adaptation. *Pacific Affairs*, October 1928:1-5.

_____. 1934. *Modern Samoa: its Government and Changing Life*. London: George Allen & Unwin.

Kiple, Kenneth F. 1984. *The Caribbean Slave: a Biological History*. Cambridge: Cambridge University Press.

Knapman, Claudia. 1986. *White Women in Fiji 1835-1930*. Sydney: Allen & Unwin.

Lal, Brij. 1992. *Broken Waves: a History of the Fiji Islands in the Twentieth Century*. Honolulu: University of Hawaii Press.

Lalor, Myles. 2000. *Wherever I Go: Myles Lalor's 'Oral History'*, ed. Jeremy Beckett. Carlton South, VIC: Melbourne University Press.

Lawry, Walter. 1850. *Friendly and Fiji Islands: a Missionary Visit to Various Stations in the South Seas*. London: John Mason.

Leahy, Michael J. [1933-4]. Collection of Photographs of New Guinea. Photographs. PIC/6102 Roll 85 A3/23 LOC ALBUM 801/24. Canberra: National Library of Australia.

Lukere, Victoria. 1997. Mothers of the Taukei: Fijian Women and 'the Decrease of the Race'. PhD thesis. Canberra: Australian National University.

McArthur, Norma. 1967. *Island Populations of the Pacific*. Canberra: Australian National University Press.

McGrath, Ann. 1987. *Born in the Cattle: Aborigines in Cattle Country*. Sydney: Allen & Unwin.

_____. 2003. The Silken Threads of Kinship: Mixed Marriages between Asians and Aborigines during Australia's Federation Era. In *Lost in the Whitewash: Aboriginal-Asian Encounters in Australia, 1901-2001*, ed. Penny Edwards and Shen Yuanfang, 37-58. Canberra: Humanities Research Centre, Australian National University.

McGregor, Russell. 1997. *Imagined Destinies: Aboriginal Australia and the Doomed Race Theory, 1880-1939*. Carlton South, VIC: Melbourne University Press.

_____. 1993. Representations of the 'Half-caste' in the Australian Scientific Literature of the 1930s. *Journal of Australian Studies* 36:51-64.

Mann, Cecil B. 1937. *Objective Tests in Fiji*. Suva, Fiji: Government Printer.

Manne, Robert. 2001. In Denial: the Stolen Generations and the Right. *Australian Quarterly Essay* 1:1-113.

Markus, Andrew. 1982. After the Outward Appearance: Scientists, Administrators, and Politicians. In *All that Dirt: Aborigines 1938*, ed. Bill Gammage and Andrew Markus, 83-106. Canberra: History Project Incorporated, Research School of Social Sciences, Australian National University.

Meleisea, Malama. 1987. *The Making of Modern Samoa: Traditional Authority and Colonial Administration in the History of Western Samoa*. Suva, Fiji: Institute of Pacific Studies, University of the South Pacific.

Nash, Walter. 1927. A New Zealand Outlook on Pacific Affairs. *News Bulletin, Institute of Pacific Relations* August 1927:31-6.

Neville, A.O. [1947]. *Australia's Coloured Minority: Its Place in the Community*. Sydney: Currawong Publishing.

Newman, Alfred. 1881. A Study of the Causes Leading to the Extinction of the Maori. *Transactions and Proceedings of the New Zealand Institute* 14:459-77.

New Zealand, Department of Island Territories. 1919-40. IT series. Wellington: National Archives of New Zealand.

Ngata, Apirana. 1929a. Speech on the Mandated Territory of Western Samoa. In New Zealand, *Parliamentary Debates: Legislative Council and House of Representatives*, vol. 222, 903-7. Wellington: Government Printer.

_____. 1929b. Anthropology and the Government of Native Races. In *New Zealand Affairs*, ed. Apirana Ngata, et al., 22-44. Christchurch: New Zealand Branch of the Institute of Pacific Relations.

Nordyke, Eleanor. 1989 [1977]. *The Peopling of Hawai'i*. 2nd edition. Honolulu: University of Hawai'i Press.

N.Z. Samoa Guardian. 1929-. Auckland: N.Z. Samoa Guardian Ltd.

O'Callaghan, Mary-Louise. 2000. Fiji's Future Mired in Mistrust. *Australian*, 22 May 2000.

Orange, Claudia. 1987. *The Treaty of Waitangi*. Wellington: Bridget Williams Books.

Orizio, Riccardo. 2001. *Lost White Tribes: Journeys among the Forgotten*, tr. Avril Bardoni. London: Vintage.

Owens, J.M.R. 1992. New Zealand before Annexation. In *The Oxford History of New Zealand*, ed. Geoffrey W. Rice, 28-53. Auckland: Oxford University Press.

Parry, Suzanne. 1995. Identify the Process: the Removal of 'Half-caste' Children from Aboriginal Mothers. *Aboriginal History* 19:141-53.

Paul, Diane B. 1995. *Controlling Human Heredity: 1865 to the Present*. Atlantic Highlands, NJ: Humanities Press.

Pitt-Rivers, George H. L.-F. 1927. *The Clash of Culture and the Contact of Races: an Anthropological and Psychological Study of the Laws of Racial Adaptability, with Special Reference to the Depopulation of the Pacific and the Government of Subject Races*. London: George Routledge & Sons.

Ritvo, Harriet. 1996. Barring the Cross: Miscegenation and Purity in Eighteenth and Nineteenth Century Britain. In *Human, All Too Human,* ed. Diana Fuss, 37-57. New York and London: Routledge.

Roberts, Stephen H. 1927. *Population Problems of the Pacific.* London: George Routledge & Sons.

Salesa, Damon Jeremia. 1997. Troublesome Half-Castes: Tales of a Samoan Borderland. MA thesis. Auckland: University of Auckland.

Salesa, Toeolesulusulu D. 2000. Half-castes between the Wars: Colonial Categories in New Zealand and Samoa. *New Zealand Journal of History* 34:98-116.

Scarr, Deryck. 1984. *Fiji: a Short History.* Sydney: George Allen & Unwin.

Shankman, Paul. 2001. Interethnic Unions and the Regulation of Sex in Colonial Samoa, 1830-1945. *Journal of the Polynesian Society* 110:119-47.

Shiels, Drummond. 1933. *Social Hygiene and Human Welfare II: The Task of Colonial Administration.* Health and Empire 7:319-31.

Simpson, J.A., and E.S.C. Weiner, ed. 1989. *Oxford English Dictionary,* 20 vols. 2nd edition. Oxford: Clarendon Press.

Simpson, Sam. 1974. *The Part-European Community in Fiji.* Suva, Fiji: South Pacific Social Sciences Association.

Sinclair, Keith. 1971. Why Are Race Relations in New Zealand Better than in South Africa, South Australia or South Dakota? *New Zealand Journal of History* 5:121-27.

Sorrenson, M.P.K. 1973. Review of J.B. Condliffe, *Te Rangi Hiroa: the Life of Sir Peter Buck. New Zealand Journal of History* 7:192-4.

_____. 1979. *Maori Origins and Migrations: the Genesis of Some Pakeha Myths and Legends.* Auckland: Auckland University Press.

Stepan, Nancy. 1985. Biological Degeneration: Races and Proper Places. In *Degeneration: the Dark Side of Progress,* ed. J. Edward Chamberlin and Sander L. Gilman, 97-120. New York: Columbia University Press.

Stewart, James, Bolton Glanville Corney, and Basil Thomson. 1896. *Report of the Commission Appointed to Inquire into the Decrease of the Native Population.* Suva, Fiji: Government Printer.

Stoler, Ann. 1995. 'Mixed-Bloods' and the Cultural Politics of European Identity in Colonial Southeast Asia. In *The Decolonization of Imagination: Culture, Knowledge and Power,* ed. Jan Nederveen and Bhikhu Parekh, 128-48. London: Zed Books Ltd.

Sukuna, Lala. 1983. *Fiji, the Three Legged Stool: Selected Writings of Ratu Sir Lala Sukuna,* ed. Deryck Scarr. London: Macmillan Education Limited.

Taylor, Griffith. 1928. White and Black Races in Australia. *Pacific Affairs*, July 1928:1-3.

Te Rangi Hiroa [Peter Buck]. 1924. The Passing of the Maori. *Transactions and Proceedings of the New Zealand Institute* 55:362-74.

_____. 1938. *Vikings of the Sunrise*. New York: Frederick A. Stokes.

Teaiwa, Teresia. 2000. There Is No Poetry. In Teresia Teiawa and Sia Figiel, *Terenesia*. CD recording, track 14. Honolulu: Hawai'i Dub Machine and 'Elapaia Press.

Thomson, Basil. 1908. *The Fijians: a Study in the Decay of Custom*. London: William Heinemann.

Tindale, Norman B. 1941. *Survey of the Half-Caste Problem in South Australia*. Adelaide: Royal Geographical Society, S.A. Branch.

Walker, David. 1999. *Anxious Nation: Australia and the Rise of Asia 1850-1939*. St Lucia, QLD: University of Queensland Press.

Walker, Ranginui. 1990. *Ka Whawhai Tonu Mātou: Struggle Without End*. Auckland: Penguin Books (NZ).

_____. 1996. *Ngā Pepa a Ranginui: the Walker Papers*. Auckland: Penguin Books (NZ).

Wareham, Evelyn. 2002. *Race and Realpolitik: the Politics of Colonisation in German Samoa*. Frankfurt am Main: Peter Lang.

Webb, T.T. n.d. [early 1940s]. *A Future for the Half-Caste*. Sydney: Methodist Overseas Missions.

Wilson, Ronald. 1997. *Bringing Them Home: National Inquiry into the Separation of Aboriginal and Torres Strait Islander Children from Their Families*. Sydney: Human Rights and Equal Opportunity Commission.

Wolfe, Patrick. 1999. *Settler Colonialism and the Transformation of Anthropology: the Politics and Poetics of an Ethnographic Event*. London and New York: Cassell.

_____. 2001. Land, Labor, and Difference: Elementary Forms of Race. *American Historical Review* 106:866-905.

Yarwood, A.T. 1991. Sir Raphael Cilento and the White Man in the Tropics. In *Health and Healing in Tropical Australia*, ed. Roy MacLeod and Donald Denoon, 47-63. Townsville: James Cook University.

Young, Robert J.C. 1995. *Colonial Desire: Hybridity in Theory, Culture and Race*. London and New York: Routledge.

Notes

[1] Despite the ugly implications of terms like 'half-caste' and 'mixed race', I use them freely in this discussion because of their historical aptness. Inverted commas are omitted except when quoting but are always implied.

[2] See, e.g., Keesing 1934; Pitt-Rivers 1927; Roberts 1927; Tindale 1941.

[3] The record is lost but the song was composed in 1930 (Coward 1982:396).

[4] I am grateful for comments on this subject from Tim Rowse, referring particularly to doctoral research currently being done by Mark Hannah at The Australian National University on the regulation of Aboriginal marriage, and from Donald Denoon. See also Markus 1982.

[5] Most of the etymological information derives from the second edition of the *Oxford English Dictionary* (Simpson and Weiner 1989, II:953-4; III:55; VI:1035).

[6] See Boxer 1963; Henriques 1974; Stoler 1995.

[7] See, e.g., G.S. Richardson, Private Notes on Administration of Western Samoa, n.d., in New Zealand Department of Island Territories 1919-40: IT 1 Ex1/42 pt 1. For a general discussion of similar themes, see McGrath 1987:70-2.

[8] Patrick Wolfe (1991:179-81), however, construed the half-caste as a grave threat to white identity in Australia while Cecil Cook, who features in the main text of this discussion, was one contemporary who feared the male half-caste as a dangerous element in the population of the Northern Territory (Austin 1990:113, 115, 116, 117, 119).

[9] Connolly and Anderson 1987:242-3.

[10] Leahy [1933-4].

[11] Connolly and Anderson 1987:278.

[12] Children of mixed but non-European ancestry raise questions that will scarcely be touched here (but see Lukere 1997:211-34; see also McGrath 2003; Shankman 2001; Wareham 2002). To say that the ancestry of the European half-caste is archetypically white on the father's side and coloured on the mother's can, of course, travesty the ancestry of individuals whose parents might both have had European forebears. Half-castes of later generations classified as 'Europeans', however, as a general rule inherited this status, along with a European surname, through a legally recognized patriline.

[13] Resolution 10 Concerning Jese Tagivaitana, Report of the Provincial Council of Tailevu, Nausori, 20 January 1892, in Colony of Fiji 1874-1941c: Resolutions 1892-94, Book No. 1, Tailevu.

[14] Superintendent of Police, Recommendation of the Removal of Mrs Murdock from the Colony, 17 January 1878, in Colony of Fiji 1874-1941a: Colonial Secretary's Office, CSO 78/93.

[15] Tindale 1941:82, figure 4.

[16] Lawry's vision of miscegenation can also be seen in terms of the Christian Evangelical tradition which contained within it creeds opposed to the racial compartmentalization of humanity. See Chapters Six (Gardner) and Seven (Weir), this volume.

[17] Cilento (1959:437) remarked that the Australasian Medical Congress in 1920 had, in opposition to traditionalists, affirmed the feasibility of the white colonization of the tropics. Aside from 'traditionalists' within medical circles, some prominent geographers remained doubtful and, as David Walker (1999:153) observed, 'the stigma of tropicality' persisted until the late 1930s. For a fuller discussion of perduring misgivings, see Anderson 2002:164-74.

[18] Cook, quoted in McGregor 1997:169; Yarwood 1991:54-5.

[19] During the interwar era, Cuba and Puerto Rico were virtually the only colonies within the tropics where people of predominantly European descent comprised the majority (Kiple 1984:7). In New Caledonia and Hawaii, the Pacific Island groups with the largest European populations at that time, whites were — and remain still — a minority (Connell 1987:97; Nordyke 1989:178-9). For these reasons, Cilento (1933:432) stressed Australia's uniqueness: 'we have a greater population, purely white, living in the tropics than any other country in the world can boast'.

[20] For a general discussion of pejorative characterizations of people of mixed race, see Stepan 1985:104-12. See Chapter One (Douglas), this volume, on the key status of racial mixing in scientific debates about the unity or plurality of human species from the mid-eighteenth century and on the racialism of arguments both in favour of and against human hybridity.

[21] Defoe quoted in Dover 1937:99; Thomson 1908:ix; see also Barkan 1992:23.

[22] Ritvo 1996:41; Stepan 1985:106; Young 1995:8.

[23] Paul 1995:110-11; Ritvo 1996:45; Stepan 1985:106, 108; Young 1995:11-12. The question of the infertility or otherwise of hybrids was pivotal in naturalists' debates on the concept of species at least from the mid-eighteenth century. The French anatomist and anthropologist Paul Broca (1824-1880) based his influential short monograph on human hybridity — the first systematic study of the subject, quickly translated into English (1864) — on a thorough study of hybridity in animals. See Chapter One (Douglas), this volume.

[24] See Chapters Two (Douglas), Four (Turnbull), and Five (Anderson), this volume.

[25] Anderson 2002; Hage 2003:47-68; Ballara 1986; Belich 2001:223-31.

[26] Hasluck 1938:24; Hegarty 1999:7-8; Lalor 2000:38-41; Tindale 1941:76; Wilson 1997:135.

[27] For a discussion of problems relating to data for Aboriginal populations in Western Australia and Queensland in the period from 1900 to 1940, see Briscoe 2003:1-78.

[28] Quoted in Neville [1947]:27, original emphasis.

[29] Tindale 1941:116-24, 125-35; Wilson 1997:39-150.

[30] Hasluck 1938:16-17; Wilson 1997:212-20.

[31] Australian Broadcasting Commission 2003.

[32] Connolly and Anderson 1987:276-7.

[33] Joseph Waterhouse, Drawing Attention to the Fact that Two White Children are Living under the Care and Control of Native Polynesians, 18 April 1878, in Colony of Fiji 1874-1941a: CSO 78/93. Waterhouse had inherited a set of Christian and humanitarian values that often stressed the fundamental unity of humankind and discounted the spiritual significance of racial divisions. See Chapters Six (Gardner) and Seven (Weir), this volume. Nevertheless, as this instance illustrates, racial markers such as skin colour could continue to be used as signifiers of cultural difference and social status.

[34] Jones 1934:39-40; Tindale 1941:79-81.

[35] Anderson 2002:181-215; McGregor 1997:156-61; Tindale 1941:87.

[36] Anderson 2002:199-206; Taylor 1928:3.

[37] Sorrenson 1979:19-33; Ballantyne 2002:56-82. This is what James Belich (1996:20) called the 'white' lens of the 'race-bow' through which white New Zealanders saw Maori as 'quite European-like', 'the best of savages'.

[38] Cocker 1927; Nash 1927; Te Rangi Hiroa 1924; see also Sinclair 1971:124.

[39] Allen 1994; Te Rangi Hiroa 1938:14-15.

[40] Maori transliterated the term half-caste and Te Rangi Hiroa on occasion publicly described himself as 'half-caste' (Allen 1994:20). Mixed ancestry was also an important feature of Carroll's personal and public identity. Pomare and Ngata had European forebears on the maternal side but their white ancestry was less stressed. For a detailed biography of Te Rangi Hiroa, see Condliffe 1971.

[41] A few years after Te Rangi Hiroa's repudiation of Newman, the anthropologist Felix Keesing (1902-1961) in turn percipiently challenged the prognosis of a fully acculturated and assimilated future for Maori (1928:5). He foresaw educated Maori, including those with European ancestors, rejecting 'passive absorption' and promoting among Maori 'the fire of race-consciousness and vitality'. Keesing also observed, at odds with the tendency to celebrate miscegenation, that interracial marriages in New Zealand were now fewer due to racial prejudice.

[42] The wave of revisionist historiography since the 1970s includes the writings of Maori like Ranginui Walker (1990), who stressed the brutal impact of European colonization on Maori and an uninterrupted history of their resistance; and a series of critical studies by Belich who, beginning with *The New Zealand Wars* (1986), endeavoured to place New Zealand's colonial history within a broader comparative framework (1996, 2001).

[43] This chapter was first written without the benefit of Toeolesulusulu Salesa's sensitive meditation on half-castes in New Zealand and Western Samoa between the wars. Whereas Salesa (2000:99) at the outset stressed the ways in which the fortunes of half-castes in each context shaped each other, my starting-point has been the disjunctions between these histories.

[44] For a discussion of the legal complexities, however, see Shankman (2001) and Wareham (2002).

[45] See, e.g., Juxon Burton, Minute on Tourists and Fijians, 29 July 1936, in Colony of Fiji 1874-1941b: CF 50/12.

[46] In the context of this volume, Fiji is an interesting case because its native policy was founded on a conscious rejection of the nineteenth-century conviction that races like the Fijians were congenitally doomed (Lukere 1997:29-50).

47 For a history well attuned to the racial dimensions of Fiji's twentieth century, see Lal 1992.

48 Andrews 1937:114; Mann 1937:7-8; Scarr 1984:143, 156.

49 Davidson 1967:76-113; Meleisea 1987:48-51, 128-30.

50 A further 959 'Europeans' were Chinese. Under the Samoa Act of 1921, 'A European is any person other than a Samoan' (quoted in McArthur 1967:118). The actual ethnic composition of the 'European' category was therefore difficult to analyze precisely (Keesing 1934:32).

51 Keesing 1934:37-40; Wareham 2002:177-178.

52 Gilson 1970; Salesa 1997; Shankman 2001.

53 See, e.g., comments by the Military Administrator of Western Samoa: Robert Logan, Report for Governor General on Administration of Samoa, 8 July 1919, in New Zealand Department of Island Territories 1919-40: IT1/10: 32-3.

54 Stephen S. Allen, Telegram to Department of External Affairs, 3 April 1930, in New Zealand Department of Island Territories 1919-40: IT 1 Ex1/23/8 pt 18.

55 Ian Campbell's reassessment of the Mau (1999) came close to the contemporary official interpretation of Nelson's involvement and also recognized New Zealand's good intentions under the terms of the mandate.

56 See Richardson to Sir Frances Bell, 27 December 1926; Richardson to Minister of External Affairs, 13 December 1926; Richardson to Nosworthy, 26 July 1927; G.S. Richardson, Memo to Minister for External Affairs, 24 June 1927; and Bell to Richardson, 29 January 1925, in New Zealand Department of Island Territories 1919-40: IT 1 1/33/1 pt 1; IT 1 Ex1/23/8 pt 2; IT 1 Ex 1/33/1 pt 1. While anti-German feeling had been inflamed by the war and New Zealand officials were, for other reasons, mistrustful of German elements within Western Samoa and acutely sensitive to unfavourable comparisons with the earlier German regime, these anti-German sentiments cannot totally explain the administration's hostility towards half-castes in Samoa, as the parallels with Fiji, where the British did not have a comparable German element or legacy, suggest.

57 *N.Z. Samoa Guardian*, 12 December 1929:1.

58 For a discussion of the policies towards miscegenation in Western Samoa during the German administration, see Shankman (2001) and Wareham (2002).

59 Ngata 1929a:906; see also 1929b:43-4.

60 Neville 1947:72; Tindale 1941:122.

61 See, e.g., Walker 1996:110, 164-7, 168-9.

62 In Fiji, the English word half-caste is often used though the Fijian term is *kai loma*, 'person in the middle'. In Samoan, the words are *totolua*, 'two blood', or *'afakasi*, the latter transliterating the English word.

63 Meleisea 1987:179-80; Simpson 1974:19.

64 Brown 2000; Sitiveni Rabuka quoted in O'Callaghan 2000.

Epilogue

The Cultivation of Difference in Oceania

Chris Ballard

This volume marks the first attempt to assemble the writings of a group of scholars with a common interest in the history of racial thought in Oceania. If some of the contributors refuse to be definitive, the collection nevertheless yields some unanticipated results. As a group, we were led to the topic by a preliminary sense — now largely confirmed — of the scarcity of original scholarship on race in Oceania, as distinct from the uncritical repetition of a small litany of received truths. What we failed to anticipate was the degree of significance of Oceanic materials in the development of metropolitan raciological thought, a theme partially documented in this volume, or the extent to which Oceania was promoted as a potential source of authoritative solutions to questions generated elsewhere. Equally as surprising was the paucity of scholarship on a global scale upon which to draw in framing our regional accounts. Bronwen Douglas's groundbreaking investigation in Chapter One into the etymology and shifting connotations of the term 'race' is perhaps the most obvious example of the need to undertake fundamental historical research in a worldwide field that we had naively assumed to be comprehensively charted and documented.

The regional scope of the volume provides a critical focal length for questions about the relationship between field and metropole in the development of theories of human difference, bridging the particularism of local or national accounts and the abstraction of global narratives. The geographical contiguities within a region enable us to follow trans-local connections, to identify interactions and exchanges between individuals, and to trace the evolution of specifically regional grammars of distinction — a process further enhanced by the emergence of regional metropolitan centres such as Singapore, Sydney, and Honolulu. If regional perspectives have the capacity to challenge and even reconfigure the form of metropolitan histories of raciology, the contributors to this volume would also contend that Oceania offers a number of distinctive possibilities. The earliest documented encounters between Europe and Oceania are of an antiquity not dissimilar to those between Europe and the Americas and sub-Saharan Africa. Yet from the early sixteenth century, the slow and sporadic unfolding of European exploration and colonial acquisition in Oceania, which would see 'first contacts' extend as late as the 1960s in parts of interior New Guinea, has produced an exceptionally long sequence of engagements between changing metropolitan ideas about difference and ongoing encounters with 'new' peoples. The range of apparent variation in human forms and cultures across broadly similar latitudes and environments within Oceania has also provided a critical stimulus for European thought: witness the unsavoury sobriquet of 'natural laboratory' which continues to feature in scholarly writing on the region.

We do not pretend that the volume provides the final word on such questions but see it as also plotting the outliers of a new archipelago of enquiry. This epilogue briefly considers four specific areas for further investigation: the relationship between raciological elaboration and the politics of settler colonialism; the legacy and imprint of raciology in Oceania beyond the early twentieth century; the focus on embodied encounters as a critical locus or moment in both the performance and production of raciological knowledge; and the nature of indigenous Oceanian adoption, reworking, and subversion of raciological ideas.

First, however, it is necessary to address the problem of writing at all about raciology as a science or a system of knowledge. The attribution of 'slipperiness' to race presumes a substance or content, however labile, that might ultimately be grasped. As an enterprise of contested knowledge in which any verifiable results of scientific consequence have been outweighed so overwhelmingly by the sheer mass of intellectual and other investments, the science of race is perhaps challenged only by pre-Enlightenment alchemy. How then are we to write of the history of racial thinking in the progressive terms deemed appropriate to other sciences? In what respects might Cuvier be said to 'improve' upon Buffon, or Wallace upon Crawfurd? How are we to account for the hydra-like quality of the naturalized idea of race which sees individual elements of racialist theories repeatedly slain, only to rise again, perhaps euphemized but seemingly unharmed and multiplied?

Much of the power of raciology as an institutionalized system of knowledge has derived from its capacity to inform, and to be informed by, both popular understandings of difference and the machinery of state and colonial administrations. Few other branches of science have been so promiscuously engaged with popular discourses or so susceptible to the fashions and demands of settler and colonial politics. In the most banal of terms, while race may not have achieved much as a science, it has certainly done work in the world. What this suggests is that we need to appreciate the visceral efficacy of the fundamental logic of raciology which extends beyond its pretensions as a science to cater to more profound and more widely shared understandings of human difference and identity. An account of the history of racialist thinking which is capable of exposing the underlying structures of differentiation, such as the role of dualisms or the function of hierarchy in the comparison of different individuals or populations, might dispel any impulse to seek order and progress in the development of racialist ideas. Such an approach offers the added advantage of allowing for the incorporation of indigenous Oceanian and foreign theories of difference within a single frame of analysis. To what extent did Oceanian and European modes of distinction resemble each other and how might this have enabled the mutual exchange and adoption of concepts of difference?

With respect to the presumed but not systematically historicized nexus of raciology and settler colonialism, a closer correlation is needed of the changing tone of raciology and the political and economic imperatives that accompanied the transition to settler colonialism. The common observation that raciology hardened as the colonial demand for land stepped up the requirement for moral legitimation is itself in need of more extensive empirical demonstration. Can it be shown that discourses of race particular to different colonies in Oceania transformed not so much in step with developments in global thought but rather at a pace with changes in the local politics of land?

The relatively long time depth and extraordinary persistence of fundamental raciological precepts invite consideration of the possibility that many of these precepts still endure in scholarly, as well as in popular conception. Just as the history of nineteenth-century raciology in Oceania has been largely neglected, so too its legacy and subsequent imprint is an open-ended and largely unconsidered field. This lack makes recent scholarly discourse on difference in Oceania an obvious area for further attention. The gradual unravelling of consensus on the biological concept of race between the World Wars and the explicit post-war rejection of race as a valid social concept, enshrined in the 1952 UNESCO statement on race, might have lifted a burden of guilt from the social sciences but also encouraged a collective amnesia about anthropology's intellectual antecedents. The euphemization and sublimation of race as 'ethnicity' or even 'identity' leave scholarly debates on these themes open to the forms of analysis employed in this volume to characterize eighteenth- and nineteenth-century thinking. There is no reason to suspect that late twentieth-century anthropology, for example, is any more immune to popular conceptions of difference than were its predecessors. The expression of difference in fiction, encyclopaedias, school texts, photography, and cinema should form part of any comprehensive analysis of that intellectual history.

A quick survey of post-war Oceanic anthropology will yield any number of statements about Negritos and other primordial, dark-skinned inhabitants of island interiors; casual analogies asserted between contemporary Oceanic communities or practices and the Pleistocene or Neolithic Europe; and comparisons between the tool-making skills of chimpanzees and Tasmanian Aborigines. But these are simply the more clumsy and egregious instances of a discipline painfully and often wilfully ignorant of its own past. French racial cartographies developed for Oceania during the late eighteenth and early nineteenth centuries have furnished the region with perhaps the most powerful of legacies, commonly condensed into the binary contrast between Melanesia and Polynesia. Many of the region's classic ethnographic distinctions such as egalitarianism and hierarchy, big-men and chiefs, diversity and homogeneity, and gender antagonism and complementarity are aligned along this axis. If ideas about race were never free of culture, can theories of culture ever be free from race? The crania of human beings — living and dead — continue to be measured (if not collected) into the present but, since 1945, confidence about our ability to fix human difference has shifted from metrical studies of anatomy to blood group analysis and, most recently, to genetics. The particular quality of confidence expressed during the late eighteenth and nineteenth centuries by anatomists and then anthropologists, for whom the biologization of difference removed analysis from the realm of subjective speculation, is closely echoed in the conviction of contemporary geneticists that the answers to our questions will be definitively resolved. The longer historical perspective promoted in this volume would suggest that, while the increasing sophistication of technologies of differentiation is evident, elaboration of the questions being posed might not have kept pace. The need for a sustained cross-disciplinary encounter between geneticists and historians and other social scientists has never been more pressing.

The centrality of embodied encounters in the constitution of raciological knowledge about Oceania emerges clearly from each of the contributions as a focus for further close analysis. It forms the theme of the editors' ongoing Australian Research Council Discovery project on 'European Naturalists and the Constitution of Human Difference in Oceania: Crosscultural Encounters and the Science of Race, 1768-1888'. Raciology shares with most other field sciences the tendency to expunge all traces of subjectivity in the extraction of its raw material, writing out from its published accounts all the performative qualities of the encounter. Yet race (on both sides) is, foremost, a perception of performed qualities: of civility or savagery, of bodily decoration and the arrangement of clothing and hair, of the relations between men and women or between social categories. European observations on the colour of skin often appear as summary statements on all these other perceived qualities and commonly vary considerably from one member of an expedition to another. Much as indigenous agency is now acknowledged and sought in the composition of artefact collections, so too the data of raciology must be interrogated for evidence of what Bronwen Douglas has called indigenous countersigns, for a more nuanced and often more troubling sense of connections and missed connections in the encounter.

For many states, communities, and individuals in contemporary Oceania, the categories of distinction received from raciology have assumed new forms of significance, whether through challenge, reclamation, or subversion. Bernard Narakobi's philosophy of a Melanesian Way, the Anglican order of the Melanesian Brotherhood, and the international cross-state Melanesian Spearhead Group, along with Polynesian Airlines, the Polynesian Society, and the Polynesian Cultural Center have all embraced the contours of a French geography elaborated from the mid-eighteenth century. Papuan nationalists in the Indonesian half of New Guinea, long subject to racist discrimination under Dutch colonial and later Indonesian rule, themselves repeat the distinctions advanced by Crawfurd, Earl, and Wallace when they insist on dichotomizing black-skinned, curly-headed Papuans and their straight-haired Indonesian Malay opponents. But while there may be some liberal discomfort about the uses to which these categories are now put, any awkwardness about their historical origins is a problem only for scholars. These days, as in the past, the question to be posed in addressing any classification or hierarchy is what purpose and which agenda it serves, rather than seeking to determine its fit with any presumed reality.

Index

www.ingramcontent.com/pod-product-compliance
Lightning Source LLC
Chambersburg PA
CBHW061238270326

41928CB00033B/3356